GREATER DUBLIN
Streetfinder Atlas

Contents

Tourist & travel information 2
Key to map symbols 3
Key to map pages 4-5
Distance chart 4
Route planner (8 miles to 1 inch) 6-7
Dublin approaches (4 miles to 1 inch) 8-9
Main Dublin maps (4 inches to 1 mile) 10-143
Central Dublin map (6.6 inches to 1 mile) 144-145
Guide to central Dublin 146-165
Index to place names 166
Index to street names 166-200

Published by Collins
An imprint of HarperCollins Publishers
77-85 Fulham Palace Road, Hammersmith, London W6 8JB

www.harpercollins.co.uk

Copyright © HarperCollins Publishers Ltd 2009

Collins® is a registered trademark of HarperCollins Publishers Limited

Mapping generated from Collins Bartholomew digital databases

Based on Ordnance Survey Ireland by permission of the Government of Ireland. Ordnance Survey Ireland Permit No. 8407
© Ordnance Survey Ireland/Government of Ireland

Fixed speed camera information supplied by PocketGPSWorld.Com Ltd
Speed Enforcement Zone information supplied by An Garda Síochána and the National Roads Authority.

Printed in Hong Kong   ISBN 978 0 00 731282 5   Imp 001   WI12439 / CDL
e-mail: roadcheck@harpercollins.co.uk

D0184211

Tourist and travel information

Air travel

Dublin Airport
☎ 01 814 1111.
www.dublinairport.com

The airport is 12km (8 miles) north of the city centre with Dublin Bus operating many services to and from the airport including the **'Airlink'** express coach service operating between the airport, the central bus station in Store Street (Bus Áras) and the two mainline rail stations, Connolly and Heuston. It runs every 10-15 mins (15-20 mins on Sundays) between 05.45 (07.15 on Sundays) and 23.30 from the airport and between 05.15 (07.35 on Sundays) and 22.50 from O'Connell Street in the centre of Dublin. ☎ 01 873 4222 www.dublinbus.ie.

'Aircoach' runs between the airport and Dublin City and South Dublin City stopping at major hotels. The 24 hour service operates every 10-20 minutes except from 24.00 and 05.00 when an hourly service operates. ☎ 01 844 7118 www.aircoach.ie.

Services at Dublin airport include Travel Information, Tourist Information and Bureau de Change.

Frequent direct flights operate between Dublin and many airports in Britain, Europe and North America. Internal flights are available to Cork, Donegal, Galway, Kerry, Knock, Shannon & Sligo and are operated by

Aer Arann	☎ 0818 210210 (R of I)
	☎ 0800 587 2324 (UK)
	www.aerarann.com
Aer Lingus	☎ 0818 365 044 (R of I)
	☎ 0870 876 2020 (UK)
	www.aerlingus.com

Other operators flying into Dublin are:

British Airways	☎ 1890 626 747 (R of I)
	☎ 0870 850 9850 (UK)
	www.britishairways.com
Flybe	☎ 00 44 1392 268529 (R of I)
	☎ 0871 522 6100 (UK)
	www.flybe.com
BMI	☎ 01 407 3036 (R of I)
	☎ 0870 6070 555 (UK)
	www.flybmi.com
Ryanair	☎ 0818 30 30 30 (R of I),
	☎ 0871 246 0000 (UK)
	www.ryanair.com

Passenger and vehicle ferries

Irish Ferries (Dublin-Holyhead).
☎ 01 855 2222 / 0818 300 400 (R of I)
☎ 08705 17 17 17 (UK)
www.irishferries.com

Norfolk Line Ferries (Dublin-Birkenhead).
☎ 01 819 2999 (R of I) ☎ 0870 600 4321 (UK)
www.norfolkline-ferries.co.uk

P & O Irish Sea (Dublin-Liverpool).
☎ 01 407 3434 (R of I) ☎ 0870 24 24 777 (UK)
www.poirishsea.com

Isle of Man Steam Packet Company (Dublin-Douglas).
☎ 1800 80 50 55 (R of I) ☎ 0871 222 1333 (UK)
www.steam-packet.com

Stena Line (Dún Laoghaire-Holyhead, Dublin-Holyhead).
☎ 01 204 7777 (R of I) ☎ 08705 70 70 70 (UK)
www.stenaline.co.uk

The ferry terminal at Dún Laoghaire is also linked to the city by the DART rail service with a 20 minute journey time.

Tourist information

Dublin Tourism Centre, Suffolk Street.
☎ 01 605 7700.
Open: (July & August) Mon-Sat 09.00-20.00, (Sept & June) Mon-Sat 09.00-19.00, (Oct-May) Mon-Sat 09.00-17.30. Open Sun & bank holidays 10.30-15.00; closed 25 & 26 Dec & 1 Jan.

Formerly St. Andrew's Church, the centre provides details of visitor attractions and events in the city as well as acting as a ticket and accommodation bureau. Transport and tour information, exchange facilities and a café are also on hand.

Other tourist information and reservation centres in Dublin (walk-in only) are located at:
Dublin Airport. Open: Mon-Sun 08.00-22.00.
Open bank holidays except 25 & 26 Dec & 1 Jan.
Dún Laoghaire Ferry Terminal.
Open: Mon-Sat 10.00-18.00, closed 13.00-14.00.

Open bank holidays except 25 & 26 Dec & 1 Jan.
Baggott Street Bridge. Open: Mon-Fri 09.30-17.00, closed 12.00-12.30. Closed bank holidays.
For accommodation reservations in Dublin and Ireland contact Ireland Reservations.
☎ 1800 363 626 (R of I) ☎ 008 002 580 2580 (UK)

Official tourism website for Dublin:
www.visitdublin.com
Email: information@dublintourism.ie
or reservations@dublintourism.ie

Irish Tourist Board Website:
www.ireland.ie

The Dublin Pass allows fast-track entry to many visitor attractions for a 1, 2, 3 or 6 day period. It can also be used on public transport and to obtain discount in some shops and restaurants. www.dublinpass.ie

Speed Enforcement Zones

An Garda Síochána, in conjunction with the National Roads Authority, have conducted an analysis of the road network and identified areas where excessive speed has been considered to be a contributory factor to a significant proportion of accidents.

Based on this analysis, Speed Enforcement Zones have been developed with the aim of raising awareness of speeding in these zones. An Garda Síochána will utilize these zones in order to direct speed enforcement activity in a proportionate and targeted manner. These zones will be reviewed and updated on an ongoing basis.

Key to map symbols

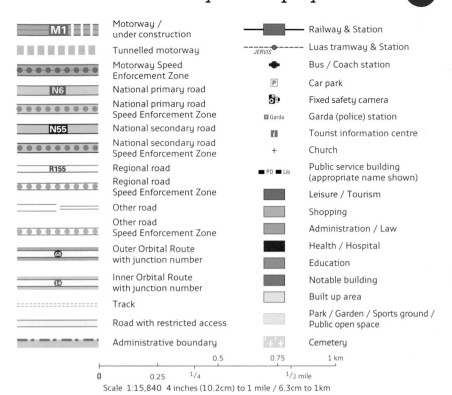

M1	Motorway / under construction		Railway & Station	
	Tunnelled motorway		*JERVIS* Luas tramway & Station	
	Motorway Speed Enforcement Zone		Bus / Coach station	
N6	National primary road		P Car park	
	National primary road Speed Enforcement Zone		Fixed safety camera	
N55	National secondary road		Garda Garda (police) station	
	National secondary road Speed Enforcement Zone		*i* Tourist information centre	
R155	Regional road		+ Church	
	Regional road Speed Enforcement Zone		PO Lib Public service building (appropriate name shown)	
	Other road		Leisure / Tourism	
	Other road Speed Enforcement Zone		Shopping	
68	Outer Orbital Route with junction number		Administration / Law	
14	Inner Orbital Route with junction number		Health / Hospital	
	Track		Education	
	Road with restricted access		Notable building	
	Administrative boundary		Built up area	
			Park / Garden / Sports ground / Public open space	
			Cemetery	

```
                              0.5        0.75      1 km
0        0.25    1/4                1/2 mile
Scale 1:15,840  4 inches (10.2cm) to 1 mile / 6.3cm to 1km
```

Key to map symbols (pages 6-9)

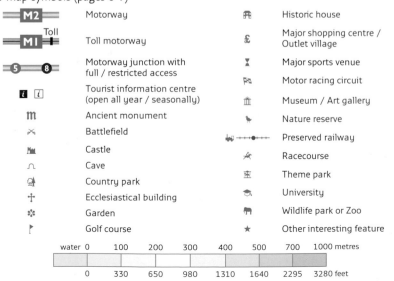

M2	Motorway		Historic house	
M1 Toll	Toll motorway		Major shopping centre / Outlet village	
5 8	Motorway junction with full / restricted access		Major sports venue	
i *i*	Tourist information centre (open all year / seasonally)		Motor racing circuit	
m	Ancient monument		Museum / Art gallery	
✕	Battlefield		Nature reserve	
Castle	Castle		Preserved railway	
∩	Cave		Racecourse	
Country park	Country park		Theme park	
†	Ecclesiastical building		University	
❋	Garden		Wildlife park or Zoo	
Golf course	Golf course		★ Other interesting feature	

```
water  0    100   200   300   400   500   700   1000 metres

       0    330   650   980  1310  1640  2295  3280 feet
```

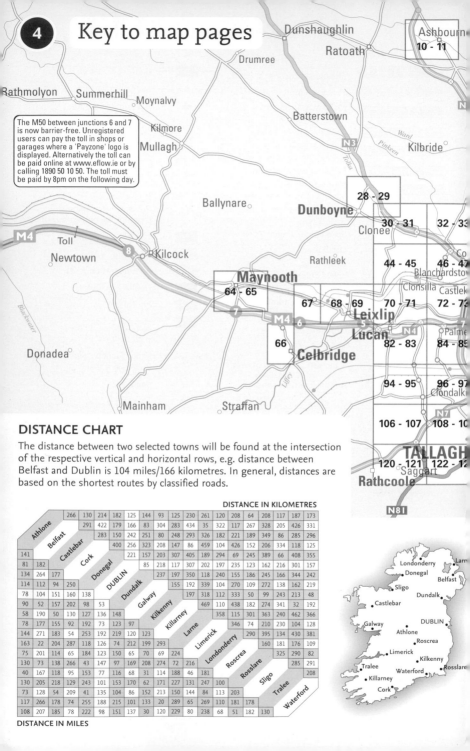

Dunshaughlin
Ashbourn
Ratoath
10 - 11
Drumree
Rathmolyon
Summerhill
Moynalvy
Batterstown

The M50 between junctions 6 and 7 is now barrier-free. Unregistered users can pay the toll in shops or garages where a 'Payzone' logo is displayed. Alternatively the toll can be paid online at www.eflow.ie or by calling 1890 50 10 50. The toll must be paid by 8pm on the following day.

Kilmore
Mullagh
Kilbride
Ballynare
Dunboyne
28 - 29
Clonee
30 - 31 **32 - 33**
M4 Toll
Newtown
Kilcock
Rathleek
44 - 45 **46 - 47**
8
Blanchardsto
Clonsilla Castlek
Maynooth
67 **68 - 69** **70 - 71** **72 - 7**
64 - 65
Leixlip
7
M4 **6** **Lucan**
66 **82 - 83** **84 - 85**
Celbridge
Donadea
94 - 95 **96 - 97**
Clondalki
Mainham
Straffan
106 - 107 **108 - 10**
N7
TALLAGH
120 - 121 **122 - 12**
Saggart
Rathcoole
N81

DISTANCE CHART

The distance between two selected towns will be found at the intersection of the respective vertical and horizontal rows, e.g. distance between Belfast and Dublin is 104 miles/166 kilometres. In general, distances are based on the shortest routes by classified roads.

DISTANCE IN KILOMETRES

Athlone	266	130	214	182	125	144	93	125	230	261	120	208	64	208	117	187	173
	Belfast	291	422	179	166	83	304	283	434	35	322	117	267	328	205	426	331
		Castlebar	283	150	242	251	80	248	293	326	182	221	189	349	86	285	296
141			Cork	400	256	323	208	147	86	459	104	426	152	206	334	118	125
81	182			Donegal	221	157	203	307	405	189	294	69	245	389	66	408	355
134	264	177			DUBLIN	85	218	117	307	202	197	235	123	162	216	301	157
114	112	94	250			Dundalk	237	197	350	118	240	155	186	245	166	344	242
78	104	151	160	138			Galway	155	192	339	104	270	109	272	138	162	219
90	52	157	202	98	53			Kilkenny	197	318	112	333	50	99	243	213	48
58	190	50	130	127	136	148			Killarney	469	110	438	182	274	341	32	192
78	177	155	92	192	73	123	97			Larne	358	115	301	363	240	462	366
144	271	183	54	253	192	219	120	123			Limerick	346	74	210	230	104	128
163	22	204	287	118	126	74	212	199	293			Londonderry	290	395	134	430	381
75	201	114	65	184	123	150	65	70	69	224			Roscrea	160	181	176	109
130	73	138	266	43	147	97	169	208	274	72	216			Rosslare	325	290	82
40	167	118	95	153	77	116	68	31	114	188	46	181			Sligo	285	291
130	205	218	129	243	101	153	170	62	171	227	131	247	100			Tralee	208
73	128	54	209	41	135	104	86	152	213	150	144	84	113	203			Waterford
117	266	178	74	255	188	215	101	133	20	289	65	269	110	181	178		
108	207	185	78	222	98	151	137	30	120	229	80	238	68	51	182	130	

DISTANCE IN MILES

Londonderry Larn
Donegal
Belfast
Sligo
Dundalk
Castlebar
DUBLIN
Galway
Athlone
Roscrea
Limerick
Kilkenny
Tralee
Waterford Rosslare
Killarney
Cork

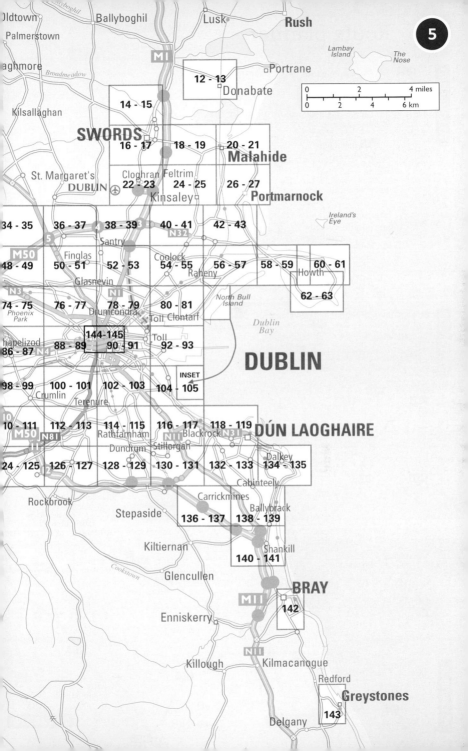

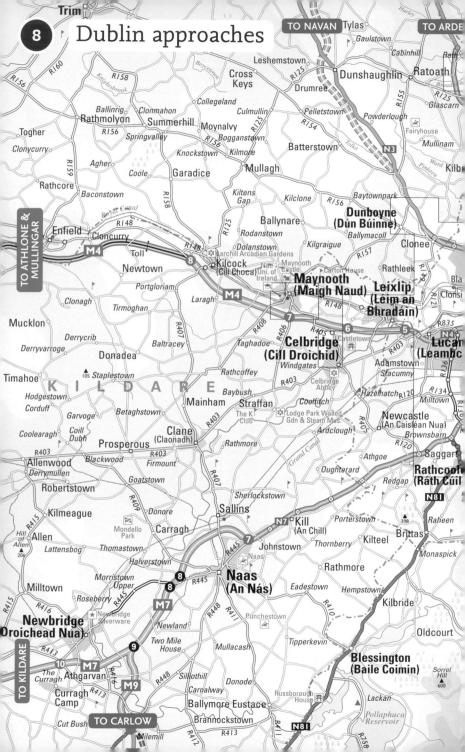

A

B

1

2

3

A

B

N2

R135

1916 Rebellion Mon.

Rath Cross
Roads

Cookstown

*ASHBOURNE
INDUSTRIAL
PARK*

RATH
LODGE

RAC
LO

RACE HILL LANE

TUDOR

TUDOR CRES

GROVE

THE ASHES

WEST
GRN

WEST
WV

BRINDLEY PK GDN

B PL
PK
SQ

BRI PK CRES

ST. JOHNS
WD PK

WD CT

ST. JOHNS

J DERRY HA

RISE

**Health
Centre**

KILL
CT

Lib

KILLEGLAND PARK

CLUAIN

ST. JOHNS WD
DR

BALLYBIN ROAD

COOKSTOWN
BRIDGE

Ballybin

ASHBOURNE

CAS

CRE

CRESTWOO
GREEN

CRESTWOOD
PARK

CEM

Killegland

WESTV

BOURNE VIEW

THE
BALEY

BOUR

BROADMEADO
GREEN

BROAD MEADOW RIVER

N2

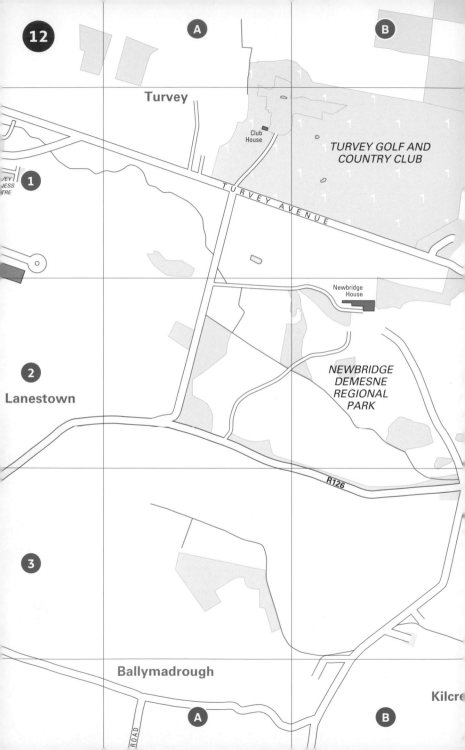

A

B

Turvey

Club House

TURVEY GOLF AND COUNTRY CLUB

1

TURVEY BUSINESS CENTRE

T U R V E Y   A V E N U E

Newbridge House

2

Lanestown

NEWBRIDGE DEMESNE REGIONAL PARK

R126

3

Ballymadrough

Kilcre

ROAD

A

B

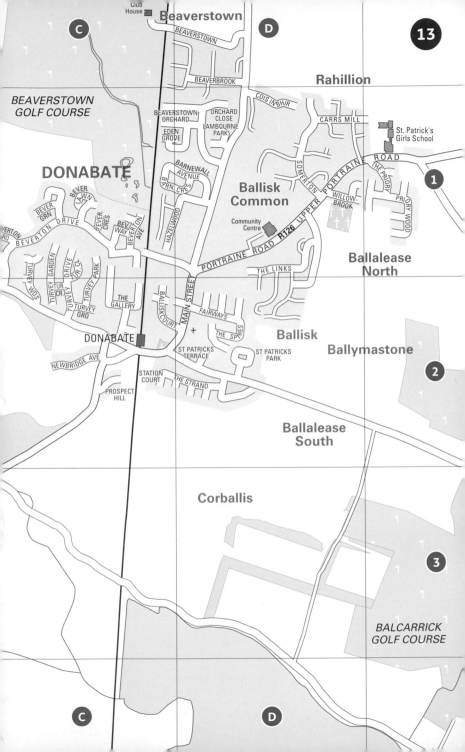

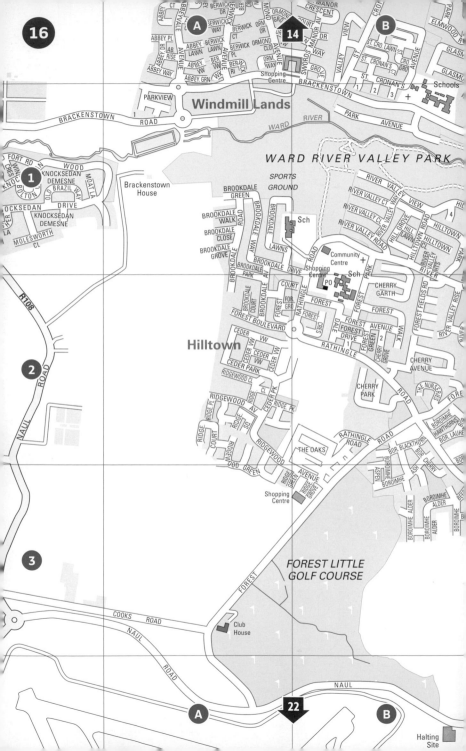

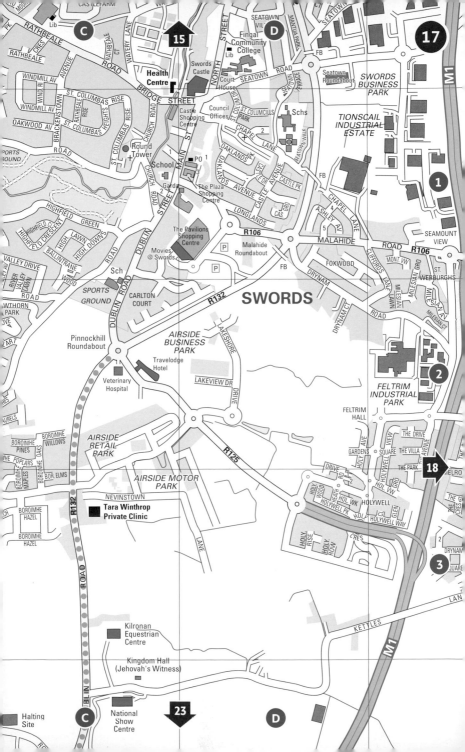

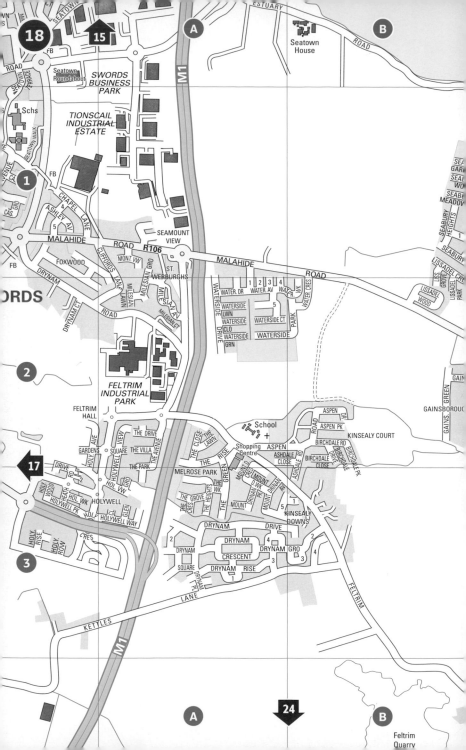

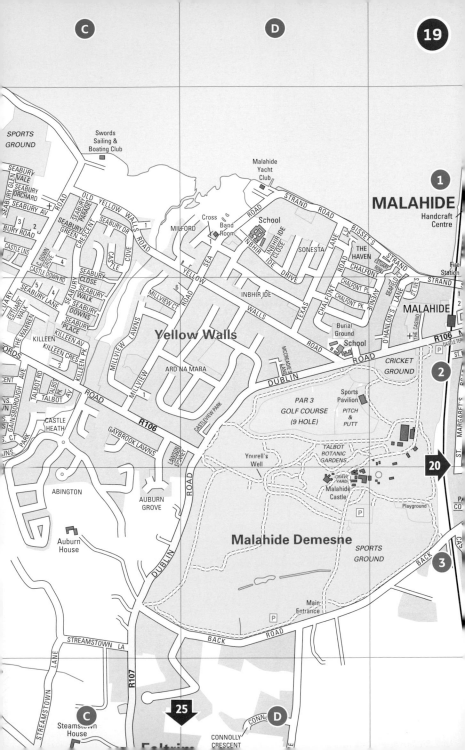

SPORTS GROUND

Swords Sailing & Boating Club

SEABURY GLEN
SEABURY VALE
SEABURY ORCHARD
SEABURY AV
BURY ROAD
CASTLE LNS
C. DOWN GROVE
Castle Down Rd
4
SEABURY CRESCENT
SEABURY PARADE
OLD YELLOW WALLS ROAD
CASTLE COVE
SEABURY DR
3
SEABURY GREEN
SEABURY CLOSE
SEABURY WALK
SEABURY DOWNS
SEABURY PLACE
SEABURY LANE
SEABURY AV
4
5
A

Malahide Yacht Club

MILFORD
Cross
Band Room
School

STRAND ROAD

INBHIR IDE
INBHIR IDE CLOSE
INBHIR IDE DRIVE
SEA ROAD
YELLOW WALLS ROAD
MILLVIEW CT
6

INBHIR IDE

SONESTA
THE HAVEN
BISSET'S LANE
CHALFONT
CHALFONT PL
CHALFONT PK
O'HANLON'S LANE
TEXAS
MCREAGH'S LANE
ESTUARY ROW
SEAFIELD
ST. IVES
STRAND

MALAHIDE

Handcraft Centre

Fire Station

MALAHIDE

THE CASINO

R106

P

CASTLE TERR.

ST.

ESTUARY WALK
THE WARREN
KILLEEN
KILLEEN AV
KILLEEN PK
KILLEEN CRES
SWORDS
GAINSBOROUGH AVE
TALBOT RD
TALBOT PK
TALBOT ROAD
CASTLE HEATH
GAYBROOK LAWNS
LAWSON SQ/WAY
CASTLEVIEW PARK

Yellow Walls

MILLVIEW LAWNS
MILLVIEW
1
ARD NA MARA

DUBLIN ROAD

R106

ABINGTON

AUBURN GROVE

Auburn House

DUBLIN ROAD

STREAMSTOWN LA

R107

Steamstown House

Burial Ground
School

CRICKET GROUND

2

PAR 3 GOLF COURSE (9 HOLE)

Sports Pavilion
PITCH & PUTT

Ynurell's Well

TALBOT BOTANIC GARDENS

GRAVE YARD
Malahide Castle
P
Playground

Malahide Demesne

SPORTS GROUND

BACK ROAD

20

ST. MARGARET'S ST.

CAS

3

Main Entrance
P

BACK ROAD

25

CONNOLLY CRESCENT

Feltrim

C · D

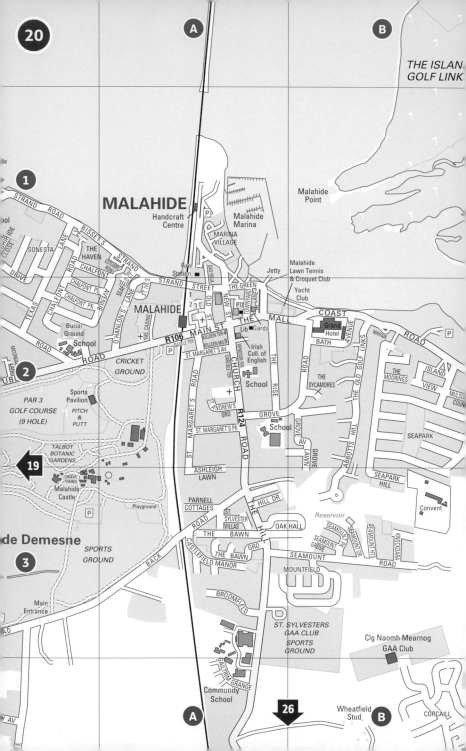

A   B

THE ISLAN
GOLF LINK

1

STRAND ROAD
BISSET'S LANE
CHALKHIDE CLOSE
SONESTA
THE HAVEN
STRAND ROAD
CHALFONT
ESTUARY ROW
DRIVE
CHALFONT PL
CHALFONT AVENUE
CHALFONT PK
TEXAS
O'HANLON'S LANE
SCARLETT
ST. ITE'S
STRAND STREET

MALAHIDE

Handcraft
Centre

MARINA
VILLAGE

Malahide
Marina

Malahide
Point

Fire
Station

Jetty

Malahide
Lawn Tennis
& Croquet Club

THE GREEN
NEW ST
OLD ST
TOWNYARD LANE
PO
Yacht
Club

COAST

MALAHIDE

Burial
Ground
School
McGRAIL
LAMBERT
Road

R106   MAIN ST

CASTLE TER
KILLEEN TER 4
KILLEEN MS 5
ST. MARGARET S AV

Lib Garda

Grand
Hotel

BATH

THE MALL

AVENUE
MAYFAIR

ROAD

P

CRICKET
GROUND

ST. MARGARET'S ROAD

CHURCH ROAD
CARLISLE TER

Irish
Coll. of
English

School

THE RISE

GROVE

THE OLD GOLF LINKS

ABBOTTS HILL

ISLAND
VIEW

THE
MOORINGS

MULDO
COUR

2

PAR 3
GOLF COURSE
(9 HOLE)

Sports
Pavilion

PITCH
& PUTT

ST. ANDREW'S
GRO

R124

GROVE

School

GROVE
AV

GROVE
LAWN

THE SYCAMORES

SEAPARK

TALBOT
BOTANIC
GARDENS

GRAVE
YARD

Malahide
Castle

Playground

ST. MARGARET S PK

ASHLEIGH
LAWN

PARNELL
COTTAGES

SEAPARK
HILL

Convent

19

P

de Demesne

SPORTS
GROUND

BACK ROAD

CASTLEFIELD ROAD

HILL DR

ST.
SYLVESTER
VILLAS

THE BAWN
GRO

THE BAWN

CASTLEFIELD MANOR

THE HILL

OAK HALL

Reservoir

SEAMOUNT
GROVE
SEAMOUNT TCE
SEAMOUNT TER
SEAMOUNT HTS

KNOCKDARA

ROAD

MOUNTFIELD

SEAMOUNT

3

Main
Entrance

BROOMFIELD

ST. SYLVESTERS
GAA CLUB
SPORTS
GROUND

Clg Naomh Mearnog
GAA Club

GAILTIN
GRANGE

Community
School

A

26

Wheatfield
Stud

B

CORCAILL

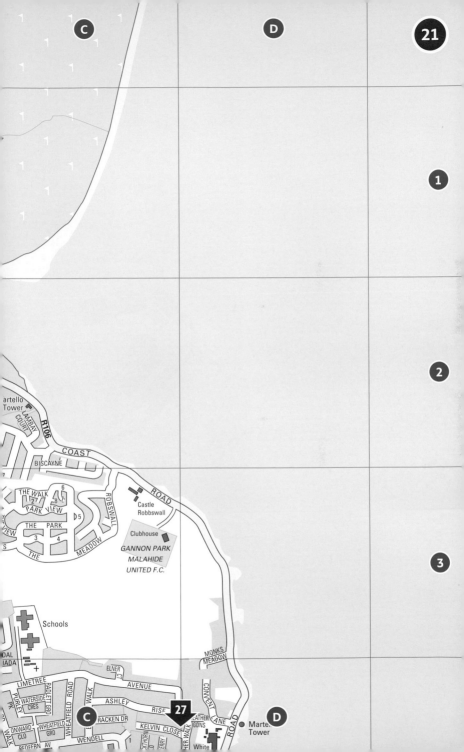

C

D

21

1

2

artello
Tower

R106

COAST

BISCAYNE

LAMBAY COURT

ROAD

Castle
Robbswall

THE WALK
27
PARK VIEW
6
8
5
ROBBSWALL

THE PARK
3
4
VIEW
THE
MEADOW

Clubhouse

GANNON PARK
MALAHIDE
UNITED F.C.

3

Schools

MONKS
MEADOW

DAL
IADA

ELNER

LIMETREE
PK
PURLEY
WATERSIDE
CRES
RADLET GRO

AVENUE

ASHLEY

RISE

WALK

27

CONVENT LANE

D

ONWARD
CLO
REDFERN AV
WHEATFIELD
GRO
WHEATFIELD ROAD
RADLET ROAD
RACKEN DR
WENDELL

C

KELVIN CLOSE

HER WALK

XTHORN
JO
ERRY

1

White

LEATHER
GDNS

ROAD

Marte.
Tower

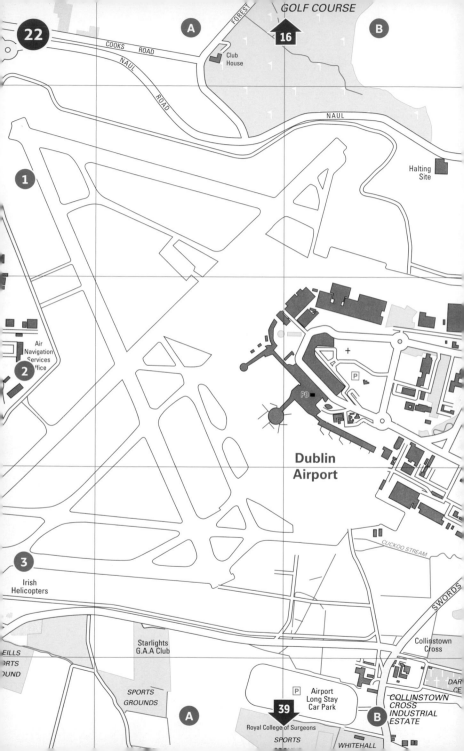

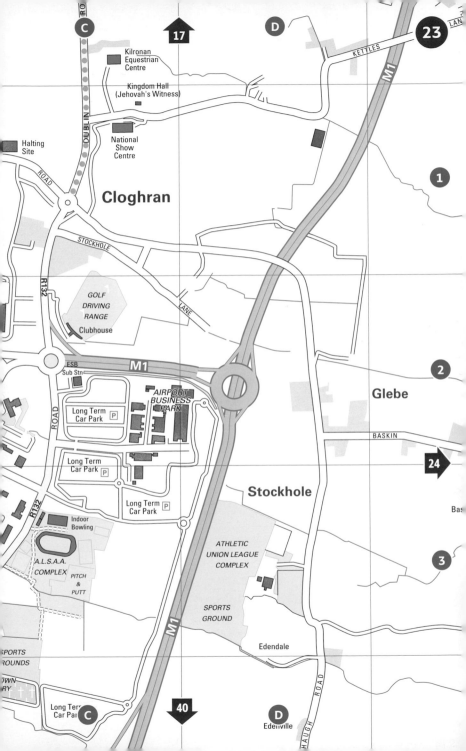

24

A

18

B

KETTLES

M1

Feltrim
Quarry

1

Greenwood

2

Glebe

ASHGROVE

Ballymac

BASKIN

23

LANE

BASKIN
COTTAGES

khole

Baskin Hill

Emsworth

3

ale

Spring Hill

HAUGH ROAD

A

41

B

ville

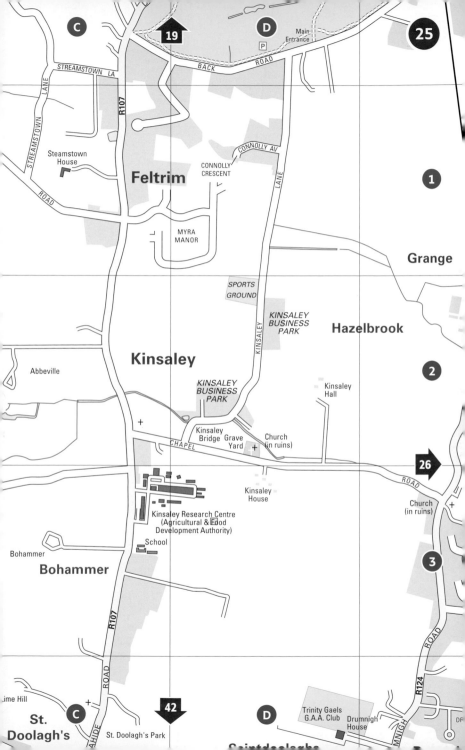

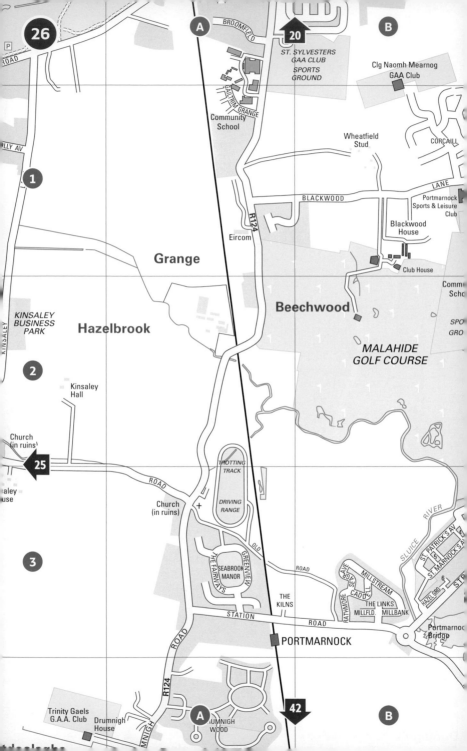

Schools

MONKS
MEADOW

ELNER
CT
LIMETREE
AVENUE

ASHLEY

PURLEY
WATERSIDE
CRES

WHEATFIELD ROAD

BRIAR WALK

RISE

BRACKEN DR

PADGETT RD

CONVENT LANE

HEATHER
GDNS

● Martello
Tower

ONWARD
CLO

WHEATFIELD
GRO

WENDELL

KELVIN CLOSE

BLACKTHORN
CLO

DEWBERRY
PK

HEATHER WALK

ROAD

White
Sands
Hotel

REDFERN AV

MARTELLO COURT

Shopping
Centre

AVENUE

CARRICKHILL

PORTMARNOCK

RISE

PORTMARNOCK CRESCENT

STRAND

CARRICKHILL

CARRICKHILL
CLOSE

PORTMARNOCK
PARK

CARRICKHILL

PORT. WLK

PORTMARNOCK WALK

CARRICKHILL

ROAD

PORTMARNOCK PARKVIEW

PORT.
RISE

PORT. GDS

HILL UPPER

DRIVE

P

PINE
CT

CARRICKHILL HEIGHTS

WOODLANDS

WOOD
CLO

1

BEACH PARK

BLACKBERRY LANE

R106

BURROW CT

Portmarnock Hotel
& Golf Links

ARDILAUN

CARRICKHILL ROAD MIDDLE

CARRICKHILL DRIVE

BLACKBERRY
RISE

GRAVE
YARD

CARRICK
COURT

CARRICKHILL
ROAD

BLACKBERRY

PORTMARNOCK

THE DUNES

PO ■

PITCH
&
PUTT

*PORTMARNOCK
GOLF LINKS*

Sch

STRANDMILL AV

GOLF

STRANDMILL RD

ROAD

Velvet Strand

LINKS

tuary
rve

ROAD

P

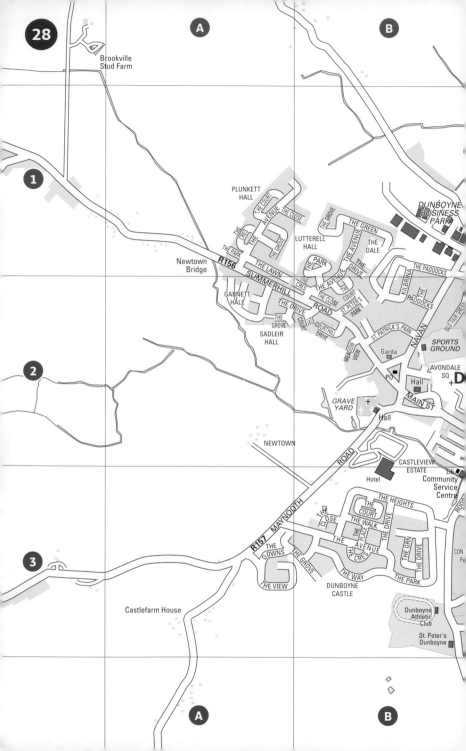

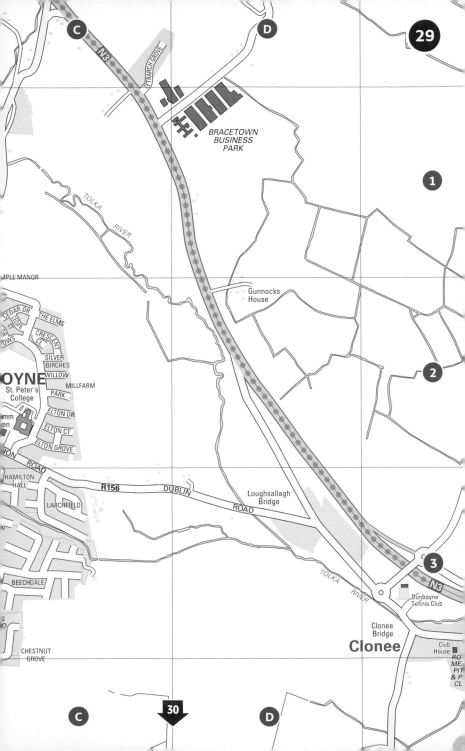

N3

RACETRARCH GROVE

BRACETOWN
BUSINESS
PARK

1

TOLKA

RIVER

MPLE MANOR

Gunnocks
House

CEDAR DR

THE ELMS

CRESCENT
CL

SILVER
BIRCHES

WILLOW

OYNE

MILLFARM

St. Peter's
College

PARK

ELTON DR

2

ELTON CT

ELTON GROVE

ON   ROAD

HAMILTON
HALL

R156

DUBLIN

Loughsallagh
Bridge

LARCHFIELD

ROAD

BEECHDALE

TOLKA

RIVER

3

N3

Dunboyne
Tennis Club

Clonee
Bridge

CHESTNUT
GROVE

Clonee

Club
House

RO
ME
PIT
& P
CL

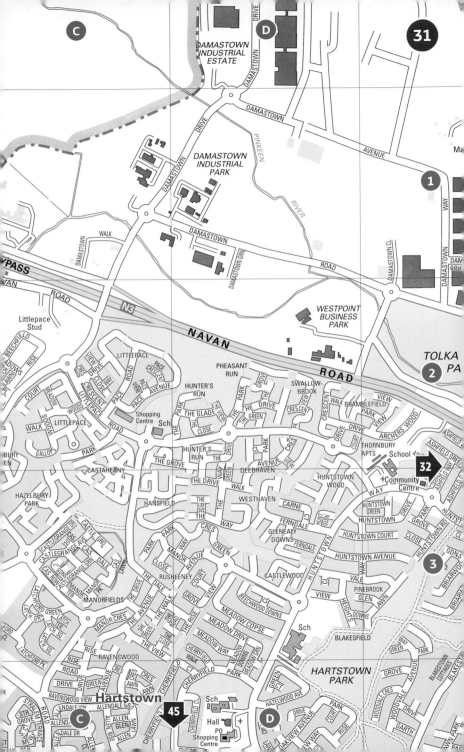

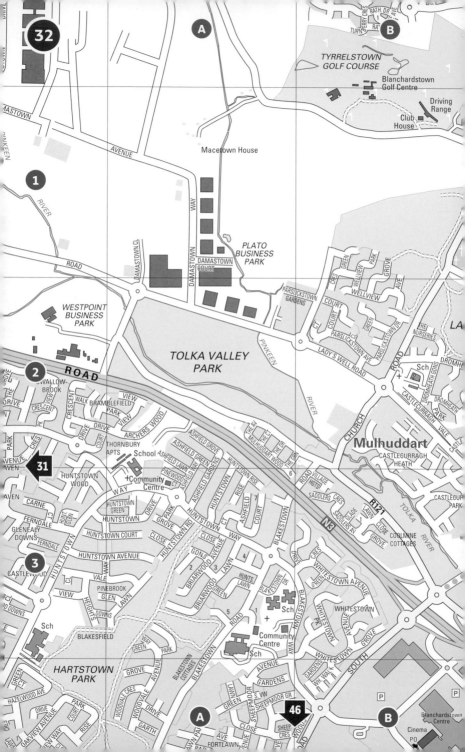

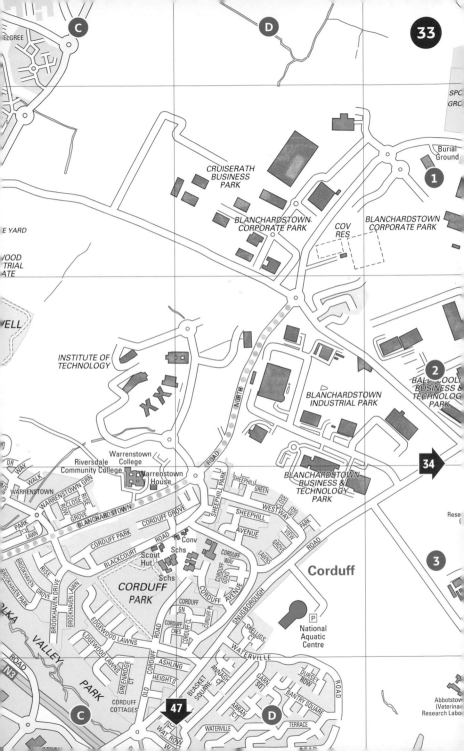

C

D

SPC
GRC

Burial
Ground

1

CRUISERATH
BUSINESS
PARK

BLANCHARDSTOWN
CORPORATE PARK

COV
RES

BLANCHARDSTOWN
CORPORATE PARK

E YARD

OOD
TRIAL
ATE

ELL

INSTITUTE OF
TECHNOLOGY

BLANCHARDSTOWN
INDUSTRIAL PARK

2

BALL COOL
BUSINESS &
TECHNOLOG
PARK

NORTH

Warrenstown
College

Riversdale
Community College

Warrenstown
House

BLANCHARDSTOWN
BUSINESS &
TECHNOLOGY
PARK

34

Rese

DR
WAY

WALK

WARRENSTOWN

WARRENSTOWN GRN

CLOSE
RISE
ROW

GROVE

BLANCHARDSTOWN

PARK
LAWN

CORDUFF GROVE

CORDUFF PARK

ROAD

Conv

Schs

BLACKCOURT

Scout
Hut

Schs

CORDUFF
PARK

SHEEPHILL PARK

SHEEPHILL
GREEN

SHEEPHILL
AVENUE

WEST WAY

CLOSE
RISE

VIEW

GROVE

LAVNS

PARK

Corduff

ROAD

3

BROOKHAVEN PARK

RISE

BROOKHAVEN GROVE

BROOKHAVEN DRIVE

BROOKHAVEN LAWN

EDGEWOOD LAWNS

EDGEWOOD LAWNS

GREENRIDGE CT

CORDUFF
COTTAGES

CORDUFF
GN

CORDUFF
ROAD

CORDUFF CL

CORDUFF
CRES

OLD CORDUFF

CORDUFF
PL

CORDUFF AVENUE

CORDUFF
GDNS

CORDUFF
WAY

SNUGBOROUGH

SKELLIGS
CT

National
Aquatic
Centre

P

OLKA

VALLEY
PARK

ROAD

N3

ASHLING

CORDUFF
HEIGHTS

BLASKET
SQUARE

ANNAGH

WATERVILLE

ARRAN
CT

GARN
SGT

DURSEY
ROW

BANTRY SQUARE

WATERVILLE

TERRACE

Abbotstown
(Veterinar
Research Labo

C

47

D

WAT ROW

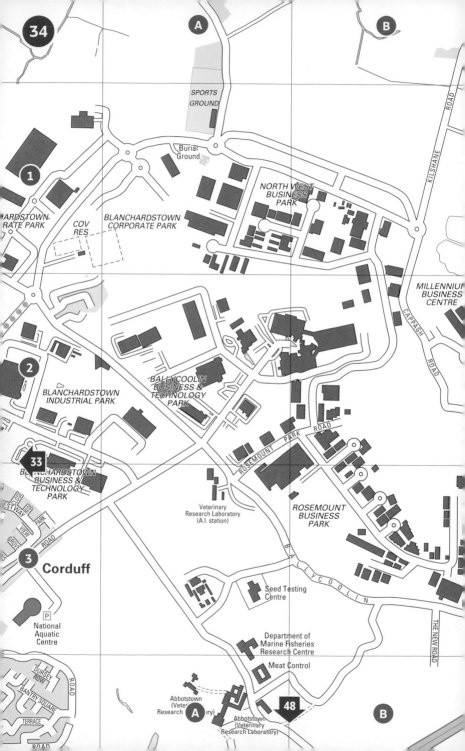

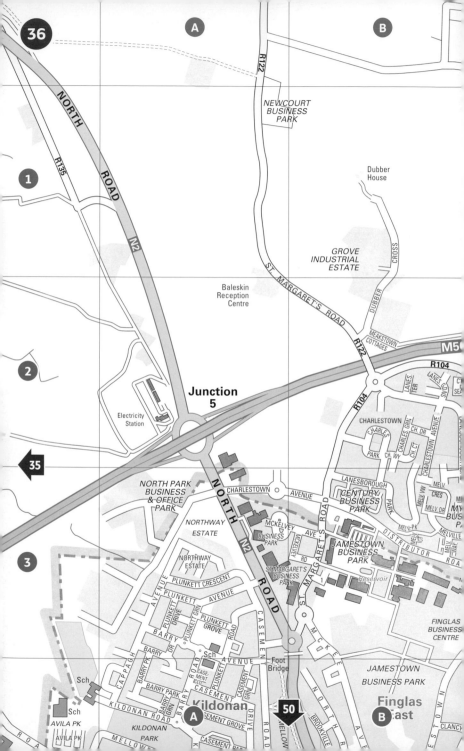

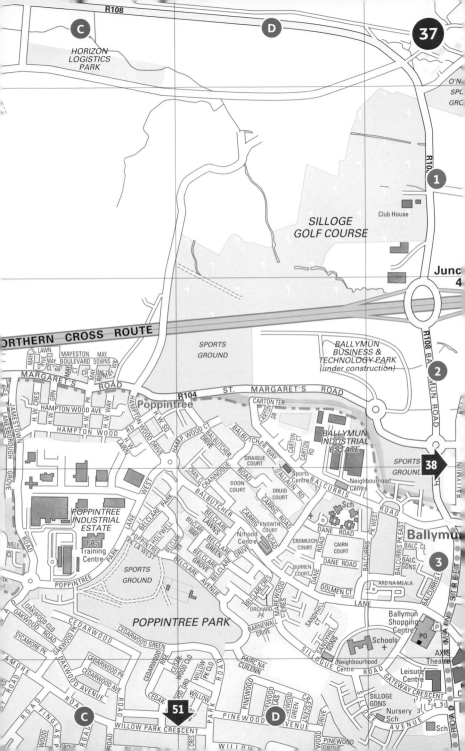

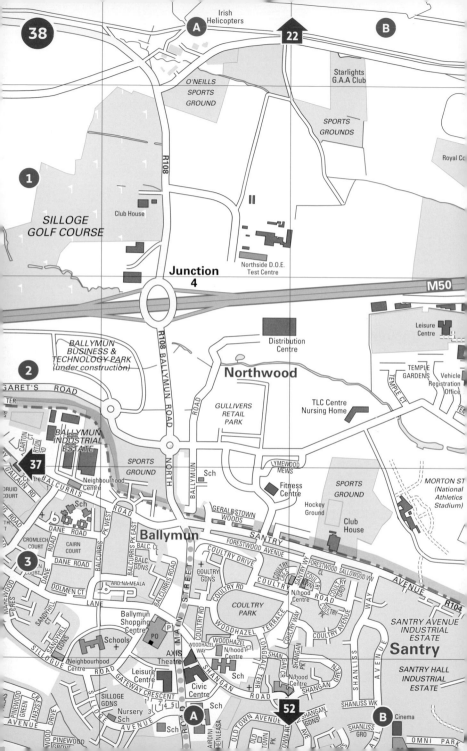

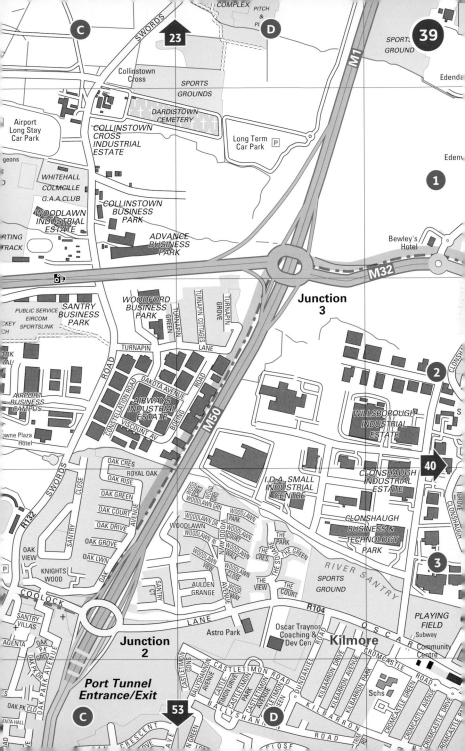

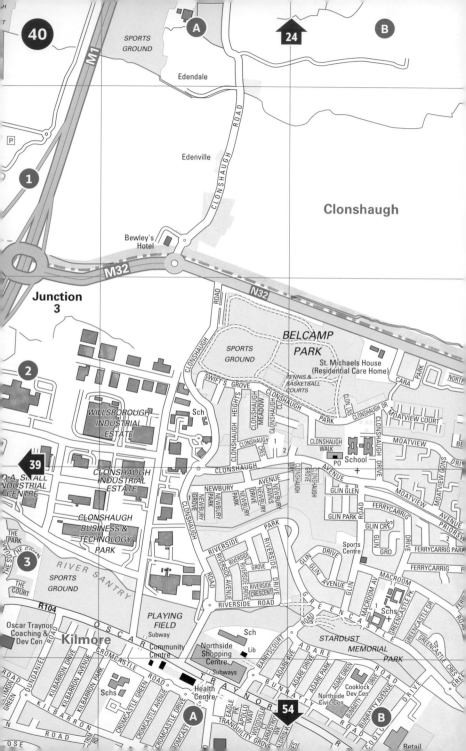

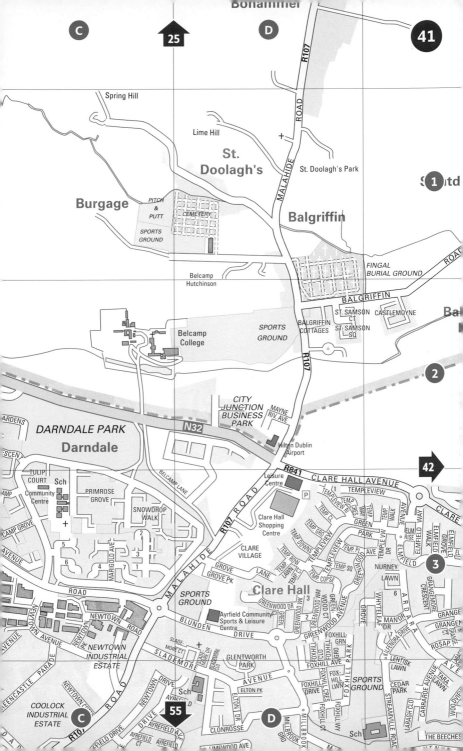

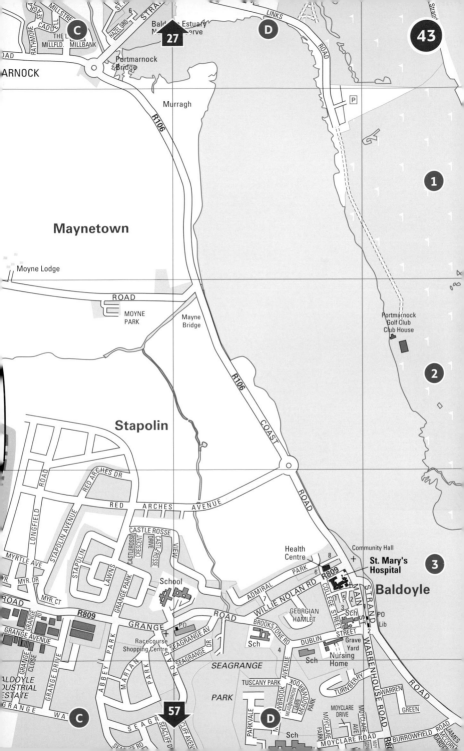

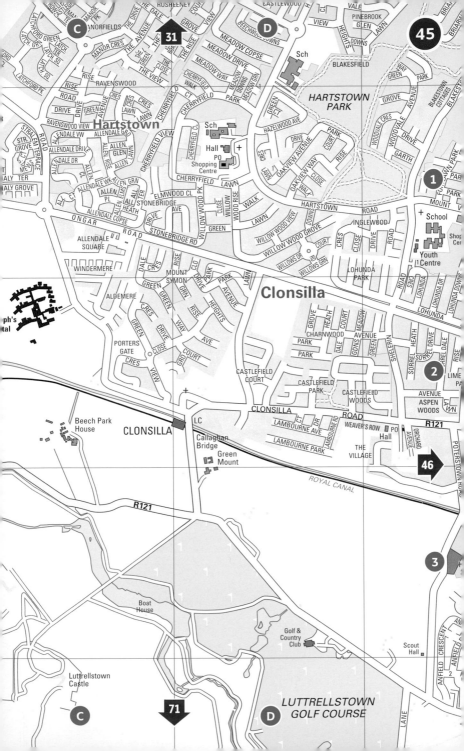

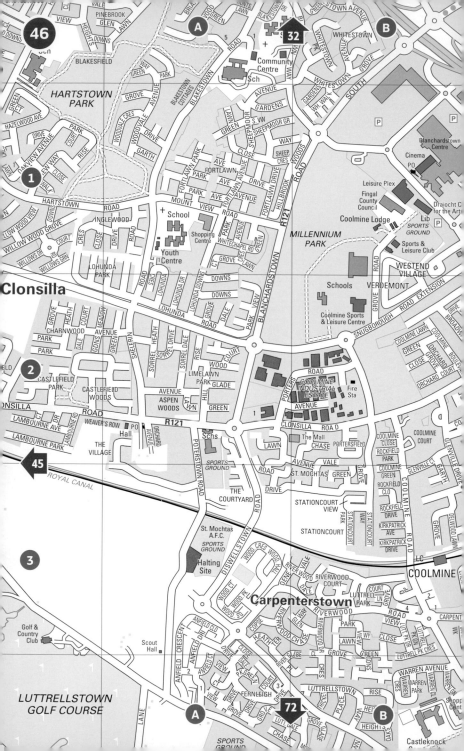

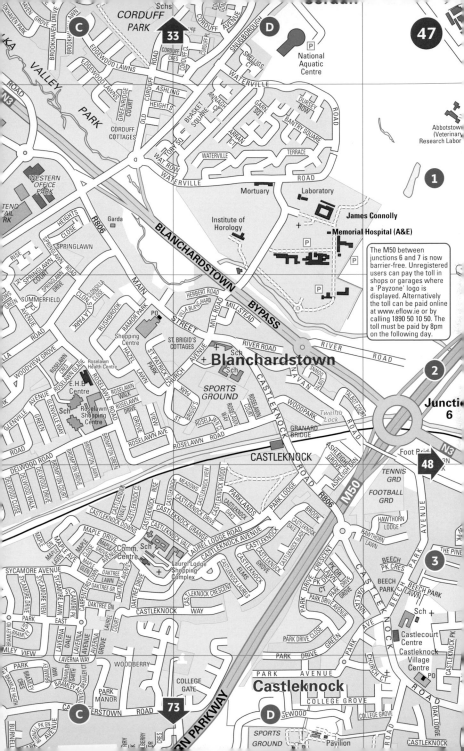

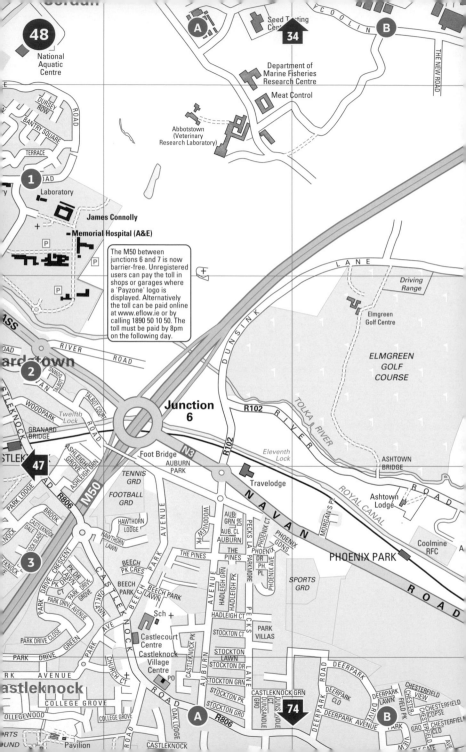

48

National Aquatic Centre

34

Seed Testing Centre

Department of Marine Fisheries Research Centre

Meat Control

Abbotstown (Veterinary Research Laboratory)

THE NEW ROAD

COOLIN

LANE

Driving Range

Elmgreen Golf Centre

1

Laboratory

James Connolly
Memorial Hospital (A&E)

The M50 between junctions 6 and 7 is now barrier-free. Unregistered users can pay the toll in shops or garages where a 'Payzone' logo is displayed. Alternatively the toll can be paid online at www.eflow.ie or by calling 1890 50 10 50. The toll must be paid by 8pm on the following day.

ELMGREEN GOLF COURSE

RIVER ROAD

...ardtown

2

DUNSINK LANE

TOLKA RIVER

Twelfth Lock

GRANARD BRIDGE

WOODPARK

TALBOT COURT

SNOWS

Junction 6

R102

R102

Eleventh Lock

ASHTOWN BRIDGE

...STLEK

47

ASHLEIGH GROVE

ASHLEIGH GRN

Foot Bridge

AUBURN PARK

N3

ROAD

Travelodge

NAVAN

ROYAL CANAL

Ashtown Lodge

ROAD

TENNIS GRD

FOOTBALL GRD

HAWTHORN LODGE

HAWTHORN LAWN

PARK LODGE

R806

M50

BROOK

PARK AVENUE

WOODVIEW PK

AUBURN

AUB. GRN DR
AUB. CL

THE PINES

AUBURN

THE PINES

PECKS LA

PARKMORE

PHOENIX
PHOENIX DR
PH. PL
PHOENIX AVE

PHOENIX GDNS

MORGAN'S PL

PHOENIX PARK

Coolmine RFC

ROAD

3

...TLEK

PARK GLADE

PARK DRIVE CRESCENT

PK DR
PK DR GN
PK DR CT

PARK DRIVE GROVE

BEECH PK CRES

BEECH PARK

BEECH PARK

BEECH LAWN

HADLEIGH GRN

HADLEIGH PK

HADLEIGH CT

PECKS LANE

SPORTS GRD

PARK DRIVE AVENUE

CASTLEKNOCK LAWN

CASTLEKNOCK PK

Sch

Castlecourt Centre

Castleknock Village Centre

STOCKTON CT

STOCKTON LAWN
STOCKTON DR

PARK VILLAS

PARK DRIVE CLOSE

PARK GREEN

PARK AVENUE

PARK DRIVE

CASTLEKNOCK AVE

CHURCH CT

ROAD

PO

OAK LODGE

AUBURN

STOCKTON GRN
STOCKTON PK
STOCKTON GRO

CASTLEKNOCK GRN

DUNSANDLE

DUNSINK

PECKS LANE

DEERPARK ROAD

DEERPARK DRIVE

DEERPARK CLO

DEERPARK LAWN

DEERPARK AVENUE

DEERPARK CLO

CHESTERFIELD VIEW

CHESTERFIELD COPSE

CHESTER FIELD PK

WEST GATE

CHESTERFIELD GRO
CHESTERFIELD CLO

A

R806

74

B

Castleknock

COLLEGE GROVE

COLLEGEWOOD

COLLEGE GROVE

Pavilion

CASTLEKNOCK

...RTS...
...UND...

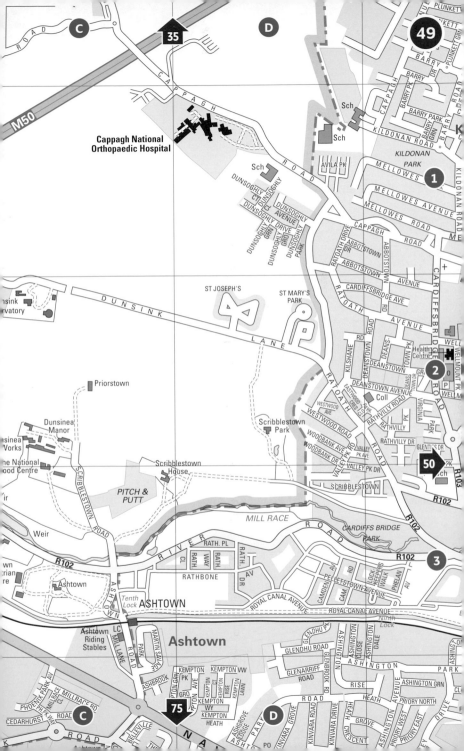

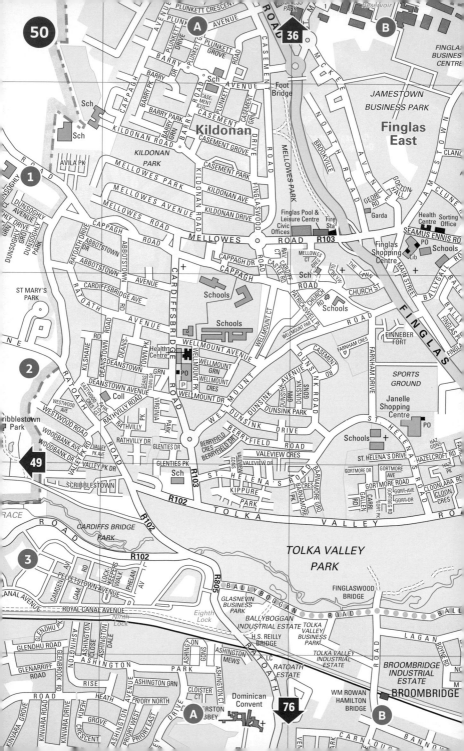

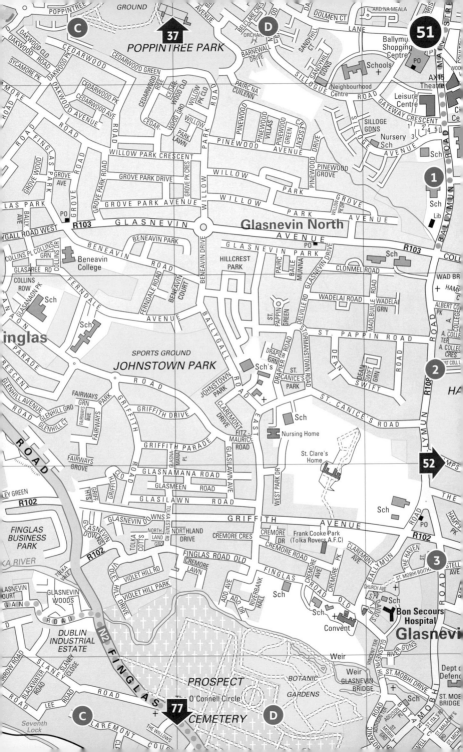

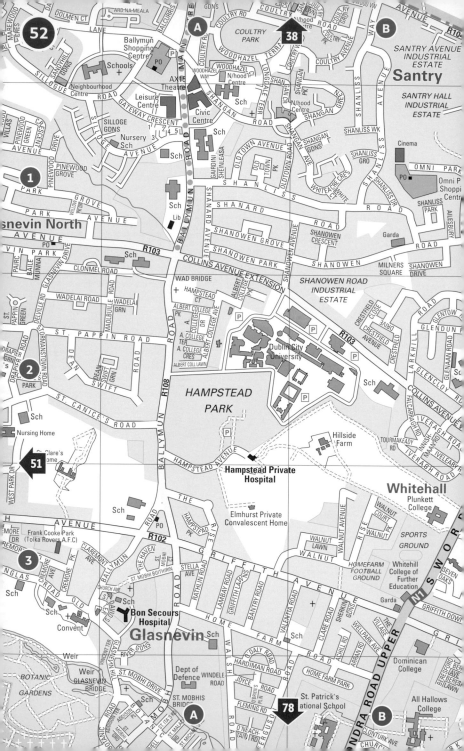

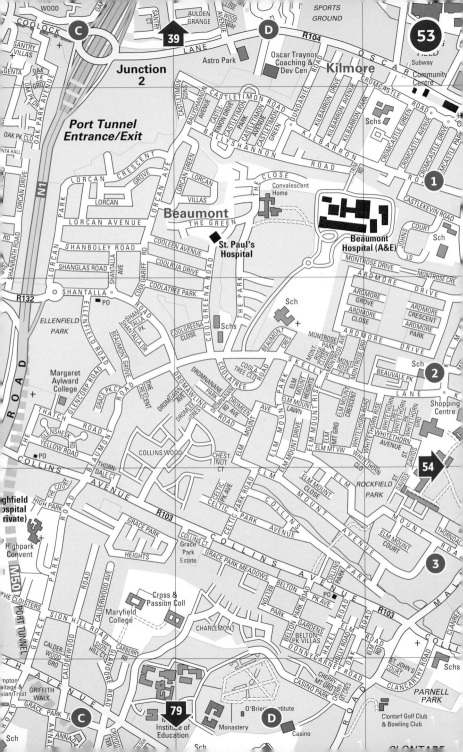

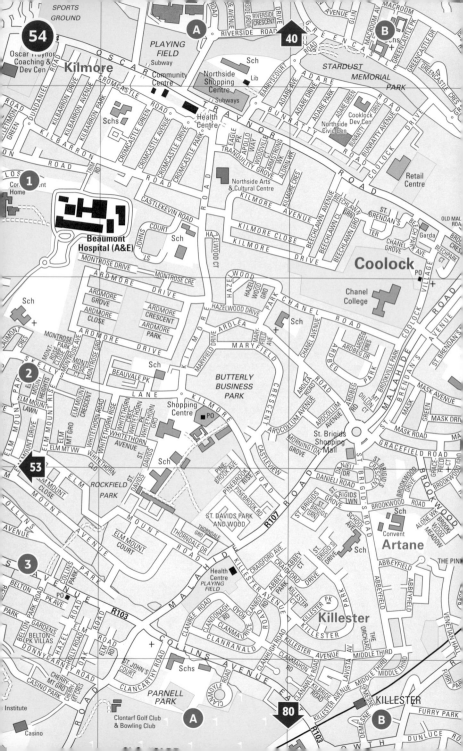

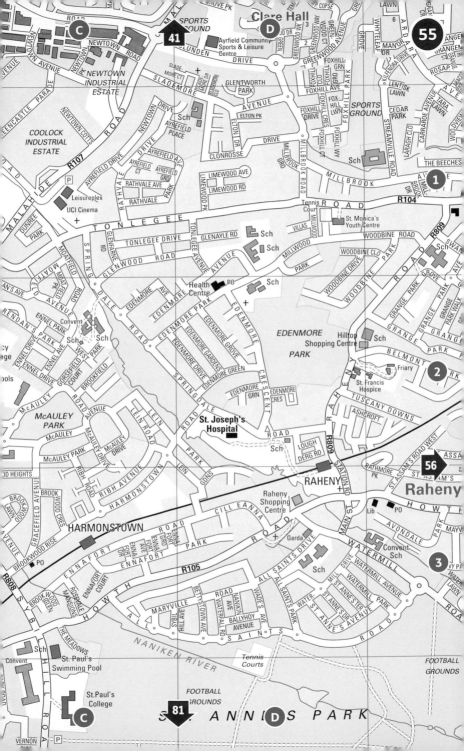

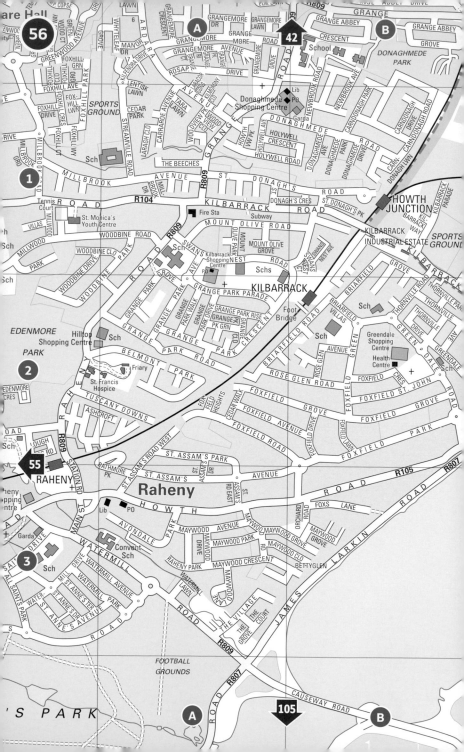

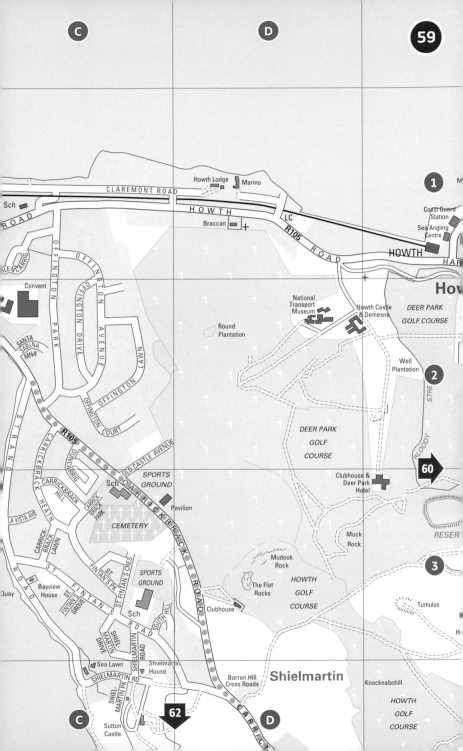

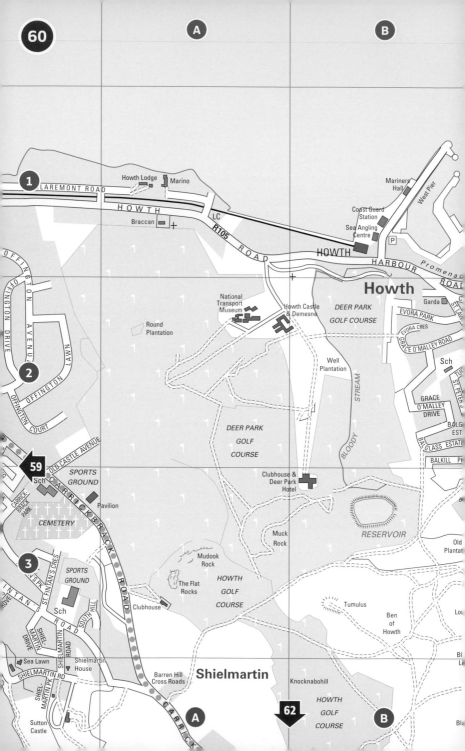

1

hthouse

WTH
BOUR

East Pier

P

Martello
Tower

BALSCADDEN BAY

ABBEY STREET

Health
Centre

BALSCADDEN   ROAD

P

Puck's Rocks

Lib

ASGARD PK.

KILROCK ROAD

NASHVILLE PARK

Kilrock

Nose
of
Howth

2

MAIN STREET

NASHVILLE RD

COWBOOTER LANE

THORMANBY

CROSSTREES

ASGARD
ROAD

THORMANBY

CANNON ROCK VIEW

UPPER

Cannon Rock
Cottage

CLIFF WALK (Fingal Way)

LAWNS

CLIFF RD.

ROAD

DUNGRIFFAN   ROAD

MARINERS
COVE

ALKIL

GREYS LANE

WOODCLIFF
HEIGHTS

CASANA VIEW

THORMANBY
LODGE

Green
Ivy

3

Rookstown

THORMANBY WOODS

WINDGATE

Ashville

Highfield

Bearna

Piper's
Gut

ROAD

Oakley Park

KITESTOWN ROAD

R105

NEW ROAD

WINDGATE RISE

CLIFF WALK

Fox Hole

ROAD

ROAD

BAILEY GRN RD.

The
Haven

om Bed

White
Water

Old Baily
Cottage

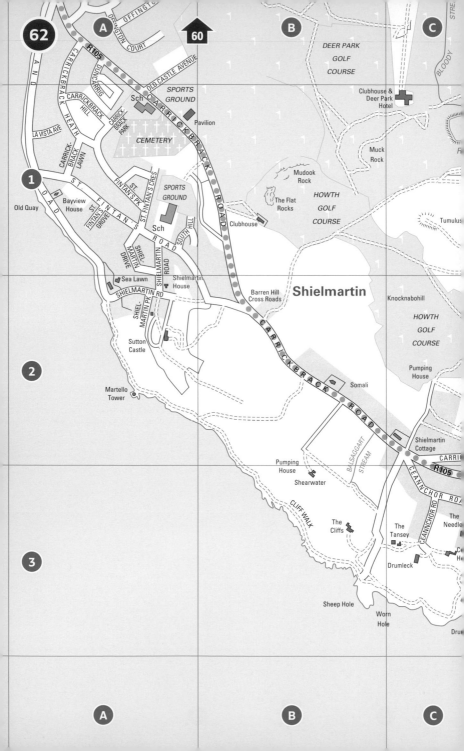

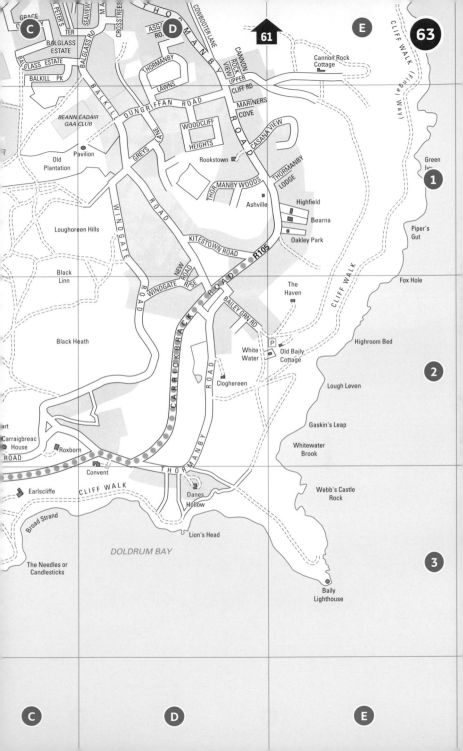

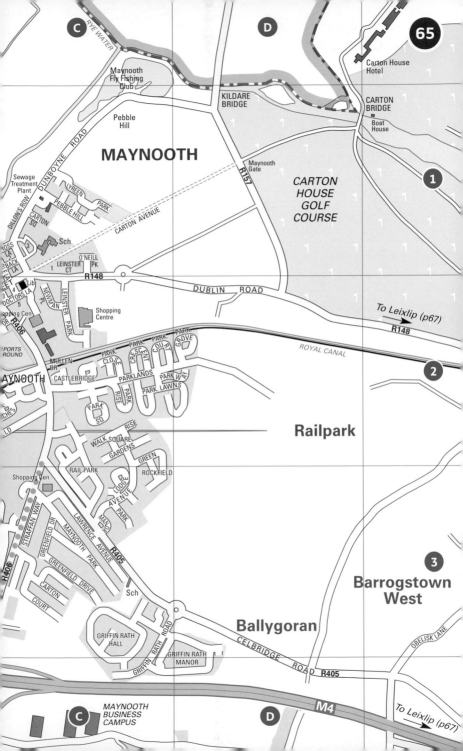

RYE WATER

Maynooth
Fly Fishing
Club

KILDARE
BRIDGE

Carton House
Hotel

CARTON
BRIDGE

Boat
House

Pebble
Hill

DUNBOYNE ROAD

MAYNOOTH

R157

Maynooth
Gate

*CARTON
HOUSE
GOLF
COURSE*

Sewage
Treatment
Plant

DILLON'S ROW

LYREEN PARK

PEBBLE HILL

CARTON SQ

Sch

CARTON AVENUE

O'NEILL PK

LEINSTER CT

1

R148

CROSS LA

BACK

STREET

Lib

DOCTORS LA

5

pping Cen

R406

Shopping
Centre

LEINSTER PL

NEWMAN PL

DUBLIN ROAD

To Leixlip (p67)

R148

1

PORTS
ROUND

MULLEN BR

AYNOOTH

CASTLEBRIDGE

PARK CLOSE

PARK CRESCENT

PARK COURT

PARK GROVE

PARKLANDS

PARK WAY

PARK LAWNS

ROYAL CANAL

2

PARK SQ

ARCHES

FIELD

PARK RISE

WALK

SQUARE

GARDENS

PARK RISE

GREEN

Railpark

RAIL PARK

ROCKFIELD

Shopping Cen

STRAFFAN WAY

GREENFIELD DR

MAYNOOTH PARK

LAWRENCE AVENUE

LODGE

AVENUE

PARK

MAIN

R405

GREENFIELD DRIVE

Sch

CARTON COURT

R406

GRIFFIN RATH HALL

GRIFFIN RATH ROAD

GRIFFIN RATH MANOR

Ballygoran

CELBRIDGE ROAD

R405

3

**Barrogstown
West**

OBELISK LANE

To Leixlip (p67)

*MAYNOOTH
BUSINESS
CAMPUS*

M4

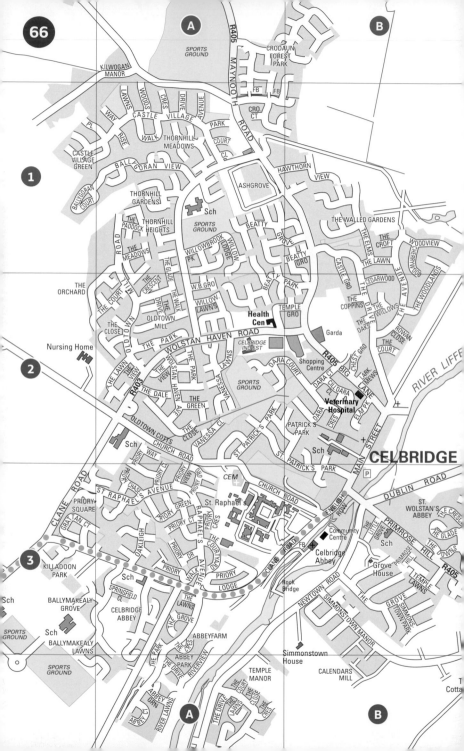

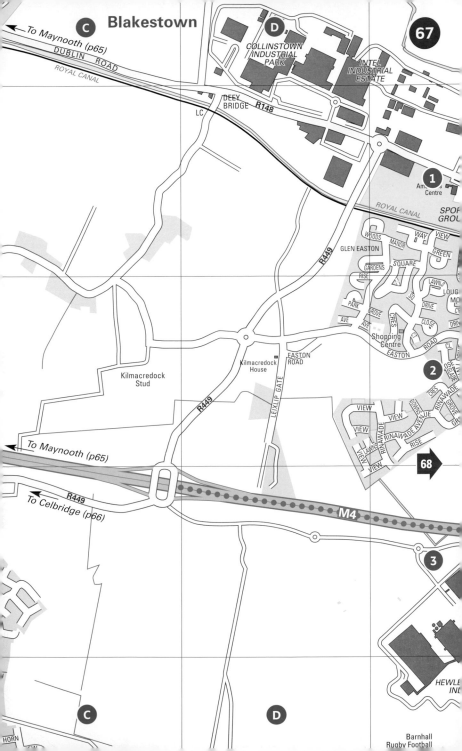

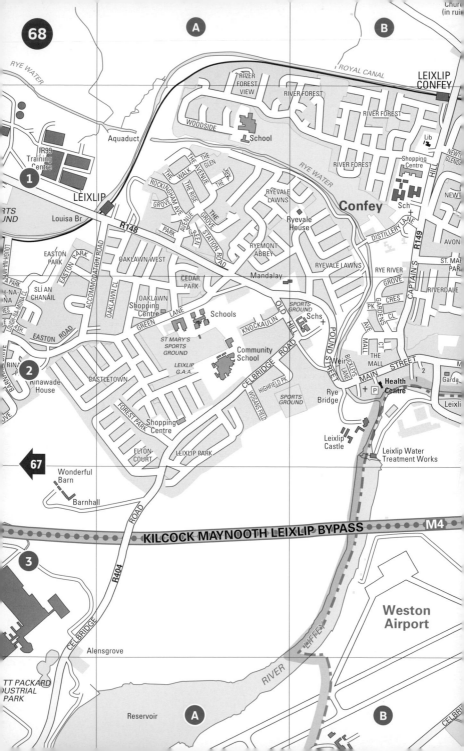

68

A

B

RYE WATER

ROYAL CANAL

LEIXLIP CONFEY

Church (in rui...)

RIVER FOREST VIEW

RIVER FOREST

RIVER FOREST

RIVER FOREST

WOODSIDE

School

Lib

Shopping Centre

Aquaduct

1

IR99 Training Centre

LEIXLIP

NEWTOWN GLENDA...

Sch

NEWT...

ROCKINGHAM AVE

THE WALK

THE AVENUE

THE GLEN

THE RISE

THE GROVE

THE DELL

RYEVALE LAWNS

Confey

RYE WATER

DISTILLERY LANE

R149

Louisa Br

R148

GROVE

PARK

AVENUE

STATION ROAD

GREEN

Ryevale House

RYEMONT ABBEY

Mandalay

RYEVALE LAWNS

AVON

ST. MAR... PAR...

EASTON PARK

EASTON PARK

ACCOMMODATION ROAD

OAKLAWN WEST

CEDAR PARK

RYE RIVER

GROVE

CAPTAIN'S

RIVERDALE

SLÍ AN CHANAIL

SLÍ-NA-... NA

OAKLAWN CL

OAKLAWN Shopping Centre

GREEN LANE

CEDAR LANE

Schools

SPORTS GROUND

KNOCKAULIN

OLD HILL

Schs

PK GARDENS CL

AVE MALL

CRES

EASTON ROAD

ASH

...RINA...

2

Rinawade House

CASTLETOWN

ST MARY'S SPORTS GROUND

LEIXLIP G.A.A.

Community School

CELBRIDGE ROAD

HIGHFIELD PK

POUND STREET

Weir

BUCKLEY'S LANE

CT THE MALL

MAIN STREET

Health Centre

Garda

Leixli...

WOGANSFIELD

SPORTS GROUND

Rye Bridge

P

67

FOREST PARK

Shopping Centre

ELTON COURT

LEIXLIP PARK

Leixlip Castle

Leixlip Water Treatment Works

Wonderful Barn

Barnhall

CELBRIDGE ROAD

R404

KILCOCK MAYNOOTH LEIXLIP BYPASS

M4

3

TT PACKARD ...DUSTRIAL PARK

CELBRIDGE

Alensgrove

Weston Airport

RIVER

LIFFEY

CELBR...

Reservoir

A

B

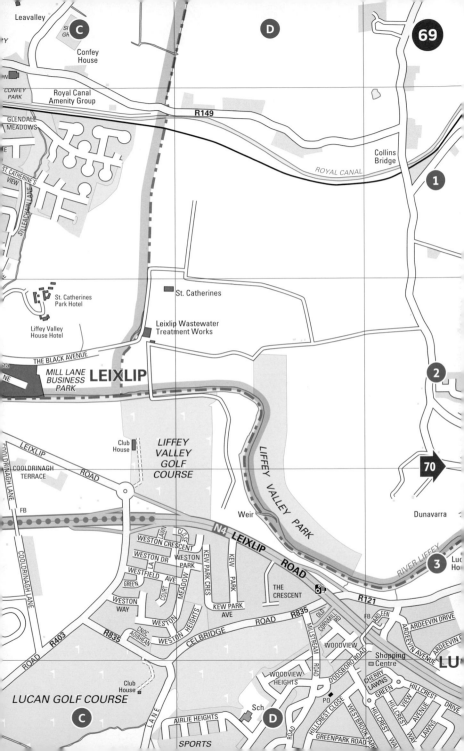

Leavalley

C
SI
GA

Confey
House

CONFEY
PARK

ST. CATHERINE'S
VIEW

GLENDALE
MEADOWS

Royal Canal
Amenity Group

R149

ROYAL CANAL

Collins
Bridge

D

69

1

St. Catherines
Park Hotel

St. Catherines

Liffey Valley
House Hotel

Leixlip Wastewater
Treatment Works

THE BLACK AVENUE

MILL LANE
BUSINESS
PARK

LEIXLIP

2

LEIXLIP
ROAD

COOLDRINAGH
TERRACE

Club
House

LIFFEY
VALLEY
GOLF
COURSE

LIFFEY VALLEY PARK

70

COOLDRINAGH LANE

FB

Weir

Dunavarra

N4 LEIXLIP ROAD

WESTON CRESCENT

WESTON DR

WESTON
PARK

CLOSE

LAWN

KEW PARK CRES

KEW
PARK

THE
CRESCENT

River Liffey

3

Luc
Ho

WESTFIELD AVE

GREEN

COURT

WESTON
MEADOW

KEW PARK
AVE

R121

WESTON
WAY

CNOC
AOIBHEAN

WESTON
HEIGHTS

WESTON

ROAD

R835 ROAD

OLD
CORNMILL
RD

FB

GREEN

ARDEEVIN DRIVE

R403

R835

CELBRIDGE

MILLSTREAM ROAD

WOODVIEW

DODSBORO ROAD

Shopping
Centre

ARDEEVIN AVENUE

ARDEEVIN

LU

LANE

Club
House

LUCAN GOLF COURSE

C

WOODVIEW
HEIGHTS

HILLCREST CLOSE

PO

Sch

D

AIRLIE HEIGHTS

WESTBROOK

GREENPARK ROAD

CHERRY
LAWNS

CHERRY
GREEN

HILLCREST
VIEW

HILLCREST
WAY

HILLCREST
LAWNS

HILLCREST
AVENUE

HILLCREST
DRIVE

SPORTS

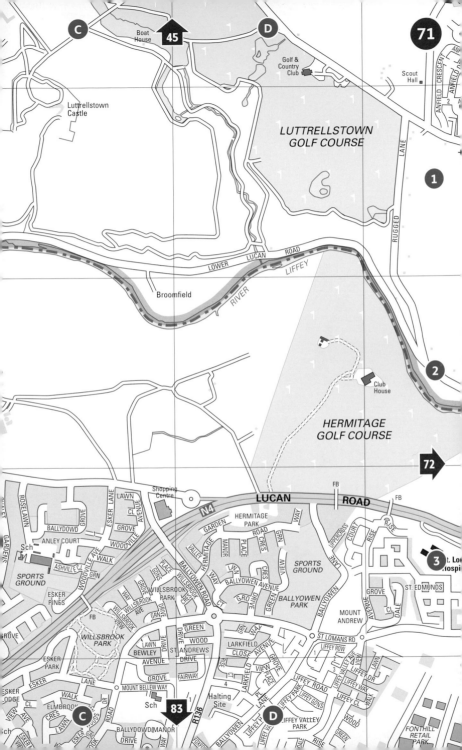

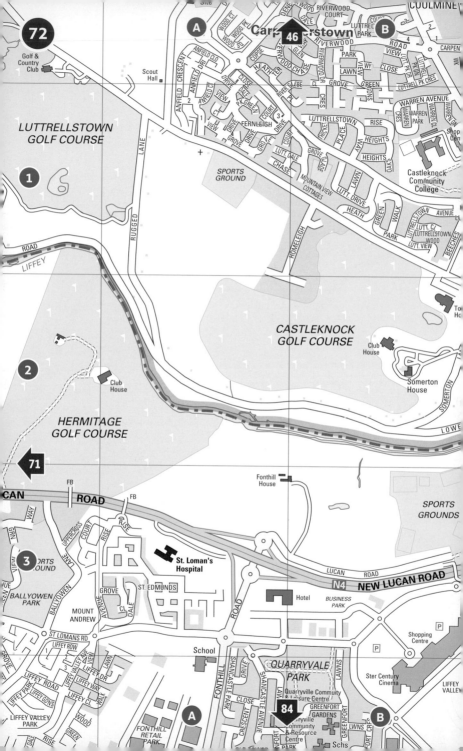

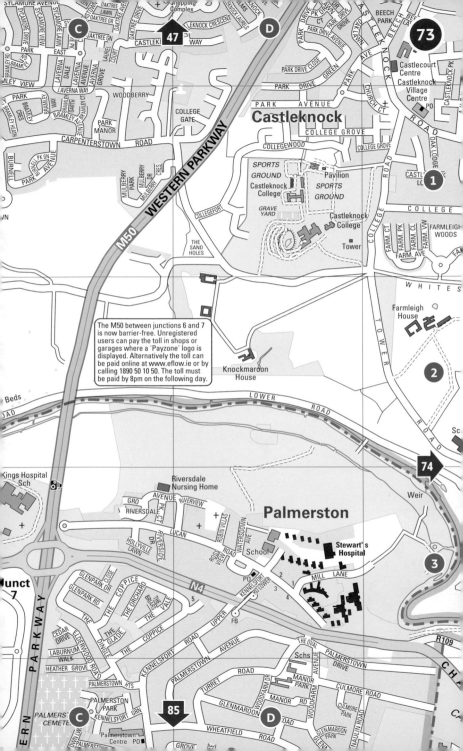

The M50 between junctions 6 and 7 is now barrier-free. Unregistered users can pay the toll in shops or garages where a 'Payzone' logo is displayed. Alternatively the toll can be paid online at www.eflow.ie or by calling 1890 50 10 50. The toll must be paid by 8pm on the following day.

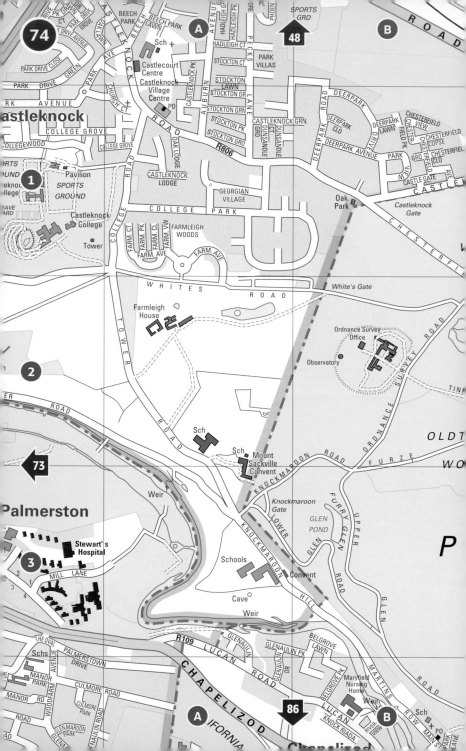

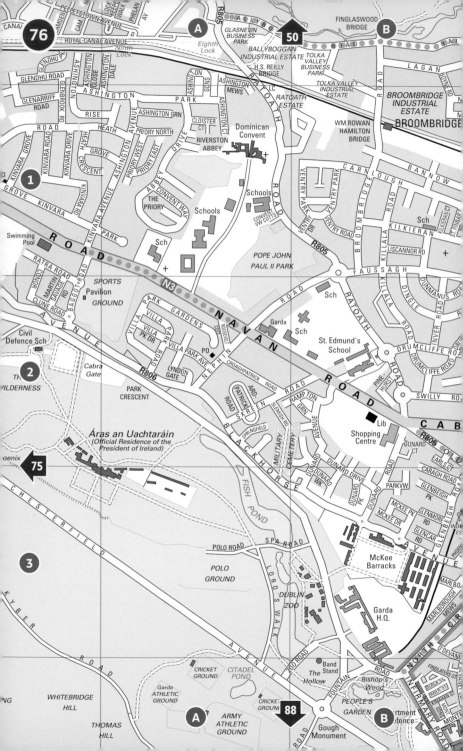

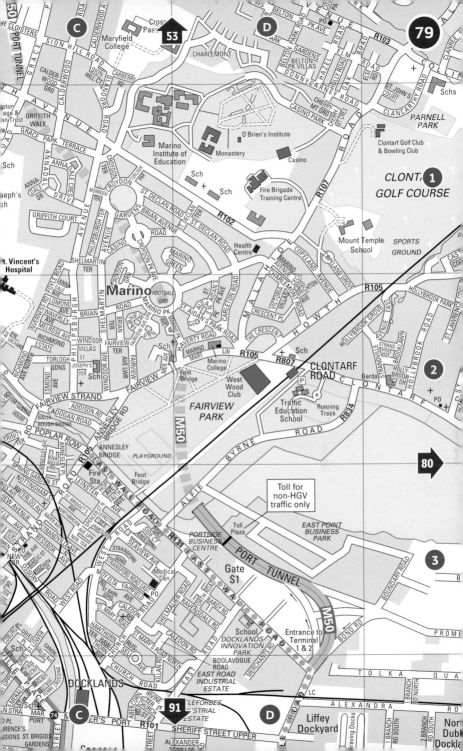

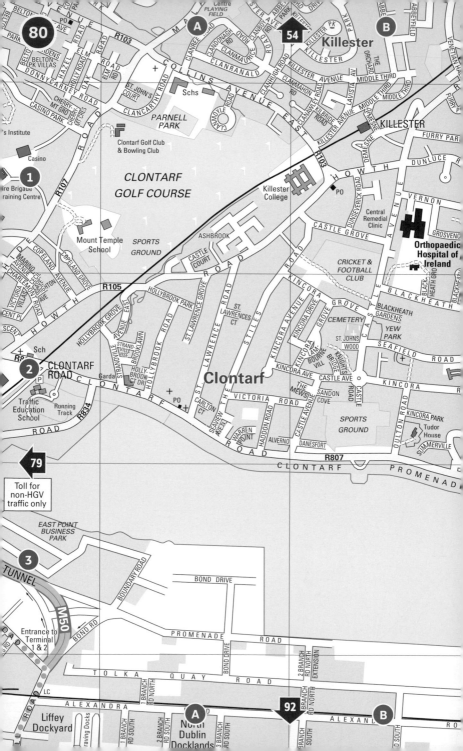

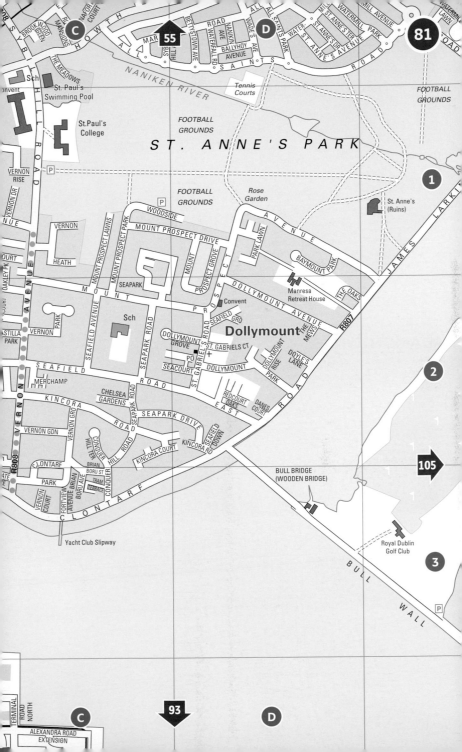

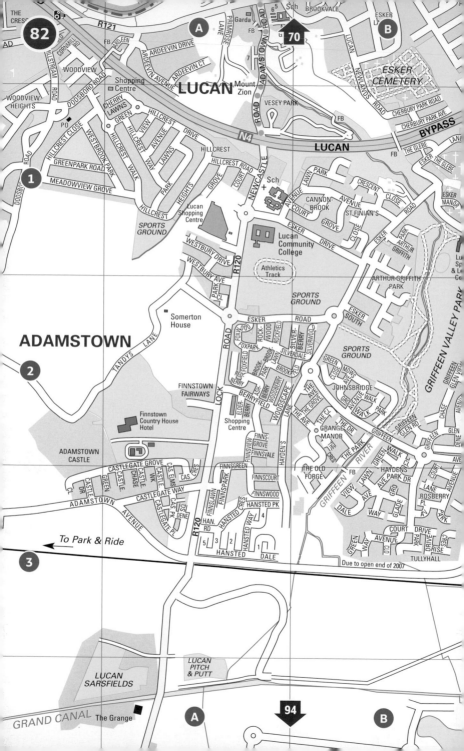

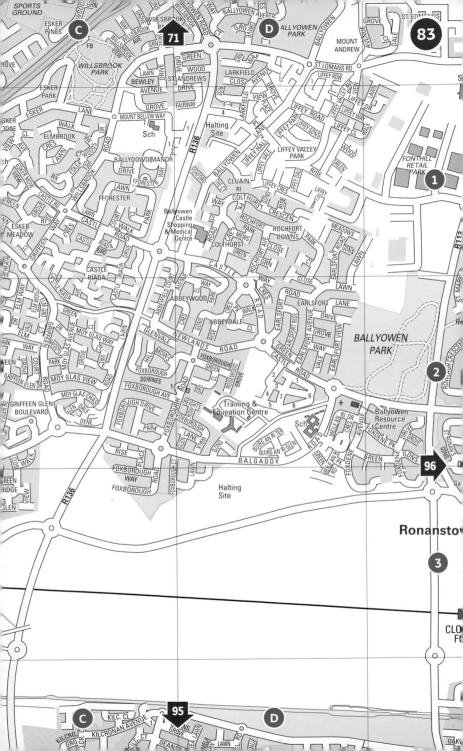

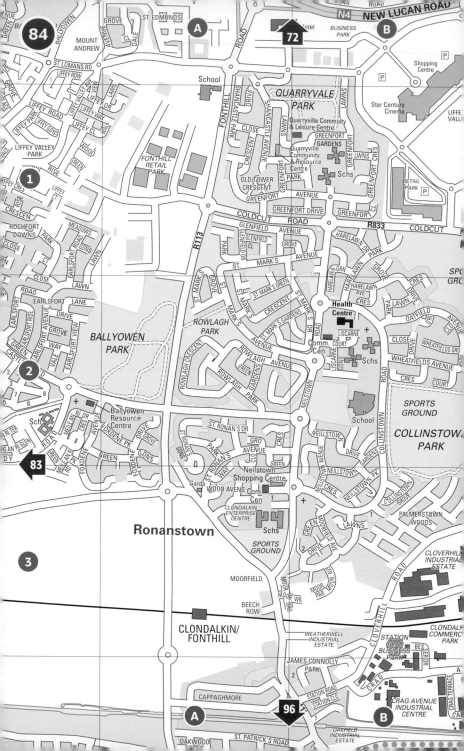

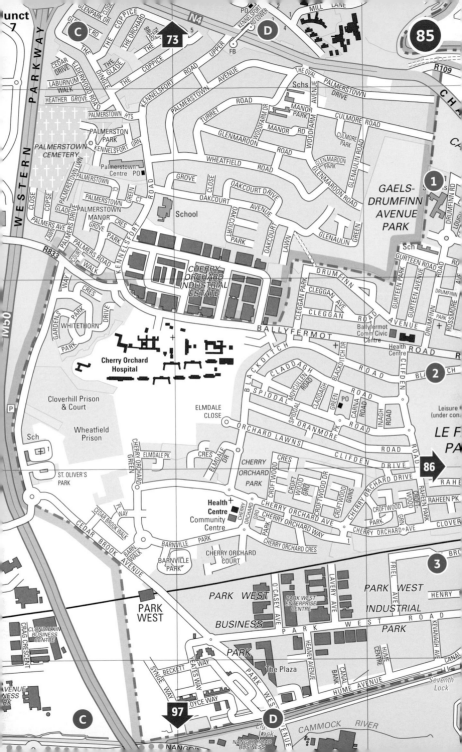

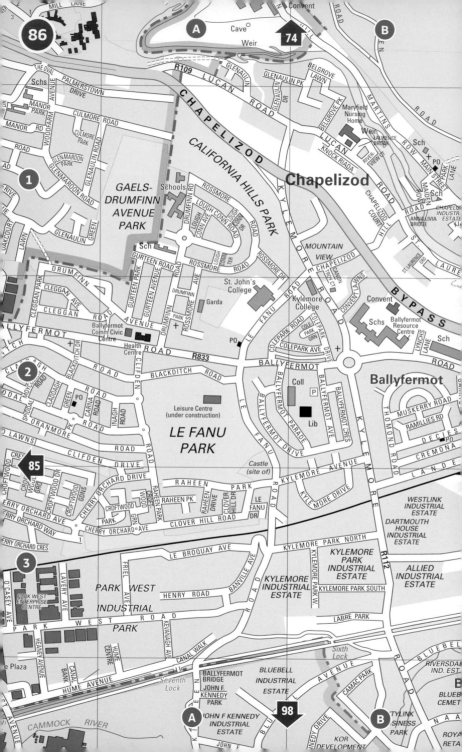

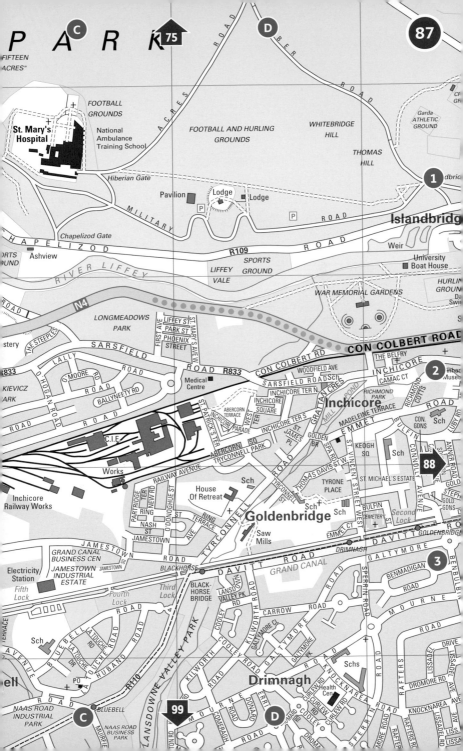

"FIFTEEN ACRES"

FOOTBALL GROUNDS

St. Mary's Hospital

National Ambulance Training School

FOOTBALL AND HURLING GROUNDS

WHITEBRIDGE HILL

THOMAS HILL

Garda ATHLETIC GROUND

Hiberian Gate

Pavilion

Lodge

Lodge

MILITARY

Chapelizod Gate

Islandbridge

ROAD

R109

Weir

University Boat House

CHAPELIZOD

Ashview

RIVER LIFFEY

SPORTS GROUND

LIFFEY VALE

WAR MEMORIAL GARDENS

HURLIN GROUN

N4

LONGMEADOWS PARK

Liffey St.
First Ave
Park St.
St. Mary's Ave
Phoenix Street

CON COLBERT ROAD

THE STEEPLES

SARSFIELD

CON COLBERT RD

THE BELFRY

INCHICORE

WOODFIELD AVE

CAMAC CT

R833

ROAD

R833

SARSFIELD RD

Sch

RICHMOND COTTS

Medical Centre

INCHICORE TER N.

INCHICORE TER S.

ABERCORN TERRACE

WEST TER

INCHICORE SQUARE

GRATTAN CRES

RICHMOND PARK

CON. GDNS

Sch

ANNER ROAD

KIEVICZ PARK

O.MOORE ROAD

O.HOGAN ROAD

BALLYNEETY RD

LALLY ROAD

ROAD

ST. PATRICK'S TER

INCHICORE PARADE

JAMES ST.

GOLDEN BR.

EMMET

MADELEINE TERRACE

BULFIN

Inchicore

KEOGH SQ

Sch

CONNOLLY AVENUE

C.I.E.

ABERCORN SQ

TRYCONNELL PARK

SPA RD

THOMAS DAVIS ST W.

St. VINCENT STREET WEST

TYRONE PLACE

St. MICHAEL'S ESTATE

88

STEPH GOLD. GDNS

Works

PARTRIDGE TER

NEW RD

O'DONOGHUE ST

RING TER

NASH ST

Sch

TYRCONNELL

Sch

BULFIN CEMETERY

Second Lock

Inchicore Railway Works

House Of Retreat

JAMESTOWN

RING TERRACE

JAMESTOWN

TYRCONNELL ROAD

Goldenbridge

Saw Mills

EMMET CT

DAVITT

Goldenbridge

Electricity Station

GRAND CANAL BUSINESS CEN

JAMESTOWN INDUSTRIAL ESTATE

JAMESTOWN

BLACKHORSE

DAVITT

ROAD

GRAND CANAL

DRIMNAGH

GALTYMORE

3

BENMADIGAN ROAD

Fifth Lock

Fourth Lock

Third Lock

BLACK-HORSE BRIDGE

LANSO'S VALLEY PK

COOLEY RD

GALTYMORE RD

CARROW

SPERRIN RD

MOURNE ROAD

BENBULBIN

Sch

BLUEBELL LA TOUCHE RD

LA TOUCHE DR

HUBAND ROAD

ROAD

Fourth Lock

KILWORTH

COOLEY ROAD

GALTYMORE CL

GALTYMORE

KNOCKNAREA

Schs

DRIVE

LISSADE

DROMORE RD

AVENUE

ROAD

PO

BLUEBELL

R110

LANSDOWNE VALLEY PARK

KILWORTH ROAD

MOURNE

ERRI

DONARD

COOLEY

COMERAGH

Drimnagh

CURLEW

Health Cen

COOLEY

DRONT

SPERRIN ROAD

RAFTERS

KNOCKNAREA AVE.

LISSADEL RD

ROAD

NAAS ROAD INDUSTRIAL PARK

99

NAAS ROAD BUSINESS PARK

C

D

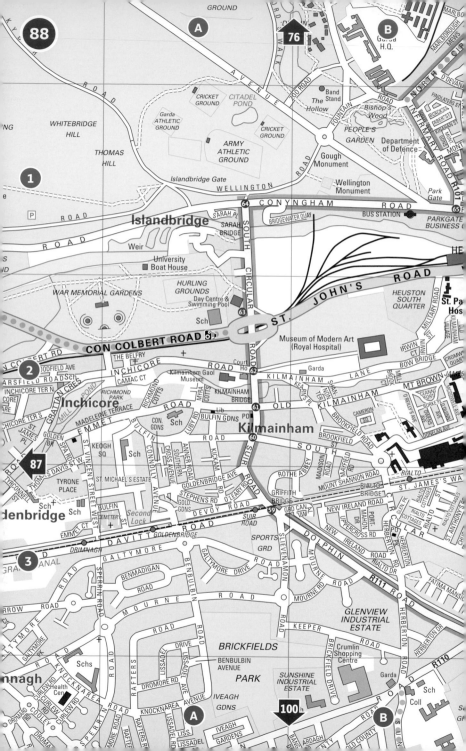

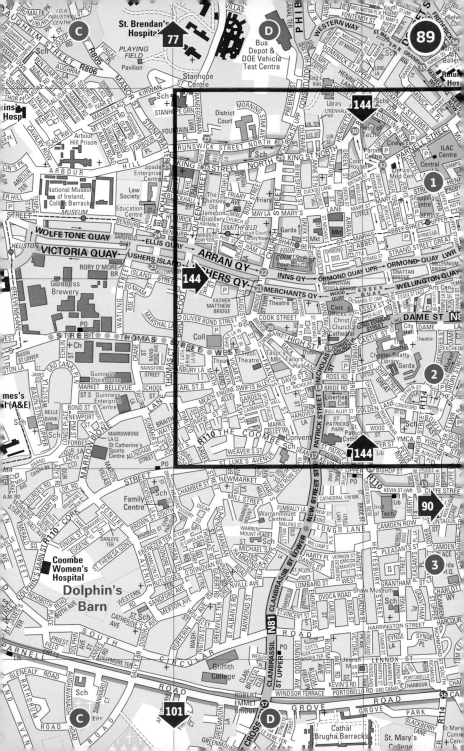

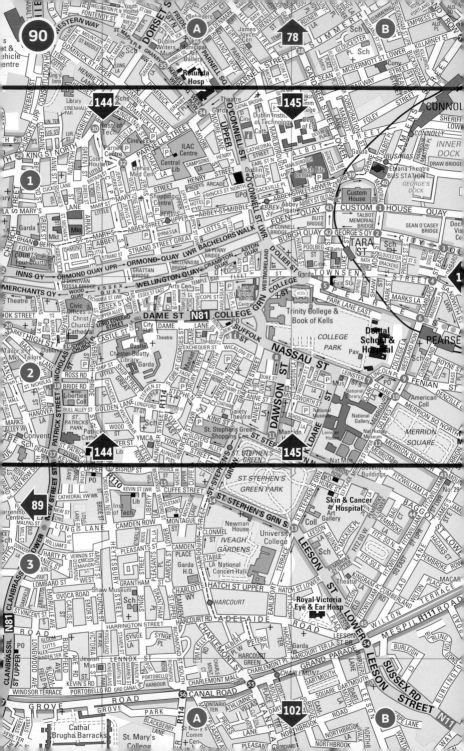

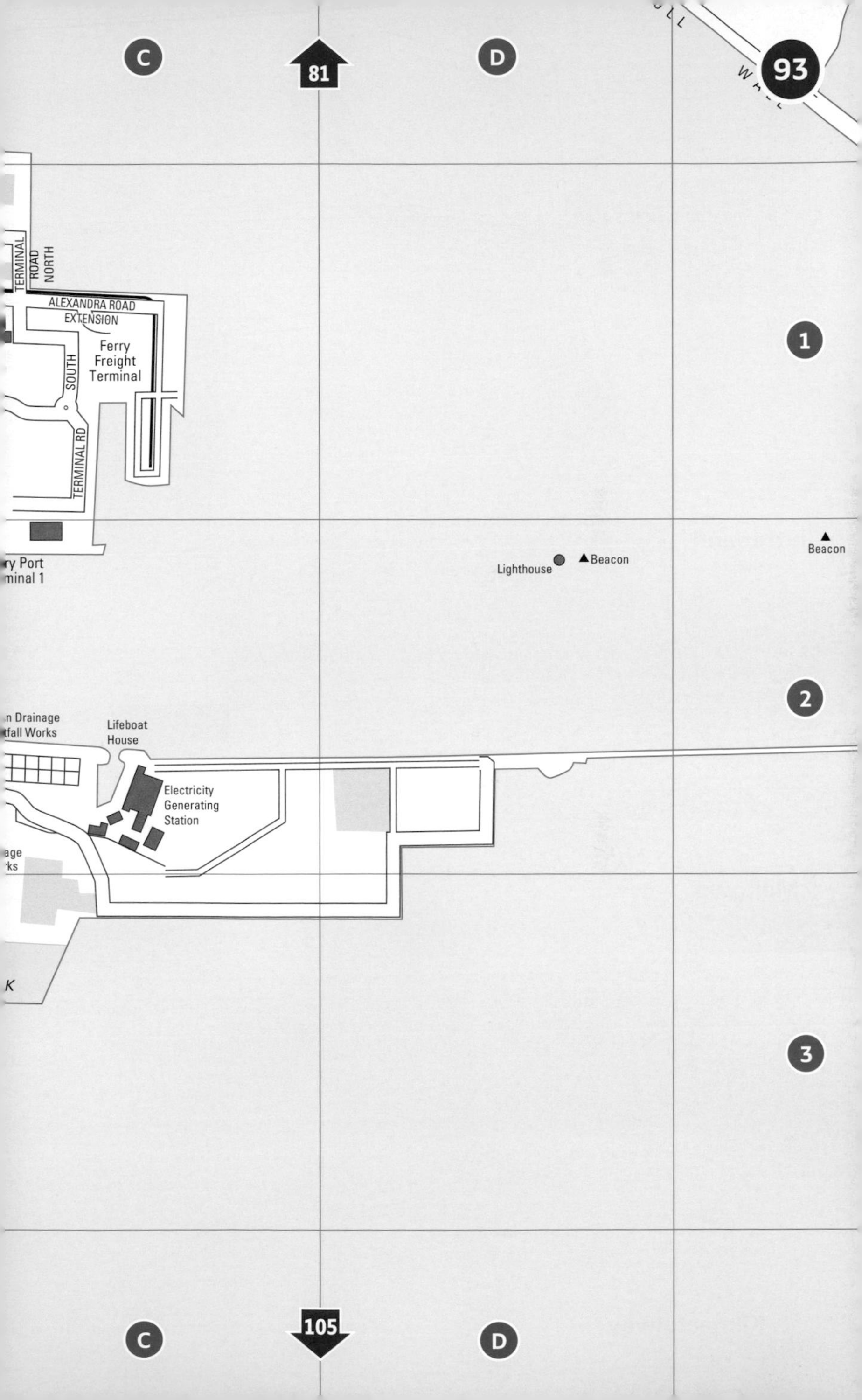

TERMINAL ROAD NORTH

ALEXANDRA ROAD
EXTENSION

Ferry
Freight
Terminal

SOUTH

TERMINAL RD

1

ry Port
minal 1

Lighthouse ● ▲ Beacon

▲
Beacon

2

n Drainage
tfall Works

Lifeboat
House

Electricity
Generating
Station

age
ks

K

3

A

82

B

LUCAN
PITCH
& PUTT

LUCAN
SARSFIELDS

GRAND CANAL The Grange

1

R120

Clutterland

Ballybane
Pitch & Putt

GRANG
INTER
BU

KILCARBERRY
INDUSTRIAL
ESTATE

THE COURTYA
BUSINESS
PARK

2

R120

R134

NANGOR ROAD

R13

Milltown

3

Castle
Bagot
House

Burial
Ground

Kilmactalway

A

106

B

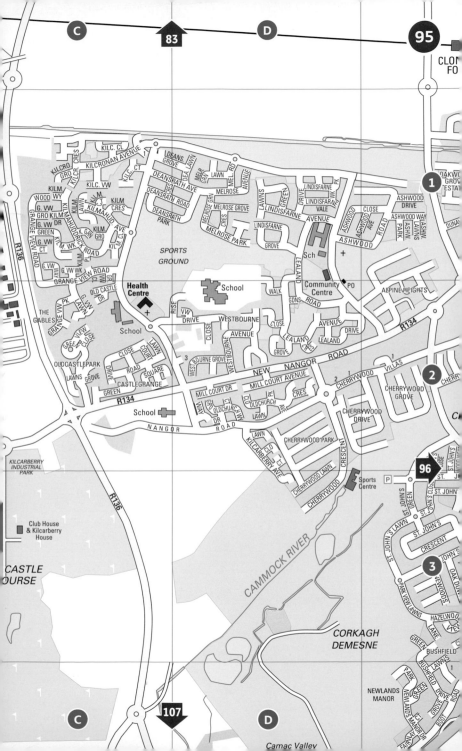

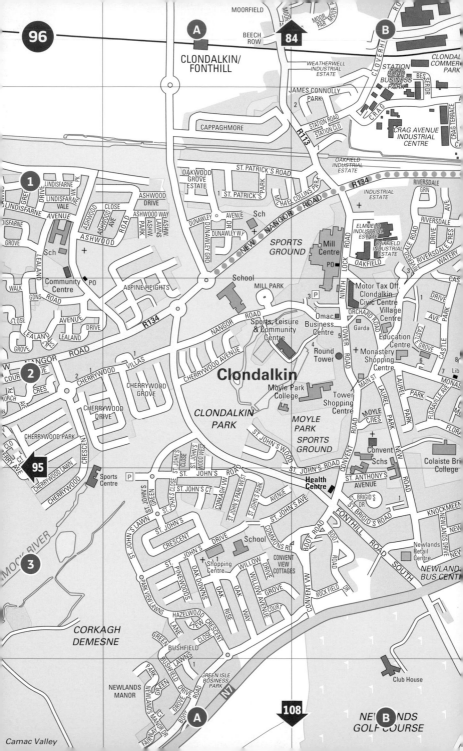

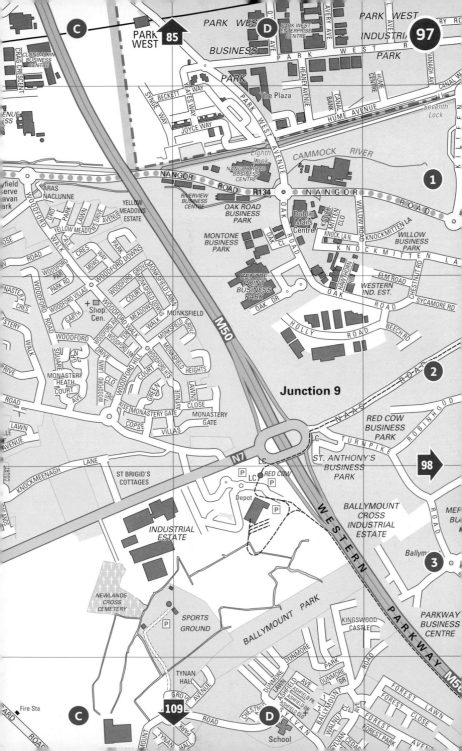

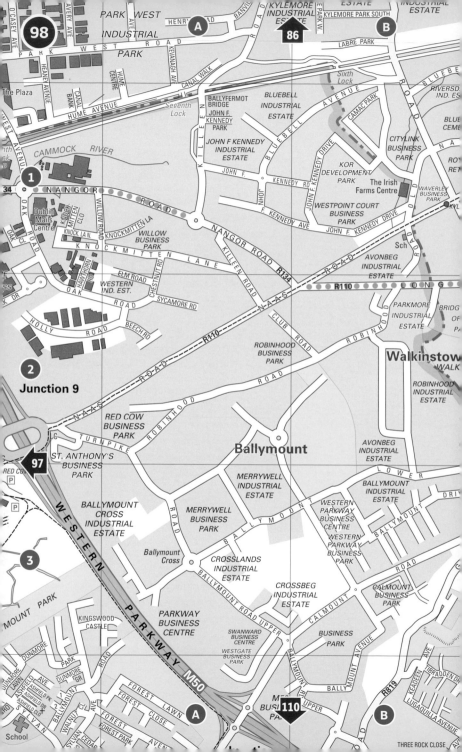

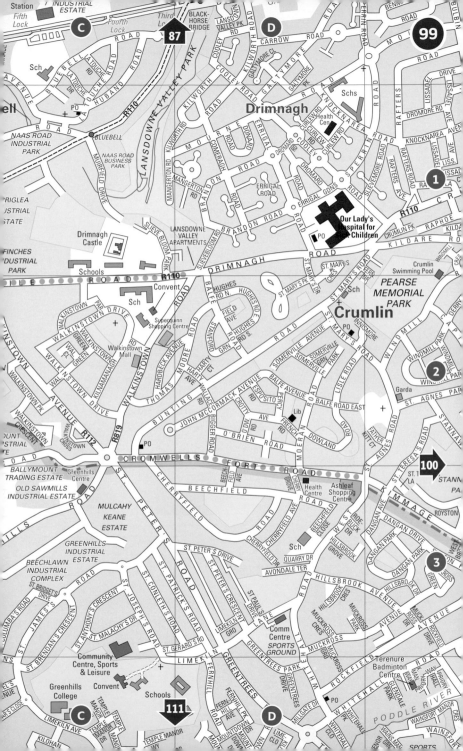

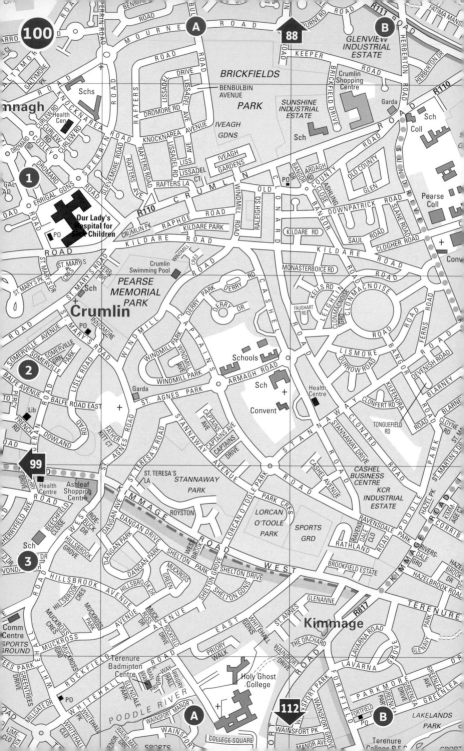

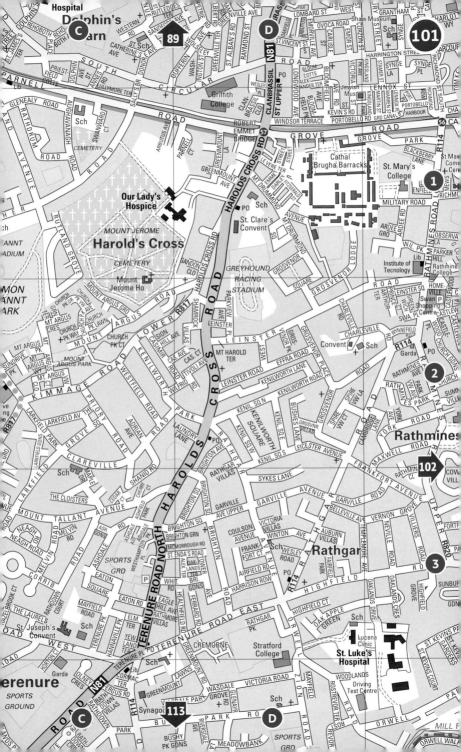

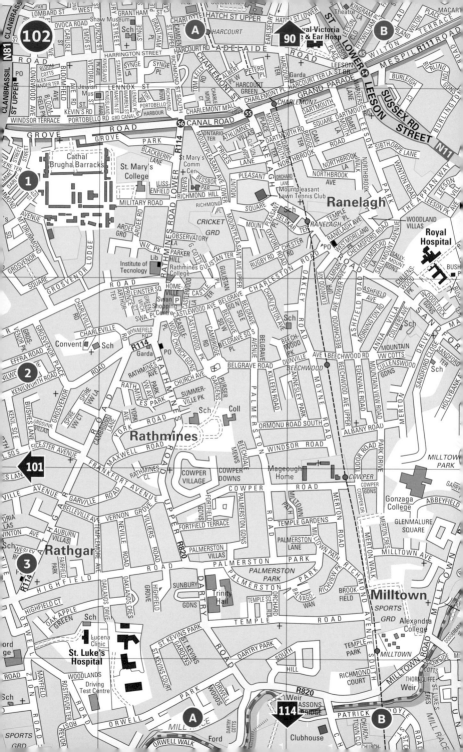

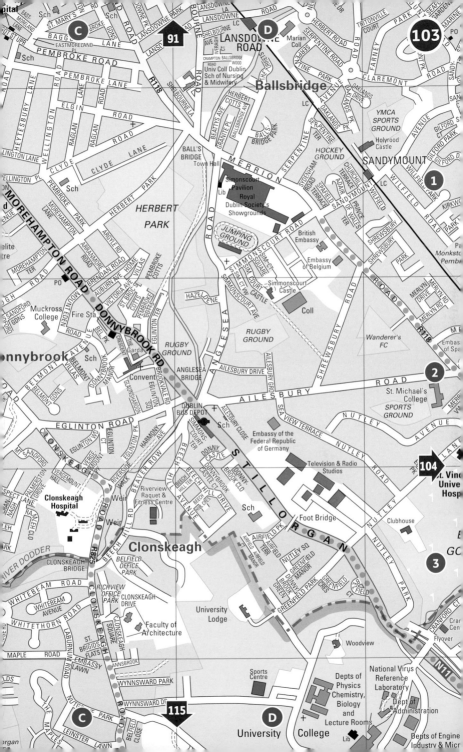

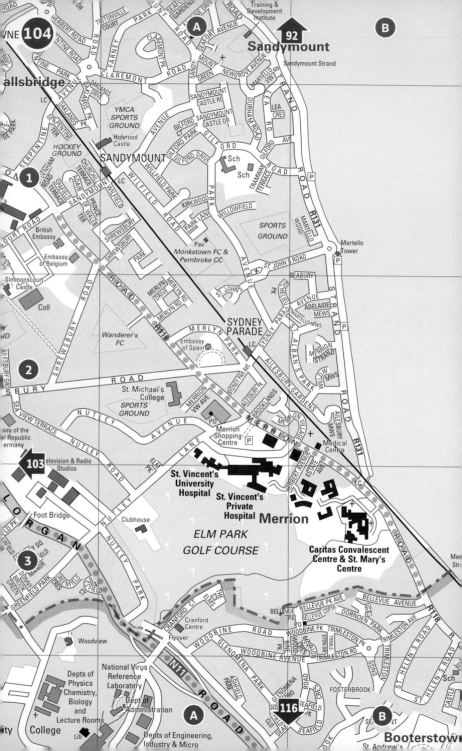

C
56
D
1
81
2
3
ERSTOWN
117
C
D

North

FOOTBALL
GROUNDS

R809
R807

JAMES LARKIN ROAD

CAUSEWAY ROAD

St. Anne's
(Ruins)

R O Y A L   D U B L I N   G O L F   C O U R S E

Interpretive
& Visitors
Centre

P

WATER LANE
MAYWOOD
THE VILLAGE
THE GROVE
THE COURT

Royal Dublin

P

School

Martello Tower

Williamstown

ROAD

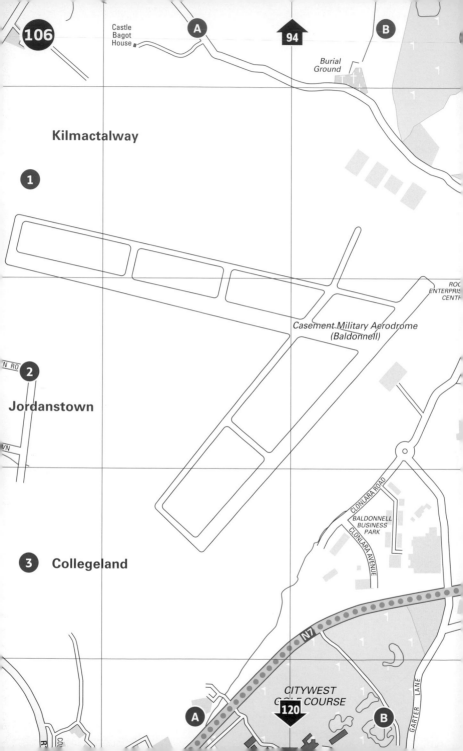

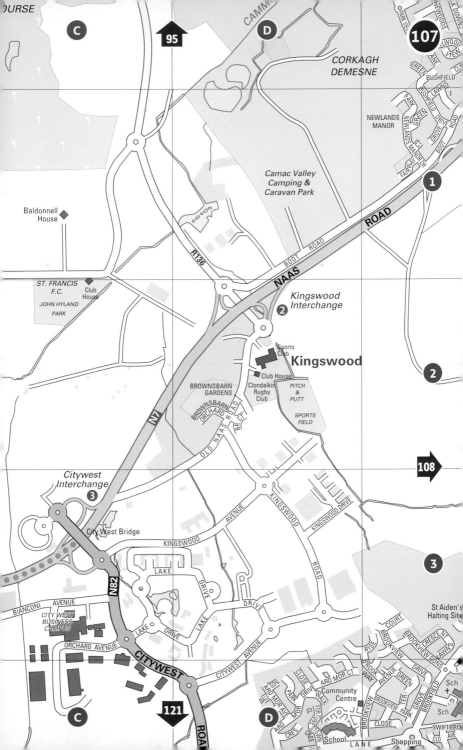

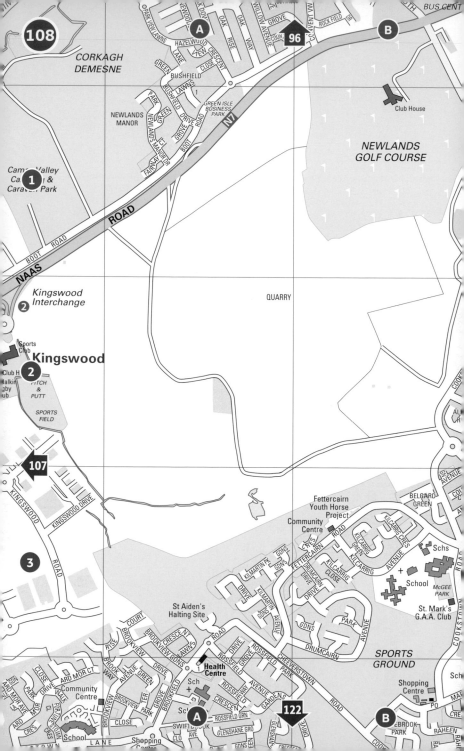

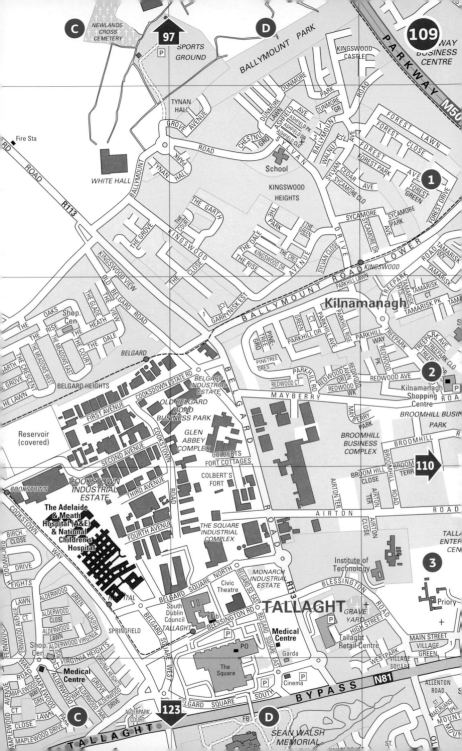

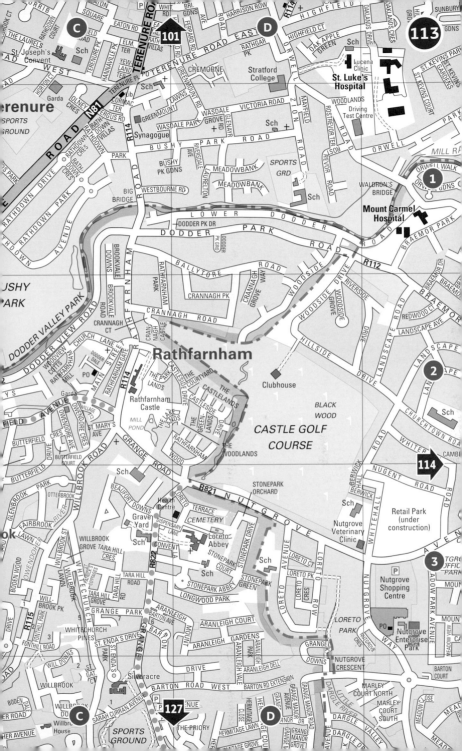

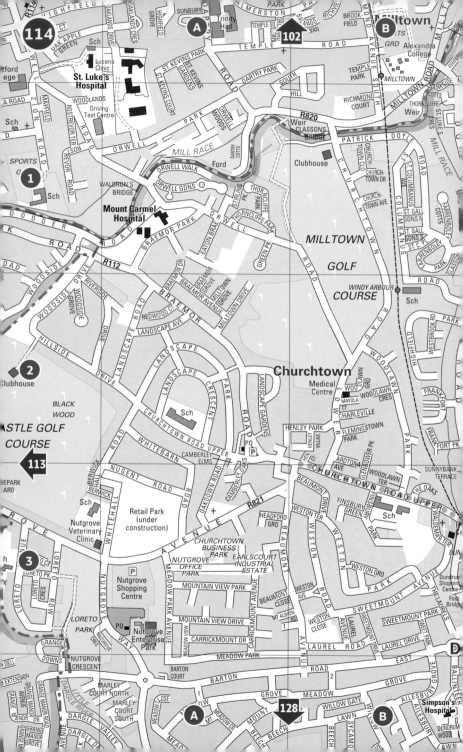

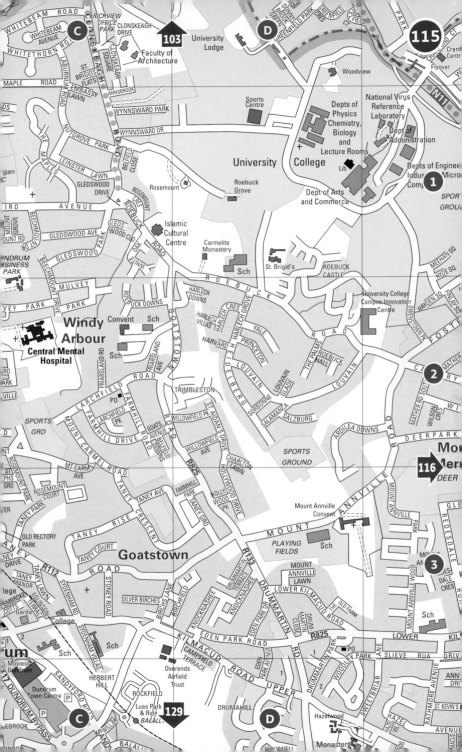

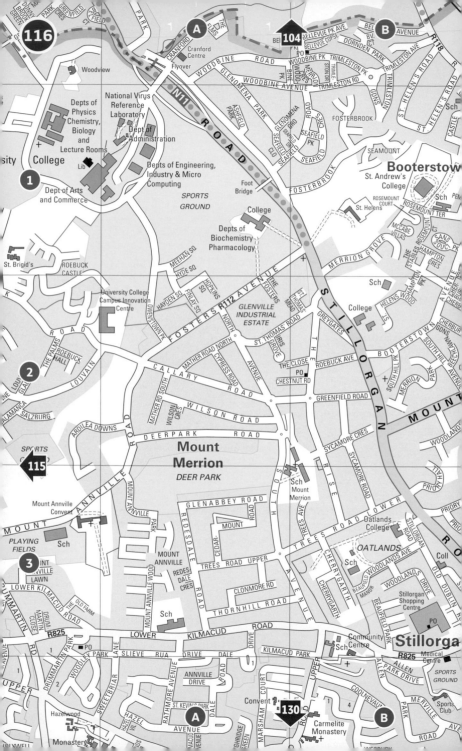

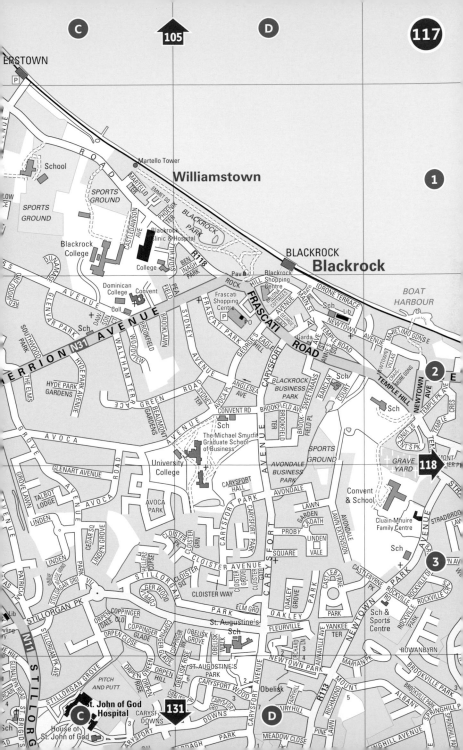

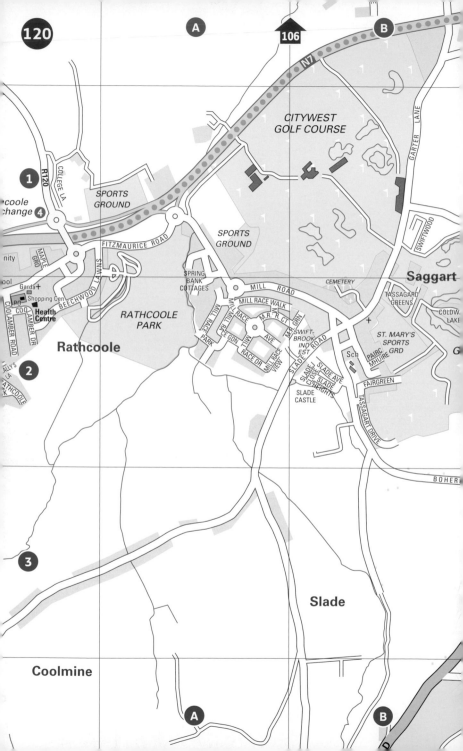

A

B

106

N7

CITYWEST
GOLF COURSE

GARTER LANE

R120

COLLEGE LA

1

SPORTS
GROUND

coole
change 4

SWIFTWOOD

MAPLE
GRO

nity

FITZMAURICE ROAD

SPORTS
GROUND

SPRING
BANK
COTTAGES

MILL   ROAD

Saggart

CEMETERY

TASSAGARD
GREENS

COLDW.
LAKE

ool

Garda

LPO
COO

BEECHWOOD LAWNS

Shopping Cen

Health
Centre

MILL RACE WALK

MILL RACE

M.R. R CT.

M.R. GRN

ST. MARY'S
SPORTS
GRD

G

COOLAMBER ROAD

AMBER DR

RATHCOOLE
PARK

MILL RACE GDN

MILL RACE PARK

AVE

SWIFT-
BROOK
IND
EST

MILL ROAD

Sch

PAIRC
MHUIRE

Rathcoole

ALLY'S

LA

ATHCOOLE

2

MILL RACE DR

MILL RACE VIEW

SLADE

SLADE AVE

SLADE
CLOSE

SLADE
HEIGHTS

FAIRGREEN

SLADE
CASTLE

TASSAGART DRIVE

BOHER

3

Slade

Coolmine

A

B

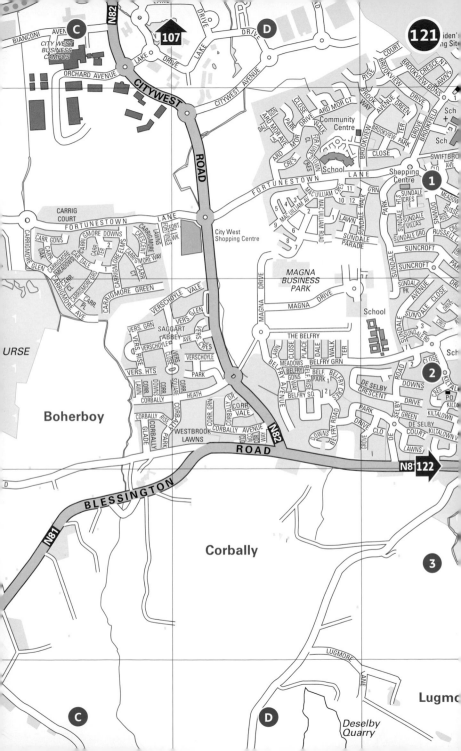

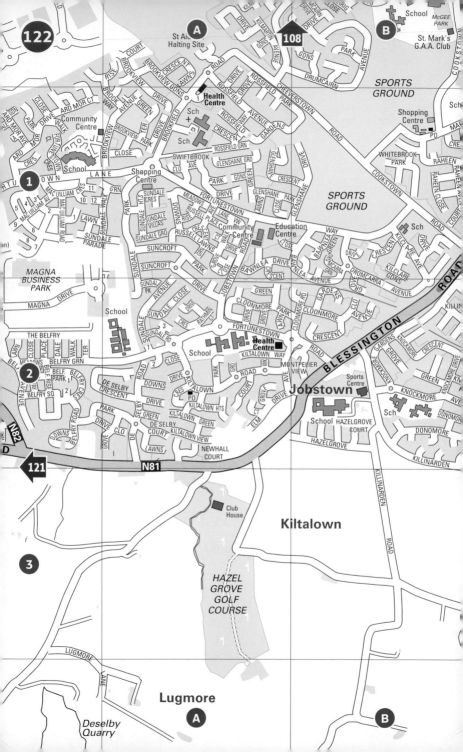

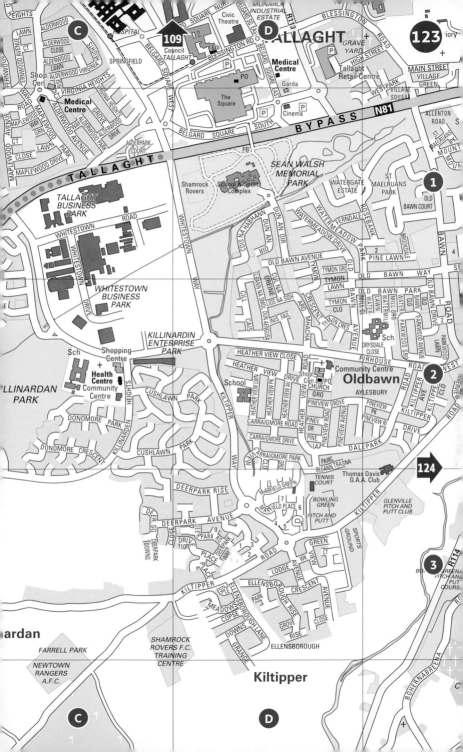

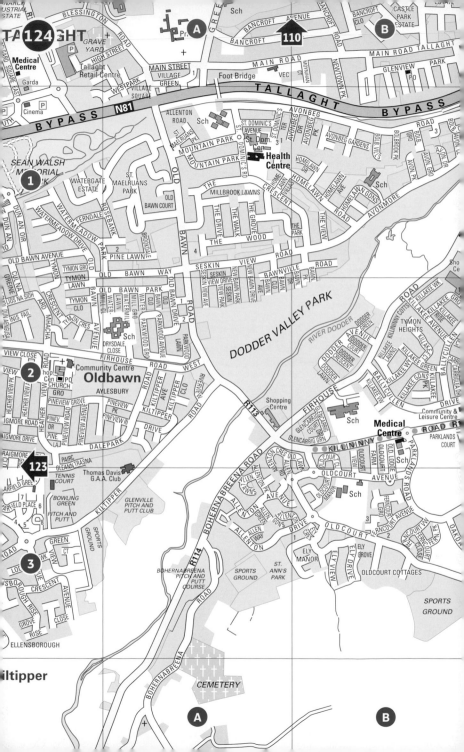

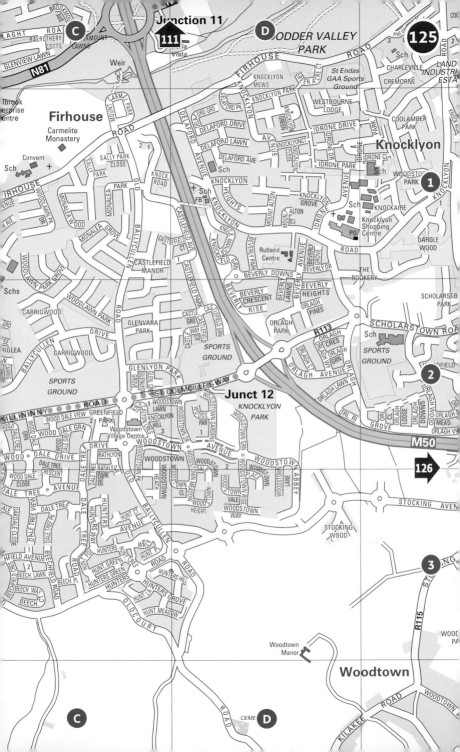

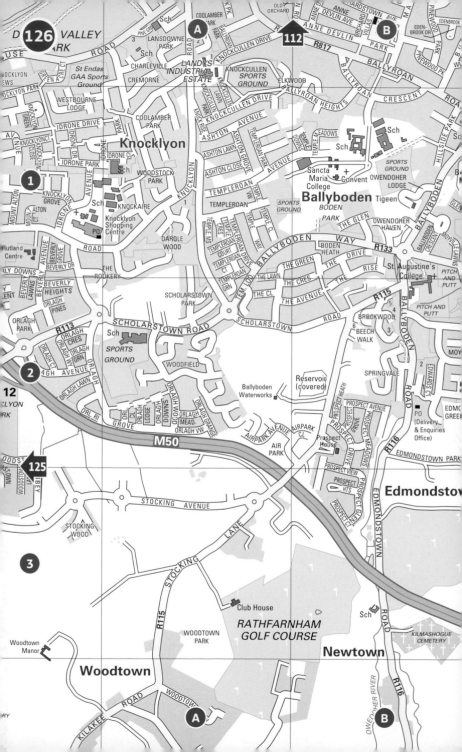

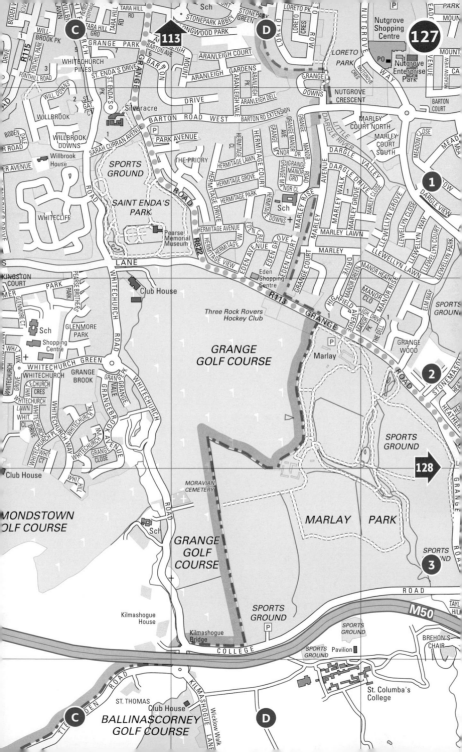

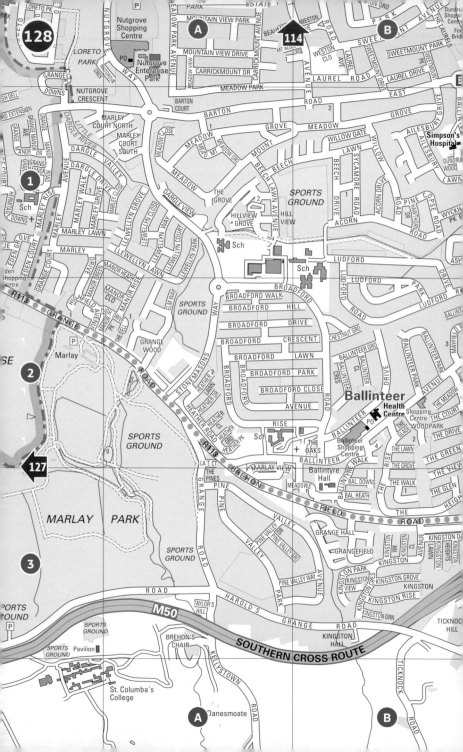

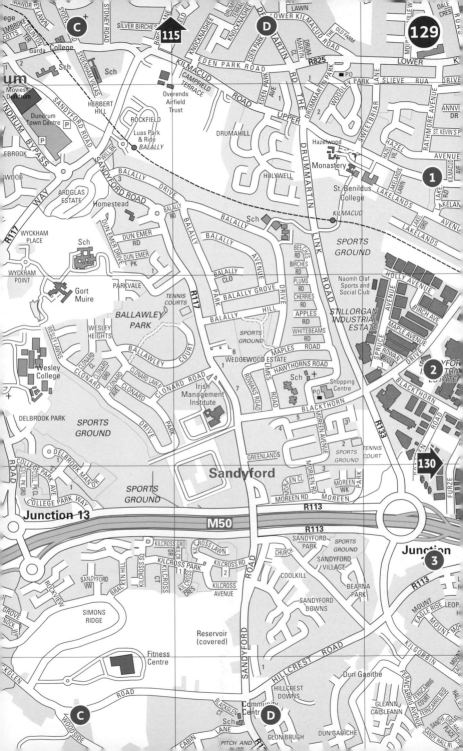

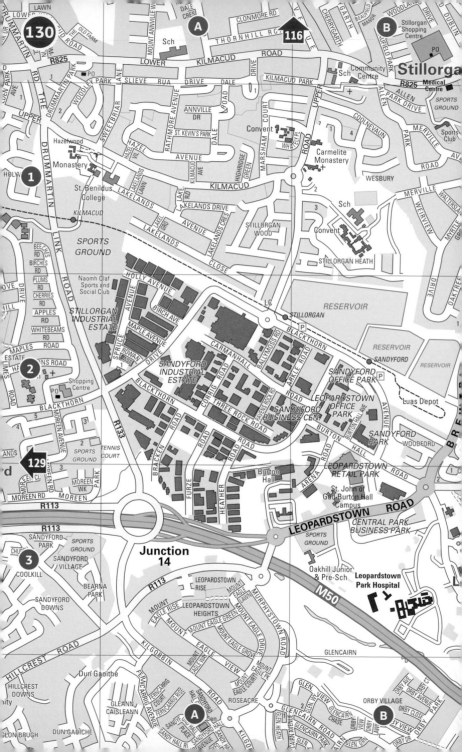

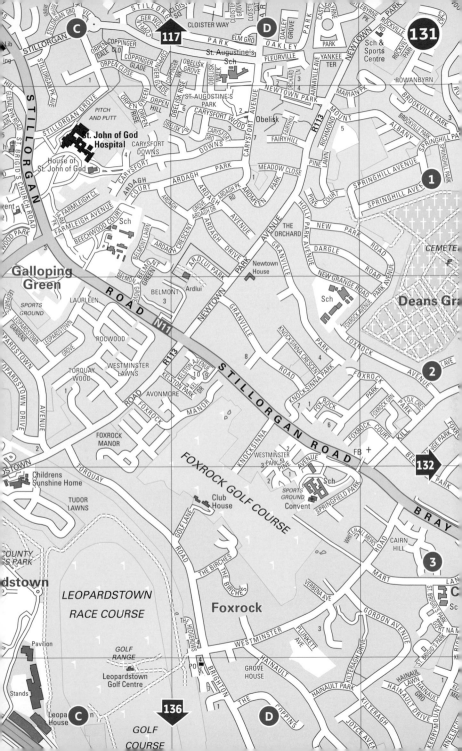

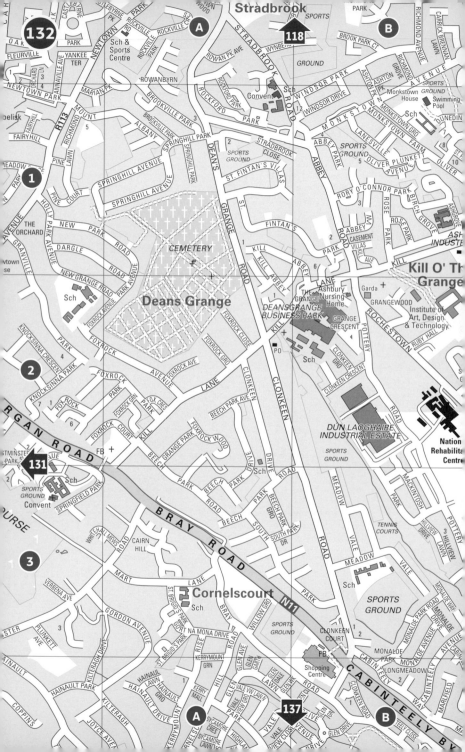

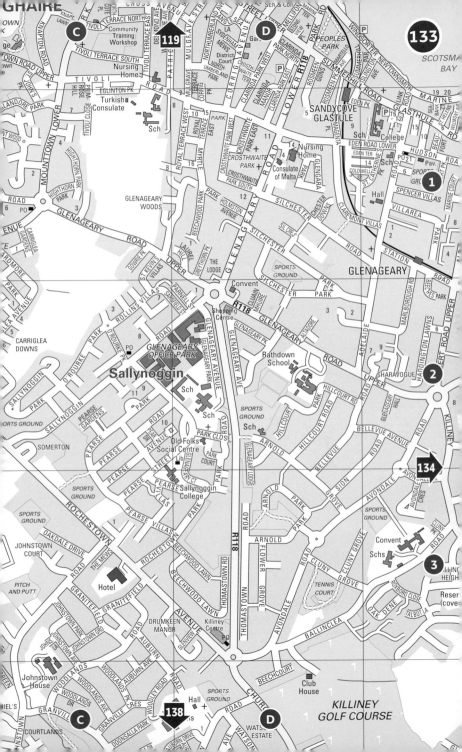

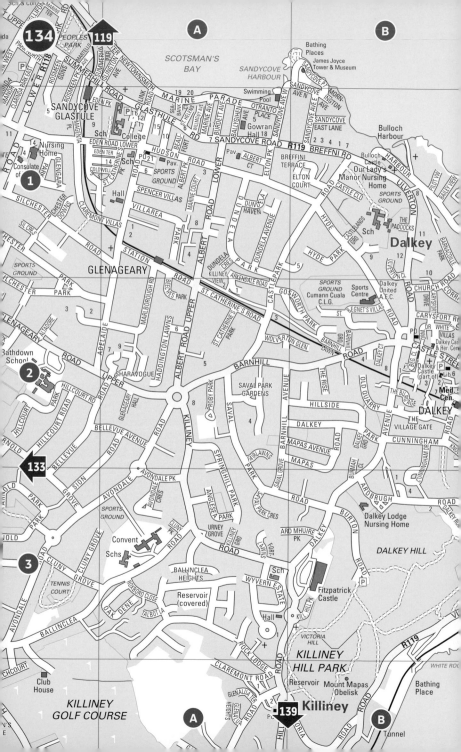

ace

1

Schs

Loreto
Abbey School

SPORTS
GROUNDS

MAIDEN ROCK

Pier

LORETO AVENUE

'EMORE   10

RE RD   11

'NTO   8

' DRIVE   7

VICTORIA ROAD

HEANY AVE

DALKEY SOUND

GREAT RD

R119

Martello
Tower

Coliemore
Harbour

2

LAMB ISLAND

MUGLINS

4

KNOCK-NA-CREE
GROVE

-NA-CREE

NERANO RD

NERANO RD

COLIEMORE ROAD

ROAD

DALKEY SOUND

Promontory
Fort
✝

MOUNT SALUS RD

Tunnel

*SORRENTO
PARK*

SORRENTO ROAD

ROAD

Martello
Tower

ROAD

*SORRENTO
POINT*

DALKEY ISLAND

3

3

HAWK CLIFF

STLE

C   D

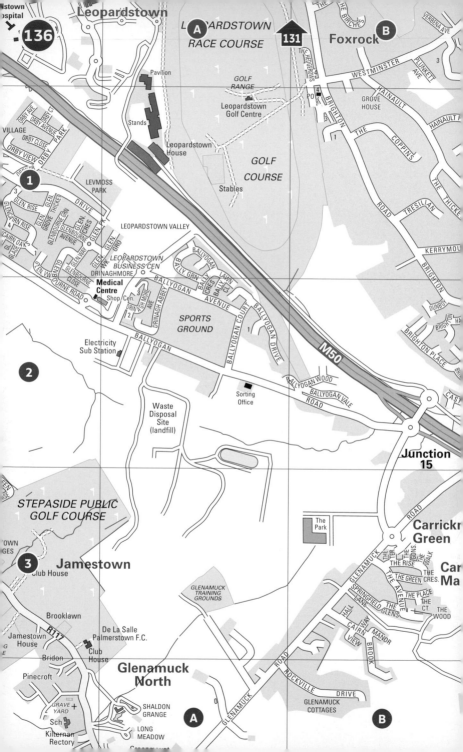

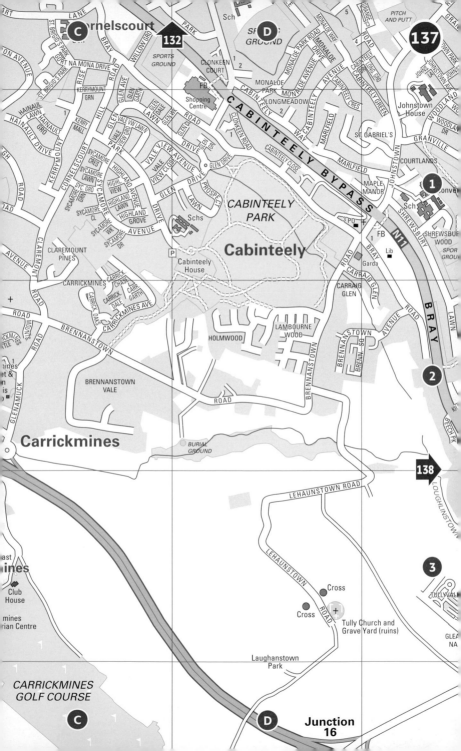

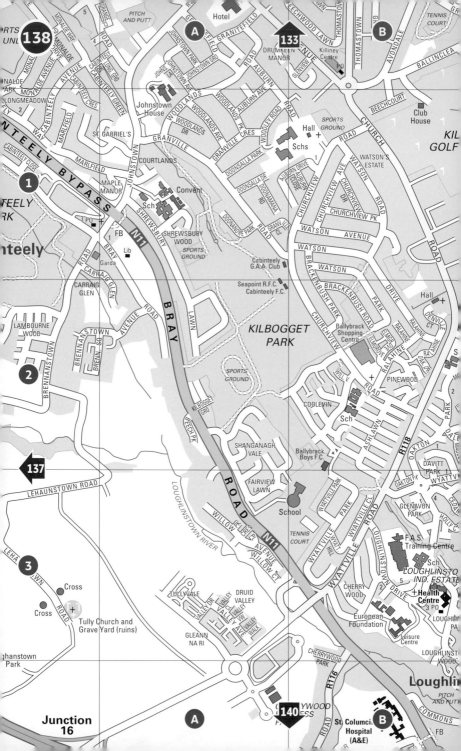

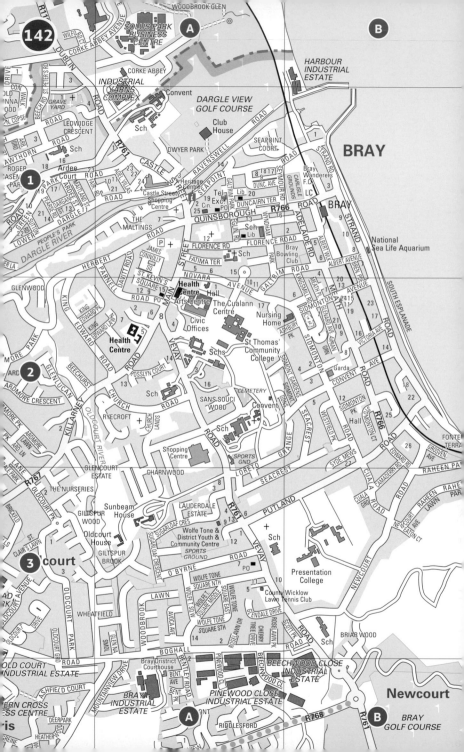

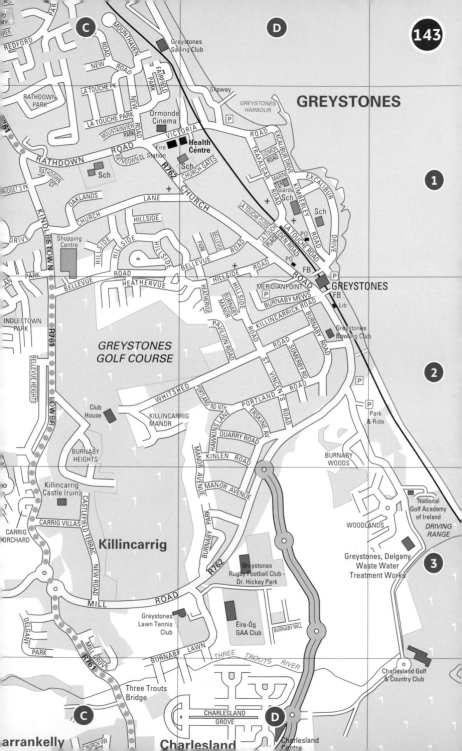

REDFORD

PARK

RATHDOWN PARK

LA TOUCHE PK

LA TOUCHE PARK

MOUNTHAVEN ROAD

NEW ROAD

FAIRFIELD PARK

Greystones Sailing Club

Shipway

Greystones Harbour

GREYSTONES

MOUNTAINVIEW PARK

NEW ROAD

Ormonde Cinema

Victoria

Fire Station

Health Centre

Sch

Church Gates

RATHDOWN ROAD

RATHDOWN CL.

RATHDOWN CT

R762

ROAD

EXCALIBUR DRIVE

SIOMON ROAD

TRAFALGAR

MARINE TERR

Garda

Sch

KIMBERLEY ROAD

Sch

EXCALIBUR ROAD

OAKLANDS LANE

CHURCH LANE

CHURCH ROAD

HILLSIDE

LA TOUCHE CLOSE

LA TOUCHE ROAD

EDEN ROAD

LA TOUCHE PLAZA

PO

DRIVE

HILLSIDE ROAD

HILLSIDE

BELLEVUE

PARK

BELLEVUE ROAD

ROAD

PO

FB

P

GREYSTONES

FB

Lib

KINDLESTOWN DRIVE

Shopping Centre

PARK

BELLEVUE ROAD

HEATHERVUE

HILLSIDE ROAD

HEATHERVUE

BURNABY MANOR

HILLSIDE ROAD

MERIDIANPOINT

P

BURNABY MEWS

KILLINCARRICK ROAD

BURNABY ROAD

Greystones Bowling Club

RIDGET'S PK

GREYSTONES GOLF COURSE

PAVILION ROAD

ROAD

ST. VINCENTS

SOMERBY RD

BURNABY ROAD

P

INDLESTOWN PARK

R761

WHITSHED

PORTLAND RD NTH

PORTLAND ROAD

ERSKINE AV

P

Park & Ride

BURNABY WOODS

Club House

KILLINCARRIG MANOR

HAWKINS LANE

QUARRY ROAD

BELLEVUE HEIGHTS

LOWER

BURNABY HEIGHTS

KINLEN ROAD

MANOR AVENUE

MANOR AVENUE

BURNABY PARK

National Golf Academy of Ireland

WOODLANDS

DRIVING RANGE

Killincarrig Castle (ruin)

CASTLEFIELD TERRACE

Killincarrig

CARRIG ORCHARD

CARRIG VILLAS

NEW ROAD

R762

Greystones Rugby Football Club - Dr. Hickey Park

Greystones, Delgany Waste Water Treatment Works

DELGANY PARK

MILL GROVE

MILL ROAD

Greystones Lawn Tennis Club

Éire-Óg GAA Club

BURNABY MILL

BURNABY LAWN

R761

Three Trouts Bridge

CHURCH VW

THREE TROUTS RIVER

CHARLESLAND GROVE

Charlesland Golf & Country Club

arrankelly

Charlesland

Charlesland Centre

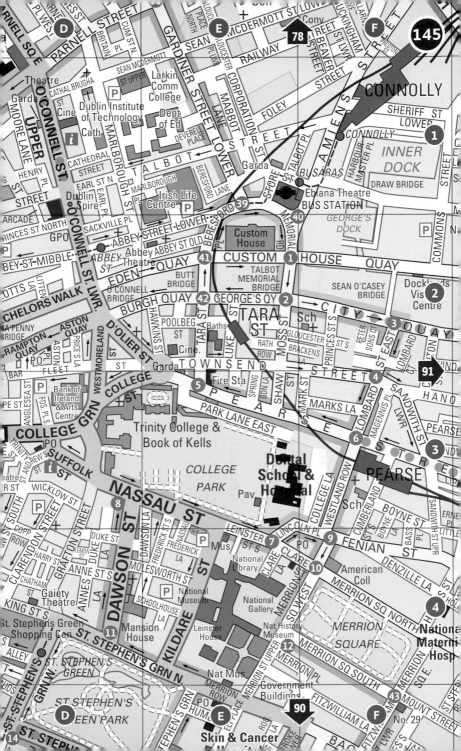

The telephone numbers beginning with '01' are Dublin numbers. To telephone these numbers from the UK replace the initial '0' with '00 353'

History

The ford over the River Liffey has been important since Celtic times and there was a thriving Christian community here from the 5thC, following their conversion by St Patrick in AD448. Marauding Vikings landed here in AD840, established a garrison port by the Dark Pool or Dubbh Linn, and within a few years had built a fortified town on the high ground above the estuary. Originally a base for raiding sorties, Dublin soon became a flourishing trading port as well, until Viking dominance was curtailed following a defeat by Brian Boru at the Battle of Clontarf in 1014.

Many of the Vikings had inter-married with the Irish and converted to Christianity but they were finally driven out by the Anglo-Normans under Strongbow, who took Dublin by storm and executed the Viking leader Hasculf. In 1170 Henry II arrived in Dublin, defeated Strongbow and received the submission of the Irish chieftains on the site of College Green. Henry granted the city by charter to the citizens of Bristol, thereby establishing English authority in Ireland.

The city and surrounding area, established as the seat of English government and protected by an enclosing wall and strategic castles, was known as The Pale. Frequently attacked during the 12thC and 13thC by the Irish clans based in the Wicklow Mountains, it was assaulted unsuccessfully by Edward Bruce in 1316. The city witnessed the crowning of Lambert Simnel, pretender to the English throne, in Christ Church in 1486. Unmoved by the rebellion of 'Silken' Thomas Fitzgerald in 1534, the inhabitants remained loyal to the English crown, supporting King Charles during the Civil Wars. Parliamentarians captured Dublin in 1647 and at this time the city was in decline. Following the Restoration of Charles I, however, Dublin underwent a great economic and architectural expansion.

By the end of the 17thC Dublin had become a flourishing commercial centre and during the following century the city was transformed into one of the most beautiful Georgian cities in Europe. The 'Wide Streets Commission' was established in 1757 and in 1773 the Paving Board was formed. New, elegantly spacious streets and squares were planned and palatial town houses built. In 1783 the Irish Parliament led by Henry Grattan was granted a short-lived autonomy but there was growing political unrest, which erupted in the unsuccessful uprising of 1798. Lord Edward Fitzgerald died of wounds sustained resisting arrest and in 1800 the detested Act of Union was established and the fortunes of the city began to wane.

With government now in London, few of the noblemen required their fine mansions and many returned to their country estates or left for London. Bitterness increased; in 1803 the Lord Chief Justice was assassinated and Robert Emmet, the leader of an abortive insurrection, was hanged. The newspaper The Nation was established by Charles Gavan Duffy in 1842, the heyday of the Repeal Movement. Daniel O'Connell was elected Lord Mayor in 1841 but only three years later he was interned in Richmond Gaol for campaigning for the repeal of the Union and the restoration of Grattan's 'Irish Parliament'. In 1873 the first great Home Rule Conference was held and in 1879 the Land League was formed, whose leaders, including Parnell and Davitt, were imprisoned as a consequence. In 1882 the new Chief Secretary, Lord Frederick Cavendish, and his Under-Secretary were assassinated in Phoenix Park by the Invincibles, a new terrorist organisation.

As the campaign for Home Rule gathered momentum, the Gaelic League, which started the Irish literary renaissance, was established by Douglas Hyde and Eóin MacNeill in 1893. Conceived as a means of reviving interest in the Irish language and traditional Irish life, the Gaelic League was also responsible for a remarkable literary revival resulting in the formation of the Abbey Theatre in 1904, where plays by J M Synge, Sean O'Casey and W B Yeats, amongst others, were performed.

In 1905 the Sinn Fein movement was formed, in 1909 the Irish Transport and General Workers Union was set up under the leadership of James Connolly, and in 1913 there was a massive strike, paralysing the city. The Irish Volunteers came into being in 1914, largely to combat the Ulster Volunteers who had been raised by Edward Carson in January 1913 to defend the right of Ulster to remain united with Great Britain. In 1916 the Irish Volunteers seized the General Post Office in Lower O'Connell Street as their headquarters and the Easter Rising had begun. It was quickly crushed, but so brutally that public conscience, clearly appalled, overwhelmingly elected Sinn Fein at the general election of December 1918 with Eamon de Valera as the new president.

Whilst the Dublin faction was openly in support of the guerrilla bands operating across the country, the Ulster Unionists set up their own provisional government, and the ambushes and assassinations which characterised the Anglo-Irish

War, featuring the notorious Black and Tans, began in bloody earnest. The war ended in the truce of July 1921. Despite the ratification of the Irish Free State in January 1922, a large and dissatisfied faction of leaders in the Irish movement took up arms against their former comrades and seized the Four Courts, which they held for two months. The subsequent shelling ordered by the new Dublin Government destroyed much of O'Connell Street but by the 1930s Dublin was emerging as a modern capital city and most of the public buildings had been restored.

Visiting Dublin www.visitdublin.com

Passports

Citizens of the European Union need either a valid national identity card or passport to enter the Republic of Ireland. It is recommended that visitors from the UK bring a passport as a means of identification. Nationals of other countries require a passport and may require a visa. Enquiries should be made with a travel agent or Irish Embassy before travelling. The address of the Irish Embassy in London is 17 Grosvenor Place, SW1X 7HR ☎ 020 7235 2171

The Irish Passport & Visa Office is at Montpelier House, 106 Brompton Road, London SW3 1JJ ☎ 020 7225 7700
www.dfa.ie

Banks

In February 2002 the Irish Punt (IEP) was withdrawn from circulation and the Euro (€) became the Irish unit of currency.

Banks open Monday–Friday from 10.00–16.00 and in Dublin most branches remain open until 17.00 on Thursdays. Major banks have 24 hour ATM machines which accept Plus and Cirrus symbols. All major credit cards are widely accepted in shops, petrol stations, restaurants and hotels. Personal cheques from banks outside the Republic of Ireland are not accepted in the country without prior arrangement.

Bureaux de Change

Banks and Bureaux de Change generally offer the best exchange rates, although post offices, hotels, travel agents and some department stores offer exchange facilities.

There is a Bureau de Change at Dublin Airport and Dún Laoghaire ferry terminal. Dublin Airport also has a 24 hour Bank of Ireland foreign currency note exchanger and multi-currency Pass machines. Foreign exchange facilities are also to be found at the central bus station (Busárus), Connolly railway station and at the Dublin Tourism Centre in Suffolk Street.

Language

English is spoken by everyone in Ireland. The country is officially bilingual with Irish (Gaelic) also spoken.

Customs and excise

The Republic of Ireland is a member of the European Union and, in accordance with EU regulations, travellers within the Community can import 90 litres of wine, 110 litres of duty paid beer and 800 cigarettes without question. Duty free sales of goods amongst European community members are now abolished. There are restrictions on taking certain food items into Ireland and checks should be made beforehand with the Irish Embassy or travel agent. Pets may not be brought into the country unless travelling from the UK, all other animals entering the country have to undergo quarantine.

Emergency

If you are involved in an emergency and require the services of the Police, Fire Brigade, Ambulance Service, or Coastguard, dial 999 or 112.

Medical treatment

Visitors to Ireland from European Community countries are entitled to free treatment by a general practitioner, medicines on prescription and treatment on a public ward in a hospital. British citizens need only show some form of identification such as a passport or driving licence to the doctor or hospital and request treatment under the EU health agreement. Visitors from other EU countries need to present form E111 (available from social security offices prior to departure). Health Insurance is recommended for visitors from outside the EU. No inoculations are required for travellers to Ireland.

Disabled visitors

The Irish Wheelchair association can offer advice and can arrange wheelchair hire.
☎ 01 818 6400 (Mon–Fri 09.00–17.00).
www.iwa.ie

Irish Rail publishes a 'Guide for Mobility Impaired Passengers' which details the accessibility of all railway and DART stations. Obtainable at all manned stations or from the Access and Liaison officer, ☎ 01 703 2634. Most of the Dublin Bus fleet is low floor easy access, and the buses run by Bus Éireann – Ireland's national bus company – are largely wheelchair accessible. Discounts on many ferry sailings from Britain are available to disabled drivers who wish to take their own car to Ireland. Drivers should contact the Disabled Drivers' Association or Motor Club in Britain to obtain the relevant form. This form should then be sent to the ferry company.

Phones

Most calls are dialled direct with cheaper call charge rates between 18.00 and 08.00 Mon–Fri and all day Saturday, Sunday and bank holidays. The dialling code for Dublin is *01* and so for calls within Dublin omit *01* at the beginning of a number. To dial Dublin from abroad dial the access code for Ireland *(00353)* plus the area code for Dublin *(01)* but omit the zero. For directory enquiries, including Northern Ireland, dial *11811*; for Great Britain or International numbers dial *11818*. For operator assistance dial *10* (Ireland and UK) or *114* for the international operator. Card phones are cheaper than payphones and are widely available. Callcards are obtainable at post offices, newsagents and supermarkets. Mobile phones can be brought into Ireland but visitors need to ensure their phone company has a roaming agreement with the Irish network operators.

Transport

Driving *See pages 2 & 4 for additional information*

Driving is on the left-hand side of the road in Ireland as in the UK; at roundabouts give way to traffic from the right. All drivers and front seat passengers must wear seat belts, and rear belts if they are fitted. Children under twelve must have a suitable restraint. Helmets are compulsory for motorcyclists. The maximum speed limit is 97kph (60mph) outside urban areas and the motorway speed limit is 110kph (70mph). In urban areas the limit is usually 50kph (30mph). There are on-the-spot fines for speeding and drink driving laws are strict. Parking infringements are taken seriously and illegally parked cars in Dublin City are liable to be clamped or towed away to the Corporation pound with a recovery charge payable.

Distances and speed limits are now both measured in kilometres (speed limit signs changed on 20th January 2005). Place names are generally in English and Irish. Unleaded petrol and diesel are widely available. Recorded weather information is available for Dublin by calling the Meteorological Service ☎ *1550 123 854*. There is a charge for this call.

Car hire

Car hire is readily available in Dublin, although in July and August there is a high demand and it is best to book in advance. You must have held a full licence for 2 years and be under 70 and over 23. Some companies make exceptions to this but charges may be higher. A full valid driving licence of your country of residence (which you must have held for at least two years without endorsements) must be presented at the time of hiring.

Most international car rental companies have offices in Dublin and cars can also be hired at the airport and Dún Laoghaire ferry terminal. The cost of hire will depend on the type of car and time of year and it is worthwhile shopping around. It is important, however, to check the insurance details and ensure Collision Damage Waiver is included. A deposit is usually payable at the time of booking or before you drive away. Fly-drive or rail-sail-drive packages arranged by travel agents or the air and ferry companies can be an economical and easy way of hiring a car.

Public transport

Dublin is linked with the cities and towns of Ireland by a network of rail and bus services overseen by Córas Iompair Éireann (CIE), which is Ireland's National Transport Authority. The CIE organises Iarnród Éireann (Irish Rail), Bus Éirean (Irish Bus) and Dublin Bus. Bus and rail timetables can be bought at most newsagents. Unlimited use period tickets are available for use on rail and/or bus services.

Bus and coach travel

Dublin Bus (Bus Átha Cliath) operates the public bus services in Dublin and the surrounding area. Pre-paid tickets can be bought for periods of time ranging from one day to one month and are good value for money. They can be bought at any of the many bus ticket agencies in the city, from the CIE information desk at Dublin Airport or at Dublin Bus head office at 59 O'Connell Street Upper. Many routes operate an exact fare only policy. Dublin Bus also operates late night services (Nitelink) to most suburban areas on Thursdays, Fridays and Saturdays; some services also operate Monday to Wednesday. They also operate links to the airport (Airlink), ferry ports, railway stations and sightseeing tours.

59 O'Connell Street ☎ *01 872 0000*
Open Mon 08.30-17.30; Tues-Fri 09.00-17.30;
Sat 09.00-13.00.
Information ☎ *01 873 4222*
Mon-Sat 09.00-19.00
www.dublinbus.ie

Irish Bus (Bus Éireann) and many private companies operate national bus services between Dublin, Dublin Airport and many major cities and towns. Bus Éireann also operate combined bus and ferry services between Britain and Ireland. This service operates under the 'Eurolines' brand www.eurolines.com

Dublin Bus Station (Busáras), Store Street.
☎ *01 836 6111*
www.buseireann.ie

Scheduled daily hop-on hop-off city sightseeing tours are operated by Gray Line www.grayline.com and City Sightseeing www.guidefriday.com. Buses depart every 6-15 minutes 09.30-17.30; also

available are seasonal half and full day excursions further afield including to Newgrange and the Boyne Valley, Powerscourt Gardens, Glendalough and Wicklow. 3 & 4 day trips to Kerry and Dingle are also available. Information and tickets from the Desk 1 at the Dublin Tourism Centre, Suffolk Street.
☎ 01 605 7705
www.irishcitytours.com
Email: info@irishcitytours.com

Taxis
Taxis are available at taxi ranks or by phoning one of the many radio-linked taxi companies. There are numerous taxi ranks including ones on O'Connell Street, Dame Street, and St. Stephen's Green West.
Taxi companies are listed in the Golden Pages classified telephone directory.

Rail travel
Dublin Connolly and Dublin Heuston are the two mainline railway stations and Irish Rail (Iarnród Éireann) operates an excellent service to most towns and cities in Ireland. Irish rail also operates the suburban rail network in Dublin and DART (Dublin Area Rapid Transit) with 26 stations between Howth on the north of Dublin Bay to Bray in the south.
☎ 01 850 366222
www.irishrail.ie
LUAS is the Light Rail Transit System in Dublin operated by Veolia Transport Ireland. There are two lines; the red line runs from Tallaght to Connolly Station and the green line runs from Sandyford to St. Stephen's Green. Tickets are available at each stop at vending machines.
☎ 1800 300 604 (Freephone, Dublin only) Mon-Fri from 07.00-19.00; Sat 10.00-14.00.

Bike hire
Belfield Bike Shop, University College Dublin.
☎ 01 260 0749
www.cyclingsafaris.com
Cycleways, 185/186 Parnell Street
☎ 01 873 4748
www.cycleways.com
Hollingworth Cycles, Templeogue Road, Templeogue
☎ 01 490 5094
Drumartin Road, Kilmacud Road Lower, Stillorgan
☎ 01 296 0225
www.hollingsworth.ie
Tracks Bikes, Botanic Road, Glasnevin.
☎ 01 850 0252

Lost property
Enquire at the nearest police station or: Dublin Airport. Open 07.30-22.30.
☎ 01 814 5555

Dublin Bus. Open Mon-Fri 08.45-17.00.
☎ 01 703 1321
Irish Bus. Open Mon-Fri 09.00-17.00.
☎ 01 836 6111
Irish Rail (Connolly Station). Open Mon-Fri 09.00-17.00.
☎ 01 703 2362
Irish Rail (Heuston Station). Open Mon-Fri 09.00-17.00. ☎ 01 703 2102 / 2126

Places of interest
Arbour Hill Cemetery, Arbour Hill.
The leaders of the Easter Rising are buried here.

Bank of Ireland, College Green.
Designed by Sir Edward Lovett Pearce in 1729, it was later enlarged by James Gandon and Robert Parke between 1785-1794. Originally the Parliament House, the first of a series of great public buildings erected in 18thC Dublin, it was taken over by the Bank of Ireland in 1804. A statue of Henry Grattan, leader of the Irish parliament of 1782, stands outside on the lawn of College Green. Two huge 18thC tapestries commemorating the Siege of Londonderry and the Battle of the Boyne hang in the oak-panelled chamber of the former House of Lords.
There are guided tours of the House of Lords on Tuesdays at 10.30, 11.30, and 13.45. The House of Commons is now the banking hall.
Admission free. Disabled access.
☎ 01 671 1488

Bank of Ireland Arts Centre, Foster Place.
An arts centre which presents classical concerts and recitals and houses an interactive museum. The museum illustrates the history of the adjoining College Green buildings where many of the dramatic events of Irish history were played out in the Irish parliament. The museum also reflects the role played by the Bank of Ireland in the economic and social development of Ireland.
Open Tues-Fri 10.00-16.00.
Disabled access.
☎ 01 671 1488

Belvedere House, North Great George's Street.
One of the best 18thC mansions in Dublin. Taken over by Jesuit Belvedere College in 1841; James Joyce went to school here between 1893-1898. Not open to the public.

Casino, off Malahide Road, Marino.
A miniature 18thC neo-classical masterpiece designed by Sir William Chambers and recently restored. Casino means 'small house'. It was built as a pleasure house beside Marino House (now demolished), Lord Charlemont's country residence, for the enormous sum of £60,000. It is a compact building, remarkably containing 16 rooms, with

many interesting architectural features. The interior circular hall, ringed by columns, is crowned by a coffered dome. The graceful roof urns disguise chimneys while the columns conceal drainpipes.

Open May-Oct daily 10.00-17.00 (Jun-Sept 18.00); Jan-Apr, Nov-Dec Sat & Sun only 12.00-16.00 (Apr 17.00). Access by guided tour only. Last tour leaves 45 mins before closing. Access to interior by stairway.

☎ 01 833 1618

City Hall, Dame Street.
Completed in 1779, this fine building was designed as The Royal Exchange. Subsequent use included a prison and corn exchange before being taken over by the city in 1852. Presently used by Dublin City Council. It features a beautiful Corinthian coffered dome and portico. The archives include the original charter of 1171 in which Henry II granted Dublin to the citizens of Bristol.
Open Mon-Sat 10.00-17.15, Sun 14.00-17.00.
☎ 01 222 2204

Custom House Visitor Centre,
Custom House Quay.
The Custom House, with a magnificent long river frontage, is an architectural masterpiece designed by James Gandon and completed in 1791. Exhibits relate to James Gandon and the history of the Custom House itself, with illustrations of how the building was restored after it was gutted by fire in 1921. The building is best viewed from the south bank of the River Liffey.
Open: Wed-Fri (Nov-16 Mar) & Mon-Fri (17 Mar-Nov) 10.00-12.30, Sat & Sun 14.00-17.00. Disabled access by prior arrangement.
☎ 01 888 2538

Drimnagh Castle, Long Mile Road.
Ireland's only castle with a flooded moat. This Norman castle has a fully restored Great Hall, medieval undercroft and 17thC style formal garden.
Open Wed 12.00-17.00; Sun 14.00-17.00. Open at other times by appointment.
☎ 01 450 2530
Email: drimnaghcastle@eircom.net

Dublin Castle, off Dame Street.
The Castle was originally built between 1204-1228 as part of Dublin's defensive system. The Record Tower is the principal remnant of the 13thC Anglo-Norman fortress and has walls 5 metres (16ft) thick but what remains today is largely the result of 18thC and 19thC re-building. It now contains the Garda (Police) Museum. The 15thC Bermingham Tower was once the state prison where Red Hugh O'Donnell was interned in the 16thC; it was rebuilt in the 18thC. The State

Apartments, Undercroft and ornate Chapel Royal are open to the public. The State Apartments, dating from the British Administration, were once the residence of the English Viceroys and are now used for Presidential Inaugurations and state receptions. Within these apartments are the magnificent throne room and St Patrick's Hall, 25 metres (82ft) long with a high panelled and decorated ceiling. In the undercroft can be seen the remains of a Viking fortress, part of the original moat, and part of the old city wall. The Chester Beatty Library exhibits art treasures from around the world.
Open: Mon-Fri 10.00-16.45, Sat & Sun 14.00-16.45. Access by guided tour only. Disabled access/toilets.
☎ 01 645 8813
www.dublincastle.ie
Email: info@dublincastle.ie

Dublin Writers Museum, Parnell Square.
Tracing the history of Irish literature from its earliest times to the 20thC, this museum is a celebration of this literary heritage. Writers and playwrights including Jonathan Swift, George Bernard Shaw, Oscar Wilde, W B Yeats, James Joyce and Samuel Beckett are brought to life through personal items, portraits, their books and letters. There is also a room dedicated to children's authors. The museum is housed in a restored 18thC Georgian mansion with decorative stained-glass windows and ornate plaster-work.
Open Mon-Sat 10.00-17.00 (18.00 Jun-Aug), Sun 11.00-17.00. Disabled access to ground floor. Last entry 45 mins before closing.
☎ 01 872 2077
www.writersmuseum.com
Email: writers@dublintourism.ie

Dublinia & Viking World,
Christ Church, St. Michael's Hill.
A multi-media recreation of Dublin life in medieval times from the Anglo-Norman arrival in 1170 to the dissolution of the monasteries in 1540. There is a scale model of the medieval city, a life size reconstruction of a merchant's house, and numerous Viking and Norman artefacts from excavations at nearby Wood Quay. The building is the old Synod Hall and is linked to Christ Church Cathedral by an ornate Victorian pedestrian bridge.
Open Mon-Fri 10.00-17.00 (Oct-Mar 11.00-16.00); Sat & Sun 10.00-16.00. Disabled access.
☎ 01 679 4611
www.dublinia.ie
Email: marketing@dublinia.ie

Dublin Zoo, Phoenix Park.
The Zoo is well known for its captive-breeding programme and is committed to the conservation and protection of endangered species. The 'big

cats', living in enclosures which simulate their natural habitats, include lions, tigers, jaguars and snow leopards. Attractive gardens surround two natural lakes where pelicans, flamingos, ducks and geese abound, while the islands in the lakes are home to chimps, gibbons, spider monkeys and orang-utans. A recent development 'Fringes of the Arctic' has provided a state of the art enclosure for the polar bears and is home to wolves, arctic foxes and snowy owls. The zoo doubled in size in 2000 and an African Plains area has been developed providing greater space and freedom for giraffe, hippo, rhino and other African animals and birds. The city farm and pets' corner provide encounters with Irish domestic animals. Other attractions include a zoo train, discovery centre, and 'meet the keeper' programme.

Open: Mon–Sat 09.30–17.30, Sun 10.30–17.30. Last admission 1hr before closing. Closes at dusk in winter.

☎ 01 474 8900

www.dublinzoo.ie

Email: info@dublinzoo.ie

Dunsink Observatory, Castleknock, Dublin 15.

Founded in 1783, it is one of the oldest observatories in the world and houses the astronomy section of the School of Cosmic Physics. Public open nights are held on the first and third Wednesdays of each month from October to March inclusive at 20.00. Requests for tickets for the open nights must be made by post to the Observatory.

☎ 01 838 7911

www.dunsink.dias.ie

Email: cwoods@dunsinkdias.ie

Four Courts, Inns Quay.

Originally designed by James Gandon in 1785, it was partially destroyed by a fire in 1922 in the struggle for Irish independence but restored again by 1932. The Four Courts has a 137 metre (450ft) river frontage and the building is fronted by a Corinthian portico with six columns. The square central block with circular hall is crowned by a copper-covered lantern-dome. Housed here are the Irish Law Courts and Law Library.

☎ 01 888 6000

www.courts.ie

Fry Model Railway, Malahide Castle, Malahide.

Covering 233 square metres (2,500sq.ft) this is one of the world's largest working miniature railways and is a delight for children and adults alike. Besides the track, the railway has stations, bridges, trams, buses and barges and includes the Dublin landmarks of Heuston station and O'Connell Bridge. On display are the hand constructed models of Irish trains by Cyril Fry, draughtsman and railway engineer, who made

them from the 1930s until his death in 1974. Perfectly engineered, the models represent the earliest trains to those of more modern times. Situated in the grounds of Malahide Castle, 13km (8 miles) north of Dublin city centre.

Open (Apr-Sept) Mon-Sat 10.00-17.00 closed Fridays; Sun & public holidays 14.00–18.00; Closed 13.00-14.00 and Oct-Mar.

☎ 01 846 3779

www.malahidecastle.com

GAA Museum, Croke Park.

The Gaelic Athletic Association (GAA) is Ireland's largest sporting and cultural organisation and is dedicated to promoting the games of hurling, Gaelic football, handball, rounders and camogie. The museum is at Croke Park, home of Irish hurling and football, and traces the history of Gaelic sports and their place in Irish culture right up to the present day. Interactive exhibits allow visitors the chance to try out the skills of the games for themselves. National trophies and sports equipment are also on display.

Open Mon-Sat 09.30-17.00, Sun 12.00-17.00. Last admission ½ hour before closing. Open for Cusack Stand ticket holders only on match days. All groups must be pre-booked.

☎ 01 819 2323

www.gaa.ie/museum

Email: gaamuseum@crokepark.ie

Heraldic Museum, Kildare Street.

Part of the National Library of Ireland, the museum illustrates the uses of heraldry with displays of coat of arms and banners and a collection of heraldic glass, seals, stamps, and coins.

Open Mon-Wed 10.00-20.30; Thurs-Fri 10.00-16.30; Sat 10.00-12.30. Admission is free.

☎ 01 603 0311

www.nli.ie

Email: herald@nli.ie

General Post Office, O'Connell Street.

Designed by Francis Johnston and completed in 1818. A century later the GPO became the headquarters of the 1916 Easter Rising and the Proclamation of the Irish Republic was read from the steps by Patrick Pearse. Bullet marks can still be seen on the pillars. Badly damaged in 1922 in the fight for independence, it was restored in 1929. A bronze sculpture, The Death of Cúchulainn by Oliver Sheppard, stands within the building.

☎ 01 705 7600

Email: customer.service@anpost.ie

Guinness Storehouse, St. James's Gate.

The story of Guinness is told from its beginnings in 1759, how it is made and the advertising campaigns used to make it internationally famous. Housed in St James's Gate Brewery and

spread over six floors, on the highest of which can be found the bar 'Gravity', from which a 360° view of Dublin can be enjoyed. Open all year 09.30-17.00 (last admission); Jul-Aug 09.30-19.00. Closed Christmas Eve, Christmas Day, Boxing Day, Good Friday. Disabled access.

☎ *01 408 4800*

www.guinness-storehouse.com

Email: guinness-storehouse@guinness.com

Ha'penny Bridge, Crampton Quay.

An elegant cast-iron pedestrian bridge spanning the Liffey; it was first opened in 1816 and the name derives from the toll once charged.

Irish Jewish Museum, Walworth Road

Opened by President Herzog of Israel in 1985, exhibits relate to the Jewish community in Ireland including synagogue fittings and the reconstruction of a typical Dublin Jewish kitchen of 100 years ago. Open (May–Sept) Sun, Tues, Thurs 11.00-15.30; (Oct-Apr) Sun 10.30-14.30. Admission is free.

☎ *01 490 1857*

Irish Museum of Modern Art,

Military Road, Kilmainham.

Opened in the 17thC Royal Hospital building and grounds in 1991, the museum is an important institution for the collection of modern and contemporary art. A wide variety of work by major established 20thC figures and that of younger contemporary artists is presented in an ever changing programme of exhibitions, drawn from the museum's own collection and from public and private collections world-wide. Open Tues–Sat 10.00–17.15, Sun & some bank holidays 12.00–17.15. Admission is free.

☎ *01 612 9900*

www.modernart.ie

Email: info@imma.ie

James Joyce Centre, North Great George's Street.

A museum in a restored Georgian town house, built in 1784, devoted to the great novelist and run by members of his family. Dennis J Maginni, dancing master in Joyce's novel Ulysses, ran his dancing school from this house. The library contains editions of Joyce's work and that of other Irish writers as well as biographical and critical writing. There is a set of biographies of real Dublin people fictionalised in Ulysses, and also the door from the house occupied by the central character of the novel, Leopold Bloom and his wife Molly. The centre hosts readings, lectures and debates on all aspects of Joyce and his literature and conducts guided city tours. Open Tues–Sat 10.00–17.00.

☎ *01 878 8547*

www.jamesjoyce.ie

Email: info@jamesjoyce.ie

James Joyce Museum, Sandycove.

The museum is housed in the Martello Tower which Joyce used as the setting for the opening chapter of Ulysses, his great work of fiction which immortalised Dublin. Joyce stayed here briefly in 1904 and the living room and view from the gun platform remains much as he described it in the novel. The museum collection includes personal possessions, letters, photographs, first editions and items that reflect the Dublin of Joyce. Situated 13km (8 miles) south of Dublin city centre, the tower was one of 15 defensive towers built along Dublin Bay in 1804 to withstand a threatened invasion from Napoleon. Open (Mar–Oct) Mon–Sat 10.00–17.00, Sun 14.00–18.00. Closed 13.00–14.00. Open Nov-Mar by arrangement.

☎ *01 280 9265*

Kilmainham Gaol, Inchicore Road, Kilmainham.

Built as a gaol in 1796, Kilmainham is now dedicated to the Irish patriots imprisoned there from 1792–1924, including Emmet and his United Irishmen colleagues, the Fenians, the Invincibles and the Irish Volunteers of the Easter Rising. Patrick Pearse and James Connolly were executed in the prison yard and Eamon de Valera, later Prime Minister and then President of Ireland, was one of the last inmates. After its closure in 1924 Kilmainham re-opened as a museum in 1966. It is one of the largest unoccupied gaols in Europe with tiers of cells and overhead catwalks. Access is by guided tour only and features an exhibition and audio-visual show on the political and penal history of the gaol. Open daily (May–Sept) 09.30–17.00; (Oct–Mar) Mon–Fri 09.30–16.00, Sun 10.00–17.00. Disabled toilets. Tours for visitors with special needs by prior arrangement.

☎ *01 453 5984*

King's Inns, Henrietta Street.

The Dublin Inns of Court is a glorious classical building, partly built to the plans of James Gandon at the end of the 19thC. The library was founded in 1787 and contains a large legal collection with about 100,000 books. The courtyard opens into Henrietta Street, where Dublin's earliest Georgian mansions remain.

☎ *01 872 6048*

www.kingsinns.ie

Leinster House, Kildare Street.

Originally a handsome town mansion designed by Richard Castle for the Duke of Leinster in 1745; it has been a Parliament House since 1922. The Dáil Éireann (House of Representatives) and Seanad Éireann (Senate) sit here. The house has two contrasting facades: an imposing formal side facing Kildare Street while from Merrion Square the

building has more of the appearance of a country residence. Anybody wanting a tour of Irish Parliament must contact their respective embassy in Dublin where arrangements can be made. Advance notice is required.
☎ 01 618 3000

Malahide Castle, Malahide.
Originally built in 1185, it was the seat of the Talbot family until 1973 when the last Lord Talbot died; the history of the family is detailed in the Great Hall alongside many family portraits. Malahide also has a large collection of Irish portrait paintings, mainly from the National Gallery, and is furnished with fine period furniture. Within the 100 hectares (250 acres) of parkland surrounding the castle is the Talbot Botanic Gardens, largely created by Lord Milo Talbot between 1948 and 1973. The grounds include walled gardens and a shrubbery with a collection of southern hemisphere plants. Malahide is situated 13km (8 miles) north of Dublin city centre.
Open Mon-Sat 10.00-17.00; Sundays & Bank Holidays 11.00-17.00 (18.00 Apr-Sept); Closed for tours 13.00-14.00.
Combined tickets with Fry Model Railway are available.
☎ 01 846 2184
www.malahidecastle.com
Email: malahidecastle@dublintourism.ie

Mansion House, Dawson Street.
Built in 1705, this Queen Anne style house has been the official residence of the Lord Mayor of Dublin since 1715. The first Irish parliament assembled here in 1919 to adopt Ireland's declaration of Independence and ratify the 1916 proclamation of the Irish Republic. Not open to the public.

National Museum of Ireland
☎ 01 677 7444 / 1890 687 386
www.museum.ie
Open Tues-Sat 10.00-17.00, Sun 14.00-17.00. Admission is free. A Museumlink bus linking the three sites of the National Museum operates regularly throughout the day.

The three national museum sites are:
  Archæology and History, Kildare Street.
Houses a fabulous collection of national antiquities including prehistoric gold ornaments, and outstanding examples of Celtic and medieval art. The 8thC Ardagh Chalice and Tara Brooch are amongst the treasures. The entire history of Ireland is reflected in the museum with 'The Road to Independence Exhibition' illustrating Irish history from 1916-1921. Additionally, there is an Ancient Egypt exhibition.

Decorative Arts and History (Collins Barracks), Benburb Street.
Ireland's museum of decorative arts and economic, social, political and military history, based in the oldest military barracks in Europe. Major collections include Irish silver, Irish country furniture, and costume jewellery and accessories. The work of museum restoration and conservation is explained and the Out of Storage gallery provides visitors with a view of artefacts in storage.

Natural History, Merrion Street.
First opened in 1857 and hardly changed since then, the museum houses a large collection of stuffed animals and the skeletons of mammals and birds from both Ireland and the rest of the world. The exhibits include three examples of the Irish Great Elk which became extinct over 10,000 years ago and the skeleton of a Basking Shark. Fascinating glass reproductions of marine specimens, known as the Blaschka Collection, are found on the upper gallery.

National Print Museum, Haddington Road.
Situated in the former Garrison Chapel in Beggars Bush Barracks, the museum illustrates the development of printing from the advent of printing to the use of computer technology with a unique collection of implements and machines from Ireland's printing industry.
Open Mon-Fri 09.00-17.00, Sat-Sun 14.00-17.00. Closed Bank Holiday weekends.
☎ 01 660 3770

National Sea Life Centre, Bray.
Features marine life from the seas around Ireland including stingrays, conger eels, and sharks; also freshwater fish from Irish rivers and streams. A touch pool gives children the opportunity to pick up small creatures such as starfish, crabs and sea anemones. By way of contrast is the fascinating 'Danger in the Depths' tank with many sea creatures from around the world which have proved harmful or fatal to humans.
Open (May-Sept) Mon-Fri 10.00-18.00, Sat & Sun 10.00-18.30; (Oct-Apr) Mon-Fri 11.00-17.00, Sat & Sun 11.00-18.00.
☎ 01 286 6939
www.sealifeeurope.com

National Transport Museum, Howth.
A collection of buses, trams, trucks, tractors and fire engines, some dating back to 1880, along with other memorabilia from the transport industry.
Open (Jun-Aug) Mon-Fri 10.00-17.00, Sat & Sun 14.00-17.00; (Sept-May) Sat & Sun only 14.00-17.00. Bank holidays 14.00-17.00.
☎ 01 848 0831
www.nationaltransportmuseum.org
Email: info@nationaltransportmuseum.org

National Wax Museum, Grafton Street.
Over 300 life-size wax figures of well-known people and personalities from the past and present ranging from Eamon De Valera to Elvis Presley. Also a dimly lit Chamber of Horrors.
Open Mon-Sat 10.00-17.30; Sun 12.00-17.30
☎ 01 872 6340

Newbridge House, Donabate.
Built in 1737 for Archbishop Charles Cobbe, and still the residence of his descendants, Newbridge has one of the most beautiful period manor house interiors in Ireland and is set within 142 hectares (350 acres) of parkland. A fully restored 18thC farm lies on the estate together with dairy, forge, tack room, and estate worker's house. Situated 19km (12 miles) north of Dublin.
Open (Apr–Sept) Tues–Sat 10.00–17.00, Sun & bank holidays 14.00–18.00; (Oct–Mar) Sat, Sun & bank holidays 12.00–17.00.
☎ 01 843 6534

Newman House, St Stephen's Green.
Newman House is made up of two splendid Georgian mansions, No 85 and No 86, which were once part of the buildings of the Catholic University of Ireland and named after Cardinal Newman, the first rector of the university. They are now owned by University College Dublin. No 86 was built in 1765 for Richard Whaley MP with marvellous stucco by Robert West, the house has also been owned by the celebrated gambler Buck Whaley. The smaller house, No 85, was designed by Richard Castle in 1739 with beautiful plasterwork by the Swiss La Franchini brothers and includes the Apollo Room with a figure of the god above the mantle. Gerald Manley Hopkins was Professor of Classics here at the end of the 19thC and his study is on view. Also open to the public is a classroom furnished as it would have been when James Joyce was a pupil here from 1899–1902. A guided tour explains the history and heritage of the house and how it was restored.
Open (Jun, Jul, Aug) Tues–Fri 14.00–17.00.
☎ 01 716 7422

Number 29, Lower Fitzwilliam Street.
This elegant four-storey house has been restored and furnished exactly as it would have been between 1790–1820 by any well-to-do middle class family. Everything in the house is authentic with period items from the National Museum. The wallpaper was hand-made for Number 29 using 18thC methods. Among the rooms in the house are a kitchen, pantry, governess' room, nursery and boudoir.
Open Tues–Sat 10.00–17.00, Sun 13.00–17.00.
Closed for about 2 weeks preceding Christmas.
☎ 01 702 6165

Old Jameson Distillery,
Bow Street, Smithfield Village.
The art of Irish Whiskey making shown through an audio-visual presentation, working models of the distilling process, and guided tour of the old distillery which was in use between 1780–1971.
Open daily 09.30–17.30 (tours only). Disabled access.
☎ 01 807 2355

Pearse Museum,
St. Enda's Park, Grange Road, Rathfarnham.
Housed in the former school run by nationalist Patrick Pearse from 1910–1916, it includes an audio-visual presentation and a nature study room with displays on Irish flora and fauna. Pearse was executed in 1916 for his part in the Easter Rising. Due to reopen mid 2008 after renovation.
Open (Feb-Apr) 10.00-17.00; (May-Aug) 10.00-17.30; (Sept-Oct) 10.00-17.00; (Nov-Jan) 10.00-16.00; closed 13.00-14.00. Admission is free.
Disabled access to ground floor/toilet.
☎ 01 493 4208

Phoenix Park Visitor Centre, Phoenix Park.
The visitor centre illustrates the history and wildlife of the park with an audio-visual display, a variety of fascinating exhibits and temporary exhibitions. Adjoining the centre is a restored medieval tower house, Ashtown Castle. On Saturdays there are free guided tours to the Irish President's House which is situated in the Park.
Open (Mar-Oct) daily 10.00-17.30 (18.00 Apr-Sept); (Nov-Sept) Wed-Sun 10.00-17.00. Last admission 45 minutes before closing. Toilet for people with disabilities.
☎ 01 677 0095

Powerscourt Centre, South William Street.
A lively three storey centre of craft shops, galleries, boutiques and cafés, converted from Powerscourt Townhouse, a classical style mansion designed by Robert Mack and built between 1771–74. It features the original grand wooden staircase and finely detailed plasterwork.
Open Mon-Fri 10.00-18.00 (Thurs 20.00),
Sat 09.00-21.00, Sun 12.00-18.00.
☎ 01 671 7000
www.powerscourtcentre.com

Powerscourt House & Gardens,
County Wicklow.
First laid out in the 1740s, the 18 hectare (45 acre) gardens, perhaps the finest in Ireland, include sweeping terraces cut into a steep hillside, statues and ornamental lakes. A spectacular Italian style stairway leading down to the main lake was added in 1874. Secluded Japanese gardens with bamboo and walled gardens are also notable and there is a huge variety of trees and shrubs. The house

suffered a serious fire in 1974 and is no longer lived in. Visitors may walk through the old ballroom, and an exhibition area illustrates the history of the construction of the house and there are models of some of the rooms as they would have been before the fire. The house dates back to the 18thC when in 1731 architect Richard Castle was commissioned by Richard Wingfield to transform the medieval Powerscourt Castle into a grand Palladian style mansion; the castle walls were used to form the main structure and the central courtyard was converted into an entrance hall. Powerscourt is in the foothills of the Wicklow mountains, 19km (12 miles) south of Dublin. Open daily 09.30–17.30.
Powerscourt Waterfall is a separate attraction and is the highest in Ireland at 121m (398ft). Open daily 09.30-17.30. Gardens & waterfall close at dusk in the winter.
☎ 01 204 6000
www.powerscourt.ie

Rathfarnham Castle, Rathfarnham.
Dating from around 1583, this castle has 18thC interiors by Sir William Chambers and James Stuart and is presented to visitors as a castle undergoing conservation. Restricted access to the castle for people with disabilities.
Open daily from May–Oct 09.30–17.30 (last tour 16.30).
☎ 01 493 9462

Royal Hospital, Military Road, Kilmainham.
The Royal Hospital was built as a home for army pensioners and invalids by Charles I, and continued in use for almost 250 years. Designed by Sir William Robinson in 1684, it has a formal facade and large courtyard and bears similarities to Les Invalides in Paris and The Royal Hospital in Chelsea. The restored building has one of Dublin's finest interiors and houses the Irish Museum of Modern Art in which there is an audio-visual presentation "The Story of the Royal Hospital Kilmainham". The grounds, including a formal garden, are open to the public.
Open (Jun–Sept) Tues-Sat 12.00-17.30, Sun & bank holidays 12.00-17.30
☎ 01 612 9900

Shaw Birthplace, Synge Street.
This delightful Victorian terrace home was the birthplace of one of Ireland's four Nobel prize-winners for literature, George Bernard Shaw. Restored to give the feeling that the Shaw family is still in residence, the home provides an insight into the domestic life of Victorian Dubliners.
Open (May–Sept) Mon–Fri 10.00–17.00, Sat & Sun 14.00–17.00. Closed Weds & 13.00–14.00.
☎ 01 475 0854

Tara's Palace, Malahide Castle.
The centrepiece of this museum is the one-twelfth size scale model house reflecting the splendour of 18thC Irish mansions. Conceived by Ronald and Doreen McDonnell in 1980, it was ten years in the making. Irish craftsmen paid meticulous attention to detail, with unique miniature furniture and paintings adorning the walls. The museum also has rare pieces of porcelain, miniature glass and silver. Dolls houses of the 18thC and 19thC are displayed, together with dolls and antique toys.
Open (all year) Sat, Sun, bank holidays 11.30-17.30, (Apr-Sept) Mon-Fri 10.45-16.45.
☎ 01 846 3779

Temple Bar
Named after a 17thC landowner, Sir William Temple, this charming neighbourhood is Dublin's cultural quarter. With its narrow cobbled streets running close to the Liffey, Temple Bar is full of character and home to many artists and musicians. The area has been regenerated in recent years and boasts a wide variety of cultural venues and events and an eclectic mix of studios, galleries, shops, markets and eating-places. Modern architecture now blends with the historic. Many free open-air events take place in summer at Meeting House Square and Temple Bar Square, including circus acts, concerts and the outdoor screening of films. Temple Bar is bounded by the south quays of the Liffey, Dame Street, Westmoreland Street and Fishamble Street.
Temple Bar Information Centre, 12 Essex Street East.
Open Mon-Fri 09.00-17.30 (19.00 Jun-Sept), Sat 10.00-18.00, Sun 12.00-16.00 (18.00 Jun-Sept).
☎ 01 677 2255
www.temple-bar.ie

The Chimney, Smithfield Village.
Originally built in 1895, this 53 metre (175ft) chimney which belonged to the Jameson Whiskey Distillery now provides a 360 degree panoramic viewpoint over the city. A glass walled lift takes visitors up the side of the chimney to two viewing galleries at the top.
Open daily 10.00–17.30 (opens 11.00 on Sundays).
☎ 01 817 3838

Trinity College, College Green.
The original Elizabethan college was founded in 1592 but the present building was largely built between 1755–1759. The cruciform complex surrounding cobbled quadrangles and peaceful gardens has an impressive 91 metre (300ft) Palladian facade designed by Henry Keene and John Sanderford. One of the most notable features within the main college square is the 30 metre (98ft) Campanile or bell tower built in 1853 by Sir

Charles Lanyon. The oldest surviving part of the college is the red brick apartment building from 1700 known as The Rubrics. Originally a Protestant College, Catholics did not start entering Trinity until the 1970s. The Library has over a million books and a magnificent collection of early illuminated manuscripts, including the famous Book of Kells; areas open to the public include the Colonnades, the Treasury, and the Long Room Library. Edmund Burke, Oliver Goldsmith and Samuel Beckett are among famous former Trinity College students.
www.tcd.ie

Waterways Visitor Centre, Grand Canal Quay.
A modern centre built on piers over the Grand Canal, housing an exhibition about Ireland's inland waterways. Working models of various engineering features are displayed and there is an interactive multimedia presentation.
Open (Jun–Sept) daily 09.30–17.30; (Oct–May) Wed–Sun 12.30–17.00. Last admission 45 minutes before closing. Access to ground floor for people with disabilities.
☎ 01 677 7510

Cathedrals and churches

Augustinian Church, Thomas Street.
Designed by E W Pugin and G C Ashlin in 1862, it has a mountainous exterior with lofty side aisles to the nave and a 49 metre (160ft) high tower crowned by a spire.

Christ Church Cathedral, Christchurch Place.
The Cathedral was established by Strongbow and Archbishop Laurence O'Toole in 1173 on the site of the cathedral founded around 1030 by the Norse King Sitric Silkenbeard. Lambert Simnel, pretender to the English throne, was crowned here as Edward VI in 1487. It was extensively restored between 1871–78 by George Edmund Street and is one of the best examples in Ireland of early Gothic architecture. The medieval crypt is one of the oldest and largest in Ireland.
Open 09.45-17.00 (Jun-Aug 09.00-18.00).
☎ 01 677 8099
www.cccdub.ie
Email: welcome@cccdub.ie

Franciscan Church,
(Adam and Eve's) Merchants Quay.
Designed by Patrick Byrne in 1830.

St. Ann's Church, Dawson Street.
Designed by Isaac Wells in 1720 with a Romanesque-style facade added by Sir Thomas Deane in 1868. Much of the colourful stained glass dates back to the mid 19thC. Wooden shelves behind the altar were once used to take bread for distribution to the poor. Music recitals are held in the church.
☎ 01 676 7727
www.stannschurch.ie

St. Audoen's Church, High Street.
Dublin's only surviving medieval parish church with a 12thC font and portal. The bell tower restored in the 19thC, has three 15thC bells. The guild chapel has an exhibition on the importance of the church in the life of the medieval city. Dublin's only surviving city gate, known as St Audoen's Arch, stands nearby.
Open Jun–Sept 09.30 (10.15 on Sun)–16.45. Toilet for people with disabilities and church partly accessible.
☎ 01 677 0088

St. Audoen's RC Church, High Street.
Designed by Patrick Byrne in 1841–47, it has a monumental, cliff-like exterior with a huge Corinthian portico added by Stephen Ashlin in 1898.

St. George's, Temple Street.
This neo-classical church was designed by Francis Johnston in 1802 and has a 61 metre (200ft) high steeple modelled on St. Martin-in-the-Fields, London.

St. Mary's Church, Mary Street.
A handsome galleried church designed by Thomas Burgh in 1627. Wolfe Tone, leader of the United Irishmen, was baptised here in 1763 and Sean O'Casey in 1880.

St. Mary's Abbey, Meetinghouse Lane.
Established originally as a Benedictine foundation in 1139, it became Cistercian eight years later. Until the 16thC it was one of the largest and most important monasteries in Ireland. The remains include a fine vaulted Chapter House of 1190 and there is an interesting exhibition about the history of the abbey.
Open mid June–mid Sept, Wed and Sat 10.00–17.00. Last admission 45 minutes before closing.
☎ 01 872 1490

St. Mary's Pro-Cathedral, Marlborough Street.
A Greek Doric style building with the interior modelled on the Church of St. Philippe de Roule in Paris, designed by John Sweetman and built between 1815–1825. St. Mary's is Dublin's most important Catholic Church and is used on State occasions. Tenor John McCormack was once a member of the Palestrina choir that sings a Latin mass every Sunday at 11.00.
Open Mon-Fri 07.30-18.45, Sat 07.30-19.15, Sun 09.00-13.45 and 17.30-19.45.
☎ 01 874 5441
www.procathedral.ie

St. Michan's Church, Church Street.
Founded in 1095 as a Viking parish church, largely rebuilt in 1685 and restored in 1828. Famous for the 17thC mummified bodies in the crypt which are preserved with skin and hair because of the dry atmosphere created by the limestone walls. Handel is thought to have played on the organ which dates from 1724.
Open (March/April-Oct) Mon-Fri 10.00-12.45 and 14.00-16.45; (Nov-March) Mon-Fri 12.30-15.30; all Saturdays 10.00-12.45. Vaults closed on Sundays.
☎ 01 872 4154

St. Patrick's Cathedral, St. Patrick's Close.
The National Cathedral of the Church of Ireland, it was built in the late 12thC on the site of the pre-Norman parish church of St. Patrick. It gained and lost cathedral status more than once in its chequered history and Cromwellian soldiers stabled horses here in the Civil War. Architect John Semple added a spire in 1749 and St. Patrick's was fully restored in the 19thC with finance from the Guinness family. The massive west tower houses the largest ringing peel of bells in Ireland. The cathedral is full of memorial brasses, busts and monuments to famous Irishmen. Jonathan Swift was Dean here from 1713-1745; there are memorials to Swift and his beloved Stella (Esther Johnson) and Swift's pulpit contains his writing table and chair, and portrait.
Usually open daily 09.00-17.00. Wheelchair access by arrangement.
☎ 01 453 9472
www.stpatrickscathedral.ie
Email: admin@stpatrickscathedral.ie

St. Saviour's, Dominick Street.
Designed by J J McCarthy in 1858, this extravagant French style Gothic edifice has a bold west door under a triangular hood, crowned by a large rose window.

St. Stephen's (Pepper Canister),
Mount Street Crescent.
This handsome neo-classical church, designed by John Bowden in 1824, has a Greek style portico.
www.peppercanister.ie

St. Werburgh's Church, Werburgh Street.
Originally the site of an Anglo-Norman foundation, the present church was built in 1715-19 and rebuilt in 1759 following a fire. St. Werburgh's was the Chapel Royal until 1790. Lord Edward Fitzgerald, one of the leaders of the 1798 rebellion, is buried in the vaults.

Whitefriar Street Carmelite Church,
Aungier Street.
19thC church standing on the site of a 16thC Carmelite Priory. The remains of Saint Valentine are buried here and there is a 15thC oak statue of the Virgin and Child, thought to be the only surviving Pre-reformation statue of its kind.
☎ 01 475 8821

Libraries

Central Catholic Library, Merrion Square.
Of religious and general interest, with a large Irish section.
Open Mon-Fri 11.00-18.00, Sat 11.00-17.30.
☎ 01 676 1264
www.catholiclibrary.ie

Central Library, Ilac Centre.
☎ 01 873 4333.
Enquiries about other Dublin City Public Libraries (lending, reference and special collections).
Open Mon-Thurs 10.00-20.00, Fri-Sat 10.00-17.00, Sun closed.
☎ 01 674 4800
Email: dublinpubliclibraries@dublincity.ie

Chester Beatty Library,
Dublin Castle, Dame Street.
Reopened in 2000 in a purpose designed home in the Clock Tower building of Dublin Castle, the library is a treasure of manuscripts, books, prints and textiles collected by American scholar Sir Alfred Chester Beatty. It has some of the rarest original manuscripts still in existence. The collection reflects the art of manuscript production and printing from many parts of the world and from early to modern times with picture scrolls, jade books and woodblock prints from the Far East, around 4,000 Islamic manuscripts, and fine books, bindings and manuscripts from Western Europe. With many Early Christian papyri, the library is a major resource for the study of the Old and New Testaments.
Open Mon-Fri 10.00-17.00, Sat 11.00-17.00, Sun 13.00-17.00. Oct-Apr closed Mondays. Admission is free.
☎ 01 407 0750
www.cbl.ie
Email: info@cbl.ie

Genealogical Office, Kildare Street.
Part of the National Library, the genealogical office offers a service to assist in the task of tracing family history, familiarising people with the relevant records and procedures.
Open Mon-Fri 10.00-17.00, Sat 10.00-12.30.
☎ 01 603 0200

Gilbert Library, Pearse Street.
Books and manuscripts relating to Dublin which were accumulated by 19thC Dublin historian Sir John T Gilbert and now in the care of Dublin Corporation. The collection includes rare early Dublin newspapers, 18thC bindings, Irish Almanacs,

manuscripts of the municipal records of the City of Dublin and the records of the Dublin guilds.
☎ 01 674 4800

Goethe Institute Library, Merrion Square.
German cultural information centre and reference library.
Open Tues-Thurs 12.00–20.00, Fri 10.00-14.30, Sat 10.00-13.30.
☎ 01 661 1155
www.goethe.de

Irish Architectural Archive, Merrion Square.
Records of Irish architecture are preserved and can be examined free of charge with no appointment at the discretion of the staff.
Open Tues–Fri 10.00-17.00.
☎ 01 663 3040
www.iarc.ie

Marsh's Library, St Patrick's Close.
Given to the city by Archbishop Narcissus Marsh and opened in 1701, this is Ireland's oldest public library containing many rare books still in their original carved bookcases. The building was designed by Sir William Robinson who was also the architect of the Royal Hospital, Kilmainham. To prevent the theft of rare books readers were locked in wire cages and three of these cages survive.
Open Mon-Fri 10.00-17.00 (closed 13.00-14.00); Sat 10.30-13.00; closed Tuesdays.
☎ 01 454 3511
www.marshlibrary.ie
Email: keeper@marshlibrary.ie

National Library of Ireland, Kildare Street.
Offers over half a million books, a vast collection of maps, prints and manuscripts and an invaluable collection of Irish newspapers and periodicals. The impressive Victorian building has been home to the Library since 1890, and there is a large domed reading room. Holds temporary exhibitions on Irish writers and books.
Open: Mon–Wed 10.00-21.00,
Thurs–Fri 10.00-17.00, Sat 10.00-13.00.
☎ 01 603 0200
www.nli.ie Email: info@nli.ie

National Photographic Archive,
Meeting House Square.
Only established in 1998, it has over 600,000 photographs recording people, political events, and scenes of Irish cities, towns and countryside. Images from the collection are always on view. There is also a reading room and darkrooms.
Open: Mon–Fri 10.00-17.00. Sat 10.00-14.00 (exhibition only) Admission is free. Disabled access/toilet.
☎ 01 603 0374
www.nli.ie/fr_arch.htm
Email: photoarchive@nli.ie

Royal Irish Academy Library, Dawson Street.
One of the largest collections of ancient Irish manuscripts in the country with one usually on display together with a small exhibition. Access may be restricted depending on Royal Academy meetings and large groups need to make a prior arrangement to visit.
Open Mon–Fri 10.00-17.30 (Fri 17.00).
Admission is free.
☎ 01 676 2570
www.ria.ie

Trinity College Library, College Green.
The oldest and most famous of Dublin's libraries dating from the late 16thC. Entitled to receive a copy of every book published in Ireland, the library also contains an extensive collection of Irish manuscripts including the Book of Kells, a beautifully illuminated copy of the gospels written on vellum in Latin around the year AD800. The Book of Kells is now bound in four volumes and two are always on display in the Treasury, one open at a major ornamental page and the other to show two pages of script. An exhibition explains how the Book of Kells and other manuscripts such as the Book of Durrow (AD675) and Book of Armagh (AD807) were created and illustrates monastic life in the 8thC.
The impressive Old Library or Long Room Library is lined with marble busts of scholars and is nearly 64 metres (210ft) long. It rises two storeys with a high barrel vaulted ceiling and contains over 200,000 of the college's books.
Open Mon–Sat 09.30-17.00; Sun 09.30-16.30 (Jun–Sept), Sun 12.00-16.30 (May–Oct). Last admission 30 minutes before closing.
☎ 01 896 1661
www.tcd.ie/Library

Arts centres, galleries, and concert halls

Douglas Hyde Gallery, Trinity College.
Showing mainly temporary exhibitions of contemporary art.
Open Mon-Sat 11.00-18.00 (Thurs 19.00, Sat 16.45)
☎ 01 896 1116
www.douglashydegallery.com
Email: dhgallery@tcd.ie

Gallery of Photography,
Meeting House Square.
Exhibitions of contemporary photography. Roof terrace has views over the square.
Open Tues-Sat 11.00-18.00, Sun 13.00-18.00.
☎ 01 671 4654
www.irish-photography.com
Email: gallery@irish-photography.com

Hugh Lane Municipal Gallery of Modern Art, Parnell Square North.

19thC and 20thC paintings, mainly Impressionist works, bequeathed by Sir Hugh Lane who was drowned in the Lusitania in 1915, form the nucleus of this collection. The Lane Collection is split with the Tate Gallery in London; each half is alternated between the galleries every 5 years. There is an extensive range of Irish and international paintings, sculpture and stained glass and the acquisition of contemporary work is ongoing. Included is the London studio of Dublin-born artist Francis Bacon, which was carefully dismantled and reconstructed here. Regular Sundays at Noon' Concerts are held at the gallery apart from July and August) with everything from early music to commissioned new works; the music is often arranged to complement one of the temporary exhibitions. The classical building which houses the gallery, Charlemont House, was designed by William Chambers in 1763 for James Caulfield, later 1st Earl Charlemont. It was reconstructed in 1929 to house the Lane Collection and opened in 1933.

Open Tues–Thurs 10.00–18.00, Fri & Sat 10.00–17.00, Sun 11.00–17.00. Admission free except for special exhibitions. Disabled access.
☎ 01 222 5550
www.hughlane.ie
Email: info.hughlane@dublincity.ie

National Concert Hall, Earlsfort Terrace.
Home of the National Symphony Orchestra of Ireland, but also a venue for international artists and orchestras, jazz, contemporary and traditional Irish music. The classical building was designed for the Great Exhibition of 1865, then became the centrepiece of University College Dublin before opening as Ireland's National Concert Hall in 1981. Booking office open Mon–Sat 10.00–19.00. Disabled access/toilet.
☎ 01 417 0000
www.nch.ie
Email:info@nch.ie

National Gallery of Ireland, Merrion Square.
Paintings by illustrious 20thC European artists such as Morrisot, Bonnard, Picasso and Monet hang in the National Gallery as well as the work of Old Masters including Titian, Caravaggio, Rembrandt and Vermeer. There is the National Collection of Irish art, a room dedicated to the work of Jack B Yeats, English paintings, and over 250 sculptures. William Dargan organised the 1853 Dublin Exhibition on this site and used the proceeds to found the collection; his statue stands on the lawn.

Open Mon–Sat 09.30–17.30, Thurs 09.30-20.30, Sun 12.00–17.30. Admission free. Disabled access/toilet.
☎ 01 661 5133
www.nationalgallery.ie
Email: info@ngi.ie

Royal Dublin Society, Ballsbridge.
Venue for large events including craft and antiques fairs and Ideal Homes exhibitions.
☎ 01 668 0866
www.rds.ie

Royal Hibernian Academy Gallagher Gallery, Ely Place.
Showing both traditional and innovative work from both Irish and international artists.
☎ 01 661 2558
www.royalhibernianacademy.com
Email: www.rhagallery@eircom.net

Solomon Gallery, Powerscourt Centre.
One of Ireland's leading contemporary art galleries, situated in an 18thC Georgian townhouse.
Open Mon–Fri 10.00–17.30, Sat 11.00–14.00. Admission free.
☎ 01 679 4237
www.solomongallery.com
Email: info@solomongallery.com

Temple Bar Gallery and Studios, Temple Bar.
A large complex with studios and exhibition spaces.
Open Tues-Sat 10.00-18.00 (Thurs 19.00).
☎ 01 671 0073
www.templebargallery.com
Email: info@templebargallery.com

Temple Bar Music Centre, Curved Street.
Live music venue with recording and rehearsal studios.
☎ 01 670 9202
www.tbmc.ie
Email: info@tbmc.ie

Taylor Galleries, Kildare Street.
Contemporary art gallery, mainly Irish, with the emphasis on painting and sculpture.
☎ 01 676 6055

The Ark, Eustace Street.
A cultural centre for children aged between 3 and 14 with a programme of events and workshops from the worlds of literature, visual arts and music & dance. Plays, exhibitions, festivals, concerts, opera and dance are regularly featured with participation and interaction encouraged. Open to school groups during school times and individuals and family groups at all other times.
Open Mon-Fri 10.00-17.00 and for weekend performances and workshops.
☎ 01 670 7788
www.ark.ie Email: boxoffice@ark.ie

Parks and gardens

Garden of Remembrance, Parnell Square East.
The Garden of Remembrance, opened in 1966, is dedicated to all those who died in the cause of Irish Freedom.
Open (Oct-Mar) 09.30-1600, (Apr-Sept) 08.30-18.00.
☎ 01 874 3074 / 01 647 2498

Iveagh Gardens, Clonmel Street.
Designed by Ninian Niven in 1863, this is one of the least known and most tranquil of Dublin's parks. Features include a rustic grotto, cascade, fountains, maze, archery grounds, wilderness and woodlands.
Opening according to daylight hours.
☎ 01 475 7816

Marlay Park, Rathfarnham.
This large park situated at the foot of the Dublin Mountains contains areas of woodland, a large pond, nature trail and model railway. It is also a popular open-air music venue.

National Botanic Gardens, Glasnevin.
Established in 1795, these magnificent gardens occupy an area of 20 hectares (49 acres) and contain a fabulous collection of plants, shrubs and trees. Many of the plants come from tropical Africa and South America and are housed in large Victorian glasshouses. Features include a rose garden, rockery and wall plants, herbaceous borders, vegetable garden and arboretum.
Open Mon-Sun 09.00-18.00 (Feb-Oct), 09.00-16.30 (Nov-Jan). Admission is free but there is a small charge for the car park. Toilet for people with disabilities, and gardens largely accessible.
☎ 01 857 0909
www.botanicgardens.ie

Phoenix Park
Phoenix Park, covering over 712 hectares (1,760 acres), is Europe's largest enclosed city park. Its name is thought to derive from the Irish meaning "clear water" and a spring does rise in the park. Enclosed by an 11km (7 mile) long stone wall, the park was laid out in the mid 18thC and was the scene of the Phoenix Park murders in 1882, when the Chief Secretary and the Under-Secretary for Ireland were assassinated. A more recent event was when the Pope celebrated mass in the park in front of 1 million people; a 27 metre (90ft) steel cross marks the spot. The park includes a number of buildings, the most important of which is Áras an Uachtaráin; the Viceroy's Lodge built in 1751 but later becoming the official house of the President of Ireland when Dr Douglas Hyde moved there in 1938. Other important buildings are the American ambassador's residence and the Ordnance Survey Office. A 60 metre (205 ft) high obelisk, erected in 1817, is a memorial to the Dublin-born Duke of Wellington. The People's Garden by the main entrance on Parkgate Street is laid out with ornamental planting in ribbon borders, much as it would have been in Victorian times. Dublin Zoo is in the south-east corner. The open space known as Fifteen Acres (but actually covering more than 200) was used in the 18thC as a duelling ground. Phoenix Park is open to the public at all times but the People's Gardens usually close at sunset.

St. Anne's Park, Dollymount.
Once part of the Guinness family estate, the park covers over 110 hectares (270 acres) and is wooded with oak, pine, beech, chestnut and lime. There is a lovely rose garden, opened in 1975.

St. Enda's Park, Grange Road, Rathfarnham.
The park surrounds the Pearse Museum and includes a walled garden, riverside walks and waterfall. Open daily from 10.00, closing time varies according to daylight hours. Limited access for people with disabilities.

St. Stephen's Green
In the heart of the city, St Stephen's Green was originally an open common but was enclosed in 1663. Opened to the general public in 1877, it is laid out as a public park with flowerbeds, an ornamental pond and several sculptures. There is a garden for the visually impaired and there are summer lunchtime concerts at the bandstand.
Open daily 08.00 (Sun & bank Holidays 10.00) closes according to daylight hours.
☎ 01 475 7816

War Memorial Gardens,
South Circular Road, Islandbridge.
Dedicated to the memory of the Irish soldiers who died in the First World War, these gardens include a sunken rose garden and herbaceous borders. They were designed by Sir Edward Lutyens. The names of the 49,400 soldiers who died between 1914–1918 are contained in the granite bookrooms in the gardens, access to which is only by arrangement with the management.
Open Mon–Fri 08.00, Sat & Sun 10.00; closes according to daylight hours.
☎ 01 677 0236 (gardens)
☎ 01 647 2498 (head office)

Theatres

The **Dublin Theatre Festival,** held at many venues throughout the city, runs for two weeks every October.
☎ 01 677 8439, Box office 01 677 8899
www.dublintheatrefestival.com

The **Fringe Festival** runs for two to three weeks each September presenting theatre, dance, music

and the visual arts. Although concentrating on new and emerging local artists, contemporary international artists are usually also featured.
☎ 01 872 9433
www.fringefest.com

Abbey Theatre, Lower Abbey Street.
Ireland's National Theatre, founded by Lady Gregory and W B Yeats in 1904. The Abbey quickly became world renowned, staging plays by J M Synge and Sean O'Casey, and played a significant role in the renaissance of Irish culture. It also provoked controversy in Dublin and even riots. The present theatre was built in 1966 to replace the previous building which had been destroyed by fire. The Abbey stages classic Irish plays, while the Peacock theatre downstairs presents new and experimental drama.
☎ 01 878 7222
www.abbeytheatre.ie

Andrews Lane Theatre and Studio,
Andrews Lane.
A wide variety of works shown both in the theatre and studio.
☎ 01 679 5720
www.andrewslane.com

Civic Theatre, Tallaght.
Stages everything from drama to variety shows
☎ 01 462 7477
www.civictheatre.ie

Focus Theatre,
Pembroke Place, Pembroke Street.
Small theatre presenting classics and new writing.
☎ 01 676 3071

Gaiety Theatre, South King Street.
Restored Victorian building and Dublin's oldest theatre, founded in 1837.
☎ 01 677 1717
www.gaietytheatre.net

Gate Theatre, Cavendish Row.
Modern Irish and classical drama, also international plays. Founded in 1928.
☎ 01 874 4045
www.gate-theatre.ie

Lambert Puppet Theatre,
Clifton Lane, Monkstown.
☎ 01 280 0974
www.lambertpuppettheatre.com

Olympia Theatre, Dame Street.
Comedy, drama, pantomime, musicals, concerts.
☎ 0818 719330

Peacock Theatre, Lower Abbey Street.
New and experimental work.
☎ 01 878 7222
www.abbeytheatre.ie

Point, The North Wall Quay.
Theatre and concert venue including ballet.
☎ 01 836 3633
www.livenation.ie

Project Arts Centre, 39 East Essex Street.
Moved in 2000 into new custom designed building with performance and gallery space; generally innovative new work and everything from drama and visual arts to talks and events.
☎ 01 881 9613
www.project.ie

Samuel Beckett Theatre, Trinity College.
Trinity College School of Drama theatre with a variety of student productions during term and touring companies at other times. Venue for Festival Fringe events.
☎ 01 608 2461

Sugar Club, Lower Leeson Street.
Multimedia theatre with wide range of entertainment; drama, film, cabaret, comedy, music, events.
☎ 01 678 7188
www.thesugarclub.com

Cinemas

Cineworld, Parnell Street
☎ 01 872 8444. 17 screens.
www.cineworld.ie

IMC, Dún Laoghaire
☎ 01 230 1399. 12 screens.
www.imc-cinemas.com

Irish Film Institute, Eustace Street
Art house with 2 screens and restaurant converted from old Quaker meeting house.
☎ 01 679 3477   www.irishfilm.ie

Movies@Dundrum, Dundrum town centre
☎ 01 291 6802. 12 screens.
www.movies-at.ie

Movies@Swords, Pavilions Shopping Centre
☎ 01 870 3600. 11 screens.
www.movies-at.ie

Omniplex, Santry
☎ 01 842 8844. 11 screens.
www.omniplex.ie

Ormonde Cinema, Stillorgan
☎ 01 707 4100. 7 screens.
www.ormondecinemas.com

Savoy Cinema, O'Connell Street Upper
☎ 01 874 6000. 6 screens.
www.savoy.ie

Screen Cinema, D'Olier Street
☎ 01 672 5500. 3 screens.
www.screencinema.ie

UCI Cinema, Blanchardstown
☎ *01 8222 624.* 9 screens.

UCI Cinema, Coolock
☎ *01 848 5122.* 10 screens.

UCI Cinema, Tallaght
☎ *01 459 8400.* 12 screens.

Vue Dublin, Liffey Valley Shopping Centre,
Fonthill Road
☎ *1520 501 000.* 14 screens.

Shopping
Opening hours are generally 09.00–18.00 Mon–Sat. Many city centre shops and shopping centres remain open until 20.00 or 21.00 on Thursdays and Fridays and open 12.00–18.00 on Sundays.

The main city centre shopping areas are around Grafton Street and Nassau Street to the south of the Liffey and around Henry Street (off O'Connell Street) to the north of the river. Both Grafton Street and Henry Street are pedestrianised. Many up-market and international designer stores can be found in Grafton Street, while shops around Henry Street are generally less expensive. The Temple Bar area has a number of craft and specialist shops.

Department stores
Arnotts, Henry Street, ☎ *01 805 0400.*

Brown Thomas, Grafton Street,
☎ *01 605 6666.*

Clery and Co, O'Connell Street Lower,
☎ *01 878 6000.*

Debenhams, Jervis Centre, ☎ *01 878 1222.*

Dunnes Stores, Henry Street, ☎ *01 872 3911.*

Guiney & Co, Talbot Street, ☎ *01 878 8835.*

Marks & Spencers, Grafton Street,
☎ *01 679 7855.*

Penneys Stores, Mary Street, ☎ *01 872 7788.*

Roches Stores, Henry Street, ☎ *01 873 0044.*

Shopping centres
Dún Laoghaire Shopping Centre, Marine Road,
☎ *01 280 2981.*

Ilac Centre, Henry Street, ☎ *01 704 1460.*

Irish Life Shopping Mall, Abbey Street,
☎ *01 704 1452.*

Jervis Shopping Centre, Jervis Street,
☎ *01 878 1323.*

Powerscourt Centre, South William Street,
☎ *01 679 4144.*

St. Stephen's Green Centre, ☎ *01 478 0888.*

There are also shopping centres at Clondalkin (Liffey Valley), Blanchardstown, and Tallaght on the outskirts of Dublin.

Markets
Blackrock
Sat, Sun & bank holidays 11.00–17.30 (bric-a-brac, china and antiques).
☎ *01 283 3522*

George's Street Market Arcade
Second hand clothes, jewellery, records.
☎ *01 280 8683*

Liberty Market
Clothes, fabrics, household goods, Meath Street.
☎ *01 280 8683*

Moore Street Market
Mon–Sat (flower, fruit and vegetables), off Henry Street.

St. Michan's Street Vegetable Market
Fruit, vegetables, fish and flowers).

Temple Bar Square
Food market is open every Saturday from 09.30–18.00 selling organic fruit and vegetables, bread, cheeses, oysters, and smoked fish. Book Market is open on Saturdays from 09.30. There is also a craft and furniture market on Sundays 12.00-18.00.
☎ *01 677 2255*

Sport and leisure
International sports venues:
Athletics
Irishtown Stadium, Irishtown
☎ *01 669 7211*

Gaelic Football and Hurling
Croke Park
(Also rugby and soccer while redevelopment of Lansdowne Road takes place)
☎ *01 836 3222*

Golf (18-hole golf clubs):
Balcarrick Golf Club, Donabate, 16km (10m) north of city centre.
☎ *01 843 6957*
www.balcarrickgolfclub.com

Ballinascorney, 13km (8m) south west of city centre.
☎ *01 493 7755*
www.ballinascorneygc.com

Beaverstown Golf Club, Donabate, 16km (10m) north of city centre.
☎ *01 843 6439*
www.beaverstown.com

Castle Golf Club, Rathfarnham, 6km (4m) south of city centre.
☎ 01 490 4207
www.castlegc.ie

Citywest Golf Resort, Saggart, 16km (10m) south west of city centre.
☎ 01 401 0500
www.citywesthotel.ie

Corballis Golf Links, Donabate,16km (10m) north of city centre.
☎ 01 843 6583
www.golfdublin.com/corballis

Deerpark Hotel and Golf Courses, Howth, 14km (9m) north east of city centre.
☎ 01 832 6039
www.deerpark–hotel.ie

Druids Glen, Newmountkennedy, 32km (2m) south east of city centre.
☎ 01 287 3600
www.druidsglen.ie

Edmondstown Golf Club, Rathfarnham, 11km (7m) south of city centre.
☎ 01 493 1082
www.edmondstowngolfclub.ie

Elmgreen Golf Centre, Castleknock, 8km (5m) north west of city centre.
☎ 01 820 0797
www.golfdublin.com/elmgreen

Elm Park Golf Club, Donnybrook, 5km (3m) south of city centre.
☎ 01 269 3438
www.elmparkgolfclub.ie

Forrest Little Golf Club, Cloghean, 9km (6m) north of city centre, near to airport.
☎ 01 840 1763
www.forrestlittle.ie

Grange Castle, Clondalkin, 8km (5m) south west of city centre.
☎ 01 464 1043
www.grange-castle.com

Grange Golf Club, Rathfarnham, 6km (4m) south of city centre.
☎ 01 493 2889
www.grangegolfclub.ie

Hermitage Golf Club, Lucan, 11km (7m) west of city centre.
☎ 01 626 8491
www.hermitagegolf.ie

Howth Golf Club, Sutton, 14km (9m) north east of city centre.
☎ 01 832 3055
www.howthgolfclub.ie

Island Golf Club, Corballis, Donabate, 14km (9m) north of city centre.
☎ 01 843 6205
www.theislandgolfclub.com

Luttrellstown Castle, Castleknock, 10 km (6m) west of city centre.
☎ 01 808 9988
www.luttrellstowngc.com

Malahide Golf Club, 13km (8m) north of city centre.
☎ 01 846 1611
www.malahidegolfclub.ie

Portmarnock Golf Club, 11km (7m) north east of city centre.
☎ 01 846 2968
www.portmarnockgolfclub.ie

Portmarnock Hotel and Golf Links, 11km (7m) north east of city centre.
☎ 01 846 1800
www.portmarnock.com

Royal Dublin Golf Club, Dollymount, 5km (3m) north east of city centre.
☎ 01 833 6346
www.theroyaldublingolfclub.com

St. Anne's Golf Club, Dollymount, 5km (3m) north east of city centre.
☎ 01 833 6471
www.stanneslinksgolf.com

St. Margaret's Golf Club, 11km (7m) north of city centre.
☎ 01 864 0400
www.stmargaretsgolf.com

Swords Open Golf Course, 13km (8m) north of city centre.
☎ 01 840 9819
www.swordsgolfclub.com

Greyhound racing

Shelbourne Park Stadium, Ringsend, (Wed, Thurs, Sat at 20.00).
☎ 01 668 3502
www.shelbournepark.com

Harold's Cross Stadium, (Mon, Tues & Fri at 20.00).
☎ 01 497 1081

Horse racing

Leopardstown
10km (6 miles) south of Dublin. National Hunt and Flat racing with 22 meetings including 4 day Christmas National Hunt Festival.
☎ 01 289 0500
www.leopardstown.com

Fairyhouse

19km (12 miles) north west of Dublin. Home of the Irish Grand National.
☎ 01 825 6167
www.fairyhouseracecourse.ie

Sailing

The Irish Sailing Association, Dún Laoghaire
☎ 01 280 0239
www.sailing.ie

Sports centres

Aughrim Street, ☎ 01 838 8085

Glin Road, Coolock, ☎ 01 847 8177

Coolmine Sports Complex, Coolmine
☎ 01 821 4549

Swimming pools

Ballymun, Town Centre, ☎ 01 862 3510

Coolock, Northside Shopping Centre,
☎ 01 847 7743

Crumlin, Windmill Road, ☎ 01 455 5792

Finglas, Mellowes Road, ☎ 01 864 2584

Markievicz Pool, Townsend Street,
☎ 01 672 9121

Rathmines, Lower Rathmines Road,
☎ 01 496 1275

Sean McDermott Street
☎ 01 872 0752

Help and advice

Embassies

Apostolic Nunciature, Navan Road.
☎ 01 838 0577

Argentina, Ailesbury Drive. ☎ 01 269 1546

Australia, Fitzwilton House, Wilton Terrace.
☎ 01 664 5300

Austria, Ailesbury Road. ☎ 01 269 4577

Belgium, Shrewsbury Road. ☎ 01 205 7100

Brazil, Harcourt Street. ☎ 01 475 6000

Bulgaria, Burlington Road. ☎ 01 660 3293

Canada, St. Stephen's Green. ☎ 01 417 4100

Chile, Wellington Road. ☎ 01 667 5094

China, Ailesbury Road. ☎ 01 269 1707

Croatia, Chambers Street. ☎ 01 476 7181

Cuba, Adelaide Road. ☎ 01 475 0899 / 2999

Cyprus, Lower Leeson Street. ☎ 01 676 3060

Czech Republic, Northumberland Road.
☎ 01 668 1135

Denmark, St. Stephen's Green.
☎ 01 475 6404 / 6405

Egypt, Clyde Road. ☎ 01 660 6566

Estonia, Ailesbury Road. ☎ 01 219 6730

Ethiopia, Fitzwilliam Street Lower.
☎ 01 678 7062 / 3

Finland, St. Stephen's Green. ☎ 01 478 1344

France, Ailesbury Road. ☎ 01 277 5000

Germany, Trimleston Avenue.
☎ 01 269 3011

Greece, Pembroke Street Upper.
☎ 01 676 7254

Hungary, Fitzwilliam Place. ☎ 01 661 2902

India, Leeson Park. ☎ 01 497 0959

Iran, Mount Merrion Avenue. ☎ 01 288 0252

Israel, Pembroke Road. ☎ 01 230 9400

Italy, Northumberland Road. ☎ 01 660 1744

Japan, Merrion Centre. ☎ 01 202 8300

Korea, Clyde Road. ☎ 01 660 8800

Latvia, Lower Leeson Street. ☎ 01 662 1610

Lesotho, Clanwilliam Square. ☎ 01 676 2233

Lithuania, Merrion Road. ☎ 01 668 8292

Malaysia, Shelbourne Road. ☎ 01 667 7280

Malta, Earlsfort Terrace. ☎ 01 676 2340

Mexico, Ailesbury Road. ☎ 01 260 0699

Morocco, Raglan Road. ☎ 01 660 9449

Netherlands, Merrion Road. ☎ 01 269 3444

Nigeria, Leeson Park. ☎ 01 660 4366

Norway, Molesworth Street. ☎ 01 662 1800

Pakistan, Ailesbury Road. ☎ 01 261 3032 / 3

Poland, Ailesbury Road. ☎ 01 283 0855

Portugal, Knocksinna Mews. ☎ 01 289 4416

Romania, Waterloo Road. ☎ 01 668 1085

Russian Federation, Orwell Road.
☎ 01 492 3492

Slovak Republic, Clyde Road. ☎ 01 660 0008

Slovenia, Nassau Street. ☎ 01 670 5240

South Africa, Earlsfort Terrace.
☎ 01 661 5553

Spain, Merlyn Park. ☎ 01 269 1640

Sweden, Dawson Street. ☎ 01 474 4400

Switzerland, Ailesbury Road. ☎ 01 218 6382

Turkey, Clyde Road. ☎ 01 668 5240

Ukraine, Elgin Road. ☎ *01 668 8601 / 5189*

United Kingdom, Merrion Road. ☎ *01 205 3700*

USA, Elgin Road. ☎ *01 668 8777*

Health centres and pharmacies

Grafton Street Centre, Open Mon-Thurs 08.30-18.30, Fri 08.30-18.00.
☎ *01 671 2122*

Mercer's Medical Centre, Stephen Street Lower, Open: Mon-Thurs 09.00-17.30, Fri 09.00-16.30 (closed 12.30-14.00).
☎ *01 402 2300*

O'Connell's Late Night Pharmacy, O'Connell Street Lower.
Open daily Mon-Fri 07.30-22.00, Sat 08.00-22.00, Sun 10.00-22.00.
☎ *01 873 0427*

Garda Síochána (Police)
City centre Garda stations:

Pearse Street station, ☎ *01 666 9000*

Store Street station, ☎ *01 666 8000*

Dublin Metropolitan Area Headquarters, Harcourt Square, ☎ *01 666 9500*

Greater Dublin Area Headquarters, Phoenix Park, ☎ *01 666 0000*

Dún Laoghaire station, ☎ *01 666 5000*
www.garda.ie

Post Offices

General Post Office, O'Connell Street.
Open Mon-Sat 08.00-20.00.
☎ *01 705 7000*
www.anpost.ie

Post offices are usually open Mon-Fri 09.00-17.30 (closed 13.00-14.15) and from 09.00-13.00 on Saturdays.

Welfare organisations

Citizens Information Centre (Comhairle), 13a O'Connell Street Upper.
☎ *01 809 0633*
www.citizensinformation.ie

Irish Tourist Assistance Service, Garda Headquarters, Harcourt Square.
All referrals must go through the Garda.
☎ *01 478 5295*
www.itas.ie

Samaritans, 112 Marlborough Street.
☎ *01 872 7700 or callsave 1850 609 090*
www.samaritans.org

Social Welfare Services, Store Street.
☎ *01 874 8444*

Hospitals

The Adelaide & Meath Hospital Incorporating the National Children's Hospital, Tallaght.
☎ *01 414 2000* www.amnch.ie

Beaumont, Beaumont Road.
☎ *01 809 3000* www.beaumont.ie

Blackrock Clinic (private), Rock Road.
☎ *01 283 2222* www.blackrock-clinic.ie

Bon Secours Private Hospital, Glasnevin.
☎ *01 837 5111* www.bonsecoursireland.org

Cappagh National Orthopaedic, Cappagh Road.
☎ *01 814 0400* www.cappagh.ie

Dental Hospital, Lincoln Place.
☎ *01 612 7200* www.dentalscience.tcd.ie

James Connolly Memorial Hospital, Blanchardstown.
☎ *01 646 5000* www.connollyhospital.ie

Mater Misericordiae, Eccles Street.
☎ *01 803 2000* www.mater.ie

Mater Private, Eccles Street.
☎ *01 885 8888* www.materprivate.ie

National Maternity, Holles Street.
☎ *01 637 3100* www.nmh.ie

Our Lady's Hospital for Sick Children, Crumlin.
☎ *01 409 6100* www.olhsc.ie

Rotunda Hospital, Parnell Square.
☎ *01 873 0700* www.rotunda.ie

Royal Victoria Eye and Ear, Adelaide Road.
☎ *01 664 4600*

St. James's, James's Street.
☎ *01 410 3000* www.stjames.ie

St. Mary's Hospital, Phoenix Park.
☎ *01 677 8132*

St. Michael's, George's Street Lower, Dún Laoghaire.
☎ *01 280 6901*

St. Patrick's, James's Street.
☎ *01 249 3200* www.stpatrickshosp.ie

St.Vincent's University Hospital, Elm Park.
☎ *01 221 4000* www.st-vincents.ie

Index to place names

Archerstown	11 D3	Clonskeagh	103 C3	Hazelbrook	25 D2	Oldtown	14 B1
Artane	54 B3	Clontarf	80 A2	Hilltown	16 A2	Outlands	14 B2
Ashbourne	10 B2	Confey	68 B1	Howth	60 B2	Palmerston	73 D3
Ashtown	49 C3	Cookstown	10 A1	Inchicore	87 D2	Pelletstown	49 D3
Balgriffin	41 D1	Coolock	54 B1	Irishtown	91 D3	Phibsborough	77 D2
Balgriffin Park	42 A2	Corballis	13 D3	Islandbridge	88 A1	Poppintree	37 C2
Ballalease North	13 D1	Corbally	121 D3	Jobstown	122 B2	Portmarnock	27 C2
Ballalease South	13 D2	Corduff	33 D3	Kilbarrack	57 C2	Raheny	56 A3
Ballinteer	128 B2	Cornelscourt	132 A3	Kildonan	50 A1	Railpark	65 D2
Ballisk	13 D2	Crumlin	99 D2	Killegland	10 B3	Ranelagh	102 B1
Ballisk Common	13 D1	Dalkey	134 B1	Killester	54 B3	Rathfarnham	113 C2
Ballsbridge	103 D1	Darndale	41 C2	Killinardan	122 B3	Rathgar	101 D3
Ballyboden	126 B1	Deans Grange	132 A2	Killincarrig	143 C3	Rathmichael	140 A2
Ballybrack	139 C2	Dollymount	81 D2	Killiney	139 D1	Rathmines	102 A2
Ballyfermot	86 B2	Dolphin's Barn	89 C3	Kill O' The Grange	132 B1	Ringsend	91 D2
Ballymacartle	24 B2	Donabate	13 C1	Kilmainham	88 A2	Ronanstown	84 A3
Ballymastone	13 D2	Donnybrook	103 C2	Kilmore	39 D3	Rossmore	111 D2
Ballymount	98 A2	Drimnagh	99 D1	Kilnamanagh	109 D2	Saggart	120 B2
Ballymun	38 A3	Drumcondra	78 A1	Kiltalown	122 A3	Saintdoolaghs (east)	42 A1
Barrogstown West	65 D3	Drumnigh	42 B1	Kimmage	100 B3	St. Doolagh's (west)	41 D1
Beaumont	53 C1	Dublin Airport	22 B2	Kingswood	107 D2	Sallynoggin	133 C2
Beechwood	26 A2	Dunboyne	28 B2	Kinsaley	25 C2	Sandyford	129 D3
Blackrock	117 D1	Dundrum	114 B3	Knocklyon	126 A1	Sandymount	92 A3
Blanchardstown	47 D2	Dún Laoghaire		Laraghbryan East	64 A1	Santry	38 B3
Bluebell	98 B1	(Dunleary)	119 C3	Leixlip	69 C2	Shankill	141 C2
Bohammer	25 C3	Dunleary		Leopardstown	130 B3	Shielmartin	62 B2
Boherboy	121 C2	(Dún Laoghaire)	119 C3	Loughlinstown	140 B1	Slade	120 B3
Booterstown	116 B1	Dunreagh	11 C1	Lucan	82 A1	Snugborough	42 B2
Bray	142 B1	Edmondstown	126 B3	Malahide	20 A1	Stapolin	43 C2
Burgage	41 C1	Feltrim	25 C1	Malahide Demesne	19 D3	Stillorgan	116 B3
Cabinteely	137 D1	Finglas	51 C2	Marino	79 C2	Stockhole	23 D3
Cabra	77 C2	Finglas East	50 B1	Mayeston Hall	37 C2	Stradbrook	118 A3
Carpenterstown	46 A3	Firhouse	125 C1	Maynetown	43 C1	Sutton	58 A1
Carrickmines	137 C2	Foxrock	131 D3	Maynooth	65 C1	Swords	18 A1
Castleknock	73 D1	Galloping Green	131 C1	Merrion	104 A3	Tallaght	109 D3
Celbridge	66 B2	Glasnevin	52 A3	Milltown (Dublin 6)	102 B3	Templeogue	112 A2
Chapelizod	86 B1	Glasnevin North	51 D1	Milltown (Ashbourne)	11 C2	Terenure	113 C1
Churchtown	114 A2	Glebe	24 A2	Monkstown	118 B3	Wainsfort	112 A1
Clare Hall	41 D3	Goatstown	115 C3	Mooretown	14 A3	Walkinstown	98 B2
Cloghran	23 C1	Goldenbridge	87 D3	Mount Merrion	116 A2	Whitehall	52 B3
Clondalkin	96 A2	Grange	26 A1	Mulhuddart	32 B2	Willbrook	112 B3
Clonee	30 A1	Greenhills	110 B1	Newtown (Dublin 16)	126 B3	Williamstown	117 D1
Clongriffin	42 B2	Greenwood	24 B2	Newtown (Swords)	15 C1	Windmill Lands	16 A1
Clonshaugh	40 B1	Harold's Cross	101 C1	Northwood	38 A2	Windy Arbour	115 C2
Clonsilla	45 D2	Hartstown	45 C1	Oldbawn	123 D2	Yellow Walls	19 C2

Index to street names

General abbreviations

All	Alley	Dws	Dwellings	Junct	Junction	Rd	Road
Apts	Apartments	E	East	La	Lane	Ri	Rise
Av/Ave	Avenue	Ex	Exchange	Lo	Lodge	S	South
Bk	Bank	Ext	Extension	Lwr	Lower	Sch	School
Bldgs	Buildings	Fld	Field	Mans	Mansions	Sq	Square
Boul	Boulevard	Flds	Fields	Mkt	Market	St.	Saint
Br/Bri	Bridge	Fm	Farm	Ms	Mews	St	Street
Cem	Cemetery	Gdn	Garden	Mt	Mount	Sta	Station
Cen	Central,	Gdns	Gardens	N	North	Ter	Terrace
	Centre	Gra	Grange	No	Numbers	Vil	Villa, Villas
Cl/Clo	Close	Grd	Ground	Par	Parade	Vw	View
Coll	College	Grn	Green	Pas	Passage	W	West
Cotts	Cottages	Gro	Grove	Pk	Park	Wd	Wood
Cres	Crescent	Ho	House	Pl	Place	Wds	Woods
Ct	Court	Hosp	Hospital	Prom	Promenade	Wk	Walk
Dr	Drive	Hts	Heights	Rbt	Roundabout	Yd	Yard

District abbreviations

Abb.	Abberley	Clons.	Clonsilla	Kill.	Killiney	Mulh.	Mulhuddart
Ashb.	Ashbourne	Collins.	Collinstown	Kilsh.	Kilshane	Palm.	Palmerston
B'brack	Ballybrack	Cool.	Coolmine	Kilt.	Kiltipper	Port.	Portmarnock
Balg.	Balgriffin	Corn.	Cornelscourt	Kings.	Kingswood	R'coole	Rathcoole
Black.	Blackrock	D'bate	Donabate	Kins.	Kinsaley	Ronan.	Ronanstown
Boot.	Booterstown	D.L.	Dún Laoghaire	Leix.	Leixlip	Sagg.	Saggart
Cabin.	Cabinteely	Dunb.	Dunboyne	Leo.	Leopardstown	Sally.	Sallynoggin
Carp.	Carpenterstown	Fox.	Foxrock	Lou.V.	Louisa Valley	Sandy.	Sandyford
Carrick.	Carrickmines	G'geary	Glenageary	Lough.	Loughlinstown	Shank.	Shankill
Castle.	Castleknock	Gra M.	Grange Manor	Mala.	Malahide	Still.	Stillorgan
Celbr.	Celbridge	Grey.	Greystones	Manor.	Manorfields		
Clond.	Clondalkin	Jobs.	Jobstown	Mayn.	Maynooth		

Some streets are not named on the map due to insufficient space. In some of these cases the nearest street that does appear on the map is listed in italics. In other cases they are indicated on the map by a number which is listed here in **bold**.

L Branch Rd N	92 A1
L Branch Rd S	92 A1
2 Branch Rd N	92 B1
2 Branch Rd N Ext	92 B1
2 Branch Rd S	92 B1
3 Branch Rd S	92 A1
4 Branch Rd S	92 B1

A

Abberley	139 C3
Abbey Cotts	
off Abbey St Upr	144 C2
Abbey Ct Dublin 5	54 B3
Abbey Ct 1 D.L.	132 B1
Abbeydale	83 D2
Abbeydale Cl	83 D2
Abbeydale Cres	83 D2
Abbeydale Gdns	83 D2
Abbeydale Pk	83 D2
Abbeydale Ri	83 D2
Abbeydale Wk	83 D2
Abbey Dr	76 A1
Abbeyfarm	66 A3
Abbeyfield Dublin 5	54 B3
Abbeyfield Dublin 6	102 B3
Abbeyfield Ct	83 C2
Abbeylea Av	14 B3
Abbeylea Cl	14 B3
Abbeylea Dr	15 C3
Abbeylea Grn	14 B3
Abbey Pk Dublin 5	54 A3
Abbey Pk Dublin 5	57 C1
Abbey Pk D.L.	132 B1
Abbey Rd	132 B1
Abbey St	61 C2
Abbey St Lwr	145 D2
Abbey St Mid	145 D2
Abbey St Old	145 E2
Abbey St Sta	145 D2
Abbey St Upr	144 C2
Abbey Thea	145 D2
Abbeyvale Av	14 A3
Abbeyvale Cl	14 A3
Abbeyvale Ct	14 A3
Abbeyvale Cres	14 A3
Abbeyvale Dr	14 A3
Abbeyvale Grn	14 A3
Abbeyvale Lawn	14 A3
Abbeyvale Pl	14 A3
Abbeyvale Ri	14 A3
Abbeyvale Vw	14 A3
Abbeyvale Way	14 A3
Abbey Vw	132 B1
Abbeywood	83 C2
Abbeywood Av	83 D2
Abbeywood Cl	83 D2
Abbeywood Cres	83 D2
Abbeywood Pk	83 D2
Abbeywood Way	83 D2
Abbots Hill	20 B2
Abbotstown Av (Ascal Bhaile An Abba)	49 D1
Abbotstown Dr	49 D1
Abbotstown Rd	50 A1
Abercorn Rd	91 C1
Abercorn Sq	87 D2
Abercorn Ter Dublin 7	77 C3
Abercorn Ter Dublin 8	87 D2
Aberdeen St	88 B1
Abington	19 C3
Achill Rd Dublin 9	78 B1
Achill Rd Lough.	139 C3
Acorn Dr	128 B1
Acorn Rd	128 B1
Acres Rd	75 D3
Adair	103 D1
Adam Ct off Grafton St	145 D4
Adamstown Rd	70 A3
Adare Av	54 A1
Adare Dr	54 B1
Adare Grn	54 B1
Adare Pk	54 B1
Adare Rd	40 B3
Addison Av	51 D3
Addison Dr	51 D3
Addison Pl	78 A1
Addison Rd	79 C2
Addison Ter	78 A1
Adelaide Ms	104 B2
Adelaide Rd Dublin 2	90 A3
Adelaide Rd Bray	142 B1
Adelaide Rd D.L.	134 A2
Adelaide St	119 D3
Adelaide Ter Dublin 8	
off Brookfield St	88 B2
Adelaide Vil Bray	142 A1
Adelaide Vil 2 D.L.	134 A1
Admiral Ct 7	43 D3
Admiral Pk	43 D3
Adrian Av	101 C2
Advance Business Pk	39 C1
Aideen Av	100 B3
Aideen Dr	100 B3
Aideen Pl	100 B3
Aikenhead Ter	91 D2
Ailesbury	52 B1
Ailesbury Cl	103 D2
Ailesbury Dr	103 D2
Ailesbury Gdns	104 A2
Ailesbury Gro Dublin 4	103 D2
Ailesbury Gro Dublin 16	128 B1
Ailesbury Lawn	128 B1
Ailesbury Ms	104 B2
Ailesbury Pk	104 A2
Ailesbury Rd	103 D2
Ailsbury Gro	128 B1
Ailsbury Lawn	128 B1
Airfield Ct	103 D3
Airfield Manor	103 D3
Airfield Pk	103 D3
Airfield Rd	101 D3
Airfield Ter	103 D3
Air Pk	126 A2
Airpark Av	126 A2
Airpark Cl	126 B2
Airport Business Pk	23 C2
Airport Ind Est	39 C2
Airside Business Pk	17 C2
Airside Retail Pk	17 C2
Airton Cl	110 A3
Airton Rd	109 D3
Airton Ter	110 A3
Airways Ind Est	39 C2
Albany Av	118 B3
Albany Ct	139 C3
Albany Rd	102 B2
Albert Av	142 B1
Albert Coll Av	52 A2
Albert Coll Cres	52 A2
Albert Coll Dr	52 A2
Albert Coll Lawn	52 A2
Albert Coll Pk	52 A2
Albert Coll Ter	52 A2
Albert Ct	134 A1
Albert Ct E	91 C2
Albert Pk	134 A1
Albert Pl	
off Inchicore Rd	88 A2
Albert Pl E	91 C2
Albert Pl W	90 A3
Albert Rd Lwr	134 A1
Albert Rd Upr	134 A2
Albert Ter	
off Albert Pl W	90 A3
Albert Vil	
off Morehampton Rd	103 C1
Albert Wk	142 B1
Albion Ter	
off Inchicore Rd	88 A2
Aldborough Par	79 C3
Aldborough Pl	78 B3
Aldborough Sq	78 B3
Aldemere	45 C2
Alden Dr	56 B1
Alden Pk	57 C1
Alden Rd	56 B1
Alderbrook Downs	11 C3
Alderbrook Glen	11 C3
Alderbrook Pk	11 C3
Alderbrook Ri	11 C3
Alderbrook Vale	11 C3
Alder Ct 1	27 C1
Alderpark Ct	123 C1
Alders, The	118 A3
Alderwood Av	123 C1
Alderwood Cl	109 C3
Alderwood Ct	123 C1
Alderwood Dr	123 C1
Alderwood Grn	109 C3
Alderwood Gro	123 C1
Alderwood Lawn	109 C3
Alderwood Pk	123 C1
Alderwood Ri	109 C3
Aldrin Wk	54 A1
Alexander Ter Dublin 1	91 C1
Alexander Ter Dublin 8	89 D3
Alexander Ter 1 Bray	142 A2
Alexandra Quay	92 A1
Alexandra Rd	91 D1
Alexandra Rd Ext	93 C1
Alexandra Ter Dublin 3	
off Clontarf Rd	81 C3
Alexandra Ter Dublin 6	101 D3
Alexandra Ter (Dundrum) Dublin 14	114 B3
Alfie Byrne Rd	79 D3
Allendale Cl	45 C1
Allendale Copse	45 C1
Allendale Ct	45 C1
Allendale Dr	45 C1
Allendale Elms	45 C1
Allendale Glen	45 C1
Allendale Grn	45 C1
Allendale Gro	45 C1
Allendale Heath	45 C1
Allendale Lawn	45 C1
Allendale Pl	45 C1
Allendale Ri	45 C1
Allendale Sq	45 C1
Allendale Ter	45 C1
Allendale Vw	45 C1
Allendale Wk	45 C1
Allen Pk Dr	130 B1
Allen Pk Rd	130 B1
Allenton Av	124 A3
Allenton Cres	124 A3
Allenton Dr	124 A3
Allenton Gdns	124 A3
Allenton Grn	124 A3
Allenton Lawns	124 A3
Allenton Pk	124 A2
Allenton Rd (Oldcourt) Dublin 24	124 A2
Allenton Rd (Tallaght) Dublin 24	124 A1
Allenton Way	124 A3
All Hallows Coll	78 B1
All Hallows La	
off Drumcondra Rd Upr	78 B1
Allied Ind Est	86 B3
Allingham St	89 C2
All Saints Dr	55 D3
All Saints Pk	55 D3
All Saints Rd	55 C3
Alma Pl	118 B3
Alma Rd	118 A2
Almeida Av	
off Brookfield St	88 B2
Almeida Ter	
off Brookfield St	88 B2
Alone Wk	54 B3
Alpine Hts	96 A3
Alpine Ri	108 B2
Altadore	133 D2
Altamont Ter	77 C3
Alverno	80 A2
Amber Vale	108 B2
Amiens St	145 F1
Anastasia La	135 C2
Anfield Cl	46 A3
Anfield Ct	72 A1
Anfield Cres	72 A1
Anfield Dr	72 A1
Anfield Lawn 1	72 A1
Anfield Vw 2	72 A1
Anglesea Av	117 D2
Anglesea Br	103 D2
Anglesea Fruit Mkt	
off Green St Little	144 B2
Anglesea La	119 D3
Anglesea Pk	134 A3
Anglesea Rd	103 D2
Anglesea Row	144 B2
Anglesea St	145 D3
Anley Ct	71 C3
Annabeg 1	138 B2
Annadale Av	79 C1
Annadale Cres	79 C1
Annadale Dr	79 C1
Annagh Ct	47 D1
Annaly Ct	45 C1
Annaly Gro	45 C1
Annaly Rd	77 C2
Annaly Ter	45 C1
Annamoe Dr	77 C2
Annamoe Par	77 C3
Annamoe Pk	77 C3
Annamoe Rd	77 C3
Annamoe Ter	77 C3
Anna Vil	102 B2
Annaville Av	131 D1
Annaville Gro	114 B2
Annaville Pk	114 B2
Annaville Ter	
off Annaville Gro	115 C2
Anne Devlin Av	112 B3
Anne Devlin Dr	112 B3
Anne Devlin Pk	112 B3
Anne Devlin Rd	112 B3
Anner Rd	88 A2
Annes La	145 D4
Annesley Av	79 C3
Annesley Br	79 C2
Annesley Br Rd	79 C2
Annesley Pk	102 B2
Annesley Pl	79 C2
Anne St N	144 B1
Anne St S	145 D4
Annsbrook	115 C1
Annville Dr	130 A1
Apollo Way	54 A1
Appian Way, The	102 B1
Apples Rd	129 D2
Applewood Av	15 C2
Applewood Cl	15 C2
Applewood Cres	14 B2
Applewood Dr	14 B2
Applewood Gro	14 B2
Applewood Main St	14 B2
Applewood Sq	15 C2
Aran Av	139 C3
Aran Cl	139 C3
Aran Dr	139 C3
Aranleigh Ct	113 C3
Aranleigh Dell	127 D1
Aranleigh Gdns	113 D3
Aranleigh Mt	113 C3
Aranleigh Pk	113 D3
Aranleigh Vale	113 D3
Áras An Uachtaráin	75 D2
Aras Naclunne	97 C1
Aravon Ct 8	142 B2
Arbour Hill	89 C1
Arbour Pl	89 C1
Arbour Ter	89 C1
Arbutus Av	101 C1
Arbutus Pl	89 D3
Arcade	145 D2
Archerstown Rd	11 D2
Archers Wd	32 A2
Arches, The 11 Lough.	139 C3
Arches, The Mayn.	65 C2
Ardagh Av	131 D1
Ardagh Cl 1	131 D1
Ardagh Ct	131 C1
Ardagh Cres	131 C1
Ardagh Dr	131 D1
Ardagh Gro	131 D1
Ardagh Pk	131 D1
Ardagh Pk Rd	131 D1
Ardagh Rd	100 B1
Ardara Av	42 A3
Ardbeg Cres	54 B2
Ardbeg Dr	54 B2
Ardbeg Pk	54 B2
Ardbeg Rd	54 B2
Ardbrugh Cl 1	134 B3
Ardbrugh Rd	134 B3
Ardbrugh Vil 2	134 B3
Ardcian Pk	14 B3
Ardcollum Av	54 A2
Ardee Gro	102 A1
Ardeen	70 A3
Ardee Rd	102 A1
Ardee St	144 A4
Ardeevin Av	70 A3
Ardeevin Ct	70 A3
Ardeevin Dr	70 A3
Ardeevin Rd	134 B2

Name	Page	Ref
Ardenza Pk		
off Seapoint Av	118	A2
Ardenza Ter	118	A2
Ardglas Est	129	C1
Ardilaun	27	C2
Ardilaun Rd	78	B3
Ardilea Downs	115	D2
Ardlea Rd	54	A2
Ard Lorcain	131	C1
Ard Lorcain Vil 1	131	C1
Ardlui Pk	131	D1
Ardmeen Pk	131	D1
Ard Mhacha	123	D2
Ard Mhuire Pk	134	A3
Ard Mor Av	121	D1
Ard Mor Cl	121	D1
Ard Mor Ct	121	D1
Ard Mor Cres	121	D1
Ard Mor Dale	121	D1
Ard Mor Dr	121	D1
Ardmore Av	77	C3
Ardmore Cl	53	D2
Ardmore Cres	54	A2
Ardmore Dr	53	D2
Ardmore Gro	53	D2
Ardmore Pk Dublin 5	54	A2
Ardmore Pk D.L.	133	C1
Ard Mor Gdn	121	D1
Ard Mor La	121	D1
Ard Mor Pk	121	D1
Ard Mor Wk	121	D1
Ard Na Mara	19	C2
Ard Na Meala	38	A3
Ardpatrick Rd	76	A2
Ard Ri Pl		
off Ard Ri Rd	89	C1
Ard Ri Rd	89	C1
Ardtona Av	114	B2
Arena Rd	130	B3
Argyle Rd	103	C1
Arkendale Ct 1	134	A2
Arkendale Rd	134	A1
Arkendale Wds 2	134	A2
Arkle Hill	11	C3
Arkle Rd	130	A2
Arkle Sq 1	130	B3
Arklow St	77	C3
Armagh Rd	100	A2
Armstrong St		
off Harolds Cross Rd	101	D1
Armstrong Wk	54	A1
Arnold Gro	133	D2
Arnold Pk	133	D3
Arnott St	89	D3
Arran Ct	47	D1
Arran Grn	142	B2
Arranmore Av	78	A2
Arranmore Rd	103	C1
Arran Quay	144	A2
Arran Quay Ter	144	A2
Arran Rd	78	B1
Arran St E	144	A2
Arran St W	144	A2
Arthur Griffith Pk	82	B1
Arundel	118	B3
Ascal An Charrain Chno		
(Nutgrove Av)	113	D3
Ascal Bhaile An Abba		
(Abbotstown Av)	49	D1
Ascal Bhaile Thuaidh		
(Ballyhoy Av)	55	D3
Ascal Dun Eanna		
(Ennafort Av)	55	C3
Ascal Measc (Mask Av)	54	B2
Ascal Phairc An Bhailtini		
(Villa Park Av)	76	A2
Ascal Ratabhachta		
(Ratoath Av)	49	D2
Asgard Pk	61	C2
Asgard Rd	61	C2
Ashberry	82	A2
Ashbourne Ind Pk	10	A1
Ashbrook Dublin 3	80	A1
Ashbrook Dublin 7	75	C1
Ashbury Pk	142	A2
Ashcroft	55	D2
Ashcroft Gro 1	32	A3
Ashdale Av	101	C3
Ashdale Cl	18	A2
Ashdale Cres	11	C2
Ashdale Gdns	101	C3
Ashdale Pk	101	C3
Ashdale Rd Dublin 6W	101	C3
Ashdale Rd Swords	18	B3
Ashes, The	10	B1
Ashfield (Templeogue)	112	A2
Ashfield Av Dublin 6	102	B2
Ashfield Cl Dublin 6W		
off Ashfield	112	A2
Ashfield Cl Dublin 24	109	D1
Ashfield Ct	32	A3
Ashfield Dr	109	D1
Ashfield Gdns	32	A3
Ashfield Grn	32	A2
Ashfield Gro	32	A2
Ashfield Lawn	32	A2
Ashfield Pk (Templeogue)		
Dublin 6W off Ashfield	112	A2
Ashfield Pk (Terenure)		
Dublin 6W	101	C3
Ashfield Pk Dublin 24	109	D1
Ashfield Pk Boot.	116	A1
Ashfield Pk 7 Mulh.	32	A3
Ashfield Rd (Ranelagh)	102	B2
Ashfield Way	32	A3
Ashford Cotts		
off Ashford St	77	C3
Ashford Pl		
off Ashford St	77	C3
Ashford St	76	B3
Ashgrove Dublin 24	109	C3
Ashgrove Celbr.	66	A1
Ashgrove D.L.	132	B1
Ashgrove Ind Est	132	B1
Ashgrove Lo	75	D1
Ashgrove Ter 1	115	C3
Ashington Av	76	A1
Ashington Cl	49	D3
Ashington Ct	76	A1
Ashington Dale	76	A1
Ashington Gdns	76	A1
Ashington Grn	76	A1
Ashington Ms	50	A3
Ashington Pk	75	D1
Ashington Ri	49	D3
Ash Lawn Dublin 16	128	B1
Ashlawn B'brack	138	B2
Ashleaf Shop Cen	99	D3
Ashleigh Grn	47	D3
Ashleigh Gro Dublin 15	47	D2
Ashleigh Gro Maynh.	64	A3
Ashleigh Lawn	20	A3
Ashley Av	17	D1
Ashley Dr 5	17	D1
Ashley Gro 4	17	D1
Ashley Ri	27	C1
Ashling Cl	100	B1
Ashling Hts	47	D1
Ash Pk Av	82	B2
Ash Pk Ct	83	C2
Ash Pk Gro	83	C1
Ash Pk Heath	83	C1
Ash St	144	A4
Ashton Av	126	A1
Ashton Br	48	B2
Ashton Gro	126	A1
Ashton Lawn	126	A1
Ashton Pk	118	B3
Ashtown Br	48	B2
Ashtown Gate Rd	75	C1
Ashtown Gro	75	D1
Ashtown Rd	49	C3
Ashtown Sta	49	C3
Ashurst	139	C3
Ashville Cl	71	C3
Ashwood Av	95	D1
Ashwood Cl	95	D1
Ashwood Dr	96	A1
Ashwood Lawns	96	A1
Ashwood Pk	96	A1
Ashwood Rd	96	A1
Ashwood Way	96	A1
Aspen Dr	18	B2
Aspen Pk 1 D.L.	133	C2
Aspen Pk Swords	18	B2
Aspen Rd	18	A2
Aspen Wds	46	A2
Aspen Wds Av	46	A2
Aspen Wds Lawn	46	A2
Assumpta Pk	140	B3
Asthown Av	14	B1
Asthown Cl	14	B1
Asthown Ct	14	B1
Asthown Dr	14	B1
Asthown Grn	14	B1
Asthown Gro	14	B1
Asthown Lawns	14	B1
Asthown Ri	14	B1
Aston Pl	145	D2
Aston Quay	145	D2
Athgoe Dr	141	C2
Athgoe Rd	141	C2
Athlumney Vil	102	A1
Atmospheric Rd 3	134	A2
Aubrey Gro	141	C2
Aubrey Pk	141	C2
Auburn Av Dublin 4	103	C2
Auburn Av Dublin 15	74	A1
Auburn Av Cabin.	138	A1
Auburn Cl Dublin 15	48	A3
Auburn Cl Cabin.	138	B1
Auburn Dr Dublin 15	48	A3
Auburn Dr Cabin.	138	A1
Auburn Grn	48	A3
Auburn Gro	19	C3
Auburn Pk	48	A2
Auburn Rd Dublin 4		
off Auburn Av	103	C2
Auburn Rd Cabin.	133	C3
Auburn St	77	D3
Auburn Vil	101	D3
Auburn Wk	77	C3
Aughavanagh Rd	101	C1
Aughrim La	77	C3
Aughrim Pl	77	C3
Aughrim St	77	C3
Aughrim Vil		
off Aughrim St	77	C3
Augustine Vil 1	142	B2
Aulden Gra	39	D2
Aungier La	144	C4
Aungier St	144	C4
Austins Cotts		
off Annesley Pl	79	C2
Avalon 1	136	B1
Ave Maria Rd	136	B1
Avenue, The Dublin 6W	112	A2
Avenue, The (Ballinteer)		
Dublin 16	128	B2
Avenue, The (Ballyboden)		
Dublin 16	126	A2
Avenue, The (Carrick)	136	B3
Avenue, The (Primrose Hill)		
Celbr.	66	B3
Avenue, The (The Drive)		
Celbr.	66	B2
Avenue, The (Clons.)	30	B3
Avenue, The		
(Dunboyne Castle)		
Dunb.	28	B3
Avenue, The (Lutterell Hall)		
Dunb.	28	B1
Avenue, The (Plunkett Hall)		
Dunb.	28	A1
Avenue, The Gra M.	82	B2
Avenue, The Kins.	15	D3
Avenue, The Lou.V.	68	A1
Avenue, The 4 Mala.	21	C3
Avenue, The Manor.	31	C3
Avenue, The Mulh.	32	A2
Avenue, The Swords	15	D3
Avenue Rd	89	D3
Avila Apts 2	131	D1
Avila Pk	49	D1
Avoca Av Black.	117	C2
Avoca Av Bray	142	A3
Avoca Pk	117	C3
Avoca Pl	117	D2
Avoca Rd	117	C3
Avonbeg Ct 1	124	A1
Avonbeg Dr	124	B1
Avonbeg Gdns	124	B1
Avonbeg Ind Est	98	B1
Avonbeg Pk	124	B1
Avonbeg Rd	124	B1
Avondale	68	B1
Avondale Av	77	D3
Avondale Business Pk	117	D3
Avondale Ct 4	134	A1
Avondale Cres	134	A3
Avondale Lawn	117	D3
Avondale Lawn Ext	117	D3
Avondale Pk Dublin 5	56	A3
Avondale Pk Dalkey	134	A3
Avondale Rd Dublin 7	77	D2
Avondale Rd Dalkey	134	A3
Avondale Sq	28	B2
Avondale Ter	99	D3
Avonmore	131	C2
Avonmore Av 1	124	B1
Avonmore Cl	124	B1
Avonmore Dr	124	B1
Avonmore Gro	124	B1
Avonmore Pk	124	B1
Avonmore Rd	124	B1
Aylesbury	124	A2
Ayrefield Av	55	C1
Ayrefield Ct	55	C1
Ayrefield Dr	55	C1
Ayrefield Gro	55	C1
Ayrefield Pl	55	C1

B

Name	Page	Ref
Bachelors Wk Dublin 1	145	D2
Bachelors Wk Ashb.	11	C3
Back La Dublin 8	144	B3
Back La 3 Dublin 13	43	D3
Back La Mayn.	65	C1
Back Rd	19	D3
Baggot Cl		
off Baggot St Lwr	90	B3
Baggot Ct	90	B3
Baggot La	91	C3
Baggot Rd	75	D2
Baggot St Lwr	90	B3
Baggot St Upr	91	C3
Baggot Ter		
off Blackhorse Av	75	D2
Bailey, The	10	B3
Bailey Grn Rd	63	D2
Bailey's Row	78	B3
Bailey Vw	134	B1
Balally Av	129	C1
Balally Cl	129	D2
Balally Dr	129	C1
Balally Gro	129	D2
Balally Hill	129	D2
Balally Pk	129	D1
Balally Rd	129	C1
Balally Sta	129	C1
Balally Ter 1	129	D2
Balbutcher Dr	37	D3
Balbutcher La	37	D3
Balbutcher Way	37	D3
Balcurris Cl	38	A3
Balcurris Gdns	38	A3
Balcurris Pk E	38	A3
Balcurris Pk W	37	D3
Balcurris Rd	37	D3
Baldonnell Business Pk	106	B3
Baldoyle Ind Est	57	C1
Baldoyle Ind Est	58	A1
Balfe Av	99	D2
Balfe Rd	99	D2
Balfe Rd E	99	D2
Balfe St		
off Chatham St	145	D4
Balgaddy Rd	83	D2
Balglass Est	60	B2
Balglass Rd	61	C2
Balgriffin Cotts	41	D2
Balgriffin Rd	41	D2
Balheary Br	15	D2
Balheary Ind Pk	15	D2
Balheary Rd	15	D2
Balkill Pk	60	B2
Balkill Rd	61	C2
Ballawley Ct	129	C2
Ballinclea Hts	134	A3
Ballinclea Rd	133	D3
Ballinteer Av	128	B2
Ballinteer Cl	128	B2
Ballinteer Ct 2	128	B2
Ballinteer Cres	128	B2
Ballinteer Dr	128	B2
Ballinteer Gdns	128	B2
Ballinteer Gro	128	B2
Ballinteer Pk	128	B2
Ballinteer Rd	128	B1
Ballinteer Shop Cen	128	B2
Ballintrane Wd	17	C1

Name	Pg	Grid
Ballintyre Downs	128	B3
Ballintyre Heath	128	B3
Ballintyre Meadows	128	A3
Ballintyre Wk	128	B3
Ballintyre Wds **4**	128	B2
Balliskcourt	13	C2
Ball's Br	103	D1
Ballsbridge Av	103	D1
Ballsbridge Pk	103	D1
Ballsbridge Ter		
off Merrion Rd	103	D1
Ballsbridge Wd	91	D3
Ballyboden Cres	126	B1
Ballyboden Rd		
Dublin 14	126	B1
Ballyboden Rd		
Dublin 16	126	B1
Ballyboden Way	126	A1
Ballyboggan Ind Est	50	A3
Ballyboggan Rd	50	B3
Ballybough Av		
off Kings Av	79	C3
Ballybough Br	79	C2
Ballybough Ct		
off Kings Av	79	C3
Ballybough Rd	78	B3
Ballybrack Shop Cen	138	B2
Ballybride	140	B3
Ballybride Rd	140	B3
Ballycoolin Business &		
Tech Pk	34	A2
Ballycoolin Rd	34	A3
Ballycullen Av	124	B2
Ballycullen Dr	125	C2
Ballydowd Dr	83	C1
Ballydowd Gro	71	C3
Ballydowd Manor	83	C1
Ballyfermot Av	86	B2
Ballyfermot Br	98	A1
Ballyfermot Cres	86	B2
Ballyfermot Dr	86	A2
Ballyfermot Par	86	A2
Ballyfermot Rd (Bothar		
Baile Thormod)	86	A2
Ballygall Av	51	C1
Ballygall Cres	50	B2
Ballygall Par	50	B2
Ballygall Pl	51	C2
Ballygall Rd E	51	D2
Ballygall Rd W	50	B2
Ballygihen Av	134	A1
Ballygihen Vil **5**	134	A1
Ballygoran Vw	66	A1
Ballyhoy Av (Ascal Bhaile		
Thuaidh)	55	D3
Ballymace Grn	112	A3
Ballymanagin La **1**	96	B1
Ballymoss Par **2**	130	B3
Ballymoss Rd	130	A2
Ballymount Av		
Dublin 12	110	B1
Ballymount Av		
Dublin 24	110	B1
Ballymount Cross	98	A3
Ballymount Cross		
Ind Est	97	D3
Ballymount Dr	98	B3
Ballymount Ind Est	98	B3
Ballymount Lwr Rd	98	A3
Ballymount Rd	109	D1
Ballymount Rd Ind Est	98	B2
Ballymount Rd Upr	98	A3
Ballymount Trd Est	99	C3
Ballymun Business &		
Tech Pk	37	D2
Ballymun Ind Est	37	D2
Ballymun Rd	52	A3
Ballymun Rd N	38	A2
Ballymun Shop Cen	38	A3
Ballyneety Rd	87	C2
Ballyogan Av	136	A2
Ballyogan Cl	136	A2
Ballyogan Ct	136	A2
Ballyogan Cres	136	A2
Ballyogan Dr	136	A2
Ballyogan Est	136	A1
Ballyogan Grn	136	A1
Ballyogan Lawn	136	A1
Ballyogan Rd **1**	136	A1
Ballyogan Vale	136	B2
Ballyogan Wd	136	A2
Ballyolaf Manor **1**	129	C1
Ballyowen Av	71	D3
Ballyowen Castle Shop &		
Med Cen	83	C1
Ballyowen Ct	71	D3
Ballyowen Cres	71	D3
Ballyowen Dr	71	D3
Ballyowen Grn	71	D3
Ballyowen Gro	71	D3
Ballyowen La	71	D3
Ballyowen Lawn	71	D3
Ballyowen Rd	71	D3
Ballyowen Vw	71	D3
Ballyowen Way	71	D3
Ballyroan Ct **1**	112	A3
Ballyroan Cres	112	B3
Ballyroan Hts	126	A1
Ballyroan Pk	112	A3
Ballyroan Rd	112	A3
Ballyshannon Av	53	D1
Ballyshannon Rd	53	D1
Ballytore Rd	113	D1
Balnagowan	102	B3
Balrothery Cotts	111	C3
Balrothery Est	110	B3
Balscadden Rd	61	C2
Bancroft Av	110	A3
Bancroft Cl	110	B3
Bancroft Gro	110	B3
Bancroft Pk	110	A3
Bancroft Rd	110	B3
Bangor Dr	100	B1
Bangor Rd	100	B1
Bank of Ireland	145	D3
Bankside Cotts	114	B1
Bannow Rd	76	B1
Bann Rd	50	B3
Bantry Rd	52	A3
Bantry Sq	47	D1
Banville Av	86	A3
Barclay Ct	117	D2
Bargy Rd	79	D3
Barnacoille Pk	134	B1
Barnamore Cres	50	B3
Barnamore Gro	50	B3
Barnamore Pk	50	B3
Barnewall Av	13	D1
Barnewall Cres	13	C1
Barnewall Dr	37	D3
Barnhill Av	134	A2
Barnhill Gro	134	B2
Barnhill Lawn	134	B2
Barnhill Pk **4**	134	A2
Barnhill Rd	134	A2
Barnville Pk	85	C3
Barren Hill Cross Rds	62	B2
Barrett St	119	C3
Barrow Rd	77	C1
Barrow St	91	C2
Barry Av	36	A3
Barry Dr	36	A3
Barry Grn	50	A1
Barry La	44	B1
Barry Pk	50	A1
Barry Rd	50	A1
Barryscourt Rd	54	A1
Barton Av	113	C3
Barton Ct	128	A1
Barton Dr	113	C3
Barton Rd E	128	A1
Barton Rd Ext	127	D1
Barton Rd W (Willbrook)	127	C1
Bartra Rock **6**	134	B1
Basin St Lwr	89	C2
Basin St Upr	89	C2
Basin Vw Ter	77	D3
Baskin Cotts	24	B2
Baskin La	24	A2
Bass Pl	145	F4
Bath Av *Dublin 4*	91	D3
Bath Av *Mala.*	20	B2
Bath Av Gdns	91	D3
Bath Av Pl	91	D3
Bath La	78	A3
Bath Pl	117	D2
Bath St	91	D2
Bawn, The	20	A3
Bawn Gro, The	20	A3
Bawnlea Av	122	B1
Bawnlea Cl	122	A1
Bawnlea Cres	122	A1
Bawnlea Dr	122	A1
Bawnlea Grn	122	B1
Bawnogue Cotts **1**	95	D2
Bawnville Av	124	A2
Bawnville Cl	124	A2
Bawnville Dr	124	B1
Bawnville Pk	124	B1
Bawnville Rd	124	A1
Baymount Pk	81	D1
Bayshore La	139	C3
Bayside Boul N	57	C1
Bayside Boul S	57	C1
Bayside Pk	57	C1
Bayside Sq E	57	C1
Bayside Sq N	57	C1
Bayside Sq S	57	C1
Bayside Sq W	57	C1
Bayside Sta	57	D1
Bayside Wk	57	C1
Bayswater Ter **7**	134	B1
Bayview *Dublin 4*		
off Pembroke St	91	D2
Bayview **2** *Bray*	142	A1
Bayview *Lough.*	139	C3
Bayview Av	79	C3
Bayview Cl	139	C3
Bayview Ct	139	C3
Bayview Cres	141	C1
Bayview Dr	141	C1
Bayview Glade **1**	141	C1
Bayview Glen **4**	141	C1
Bayview Grn	139	C3
Bayview Gro	141	C1
Bayview Lawn	139	C3
Bayview Pk	139	C3
Bayview Ri **3**	141	C1
Beach Av	92	A3
Beach Dr	92	A3
Beach Pk	27	C2
Beach Rd	92	A3
Beach Vw	57	C2
Beaconsfield Ct		
off The Belfry	88	A2
Bearna Pk	129	D3
Beatty Gro	66	B1
Beatty Pk	66	A2
Beattys Av	103	D1
Beaufield	64	B3
Beaufield Av	64	B3
Beaufield Cl	64	B3
Beaufield Cres	64	B3
Beaufield Dr	64	B3
Beaufield Gdns	64	B3
Beaufield Grn	64	B3
Beaufield Gro	64	B3
Beaufield Lawn	64	B3
Beaufield Manor	116	B3
Beaufield Pk	116	B3
Beaufort	134	A1
Beaufort Downs	113	C3
Beaumont Av	114	A3
Beaumont Cl	114	A3
Beaumont Cres	53	D2
Beaumont Dr	114	B3
Beaumont Gdns	117	C2
Beaumont Gro	53	C2
Beaumont Rd	53	C2
Beau Pk Av	42	B3
Beau Pk Cres	42	B3
Beau Pk Rd	42	B3
Beau Pk Row	42	B3
Beau Pk Sq	42	B3
Beau Pk St	42	B2
Beau Pk Ter	42	B3
Beauvale Pk	54	A2
Beaver Row	103	C3
Beaverstown Orchard	13	C1
Beaver St	78	B3
Beckett Way	97	C1
Bedford Row		
off Temple Bar	145	D3
Beechbrook Gro **7**	42	A3
Beechcourt	138	B1
Beechdale	29	C3
Beechdale Ms	102	A2
Beech Dr	128	B1
Beeches, The		
Dublin 13	56	A1
Beeches, The **6**		
Dublin 14	113	C3
Beeches, The **12** *Abb.*	139	C3
Beeches, The *Black.*	118	B3
Beeches Pk	134	A2
Beeches Rd	129	D1
Beechfield	30	B2
Beechfield Av		
Dublin 12	99	D3
Beechfield Av		
Dublin 24	125	C3
Beechfield Cl		
Dublin 12	99	D3
Beechfield Cl **1**		
Dublin 24	125	C3
Beechfield Cl *Dunb.*	30	B3
Beechfield Ct *Dublin 24*	125	C3
Beechfield Ct *Clons.*	30	B3
Beechfield Cres	125	C3
Beechfield Dr	30	B2
Beechfield Grn	30	B2
Beechfield Haven **1**	141	C2
Beechfield Hts	30	B3
Beechfield Lawn		
Dublin 24	125	C3
Beechfield Lawn *Clons.*	31	C2
Beechfield Manor	141	C2
Beechfield Meadows	30	B2
Beechfield Pk **2**	125	C3
Beechfield Pl *Dublin 24*	125	C3
Beechfield Pl *Clons.*	31	C2
Beechfield Ri	31	C2
Beechfield Rd		
Dublin 12	99	D3
Beechfield Rd		
Dublin 24	125	C3
Beechfield Rd (Hartstown)		
Clons.	30	B3
Beechfield Vw	30	B2
Beechfield Way		
Dublin 24	125	C3
Beechfield Way *Clons.*	30	B2
Beech Gro *Boot.*	116	B1
Beech Gro *Lucan*	70	B3
Beech Hill		
off Beech Hill Rd	103	C3
Beech Hill Av	103	D2
Beech Hill Cres	103	D3
Beech Hill Dr	103	D2
Beech Hill Rd	103	C3
Beech Hill Ter	103	D3
Beech Hill Vil		
off Beech Hill Ter	103	D3
Beech Lawn *Dublin 16*	128	A1
Beechlawn *Boot.*	116	B3
Beechlawn Av *Dublin 5*	54	B1
Beech Lawn Av		
Dublin 16	128	A1
Beechlawn Cl	54	B1
Beechlawn Grn	54	B1
Beechlawn Gro	54	B1
Beechlawn Ind Complex	99	C3
Beechmount Dr	115	C1
Beech Pk *Dublin 15*	48	A3
Beech Pk *Cabin.*	138	A2
Beech Pk *Lucan*	70	B3
Beech Pk Av *Dublin 5*	54	B1
Beech Pk Av *Dublin 15*	48	A3
Beech Pk Av *Deans Gra*	132	A2
Beechpark Ct	54	B1
Beech Pk Cres	48	A3
Beech Pk Dr	132	A3
Beech Pk Gro	132	A3
Beech Pk Lawn	48	A3
Beech Pk Rd	132	A2
Beech Rd *Dublin 12*	98	A2
Beech Rd **3** *Shank.*	141	C3
Beech Row **3** *Clond.*	96	B2
Beech Row *Ronan.*	84	A3
Beechview **1**	126	B2
Beech Wk	126	B2
Beechwood Av Lwr	102	B2
Beechwood Av Upr	102	B2
Beechwood Cl *Bray*	142	A3
Beechwood Cl *Manor.*	31	D3
Beechwood Ct	131	C1
Beechwood Downs	31	D3
Beechwood Gro **1**	133	D1
Beechwood Lawn	133	D3
Beechwood Pk *Dublin 6*	102	A2

Beechwood Pk *D.L.* 133 D1
Beechwood Rd 102 B2
Beechwood Sta 102 B2
Belcamp Av 40 B3
Belcamp Cres 40 B2
Belcamp Gdns 40 B2
Belcamp Grn 41 C3
Belcamp Gro 41 C3
Belcamp La 41 C3
Belclare Av 37 C3
Belclare Cres 37 D3
Belclare Dr 37 D3
Belclare Grn 37 D3
Belclare Gro 37 D3
Belclare Lawns 37 D3
Belclare Pk 37 C3
Belclare Ter 37 C3
Belclare Way 37 D3
Belfield Cl 115 C1
Belfield Ct 103 D3
Belfield Downs 115 C2
Belfield Office Pk 103 C3
Belfry, The *Dublin 8* 88 A2
Belfry, The *Jobs.* 121 D2
Belfry Av 121 D2
Belfry Cl 121 D2
Belfry Dale 121 D2
Belfry Downs 121 D2
Belfry Dr 121 D2
Belfry Gdns 121 D2
Belfry Grn 121 D2
Belfry Gro 122 A2
Belfry Lawn 121 D2
Belfry Meadows 121 D2
Belfry Pk 121 D2
Belfry Pl 121 D2
Belfry Ri 121 D2
Belfry Rd 121 D2
Belfry Sq 121 D2
Belfry Ter 121 D2
Belfry Wk 121 D2
Belfry Way 121 D2
Belgard Cl **1** 109 D2
Belgard Grn 108 B3
Belgard Hts 109 C2
Belgard Ind Est 109 D2
Belgard Rd 109 D2
Belgard Sq E 109 D3
Belgard Sq N 109 C3
Belgard Sq S 123 D1
Belgard Sq W 109 C3
Belgard Sta 109 C2
Belgrave Av 102 A2
Belgrave Pl 102 A2
Belgrave Rd *Dublin 6* 102 A2
Belgrave Rd *Black.* 118 A2
Belgrave Sq E *Dublin 6* 102 A2
Belgrave Sq E *Black.* 118 B3
Belgrave Sq N *Dublin 6* 102 A2
Belgrave Sq N *Black.* 118 A2
Belgrave Sq S *Dublin 6* 102 A2
Belgrave Sq S *Black.* 118 A2
Belgrave Sq W *Dublin 6* 102 A2
Belgrave Sq W *Black.* 118 A2
Belgrave Ter *Black.*
  off Belgrave Rd 118 A2
Belgrave Ter **9** *Bray* 142 B2
Belgrave Vil **10** 142 B2
Belgrove Lawn 74 B3
Belgrove Pk 86 B1
Belgrove Rd 80 B2
Bella Av
  off Bella St 78 B3
Bella St 78 B3
Belle Bk 89 C2
Belleville 75 C1
Belleville Av 101 D3
Bellevue 89 C2
Bellevue Av *Boot.* 104 B3
Bellevue Av *Dalkey* 133 D2
Bellevue Copse 104 B3
Bellevue Ct 104 B3
Bellevue Hts 143 C2
Bellevue Pk *Boot.* 104 A3
Bellevue Pk *Grey.* 143 D1
Bellevue Pk Av 104 B3

Bellevue Rd *Dalkey* 133 D3
Bellevue Rd *Grey.* 143 D1
Bellmans Wk
  off Ferrymans
  Crossing 91 C1
Belmont 131 C2
Belmont Av 103 C2
Belmont Ct
  off Belmont Av 103 C2
Belmont Gdns 103 C2
Belmont Grn 131 C1
Belmont Gro 131 C1
Belmont Lawn 131 C1
Belmont Pk *Dublin 4* 103 C2
Belmont Pk *Dublin 5* 56 A2
Belmont Vil 103 C2
Belton Pk Av 53 D3
Belton Pk Gdns 53 D3
Belton Pk Rd 53 D3
Belton Pk Vil 53 D3
Belton Ter **3** 142 A1
Belvidere Av 78 A3
Belvidere Ct 78 A3
Belvidere Pl 78 A3
Belvidere Rd 78 A2
Belview Bldgs
  off School St 89 C2
Belvue 108 B3
Benbulbin Av 100 A1
Benbulbin Rd 88 A3
Benburb St 89 C1
Beneavin Ct 51 C2
Beneavin Dr 51 D2
Beneavin Pk 51 C1
Beneavin Rd 51 C1
Ben Edar Rd 77 C3
Bengal Ter 77 D1
Ben Inagh Pk 117 D1
Benmadigan Rd 88 A3
Benson St 91 D2
Benson St Enterprise
  Cen 91 C2
Bentley Rd 142 A3
Beresford 78 B1
Beresford Av 78 B1
Beresford La 145 E1
Beresford Lawn 78 B1
Beresford Pl 145 E2
Beresford St 144 B3
Berkeley Rd 77 D2
Berkeley St 78 A3
Berkeley Ter 91 C3
Berryfield 82 A2
Berryfield Cres 50 A2
Berryfield Dr 50 A2
Berryfield Rd 50 A2
Berwick 113 D3
Berwick Av 14 A3
Berwick Ct 14 A3
Berwick Cres 14 A3
Berwick Dr 14 A3
Berwick Gro 14 A3
Berwick Hall 113 D3
Berwick Lawn 14 A3
Berwick Pl 14 A3
Berwick Ri 14 A3
Berwick Vw 14 A3
Berwick Wk 14 A3
Berwick Way 14 A3
Berystede
  off Leeson Pk 102 B1
Bessborough Av 79 C3
Bessborough Par 102 A1
Besser Dr 84 B3
Bethesda Pl
  off Dorset St Upr 78 A3
Bettyglen 56 B3
Bettysford **7** 96 B2
Bettystown Av 55 D3
Beverly Av 125 D2
Beverly Cres 125 D2
Beverly Downs 125 D1
Beverly Dr 125 D1
Beverly Gro 125 D1
Beverly Hts 125 D2
Beverly Lawns 125 D2
Beverly Pk 125 D1
Beverly Ri 125 D2
Beverton Av 13 C1
Beverton Cl 13 C1
Beverton Cres 13 C1
Beverton Dr 13 C1

Beverton Grn 13 C1
Beverton Gro 13 C1
Beverton Lawn 13 C1
Beverton Pk 13 C1
Beverton Way 13 C1
Bewley 71 C3
Bewley Av 83 C1
Bewley Dr 71 C3
Bewley Gro 83 C1
Bewley Lawn 71 C3
Bianconi Av 107 C3
Big Br 113 C1
Bigger Rd 99 D2
Big La 66 B2
Binn Eadair Vw 58 A1
Binns Br 78 A2
Birch Av 130 A2
Birch Dale **2** *D.L.* 133 C2
Birch Dale **1** *Fox.* 131 D3
Birchdale Cl 18 B2
Birchdale Dr 18 B2
Birchdale Pk 18 B2
Birchdale Rd 18 B2
Birches, The 131 D3
Birches Rd 129 D1
Birchfield 115 C3
Birchgrove 132 B1
Birchs La 115 C3
Birchview Av 110 A2
Birchview Cl 110 A2
Birchview Ct
  off Birchview Dr 110 A2
Birchview Dr 110 A2
Birchview Hts
  off Birchview Dr 110 A2
Birchview Lawn
  off Birchview Av 110 A2
Birchview Ri
  off Birchview Dr 110 A2
Birchwood Cl 109 C3
Birchwood Dr 109 C3
Birchwood Hts 109 C3
Bird Av 115 C1
Biscayne 21 C2
Bishop St 90 A3
Bisset's Strand 19 D1
Black Av, The 69 C2
Blackberry La *Dublin 6* 102 A1
Blackberry La *Port.* 27 C2
Blackberry Ri 27 C2
Blackcourt Rd 33 C3
Blackditch Dr 85 D2
Blackditch Rd 86 A2
Blackhall La 144 A2
Blackhall Pl 89 C1
Blackhall St 89 C1
Blackheath Av 80 B2
Blackheath Ct 81 C2
Blackheath Dr 80 B2
Blackheath Gdns 80 B2
Blackheath Gro 80 B2
Blackheath Pk 80 B2
Blackhorse Av 76 A2
Blackhorse Br 87 D3
Blackhorse Gro 76 B3
Blackhorse Ind Est 76 B3
Blackhorse Sta 87 D3
Blackpitts 89 D3
Blackrock Business Pk 117 D2
Blackrock Coll 117 C1
Blackrock Shop Cen 117 D1
Blackrock Sta 117 D1
Black St 88 B1
Blackthorn Av 130 A2
Blackthorn Cl *Port.* 27 C1
Blackthorn Cl **1** *Still.* 130 A2
Blackthorn Ct **3** 129 D2
Blackthorn Dr 129 D2
Blackthorn Grn **4** 129 D2
Blackthorn Gro **2** 129 D2
Blackthorn Rd 130 A2
Blackwater Rd 77 C1
Blackwood 30 B3
Blackwood Cl 44 B1
Blackwood Cres 30 B3
Blackwood Dr 30 B3
Blackwood La 26 B1
Blackwood Lawn 44 B1
Blackwood Ms 30 B3
Blackwood Pk 44 B1
Blackwood Pl 30 B3
Blakesfield 31 D3

Blakestown Cotts 46 A1
Blakestown Dr 32 A3
Blakestown Rd 46 A1
Blakestown Way 32 B3
Blanchardstown Business
  & Tech Park 33 D3
Blanchardstown Bypass 47 C1
Blanchardstown Cen 46 B1
Blanchardstown
  Corporate Pk 33 D1
Blanchardstown Ind Pk 33 D2
Blanchardstown Rd N 33 C3
Blanchardstown Rd S 46 A2
Blarney Pk 100 B2
Blasket Sq 47 D1
Blessington Ct
  off Blessington St 78 A3
Blessington Rd
  Dublin 24 109 D3
Blessington Rd *Jobs.* 122 B2
Blessington St 77 D3
Bloom Cotts 89 D3
Bloomfield Av (Donnybrook)
  Dublin 4 102 B1
Bloomfield Av *Dublin 8* 89 D3
Bloomfield Pk 101 D1
Bluebell Av 86 B3
Bluebell Ind Est 98 A1
Bluebell Rd 99 C1
Bluebell Sta 99 C1
Blunden Dr 41 D3
Blythe Av
  off Church Rd 91 C1
Boden Dale 127 C1
Boden Heath 126 B1
Boden Mill **2** 126 B2
Boden Pk 126 B1
Boden Wd 113 C3
Boeing Rd 39 C2
Boghall Rd 142 A3
Boherboy Rd 120 B3
Bohernabreena Rd 124 A3
Bolbrook Av **2** 124 B1
Bolbrook Cl 124 B1
Bolbrook Dr **3** 124 B1
Bolbrook
  Enterprise Cen 125 C1
Bolbrook Gro 124 B1
Bolbrook Pk 124 B1
Bolbrook Vil 124 B1
Bolton St 144 B1
Bond Dr 92 A1
Bond Rd 79 D3
Bond St 89 C2
Bonham St 89 C2
Boolavogue Rd 91 D1
Booterstown Av 116 B1
Booterstown Pk 116 B2
Booterstown Sta 105 C3
Boot Rd 96 B3
Boroimhe Alder 16 B3
Boroimhe Ash 16 B3
Boroimhe Aspen 16 B3
Boroimhe Beech 16 B3
Boroimhe Birches 16 B2
Boroimhe Blackthorn 16 B2
Boroimhe Cedars 16 B2
Boroimhe Cherry 16 B2
Boroimhe Elms 17 C3
Boroimhe Hawthorns 16 B3
Boroimhe Hazel 17 C3
Boroimhe Laurels 16 B2
Boroimhe Maples 17 C3
Boroimhe Oaks 17 C3
Boroimhe Pines 17 C2
Boroimhe Poplars 17 C2
Boroimhe Willows 17 C2
Botanic Av 78 A1
Botanic Gdns 77 D1
Botanic Ms 77 D1
Botanic Pk 78 A1
Botanic Rd 77 D2
Botanic Vil
  off Botanic Rd 78 A1
Bothar An Easa
  (Watermill Rd) 55 D3
Bothar Baile Thormod
  (Ballyfermot Rd) 86 A2
Bothar Chille Na Manac
  (Walkinstown Rd) 99 C2
Bothar Cloiginn
  (Cleggan Rd) 85 D2

Name	Page	Grid
Bothar Coilbeard (Con Colbert Rd) *Dublin 8*	88	A2
Bothar Coilbeard (Con Colbert Rd) *Dublin 10*	87	D2
Bothar Dhroichead Chiarduibh (Cardiffsbridge Rd)	50	A1
Bothar Drom Finn (Drumfinn Rd)	86	A2
Bothar Loch Con (Lough Conn Rd)	86	A1
Bothar Phairc An Bhailtini (Villa Park Rd)	76	A2
Bothar Raitleann (Rathland Rd)	100	B3
Boundary Rd	80	A3
Bourne Av	10	B3
Bourne Ct	10	B3
Bourne Vw	10	B3
Bow Br	88	B2
Bow La E	144	C4
Bow La W	88	B2
Bow St	144	A2
Boyne La	145	F4
Boyne Rd	50	B3
Boyne St	145	F3
Brabazon Cotts **4**	142	A1
Brabazon Row	89	D3
Brabazon Sq *off Gray St*	144	A4
Brabazon St *off The Coombe*	144	A4
Bracetown Business Pk	29	D1
Brackenbush Pk	138	B1
Brackenbush Rd	138	B2
Bracken Dr	27	C1
Bracken Hill	129	C3
Bracken Rd	130	A3
Brackens La	145	E2
Brackenstown Av	17	C1
Braeburn Ter	15	C2
Braemor Av	114	A2
Braemor Dr	114	A2
Braemor Gro	114	A2
Braemor Pk	114	A1
Braemor Rd	114	A2
Brainborough Ter *off South Circular Rd*	89	C3
Braithwaite St	89	C3
Bramblefield	31	D2
Bramblefield Ct	31	D2
Bramblefield Cres	31	D2
Bramblefield Dr	31	D2
Bramblefield Pk	32	A2
Bramblefield Vw	32	A2
Bramblefield Wk	31	D2
Bramley Av	73	C1
Bramley Ct	73	C1
Bramley Cres	73	C1
Bramley Garth	73	C1
Bramley Grn	47	C3
Bramley Gro	47	C3
Bramley Heath	73	C1
Bramley Pk	73	C1
Bramley Rd	47	C3
Bramley Ter	15	C2
Bramley Vw	47	C3
Bramley Wk	46	B3
Bramley Way	73	C1
Brandon Rd	99	D1
Bray Head Ter **1**	142	A3
Bray Rd *Cabin.*	138	A2
Bray Rd *Corn.*	132	A3
Bray Sta	142	B1
Breakwater Rd S	92	B1
Breffini Ter	134	A1
Breffni Rd	134	B1
Bregia Rd	77	C2
Brehon Fld Rd	128	A3
Brehon's Chair	128	A3
Bremen Av	92	A2
Bremen Gro	92	A2
Bremen Rd	92	A2
Brendan Behan Ct *off Russell St*	78	B3
Brendan Rd	103	C2
Brennans Par	142	B1
Brennans Ter **7**	142	B1
Brennanstown Av	137	D2
Brennanstown Rd	137	D2
Brennanstown Sq	137	D2
Brennanstown Vale	137	C2
Brewery Rd	130	B2
Brian Av	79	C1
Brian Boru Av	81	C3
Brian Boru St	81	C3
Brian Rd	79	C2
Brian Ter	79	C2
Briarfield Gro	56	B2
Briarfield Rd	56	A2
Briarfield Vil	56	B2
Briars, The	73	C3
Briar Wk	27	C1
Briar Wd	142	B3
Briarwood Av	32	A3
Briarwood Cl	32	A3
Briarwood Gdns	32	A3
Briarwood Grn	32	A3
Briarwood Lawn	32	A3
Briarwood Pk **2**	32	A3
Briarwood Rd **3**	32	A3
Brickfield Dr	88	B3
Brickfield La	89	C3
Bride Rd	144	B4
Bride's Glen Av	14	B2
Bride's Glen Pk	14	B2
Brides Glen Rd	140	A1
Bride St	144	B4
Bridge, The	141	C2
Bridgecourt Office Pk	98	B2
Bridgefoot St	144	A3
Bridge St *Dublin 4*	91	D2
Bridge St *Ashb.*	11	C3
Bridge St *Swords*	17	C1
Bridge St Lwr	144	A3
Bridge St Upr	144	A3
Bridgeview **1**	85	C2
Bridgewater Quay	88	A1
Brighton Av *Dublin 3*	79	D2
Brighton Av *Dublin 6*	101	D3
Brighton Av *Black.*	118	B3
Brighton Av *Carrick.*	136	B3
Brighton Cotts **2**	136	B1
Brighton Ct	136	B2
Brighton Gdns	101	D3
Brighton Grn	101	C3
Brighton Hall	136	B2
Brighton Lo **3**	136	B1
Brighton Pl	136	B2
Brighton Rd *Dublin 6*	101	D3
Brighton Rd *Fox.*	136	B1
Brighton Sq	101	D3
Brighton Ter **7**	134	A1
Brighton Vale	118	A2
Brindley Pk Cres	10	B2
Brindley Pk Gdn	10	B2
Brindley Pk Sq	10	B2
Britain Pl	78	A3
Britain Quay	91	D2
Broadford Av	128	A2
Broadford Cl	128	A2
Broadford Cres	128	A2
Broadford Dr	128	A2
Broadford Hill	128	A2
Broadford Lawn	128	A2
Broadford Pk	128	A2
Broadford Ri	128	A2
Broadford Rd	128	A2
Broadford Wk	128	A2
Broadmeadow	15	C3
Broad Meadow Castle	11	C3
Broadmeadow Grn	10	B3
Broadmeadow Rd *Ashb.*	11	C3
Broadmeadow Rd *Swords*	15	C3
Broadstone	77	D3
Broadstone Av *off Royal Canal Bk*	77	D3
Broadway Dr	46	B2
Broadway Gro	46	B2
Broadway Pk	46	B2
Broadway Rd	46	B2
Brompton Ct	47	C2
Brompton Grn	47	C2
Brompton Gro	47	C2
Brompton Lawn	47	C2
Brookdale	124	A1
Brookdale Av	16	A1
Brookdale Cl	16	A1
Brookdale Ct	16	A1
Brookdale Dr	16	A1
Brookdale Grn	16	A1
Brookdale Gro	16	A1
Brookdale Lawns	16	A1
Brookdale Pk	16	A1
Brookdale Rd	16	A2
Brookdale Wk	16	A1
Brookdale Way	16	A1
Brookdene	141	C1
Brookfield *Dublin 5*	55	C2
Brookfield *Dublin 6*	102	B3
Brookfield *Black.*	117	C2
Brookfield *Lucan*	82	A2
Brookfield Av *Black.*	117	D2
Brookfield Av **25** *Bray*	142	B2
Brookfield Av *Mayn.*	64	B3
Brookfield Ct **1**	122	A1
Brookfield Est	100	B3
Brookfield Pk	64	B3
Brookfield Rd	117	D2
Brookfield Rd *Dublin 8*	88	B2
Brookfield Rd *Dublin 24*	122	A1
Brookfield St	88	B2
Brookfield Ter	117	D2
Brookhaven Dr	33	C3
Brookhaven Gro	33	C3
Brookhaven Lawn	33	C3
Brookhaven Pk	33	C3
Brookhaven Ri	33	C3
Brooklands	104	A2
Brooklawn *Dublin 3*	80	A2
Brooklawn *Black.*	117	C2
Brooklawn *Lucan*	82	A2
Brooklawn Av	118	A3
Brooklawn Wd	118	A3
Brookmount Av	111	C3
Brookmount Lawns	111	C3
Brookpark	82	A2
Brook Pk Ct	118	B3
Brookstone La **4**	43	D3
Brookstone Rd	43	D3
Brookvale	70	B3
Brookvale Downs	113	C1
Brookvale Rd *Dublin 4*	103	C2
Brookvale Rd *Dublin 14*	113	C2
Brookview Av	122	A1
Brookview Cl	122	A1
Brookview Ct	108	A3
Brookview Cres	108	A3
Brookview Dr	108	A3
Brookview Gdns	108	A3
Brookview Grn	122	A1
Brookview Gro	122	A1
Brookview Lawns	108	A3
Brookview Pk	122	A1
Brookview Ri	108	A3
Brookview Ter	122	A1
Brookview Way	122	A1
Brookville *Dublin 11*	50	B1
Brookville *Ashb.*	11	C2
Brookville Cres	54	B1
Brookville Pk (Artane) *Dublin 5*	54	B2
Brookville Pk (Coolock) *Dublin 5*	55	C1
Brookville Pk *D.L.*	132	A1
Brookwood	126	B2
Brookwood Av	54	B3
Brookwood Cres	55	C3
Brookwood Dr	54	B3
Brookwood Glen	55	C3
Brookwood Gro	54	B3
Brookwood Hts	54	B3
Brookwood Lawn	55	C3
Brookwood Meadow	54	B3
Brookwood Pk	54	B3
Brookwood Ri	55	C3
Brookwood Rd	54	B3
Broombridge Rd	76	B1
Broombridge Sta	76	B1
Broomfield	20	A3
Broomfield Ct	141	C1
Broomhill Business Complex	109	D2
Broomhill Business Pk	110	A2
Broom Hill Cl	109	D3
Broomhill Rd	110	A2
Broom Hill Ter	110	A3
Brownsbarn Ct	107	D2
Brownsbarn Gdns	107	D2
Brownsbarn Orchard	107	D2
Brown St N	144	A1
Brown St S	89	C3
Brunswick Pl *off Pearse St*	91	C2
Brunswick St N	144	A1
Brusna Cotts	117	D2
Buckingham St Lwr	78	B3
Buckingham St Upr	78	B3
Buckleys La	68	B2
Buirg An Ri Glen	83	D2
Buirg An Ri Ter	83	D2
Bulfin Gdns	88	A2
Bulfin Rd	88	A2
Bulfin St	88	A3
Bull All St	144	B4
Bullock Steps **8**	134	B1
Bunbury Gate Av	14	B2
Bunbury Gate Cres	14	B2
Bunratty Av	54	B1
Bunratty Dr	54	B1
Bunratty Rd	54	A1
Bunting Rd	99	C2
Burdett Av	134	A1
Burgage, The	134	B2
Burgess La *off Haymarket*	144	A2
Burgh Quay	145	D2
Burke Pl	88	B2
Burleigh Ct	90	B3
Burlington Gdns	90	B3
Burlington Rd	102	B1
Burmah Cl	134	B3
Burnaby Hts	143	C2
Burnaby Manor	143	D2
Burnaby Ms	143	D2
Burnaby Mill	143	D3
Burnaby Pk	143	D3
Burnaby Rd	143	D2
Burnaby Wds	143	D2
Burnell Pk Av	73	C1
Burnell Pk Grn	73	C1
Burren Ct	37	D3
Burris Ct *off School Ho La W*	144	B3
Burrow Ct	27	C2
Burrowfield Rd	58	A1
Burrow Rd	58	B1
Burton Hall Av	130	B2
Burton Hall Rd	130	B2
Burton Rd	134	B3
Busáras Sta	145	F1
Bushes La	101	D2
Bushfield	96	A3
Bushfield Av	103	C2
Bushfield Dr	108	A1
Bushfield Grn	96	A3
Bushfield Gro	108	A1
Bushfield Lawns	108	A1
Bushfield Pl	102	B3
Bushfield Ter	102	B2
Bushy Pk Gdns	113	C1
Bushy Pk Rd	113	C1
Buterly Business Pk	54	A2
Butt Br	145	E2
Buttercup Cl **1**	41	C3
Buttercup Dr	41	C3
Buttercup Pk **2**	41	C3
Buttercup Sq **3**	41	C3
Butterfield Av	112	B2
Butterfield Cl	112	B3
Butterfield Ct	113	C2
Butterfield Cres	113	C2
Butterfield Dr	113	C3
Butterfield Gro	112	B2
Butterfield Meadow	112	B2
Butterfield Orchard	113	C3
Butterfield Pk	112	B3
Byrnes La	144	C2

C

Name	Page	Grid
Cabinteely Av	137	D1
Cabinteely Bypass	137	D1
Cabinteely Cl	137	D1
Cabinteely Ct **4**	132	B3
Cabinteely Cres	132	B3
Cabinteely Dr	132	B3
Cabinteely Grn	132	B3
Cabinteely Pk **2**	137	D1

Cabinteely Way	132	B3
Cabra Dr	77	C2
Cabra Gro	77	C2
Cabra Pk	77	D2
Cabra Rd	76	B2
Caddell	26	B3
Cadogan Rd	79	C2
Cairn Brook	136	B3
Cairn Brook Hall	136	B3
Cairn Brook Manor	136	B3
Cairn Brook Vw	136	B3
Cairn Brook Way	136	B3
Cairn Ct	37	D3
Cairn Hill	132	A3
Cairnwood	108	B3
Cairnwood Av	108	B3
Cairnwood Ct	108	B3
Cairnwood Grn	108	B3
Calderwood Av	53	C3
Calderwood Gro	53	C3
Calderwood Rd	79	C2
Caledon Rd	79	C3
Callaghan Br	45	D2
Callary Rd	116	A2
Calmount Business Pk	98	B3
Calmount Rd	98	B3
Camac Ct	88	A2
Camac Pk	98	B1
Camac Ter		
off Bow Br	88	B2
Camaderry Rd	142	B3
Camberley Elms	114	A2
Camberley Oaks	114	A3
Cambridge Av	92	A2
Cambridge La	101	D2
Cambridge Rd Dublin 4	91	D2
Cambridge Rd		
(Rathmines) Dublin 6	102	A2
Cambridge Sq	91	D2
Cambridge Ter	102	B1
Cambridge Vil		
off Belgrave Rd	102	A2
Camden Av	49	D3
Camden Lock		
off South Docks Rd	91	D2
Camden Mkt		
off Camden St Lwr	90	A3
Camden Pl	90	A3
Camden Rd	49	D3
Camden Row	90	A3
Camden St Lwr	90	A3
Camden St Upr	90	A3
Cameron Sq	88	B2
Cameron St	89	C3
Campbell's Ter		
off Little Britain St	144	B1
Campbells Row		
off Portland St N	78	B3
Campfield Ter	115	D3
Canal Bk	97	D1
Canal Rd	102	A1
Canal Ter	87	C3
Canal Turn	96	B1
Canal Wk	86	A3
Cannonbrook	82	B1
Cannonbrook Av	82	A1
Cannonbrook Ct	82	B1
Cannonbrook Lawn	82	B1
Cannonbrook Pk	82	B1
Cannon Rock Vw	61	C2
Canon Lillis Av	79	C3
Canon Mooney Gdns		
off Cambridge Rd	91	D2
Canon Troy Ct	86	B3
Capel St	144	C1
Cappagh Av	50	A1
Cappagh Dr	50	A1
Cappaghmore	96	A1
Cappagh Rd	50	A1
Cappoge Cotts	35	C3
Captains Av	100	A2
Captains Dr	100	A2
Captain's Hill	68	B3
Captains Rd	100	A2
Caragh Rd	76	B3
Cara Pk	40	B2

Carberry Rd	53	C3
Cardiff Br		
off Phibsborough Rd	77	D3
Cardiff Castle Rd	50	A1
Cardiffsbridge Av	49	D2
Cardiffsbridge Gro		
off Cappagh Rd	50	A1
Cardiffsbridge Rd		
(Bothar Dhroichead		
Chiarduibh)	50	A1
Cardiffs La	91	C2
Cards La		
off Townsend St	145	E3
Caritas Convalescent Cen &		
St. Mary's Cen	104	B3
Carleton Rd	79	D2
Carlingford Par	91	C2
Carlingford Pl		
off Carlingford Par	91	C2
Carlingford Rd	78	A2
Carlisle Av	91	D3
Carlisle St	89	D3
Carlisle Ter 2 D.L.	133	C1
Carlisle Ter Mala.	20	A2
Carlton Cl Dublin 3	80	A2
Carlton Ct Swords	17	C2
Carlton Ms		
off Shelbourne Av	91	D3
Carlton Ter 5	142	A1
Carlton Vil 6	142	A1
Carmanhall Rd	130	A2
Carmans Hall	144	A4
Carmelite Cen	103	C1
Carmelite Monastery		
Dublin 14	115	D1
Carmelite Monastery		
Still.	130	B1
Carna Rd	85	D2
Carndonagh Dr	56	B1
Carndonagh Lawn	56	B1
Carndonagh Pk	56	B1
Carndonagh Rd	56	B1
Carne Ct	31	D3
Carnew St	77	C3
Carnlough Rd	76	B2
Caroline Row		
off Bridge St	91	D2
Carpenterstown Av	47	C3
Carpenterstown Pk E	46	B3
Carpenterstown Rd	73	C1
Carraig Glen	137	D1
Carraig Grennane	139	C2
Carraigmore Cl	123	D2
Carraigmore Dr	123	D2
Carraigmore Gro	123	D2
Carraigmore Pk	123	D2
Carraigmore Rd	123	D2
Carraigmore Vw	123	D2
Carraroe Av	56	A1
Carrickbrack Heath	59	C2
Carrickbrack Hill	59	C3
Carrickbrack Lawn	59	C3
Carrickbrack Pk	59	C3
Carrickbrack Rd	59	C3
Carrick Brennan Lawn	118	B3
Carrickbrennan Rd	118	B3
Carrick Ct	27	C2
Carrickhill Cl	27	C1
Carrickhill Dr	27	C2
Carrickhill Hts	27	C2
Carrickhill Ri	27	C1
Carrickhill Rd	27	C3
Carrickhill Rd Mid	27	C2
Carrickhill Rd Upr	27	C1
Carrickhill Wk	27	C1
Carrick Lawn 1	129	D1
Carrickmines	137	C2
Carrickmines Av	137	C2
Carrickmines Chase	137	C2
Carrickmines Dale	137	C2
Carrickmines Garth	137	C2
Carrickmines Grn	136	B3
Carrickmines Little	137	C2
Carrickmines Oaks	137	C2
Carrickmount Av	114	A3
Carrickmount Dr	114	A3
Carrick Ter	88	B3
Carrigallen Dr		
off Carrigallen Rd	50	B3
Carrigallen Pk		
off Carrigallen Rd	50	B3
Carrigallen Rd	50	B3

Carriglea	125	C2
Carriglea Av Dublin 24	124	B2
Carriglea Av D.L.	133	C2
Carriglea Ct Dublin 24	125	C2
Carriglea Ct 1 D.L.	133	C1
Carriglea Downs		
Dublin 24	124	B2
Carriglea Downs D.L.	133	C2
Carriglea Dr	124	B2
Carriglea Gdns	133	C1
Carriglea Gro	124	B2
Carriglea Ind Est	99	C1
Carriglea Ri	124	B2
Carriglea Vw	124	B2
Carriglea Wk	125	C2
Carrigmore Av	121	C2
Carrigmore Cl	121	C2
Carrigmore Ct	121	C2
Carrigmore Cres, The	121	C1
Carrigmore Dale	121	C1
Carrigmore Downs	121	C1
Carrigmore Elms	121	C2
Carrigmore Gdns	121	C1
Carrigmore Glen	121	C2
Carrigmore Grn	121	C2
Carrigmore Gro	121	C2
Carrigmore Lawns 2	121	C1
Carrigmore Manor 1	121	C1
Carrigmore Meadows	121	C1
Carrigmore Oak	121	C1
Carrigmore Pl	121	C2
Carrigmore Ter	121	C1
Carrigmore Way	121	C1
Carrig Orchard	143	C3
Carrig Rd	37	D3
Carrig Vil	143	C3
Carngwood	125	C2
Carrow Rd	87	D3
Carrs Mill	13	D1
Carton Av	65	C1
Carton Ct Dublin 11	37	D2
Carton Ct Mayn.	65	C3
Carton Dr	37	D2
Carton Rd	37	D2
Carton Ter	37	D2
Carysfort Av	117	D2
Carysfort Downs	131	C1
Carysfort Dr	134	B2
Carysfort Gro	131	D1
Carysfort Hall	117	D3
Carysfort Pk	117	D3
Carysfort Rd	134	B2
Carysfort Wd	131	C1
Casana Vw	61	C3
Casement Cl	50	A1
Casement Dr	50	A1
Casement Grn	50	A1
Casement Gro	50	A1
Casement Pk	50	A1
Casement Rd (Finglas S)		
Dublin 11	50	B2
Casement Rd (Finglas W)		
Dublin 11	50	A1
Casement Vil	132	B1
Cashel Av	100	B2
Cashel Business Cen	100	B3
Cashel Rd	100	A2
Casimir Av	101	C2
Casimir Ct	101	D2
Casimir Rd	101	C2
Casino Pk	79	D1
Casino Rd	79	C1
Castaheany	31	C3
Castilla Pk	81	C2
Castle Av Dublin 3	80	B2
Castle Av Clond.	96	B2
Castle Av Swords	17	D1
Castlebridge	65	C2
Castlebrook	129	C1
Castlebyrne Pk	117	D3
Castle Cl Ashb.	11	C3
Castle Cl Clond.	96	B1
Castle Cl D.L.	134	B1
Castle Cl Dublin 3	80	A1
Castle Ct 2 Dublin 16	129	C1
Castle Ct Boot.	116	B1
Castle Ct Lough.	139	C3
Castle Cove 2 Dalkey	134	B2
Castle Cove Mala.	19	C1
Castle Cres Ashb.	11	C3
Castle Cres 6 Clond.	96	B2
Castlecurragh Heath	32	B2

Castlecurragh Pk	32	B2
Castlecurragh Vale	32	B2
Castle Dawson	64	A2
Castledawson Av	117	C1
Castle Down Cft 4	19	C1
Castle Down Gro	19	C1
Castle Down Rd	19	C1
Castle Dr Clond.	96	B2
Castle Dr Swords	17	D1
Castle Elms	54	B1
Castle Fm Shank.	141	C3
Castlefarm Swords	15	C3
Castlefarm Wd	141	C3
Castlefield Av	125	D1
Castlefield Ct Dublin 16	125	C1
Castlefield Ct Clons.	45	D2
Castlefield Dr	125	D2
Castlefield Grn	125	D2
Castlefield Gro	125	D2
Castlefield Lawn 1	125	D1
Castlefield Manor		
Dublin 24	125	C1
Castlefield Manor Mala.	20	A3
Castlefield Pk Dublin 16	125	D1
Castlefield Pk Clons.	45	D2
Castlefield Ter	143	C3
Castlefield Way	125	D2
Castlefield Wds	45	D2
Castleforbes Ind Est	91	C1
Castleforbes Rd	91	D1
Castle Gate Dublin 15	74	B1
Castlegate Shank.	140	A3
Castlegate Chase	82	A3
Castlegate Cres	82	A3
Castlegate Dene	82	A3
Castlegate Elms	82	A3
Castlegate Grn	82	A3
Castlegate Gro	82	A3
Castlegate Pk	82	A3
Castlegate Pl	82	A3
Castlegate Sq	82	A3
Castlegate Wk	82	A3
Castlegate Way	82	A3
Castle Golf Course	113	D2
Castlegrange	95	C2
Castlegrange Av Clons.	31	C3
Castlegrange Av Swords	15	C3
Castlegrange Cl Clond.	95	C2
Castlegrange Cl Swords	15	D3
Castlegrange Ct	95	C2
Castlegrange Dale	31	C3
Castlegrange Dr Clond.	95	C2
Castlegrange Dr Clons.	31	C3
Castlegrange Gdns	31	C3
Castlegrange Grn Clond.	95	C2
Castlegrange Grn Clons.	31	C3
Castlegrange Gro	31	C3
Castlegrange Hts	15	C3
Castlegrange Hill	15	D3
Castlegrange Lawn		
Clond.	95	C2
Castlegrange Lawn		
Clons.	31	C3
Castlegrange Rd Clond.	95	C2
Castlegrange Rd Swords	15	C3
Castlegrange Row	31	C3
Castlegrange Sq Clond.	95	C2
Castlegrange Sq Clons.	31	C3
Castlegrange Way	15	C3
Castle Gro Dublin 3	80	B1
Castle Gro Clond.	96	B1
Castle Gro Swords	17	D1
Castle Heath	19	C2
Castlekevin Rd	54	A1
Castleknock Av	47	D3
Castleknock Brook	47	C3
Castleknock Cl	47	C3
Castleknock Coll	73	C1
Castleknock Cres	47	D3
Castleknock Dale	47	D3
Castleknock Downs	47	C3
Castleknock Dr	47	D3
Castleknock Elms	47	D3
Castleknock Glade	47	D3
Castleknock Gra	47	C3
Castleknock Grn	74	A1
Castleknock Gro	47	D3
Castleknock Laurels	47	D3
Castleknock Lo	74	A1
Castleknock Meadows	47	C3
Castleknock Oaks	47	D3
Castleknock Pk	74	A1

Name	Page	Grid
Castleknock Parklands	47	D3
Castleknock Ri	47	C3
Castleknock Rd	74	B1
Castleknock Sta	47	D2
Castleknock Vale	47	C3
Castleknock Vw	47	D3
Castleknock Village Cen	74	A1
Castleknock Wk	47	C3
Castleknock Way	47	C3
Castleknock Wd	47	D3
Castlelands 9 *Dalkey*	134	B1
Castlelands, The *Dublin 14*	113	D2
Castlelands Gro	134	B1
Castle Lawns	19	C1
Castle Lawns Est	110	B3
Castle Mkt *off Drury St*	144	C4
Castlemoyne	42	A2
Castle Pk *Dublin 24*	110	B3
Castle Pk *Ashb.*	11	C3
Castle Pk *Black.*	118	B3
Castle Pk *Clond.*	96	B2
Castle Pk *Leix.*	68	B2
Castle Pk *Swords*	17	D1
Castle Pk Est	110	B3
Castlepark Rd	134	A2
Castle Riada	83	C1
Castle Riada Av	83	C1
Castle Riada Cres	83	C1
Castle Riada Dr	83	C2
Castle Riada Gro	83	C1
Castle Rd *Dublin 3*	80	B2
Castle Rd *Lucan*	83	C1
Castle Rosse	43	C3
Castlerosse Cres	43	C3
Castlerosse Dr	43	C3
Castlerosse Vw	43	D3
Castle Shop Cen	17	D1
Castleside Dr	113	D2
Castle St *Dublin 2*	144	B3
Castle St *Ashb.*	10	B3
Castle St *Bray*	142	A1
Castle St *Dalkey*	134	B2
Castle St Shop Cen	142	A1
Castle Ter	20	A2
Castletimon Av	53	D1
Castletimon Dr	53	D1
Castletimon Gdns	53	D1
Castletimon Grn	53	D1
Castletimon Pk	53	D1
Castletimon Rd	53	D1
Castletown Ct	66	B2
Castletown Gro	66	B1
Castletown Lawn	66	B1
Castletymon Ct	110	B3
Castleview *Dublin 5*	54	A2
Castleview 3 *Dublin 16*	128	B1
Castle Vw *Carrick.*	136	B2
Castleview *Swords*	14	A1
Castleview Av	14	B2
Castleview Cl	14	B2
Castleview Ct	14	B2
Castleview Cres	14	B2
Castleview Dr	14	B2
Castleview Est	28	B2
Castleview Grn	14	B2
Castleview Gro	14	B2
Castleview Heath	14	B2
Castleview Hts	14	B1
Castleview Lawns	14	B2
Castleview Meadows	14	B2
Castleview Pk *Mala.*	19	D2
Castleview Pk *Swords*	14	B2
Castleview Pl	14	B2
Castleview Ri	14	B2
Castle Vw Rd	96	B2
Castleview Row	14	B2
Castleview Wk	14	B2
Castleview Way	14	B2
Castle Village Av	66	A1
Castle Village Cl	66	A1
Castle Village Ct	66	A1
Castle Village Cres	66	A1
Castle Village Dr	66	A1
Castle Village Lawns	66	A1
Castle Village Pk	66	A1
Castle Village Ri	66	A1
Castle Village Wk	66	A1
Castle Village Way	66	A1
Castle Village Wds	66	A1
Castle Vil 3	134	B2
Castle Way	11	C3
Castlewood	31	D3
Castlewood Av	102	A2
Castlewood Cl *off Castlewood Av*	102	A2
Castlewood La	102	A2
Castlewood Pk	102	A2
Castlewood Pl	102	A2
Castlewood Ter	102	A2
Cathal Brugha St	145	D1
Cathedral La	89	D3
Cathedral St	145	D1
Cathedral Vw Ct *off Cathedral Vw Wk*	89	D3
Cathedral Vw Wk	89	D3
Catherines La *off Church St Upr*	144	B1
Catherine St *off Ash St*	144	A4
Cats Ladder 3	135	C3
Causeway Rd	105	D1
Cavalry Row	89	C1
Cavendish Row *off Parnell St*	78	A3
Ceannchor Rd	62	C3
Ceannt Fort	88	B2
Cecil Av	79	C2
Cecilia St *off Temple La S*	144	C3
Cedar Av	109	D1
Cedar Brook Av	85	C3
Cedar Brook Pl	85	C3
Cedar Brook Wk	85	C3
Cedar Brook Way	85	C3
Cedar Ct *Dublin 6W*	101	C2
Cedar Ct *Dunb.*	29	C2
Cedar Ct *Lough.*	138	B3
Cedar Dr *Dunb.*	29	C2
Cedar Dr *Palm.*	73	C3
Cedar Gro 1	46	A1
Cedar Hall *off Prospect La*	103	C3
Cedarhurst Rd	75	C1
Cedar Lo 6	126	B2
Cedarmount Rd	116	A3
Cedar Pk *Dublin 13*	56	A1
Cedar Pk *Leix.*	68	A2
Cedars, The 13 *Abb.*	139	C3
Cedars, The *D.L.*	118	A3
Cedar Sq	117	C3
Cedar Wk	56	A2
Cedarwood	66	B2
Cedarwood Av	51	C1
Cedarwood Cl	51	C1
Cedarwood Grn	37	C3
Cedarwood Gro	51	C1
Cedarwood Pk	51	C1
Cedarwood Ri	51	C1
Cedarwood Rd	37	C3
Ceder Pk	16	A2
Ceder Vw	16	A2
Ceide Dun Eanna (Ennafort Dr)	55	C3
Ceide Gleannaluinn (Glenaulin Dr)	86	A1
Ceide Phairc An Bhailtini (Villa Park Dr)	76	A2
Celbridge Abbey	66	A3
Celbridge Rd *Leix.*	68	A2
Celbridge Rd *Lucan*	69	D3
Celbridge Rd *Mayn.*	65	D3
Celestine Av	91	D2
Celtic Pk Av	53	D3
Celtic Pk Rd	53	D3
Cenacle Gro	139	C3
Central Pk Business Pk	130	B3
Centre Pt Business Pk	97	D2
Century Business Pk	36	B3
Chalet Gdns	71	C3
Chalfont Av	19	D1
Chalfont Pk	19	D2
Chalfont Pl	19	D2
Chalfont Rd	19	D2
Chamber St	89	D3
Chancery La	144	C4
Chancery Pl	144	B2
Chancery St	144	B2
Chanel Av	54	B2
Chanel Gro	54	B1
Chanel Rd	54	A2
Chapel Av	91	D2
Chapelizod Bypass	86	A1
Chapelizod Ct	86	A1
Chapelizod Hill Rd	86	A1
Chapelizod Ind Est	86	B1
Chapelizod Rd *Dublin 8*	87	C1
Chapelizod Rd *Dublin 20*	87	C1
Chapel La *Dublin 1*	144	C1
Chapel La *Swords*	17	D1
Chapel Rd	25	D2
Charlemont	53	D3
Charlemont Av	119	D3
Charlemont Ct	102	A1
Charlemont Gdns *off Charlemont St*	90	A3
Charlemont Mall	102	A1
Charlemont Par	79	C3
Charlemont Pl	102	A1
Charlemont Rd	79	D2
Charlemont Sq *off Charlemont St*	90	A3
Charlemont Sta	102	A1
Charlemont St	90	A3
Charles La	78	B3
Charles St Gt	78	B3
Charles St W	144	B2
Charleston Av	102	A2
Charleston Rd	102	A2
Charlestown	36	A2
Charlestown Av	36	B3
Charlestown Ct	36	B2
Charlestown Dr	36	B2
Charlestown Grn	36	B2
Charlestown Pk	36	B2
Charlestown Way	36	B2
Charleville *Dublin 14*	114	B2
Charleville *Dublin 16*	112	A3
Charleville Av	78	B3
Charleville Mall	78	B3
Charleville Rd *Dublin 6*	114	B2
Charleville Rd *Dublin 7*	77	C2
Charleville Sq	112	B2
Charlotte Quay	91	C2
Charlotte Ter 2	135	C2
Charlotte Way	90	A3
Charlton Lawn	115	D2
Charnwood *Bray*	142	A1
Charnwood *Clons.*	45	D2
Charnwood Av	45	D2
Charnwood Cts	45	D2
Charnwood Dale	45	D2
Charnwood Gdns	45	D2
Charnwood Grn	46	A2
Charnwood Gro	45	D2
Charnwood Heath	45	D2
Charnwood Meadows	45	D2
Charnwood Pk	45	D2
Chase, The	130	B2
Chatham Row *off William St S*	145	D4
Chatham St	145	D4
Chaworth Ter *off Hanbury La*	144	A3
Cheaters La *off Redmonds Hill*	90	A3
Cheeverstown Cen	112	A3
Cheeverstown Rd	108	A3
Chelmsford La	102	B1
Chelmsford Rd	102	B1
Chelsea Gdns	81	C2
Cheltenham Pl *off Canal Rd*	102	A1
Cherbury Ct	116	B2
Cherbury Gdns	116	B2
Cherbury Ms	116	B2
Cherbury Pk Av	82	B1
Cherbury Pk Rd	82	B1
Cherries, The 1	128	A2
Cherries Rd	129	D2
Cherrington Cl	141	C3
Cherrington Dr	141	C3
Cherrington Rd	140	B3
Cherry Av *Carp.*	46	B3
Cherry Av *Swords*	16	B2
Cherry Ct *Dublin 6W*	101	C3
Cherry Ct 6 *Grey.*	143	C3
Cherry Ct 2 *Lough.*	138	B3
Cherry Dr	46	B3
Cherryfield Av *Dublin 6*	102	B2
Cherryfield Av *Dublin 12*	99	D3
Cherryfield Cl	45	D1
Cherryfield Ct	45	D1
Cherryfield Dr	99	D3
Cherryfield Lawn	45	D1
Cherryfield Pk	45	D1
Cherryfield Rd	99	C3
Cherryfield Vw	45	C1
Cherryfield Wk	31	D3
Cherry Gdns 7	143	C3
Cherrygarth *Still.*	116	B3
Cherry Garth *Swords*	16	B2
Cherry Gro *Dublin 12*	99	D3
Cherry Gro *Swords*	16	B2
Cherry Lawn	46	B3
Cherry Lawns	82	A1
Cherrymount Cres	79	D1
Cherrymount Gro	79	D1
Cherrymount Pk	77	D2
Cherry Orchard Av	85	D3
Cherry Orchard Ct	85	D3
Cherry Orchard Cres	85	D3
Cherry Orchard Dr	85	D3
Cherry Orchard Grn	85	C2
Cherry Orchard Gro	85	D3
Cherry Orchard Ind Est	85	D1
Cherry Orchard Par 1	85	D3
Cherry Orchard Pk	85	D3
Cherry Orchard Sta	85	D3
Cherry Orchard Way *off Cherry Orchard Av*	85	D3
Cherry Pk *Carp.*	46	B3
Cherry Pk *Swords*	16	B2
Cherry Ri	143	C2
Cherry Tree Dr	142	A3
Cherrywood *Celbr.*	66	B1
Cherry Wd *Lough.*	138	B3
Cherrywood Av	96	A2
Cherrywood Business Pk	140	A1
Cherrywood Cres	95	D3
Cherrywood Dr	95	D2
Cherrywood Gro	96	A2
Cherrywood Lawn	95	D3
Cherrywood Pk *Clond.*	95	D2
Cherrywood Pk *Lough.*	138	B3
Cherrywood Rd	140	B1
Cherrywood Vil	95	D2
Chester Downs	133	D1
Chester Av *Dublin 8*	75	D3
Chesterfield Av *Dublin 15*	74	B1
Chesterfield Cl	74	B1
Chesterfield Copse	74	B1
Chesterfield Gro	74	B1
Chesterfield Pk	74	B1
Chesterfield Vw	74	B1
Chester Rd	102	A1
Chester Sq 8	134	A1
Chester Ct	53	D2
Chestnut Ct	53	D2
Chestnut Gro *Dublin 16*	128	B2
Chestnut Gro *Dublin 24*	109	D1
Chestnut Gro *Celbr.*	66	B2
Chestnut Gro *Dunb.*	29	C3
Chestnut Pk 2	131	D2
Chestnut Rd *Dublin 12*	98	A2
Chestnut Rd *Still.*	116	A2
Chipping Row	30	B3
Chipping Ter 3	30	B3
Christ Ch Cath	144	B3
Christchurch Pl	144	B3
Church Av (Irishtown) *Dublin 4*	91	D2
Church Av (Rathmines) *Dublin 6*	102	A2
Church Av *Dublin 8*	88	B3
Church Av (Glasnevin) *Dublin 9*	52	A3
Church Av (Blanchardstown) *Dublin 15*	47	C2
Church Av *Kill.*	139	C2
Church Av 2 *Port.*	26	B3
Church Av N (Drumcondra)	78	B3
Church Ct	74	A1
Churchfields	114	B1
Church Gdns	102	A2

173

Name	Page	Grid
Churchgate Av	80	B3
Church Gates	143	D1
Church Gro	123	D2
Churchill Ms **10**	134	B1
Churchill Ter	103	D1
Church Lands Bray	142	A2
Churchlands Sandy.	129	D3
Church La Dublin 2		
off College Grn	145	D3
Church La (Rathfarnham)		
Dublin 14	113	C2
Church La Grey.	143	C1
Church La S		
off Kevin St Lwr	90	A3
Church Pk Av	101	C2
Church Pk Ct	101	C2
Church Pk Dr	101	C2
Church Pk Lawn	101	C2
Church Pk Vw	101	C2
Church Pk Way	101	C2
Church Rd Dublin 3	91	C1
Church Rd (Finglas)		
Dublin 11	50	B2
Church Rd Dublin 13	58	B2
Church Rd Bray	142	A2
Church Rd Celbr.	66	A3
Church Rd Dalkey	134	B2
Church Rd Grey.	143	D1
Church Rd Kill.	138	B1
Church Rd Mala.	20	A2
Church Rd Mulh.	32	B2
Church Rd Swords	17	C1
Church St Dublin 7	144	B2
Church St (Finglas)		
Dublin 11	50	B2
Church St (Howth)		
Dublin 13	60	B2
Church St E	91	C1
Church Ter Upr	144	B1
Church Ter Dublin 7		
off Church St	144	B2
Church Ter **7** Bray	142	A1
Churchtown Av	114	B1
Churchtown		
Business Pk	114	A3
Churchtown Cl	114	B1
Churchtown Dr	114	B1
Churchtown Rd Lwr	114	B1
Churchtown Rd Upr	114	B3
Church Vw **1**	96	A3
Churchview Av	138	B1
Churchview Dr	138	B1
Churchview Pk	138	B1
Churchview Rd	138	B2
Cianlea	14	B3
Cian Pk	78	B1
Cill Cais	123	D2
Cilldara	66	B2
Cill Eanna	55	D3
Cill Manntan Pk **2**	142	A2
City Junct Business Pk	41	D2
Citylink Business Pk	98	B1
City Quay	145	F2
Citywest Av	121	D1
City W Br	107	C3
City W Business		
Campus	107	C3
City W Shop Cen	121	D1
Claddagh Grn	85	D2
Claddagh Rd	85	D2
Claddagh Ter **8**	142	B1
Clanawley Rd	80	B1
Clanboy Rd	54	A3
Clanbrassil Cl	101	D1
Clanbrassil St Lwr	89	D3
Clanbrassil St Upr	101	D1
Clancarthy Rd	80	A1
Clancy Av	50	B1
Clancy Rd	51	C1
Clandonagh Rd	54	A3
Clanhugh Rd	80	A1
Clanmahon Rd	54	A3
Clanmaurice Rd	54	A3
Clanmawr	141	C2
Clanmoyle Rd	80	A1
Clanranald Rd	54	A3
Clanree Rd	54	A3
Clanwilliam Pl	91	C3
Clare Hall Av	41	D3
Clarehall Shop Cen	41	D3
Clare La	145	E4
Claremont Av	51	D3
Claremont Ct	77	C1
Claremont Dr	51	D2
Claremont Gro **1**	139	C1
Claremont Pk		
(Pairc Clearmont)	92	A3
Claremont Rd Dublin 4	92	A3
Claremont Rd Dublin 13	59	C1
Claremont Rd Cabin.	137	C1
Claremont Rd Kill.	139	C1
Claremont Vil	133	D1
Claremount Pines	137	C1
Claremount Ter **11**	142	B2
Clarence Mangan Rd	89	D3
Clarence St	119	C3
Clarendon Mkt		
off Chatham St	145	D4
Clarendon Row		
off Clarendon St	145	D4
Clarendon St	145	D4
Clare Rd	52	B3
Clare St	145	E4
Clare Village	41	D3
Clareville Ct	77	C1
Clareville Gro	77	D1
Clareville Pk	77	D1
Clareville Rd	101	C2
Clarinda Manor	133	D1
Clarinda Pk E	133	D1
Clarinda Pk N	119	D3
Clarinda Pk W	133	D1
Clarke Ter	89	C3
Clarkeville Ter **1**	73	D3
Classons Br	114	B1
Claude Rd	78	A2
Cleggan Av	85	D2
Cleggan Pk	85	D2
Cleggan Rd		
(Bothar Cloiginn)	85	D2
Clifden Dr	85	D2
Clifden Rd	86	A2
Cliffords La	18	A1
Cliff Ter **1**	134	B1
Cliff Wk (Fingal Way)	61	D2
Clifton Av	118	B3
Clifton La	118	B3
Clifton Ms	102	A1
Clifton Pk	141	C1
Clifton Ter	118	B3
Cliftonville Rd	78	A1
Clinches Ct	79	C3
Clogher Rd	100	B1
Cloister Av	117	D3
Cloister Ct	76	A1
Cloister Gate	117	D3
Cloister Grn	117	D3
Cloister Gro	117	D3
Cloister Pk	117	C3
Cloisters, The		
Dublin 6W	101	C3
Cloisters, The Dublin 9	53	C3
Cloister Sq	117	D3
Cloister Way	117	D3
Clonard Av	129	C2
Clonard Cl	129	C2
Clonard Dr	129	C2
Clonard Gro	129	C2
Clonard Lawn	129	C2
Clonard Pk	129	C2
Clonard Rd Dublin 12	100	A1
Clonard Rd Dublin 16	129	C2
Clonasleigh **2**	141	C2
Clondalkin		
Business Cen	85	C3
Clondalkin		
Commercial Pk	84	B3
Clondalkin		
Enterprise Cen	84	A3
Clondalkin Sta	84	B3
Clonee Br	30	B1
Clonee Bypass	30	B1
Clonfadda Wd	116	B2
Clonfert Rd	100	B2
Clonkeen Ct	132	B3
Clonkeen Cres	132	B2
Clonkeen Dr	132	A2
Clonkeen Gro	132	B2
Clonkeen Lawn **1**	132	B3
Clonkeen Rd	132	A2
Clonlara Av	106	B3
Clonlara Rd (Ringsend)		
Dublin 4	92	A2
Clonlara Rd Kings.	106	B3
Clonlea	128	B2
Clonlea Wd **3**	128	B2
Clonliffe Av	78	B2
Clonliffe Gdns	78	B2
Clonliffe Rd	78	B2
Clonmacnoise Gro	100	B2
Clonmacnoise Rd	100	B2
Clonmellon Gro **6**	42	A3
Clonmel Rd	51	D1
Clonmel St	90	A3
Clonmore Rd Dublin 3	78	B3
Clonmore Rd Still.	116	A3
Clonmore Ter	78	B3
Clonrosse Ct		
off Clonrosse Dr	55	D1
Clonrosse Dr	55	D1
Clonrosse Pk		
off Clonrosse Dr	55	D1
Clonshaugh Av	40	A3
Clonshaugh Business &		
Tech Pk	39	D3
Clonshaugh Cl	40	A2
Clonshaugh Ct **1**	40	A2
Clonshaugh Cres	40	A2
Clonshaugh Dr	40	B2
Clonshaugh Grn	40	B2
Clonshaugh Gro	40	B2
Clonshaugh Hts	40	A2
Clonshaugh Ind Est	40	A3
Clonshaugh Lawns	40	A2
Clonshaugh Meadow	40	A2
Clonshaugh Pk	40	A2
Clonshaugh Ri **2**	40	A2
Clonshaugh Rd	40	A3
Clonshaugh Wk	40	B2
Clonsilla Cl	47	C2
Clonsilla Pk	47	C2
Clonsilla Sta	45	C2
Clonskeagh Br	103	C3
Clonskeagh Dr	103	C3
Clonskeagh Rd		
Dublin 6	103	C2
Clonskeagh Rd		
Dublin 14	103	C3
Clonskeagh Sq	103	C3
Clontarf Castle		
off Castle Av	80	B2
Clontarf Golf Course	80	A1
Clontarf Pk	81	C3
Clontarf Prom	79	D2
Clontarf Rd	79	C2
Clontarf Rd Sta	79	D2
Clonturk Av	78	B1
Clonturk Gdns	78	B1
Clonturk Pk	78	B1
Cloonlara Cres	50	B3
Cloonlara Dr		
off Cloonlara Rd	50	B3
Cloonlara Rd	50	B3
Cloonmore Av	122	B2
Cloonmore Cl	122	B2
Cloonmore Cres	122	B2
Cloonmore Dr	122	B2
Cloonmore Gdns	122	B2
Cloonmore Grn	122	B2
Cloonmore Gro	122	B2
Cloonmore Lawn	122	B2
Cloonmore Pk	122	B2
Cloonmore Rd	122	B2
Close, The Dublin 6W	112	A2
Close, The Dublin 9	53	D1
Close, The (Ballinteer)		
Dublin 16	128	B2
Close, The (Ballyboden)		
Dublin 16	126	A2
Close, The (Kilnamanagh)		
Dublin 24	109	D2
Close, The (Tallaght) **4**		
Dublin 24	124	A1
Close, The (Oldtown Mill Rd)		
Celbr.	66	A2
Close, The (Wolstan Haven Av)		
Celbr.	66	A2
Close, The (Dunboyne Castle)		
Dunb.	28	B3
Close, The (Lutterell Hall)		
Dunb.	28	B2
Close, The (Plunkett Hall)		
Dunb.	28	A1
Close, The Gra M.	82	B2
Close, The Kins.	18	A2
Close, The **8** Mala.	21	C3
Close, The Manor.	31	C3
Close, The Still.	116	A2
Clover Hill Dr	86	A3
Cloverhill Ind Est	84	B3
Clover Hill Rd Dublin 10	86	A3
Cloverhill Rd Clond.	84	B3
Cloyne Rd	100	B2
Cluain Aoibhinn	64	B3
Cluain Mhuire	133	D2
Cluain Na Greine Ct	141	C2
Cluain Rí	83	D1
Cluain Ri	10	B2
Club Rd	98	A2
Clune Rd	50	B1
Cluny Gro	133	D3
Cluny Pk	134	A3
Clyde La	103	C1
Clyde Rd	103	C1
Cnoc Aoibhean	69	C3
Coast Rd Dublin 13	43	D2
Coast Rd Mala.	20	B2
Coates La **2**	65	C2
Coburg Pl	79	C3
Cois Coillte **3**	138	B3
Cois Inbhir	13	D1
Cois Na hAbhann	123	D1
Colbert's Fort	109	D3
Colberts Fort Cotts	109	D2
Coldcut Rd	84	B1
Coldwater Lakes	120	B2
Coldwell St	133	D1
Colepark Av	86	A2
Colepark Dr	86	B2
Colepark Grn	86	B2
Colepark Rd	86	A2
Coleraine St	144	B1
Coliemore Rd	135	C2
Coliemore Vil **3**	135	C2
College Business &		
Tech Pk	33	C2
College Cres	112	A1
College Dr	112	A1
Collegefort	73	D1
College Gate	73	D1
College Grn Dublin 2	145	D3
College Grn Mayn.	64	B3
College Gro	73	D1
College La	145	F3
College Pk Dublin 6W	112	A1
College Pk Dublin 15	74	A1
College Pk Av	129	C3
College Pk Cl **1**	129	C3
College Pk Ct **1**	129	C3
College Pk Dr **2**	129	C3
College Pk Gro	129	C3
College Pk Way	129	C3
College Rd Dublin 15	74	A1
College Rd (Ballinteer)		
Dublin 16	127	D3
College Sq	112	A1
College St Dublin 2	145	D3
College St Dublin 13	43	D3
College Vw **1**	110	A3
Collegewood	73	D1
Colliers Av	102	B2
Collins Av	53	D3
Collins Av E	54	A3
Collins Av Ext	52	A1
Collins Av W	52	B2
Collins Br	70	A1
Collins Ct Dublin 9	53	D3
Collins Ct Black.		
off Sweetmans Av	117	D2
Collins Dr	51	C1
Collins Grn	51	C1
Collins Pk	53	D3
Collins Pl	51	C2
Collins Row	51	C2
Collinstown Business Pk	39	C1
Collinstown Cres **1**	84	A3
Collinstown Cross		
Ind Est	39	C1
Collinstown Gro	84	B3
Collinstown Rd	84	B2
Collins Wd	53	C2

Colthurst	83	D1
Colthurst Cl	83	D1
Colthurst Cres	83	D1
Colthurst Gdns	83	D1
Colthurst Grn	83	D1
Colthurst Ms	83	D1
Colthurst Pk	83	D1
Colthurst Ri	83	D1
Colthurst Rd	83	D1
Colthurst Way	83	D1
Comeragh Rd	99	D1
Commons Rd *Clond.*	96	A3
Commons Rd *Lough.*	140	B1
Commons St	145	F2
Con Colbert Rd		
(Bothar Coilbeard)		
Dublin 8	88	A2
Con Colbert Rd		
(Bothar Coilbeard)		
Dublin 8	87	D2
Congress Gdns **10**	134	A1
Congress Hall	28	B3
Congress Pk	28	B3
Connaught St	77	D2
Connaught Ter		
off Rathgar Rd	101	D3
Connolly Av *Dublin 3*	88	A2
Connolly Av *Mala.*	25	D1
Connolly Cres	25	D1
Connolly Gdns	88	A2
Connolly Luas Sta	145	F1
Connolly Sta	145	F1
Conor Clune Rd	75	D1
Conquer Hill Rd	81	C3
Conquer Hill Ter	81	C3
Constellation Rd	39	C2
Constitution Hill	144	B1
Convent Av *Dublin 3*	79	C2
Convent Av *Bray*	142	B2
Convent Cl **1**	130	B1
Convent La *Dublin 14*	113	C3
Convent La *Port.*	27	D1
Convent Lawns	86	A2
Convent Rd *Black.*	117	D2
Convent Rd *Clond.*	96	B3
Convent Rd *Dalkey*	135	C2
Convent Rd *D.L.*	119	C3
Convent Vw **12** *Bray*	142	B2
Convent Vw *Clond.*	96	B3
Convent Vw Cotts		
Dublin 7	76	A1
Convent Vw Cotts		
Clond.	96	A3
Convent Way	76	A1
Conway Ct		
off Macken St	91	C2
Conyngham Rd	88	A1
Cookstown Br	10	A2
Cookstown Est Rd	109	C2
Cookstown Ind Est	109	C3
Cookstown Rd	108	B2
Cookstown Sta	109	C3
Cookstown Way	109	C3
Cook St	144	A3
Coolamber Ct **2**	112	A3
Coolamber Pk	112	A3
Coolatree Cl	53	C2
Coolatree Pk	53	C2
Coolatree Rd	53	C2
Cooldrinagh La	69	C3
Cooldrinagh Ter	69	C2
Cooleen Av	53	C1
Coolevin	138	B2
Coolevin La		
off Long La	89	D3
Cooley Rd	99	D1
Coolgariff Rd	53	C2
Coolgreena Cl	53	C2
Coolgreena Rd	53	D2
Coolkill	129	D3
Coolmine Boul	46	A2
Coolmine Cl	46	B2
Coolmine Cotts	32	B3
Coolmine Ct	46	B2
Coolmine Grn	46	B3
Coolmine Ind Est	46	B2
Coolmine Lawn	46	B2
Coolmine Ms **1**	46	B2
Coolmine Pk	46	B2
Coolmine Rd	46	B3
Coolmine Sta	46	B3
Coolmine Wds	46	B2

Coolnevaun	130	B1
Coolock Dr	54	B1
Coolock Ind Est	55	C1
Coolock La	39	C3
Coolock Village	54	B2
Coolrua Dr	53	C1
Coombe, The	144	A4
Copeland Av	79	D1
Copeland Gro	79	D1
Cope St	145	D3
Copper All	144	B3
Coppice, The	73	C3
Coppinger Cl	117	C3
Coppinger Glade	117	C3
Coppinger Row	145	D4
Coppinger Wk	117	C3
Coppinger Wd	117	C3
Coppins, The *Celbr.*	66	B2
Coppins, The *Fox.*	136	B1
Corballis Row		
off Kevin St Upr	144	B4
Corbally Av	121	D2
Corbally Cl	121	D2
Corbally Downs	121	C2
Corbally Dr	121	D2
Corbally Glade	121	C2
Corbally Grn	121	C2
Corbally Heath	121	C2
Corbally Lawn	121	C2
Corbally Pk	121	D2
Corbally Ri	121	C2
Corbally Sq	121	D2
Corbally Vale	121	D2
Corbally Way	121	D2
Corbawn Av	141	D1
Corbawn Cl	141	D2
Corbawn Ct	141	D2
Corbawn Dale	141	D2
Corbawn Dr	141	D2
Corbawn Glade	141	D2
Corbawn Gro	141	D2
Corbawn La	141	C2
Corbawn Lawn	141	C2
Corbawn Wd	141	C2
Corcaill	26	B1
Corduff Av	33	D3
Corduff Cl	33	D3
Corduff Cotts	47	C1
Corduff Cres	33	D3
Corduff Gdns	33	D3
Corduff Grn	33	D3
Corduff Gro	33	C3
Corduff Pk	33	C3
Corduff Pl	33	D3
Corduff Way	33	D3
Corkagh Vw	96	A3
Cork Hill	144	C3
Cork St	89	C3
Cormac Ter	113	C1
Cornelscourt Hill Rd	137	C1
Corn Ex Pl		
off Burgh Quay	145	E2
Cornmarket	144	A3
Corporation St	145	E1
Corrib Rd	100	B3
Corrig Av	133	D1
Corrig Cl		
off Lugaquilla Av	110	B1
Corrig Pk	133	D1
Corrig Rd *Dalkey*	134	B2
Corrig Rd *D.L.*	133	D1
Corrig Rd *Still.*	130	A2
Corrybeg	112	A2
Cottage Pl		
off Portland Pl	78	A2
Coulson Av	101	D3
Coultry Av	38	B3
Coultry Cres	38	A3
Coultry Dr	38	A3
Coultry Gdns	38	A3
Coultry Gro	38	B3
Coultry Lawn	38	B3
Coultry Pk	38	B3
Coultry Rd	38	A3
Coultry Way	38	A3
Coundon Gro	138	B2
Court, The *Dublin 3*		
off Clontarf Rd	80	A2
Court, The *Dublin 5*	56	A4
Court, The *Dublin 6W*	112	A2
Court, The *Dublin 9*	53	C3
Court, The *Dublin 13*	58	A1

Court, The *Dublin 16*	128	B2
Court, The *Dublin 17*	39	D3
Court, The (Cookstown)		
Dublin 24	109	C2
Court, The (Kilnamanagh)		
Dublin 24	109	D1
Court, The *Carrick.*	136	B3
Court, The *Celbr.*	66	A2
Court, The (Dunboyne Castle)		
Dunb.	28	B3
Court, The (Lutterell Hall)		
Dunb.	28	B2
Court, The (Plunkett Hall)		
Dunb.	28	A1
Court, The (Sadleir Hall)		
Dunb.	28	B2
Court, The (Ballyowen)		
Lucan	83	D1
Court, The **7** *Mala.*	21	C3
Court, The *Mulh.*	32	A2
Court, The *Swords*	15	D3
Courthill Dr	28	B2
Court Ho Sq **3**	65	C2
Courtlands	138	A1
Courtyard, The		
Dublin 14	113	D2
Courtyard, The *Celbr.*	66	A3
Courtyard, The *Cool.*	46	A3
Courtyard, The **6** *Fox.*	131	D2
Courtyard, The **1** *Mala.*	21	C3
Courtyard Business Pk,		
The	94	B2
Cove, The **1**	19	D1
Cowbooter La	61	C2
Cowley Pl	78	A2
Cow Parlour	89	C3
Cowper Downs	102	A3
Cowper Dr	102	B3
Cowper Gdns	102	B3
Cowper Rd	102	A3
Cowper Sta	102	B3
Cowper St	77	C3
Cowper Village	102	A3
Crag Av	96	B1
Crag Av Business Pk	96	B1
Crag Av Ind Cen	96	B1
Crag Cres	85	C3
Crag Ter	96	B1
Craigford Av	54	A3
Craigford Dr	54	A3
Craiglands **4**	135	C2
Craigmore Gdns	118	A2
Crampton Bldgs		
off Temple Bar	144	C3
Crampton Ct	144	C3
Crampton Quay	145	D2
Crampton Rd	91	D3
Crane La	144	C3
Crane St	89	C2
Cranfield Pl	91	D3
Cranford Ct	104	A3
Cranmer La	91	C3
Crannagh	103	D3
Crannagh Castle	113	C2
Crannagh Ct	113	C2
Crannagh Gro	113	D2
Crannagh Pk	113	D2
Crannagh Rd	113	C2
Crannagh Way	113	D2
Crannogue Cl	37	D3
Crannogue Rd	37	D3
Crawford Av	78	A2
Creighton St	145	F3
Cremona Rd	86	A2
Cremore Av	51	D3
Cremore Cres	51	D3
Cremore Dr	51	D3
Cremore Hts		
off Ballygall Rd E	51	D2
Cremore Lawn	51	D3
Cremore Pk	51	D3
Cremore Rd	51	D3
Cremorne *Dublin 6*	101	D3
Cremorne *Dublin 16*	112	A3
Crescent, The *Dublin 3*	79	D2
Crescent, The (Donnybrook)		
Dublin 4	103	C2
Crescent, The (Beaumont)		
Dublin 9	53	C2
Crescent, The (Whitehall)		
Dublin 9	53	C3
Crescent, The *Dublin 13*	58	A1

Crescent, The (Ballinteer) **1**		
Dublin 16	128	B3
Crescent, The (Ballyboden)		
Dublin 16	126	A2
Crescent, The *Dublin 17*	39	D3
Crescent, The *Dublin 24*	124	A1
Crescent, The (Cookstown)		
Dublin 24	109	C2
Crescent, The (Kilnamanagh)		
Dublin 24	109	D1
Crescent, The *Carrick.*	136	B3
Crescent, The (Abbeyfarm)		
Celbr.	66	A3
Crescent, The (Oldtown Mill)		
Celbr.	66	A2
Crescent, The (St. Wolstan's		
Abbey) *Celbr.*	66	B3
Crescent, The *Clons.*	30	B3
Crescent, The		
(Dunboyne Castle)		
Dunb.	28	B3
Crescent, The (Lutterell Hall)		
Dunb.	28	B2
Crescent, The (Plunkett Hall)		
Dunb.	28	A1
Crescent, The *Gra M.*	82	B2
Crescent, The *Kins.*	18	A3
Crescent, The *Lucan*	69	D3
Crescent, The **5** *Mala.*	21	C3
Crescent, The **3** *Swords*	17	D1
Crescent, The (Seatown Pk)		
Swords	15	D3
Crescent Gdns	79	C3
Crescent Pl	79	D2
Crescent Vil	78	A1
Crestfield Av	52	B2
Crestfield Cl	52	B2
Crestfield Dr	52	B2
Crestfield Pk		
off Crestfield Cl	52	B2
Crestwood Av	10	B3
Crestwood Grn	10	B3
Crestwood Pk	10	B3
Crestwood Rd	10	B3
Crinan Strand	91	C1
Crinken Glen	140	B3
Crinken La	140	B3
Croaghpatrick Rd	76	A2
Crodaun Ct	66	A1
Croft, The	66	B1
Crofton Av	119	C3
Crofton Rd	119	C2
Crofton Ter	119	C2
Croftwood Cres	85	D3
Croftwood Dr	85	D3
Croftwood Gdns	85	D3
Croftwood Grn	86	A3
Croftwood Gro	85	D3
Croftwood Pk	86	A3
Croke Pk Ind Est	78	B3
Cromcastle Av	54	A1
Cromcastle Dr	54	A1
Cromcastle Grn	54	A1
Cromcastle Pk	54	A1
Cromcastle Rd	54	A1
Cromlech Ct	37	D3
Cromlech Flds	141	C1
Cromwells Fort Rd	99	C2
Cromwells Quarters	88	B2
Cross & Passion Coll	53	C3
Cross Av *Boot.*	117	C1
Cross Av *D.L.*	119	C3
Crossbeg Ind Est	98	A3
Cross Guns Br	77	D2
Cross Kevin St	90	A3
Crosslands Ind Est	98	A3
Cross La	65	C1
Crosstrees	61	C2
Crosthwaite Pk E	133	D1
Crosthwaite Pk S	133	D1
Crosthwaite Pk W	133	D1
Crosthwaite Ter	119	D3
Crotty Av	99	D2
Crown All		
off Temple Bar	144	C3
Crow St	144	C3

Name	Page	Grid
Croydon Gdns	79	C1
Croydon Grn	79	C2
Croydon Pk Av	79	C1
Croydon Ter	79	C1
Cruiserath Business Pk	33	D1
Crumlin Pk	100	A1
Crumlin Rd	100	A1
Crumlin Shop Cen	88	B3
Cuala Gro	142	B3
Cuala Rd *Dublin 7*	77	C2
Cuala Rd *Bray*	142	B3
Cuckoo La	144	B2
Cuffe La	90	A3
Cuffe St	90	A3
Cullenswood Gdns	102	B2
Cullenswood Pk	102	B2
Culmore Pk	85	D1
Culmore Rd	85	D1
Cul Na Greine	123	D1
Cumberland Rd	90	B3
Cumberland St	119	C2
Cumberland St N	78	A3
Cumberland St S	145	F4
Cunningham Dr	134	B3
Cunningham Rd	134	B2
Curlew Rd	99	D1
Curragh Av **3**	32	C1
Curragh Cres **1**	33	C1
Curragh Dr **2**	33	C1
Curragh Grn **1**	32	B1
Curragh Hall	32	B1
Curragh La **4**	32	B1
Curragh Ms **2**	32	B1
Curragh Rd **4**	33	C1
Curved St *off Eustace St*	144	C3
Curzon St	89	D3
Cushlawn Pk	123	C2
Custom Ho	145	E2
Custom Ho Quay	145	E2
Cymric Rd	92	A2
Cypress Av **3**	126	B2
Cypress Ct	138	B3
Cypress Downs	112	A2
Cypress Dr	112	A2
Cypress Garth	112	A2
Cypress Gro N	112	A2
Cypress Gro Rd	112	A2
Cypress Gro S	112	A2
Cypress Lawn	112	A2
Cypress Pk	112	A2
Cypress Rd	116	A2

D

Name	Page	Grid
Dakota Av	39	C2
Dalcassian Downs	77	D2
Dale, The (Cookstown) *Dublin 24*	109	C2
Dale, The (Kilnamanagh) *Dublin 24*	109	D1
Dale, The *Celbr.*	66	A3
Dale, The *Dunb.*	28	B1
Dale, The *Manor.*	31	C3
Dale Cl **1**	130	A1
Dale Dr	116	A3
Dalepark Rd	123	D2
Dale Rd	116	A3
Dales, The	136	B3
Dale Tree	125	D3
Dale Tree Av	125	C3
Dale Tree Cres	125	C2
Dale Tree Dr	125	C3
Dale Tree Gro	125	C3
Dale Tree Pk	125	C3
Dale Tree Rd	125	C3
Dale Tree Vw	125	C3
Dale Vw	138	B2
Dale Vw Pk **3**	138	B2
Dale Vw Rd	14	B3
Dalkey Av	134	B2
Dalkey Ct	134	B2
Dalkey Gro	134	B2
Dalkey Pk	134	B2
Dalkey Rock	134	B3
Dalkey Sound	135	C2
Dalkey Sta	134	B2
Dal Riada	21	C3

Name	Page	Grid
Damastown Av	31	D1
Damastown Cl	32	A2
Damastown Ct	32	A1
Damastown Grn	31	D2
Damastown Ind Pk	31	D1
Damastown Rd	31	D1
Damastown Wk	31	C1
Damastown Way	32	A2
Dame Ct	144	C3
Dame La	144	C3
Dame St	144	C3
Dane Rd	37	D3
Danes Ct	81	D2
Danesfort	80	B2
Daneswell Rd	78	A1
Dangan Av	100	A3
Dangan Dr	100	A3
Dangan Pk	100	A3
Danieli Dr	54	B3
Danieli Rd	54	B3
Daniel St	89	D3
Dara Ct	66	B2
Dara Cres	66	B2
Dargan Ct **13**	142	B2
Dargle Dr	127	D1
Dargle Lo **1**	126	A1
Dargle Rd *Dublin 9*	78	A2
Dargle Rd *Black.*	131	D1
Dargle Valley	127	D1
Dargle Vw	128	A1
Dargle Wd	126	A1
Darley Cotts **3**	142	A2
Darleys Ter	89	C3
Darley St	101	D1
Darling Est	75	D1
Dartmouth Ho Ind Est	86	B3
Dartmouth La	102	B1
Dartmouth Pl	102	A1
Dartmouth Rd	102	A1
Dartmouth Sq	102	B1
Dartmouth Ter	102	A1
Dartmouth Wk *off Dartmouth Ter*	102	A1
Dartry Cotts	114	A1
Dartry Pk	102	A3
Dartry Rd	102	A3
David Pk	77	D2
David Rd	78	A2
Davis Pl *off Thomas Davis St S*	144	B4
Davitt Pk	138	B2
Davitt Rd *Dublin 12*	88	A3
Davitt Rd *Bray*	142	A2
Dawson Ct *Dublin 2 off Stephen St*	144	C4
Dawson Ct *Black.*	117	C2
Dawson La	145	E4
Dawson St	145	D4
Deans Ct **1**	132	A2
Deansgrange Business Pk	132	A2
Dean's Gra Rd	132	A1
Deansrath Av	95	C1
Deansrath Cres	95	C1
Deansrath Gro	95	C1
Deansrath Lawn	95	D1
Deansrath Pk	95	C1
Deansrath Rd	95	C1
Deanstown Av	49	D2
Deanstown Dr	50	A2
Deanstown Grn	50	A2
Deanstown Pk	50	A2
Deanstown Rd	50	A2
Dean St	144	B4
Dean Swift Grn	51	D2
Dean Swift Rd	51	D2
Dean Swift Sq *off Francis St*	144	A4
De Burgh Rd	88	B1
Decies Rd	86	A2
De Courcy Sq	77	D1
Deerhaven	31	D3
Deerhaven Av	31	D3
Deerhaven Cl	31	D2
Deerhaven Cres	31	D3
Deerhaven Grn	31	D3
Deerhaven Pk	31	D2
Deerhaven Vw	31	D3
Deerhaven Wk	31	D3
Deerpark	11	C3
Deerpark Av *Dublin 15*	74	B1
Deerpark Av *Kilt.*	123	C3

Name	Page	Grid
Deerpark Cl *Dublin 15*	74	B1
Deerpark Cl *Kilt.*	123	C3
Deerpark Downs	123	C3
Deerpark Dr *Dublin 15*	74	B1
Deerpark Dr *Kilt.*	123	D3
Deerpark Grn **9**	123	D3
Deerpark Lawn	74	B1
Deerpark Pl	123	D3
Deerpark Ri	123	D3
Deerpark Rd *Dublin 15*	74	B1
Deerpark Rd *Kilt.*	123	D3
Deerpark Rd *Still.*	116	A2
Deerpark Sq	123	C3
Deerpark Ter **10**	123	D3
Deerpark Way	123	D3
Deey Br	67	D1
Delaford Av	125	D1
Delaford Dr	125	D1
Delaford Gro	125	D1
Delaford Lawn	125	D1
Delaford Pk	125	D1
Delbrook Manor	129	C2
Delbrook Pk	129	C2
Delgany Pk	143	C3
Delhurst Av	44	B1
Delhurst Ct	44	B1
Delhurst Ms	44	B1
Delhurst Ter	44	B1
Dell, The	128	A2
Del Val Av	57	C2
Del Val Ct	57	C2
Delville Rd	51	D2
Delvin Rd	77	C2
Delwood Cl	47	C3
Delwood Dr	47	C3
Delwood Gro	46	B3
Delwood Lawn	46	B3
Delwood Rd	47	C3
Delwood Wk	47	C3
Demesne	80	B1
Denmark St Gt	78	A3
Denville Ct	138	B2
Denzille La	145	F4
Denzille Pl *off Denzille La*	145	F4
Department of Defence (Infirmary Rd) *Dublin 7*	88	B1
Department of Defence (St. Mobhi Rd) *Dublin 9*	78	A1
Dermot O'Hurley Av	91	D2
Derravaragh Rd	100	B3
Derry Dr	100	A2
Derrynane Gdns	91	D2
Derrynane Par	78	A2
Derry Pk	100	A2
Derry Rd	100	A2
De Selby	122	A2
De Selby Cl	122	A2
De Selby Ct	122	A2
De Selby Cres	122	A2
De Selby Downs	122	A2
De Selby Grn	122	A2
De Selby La **2**	122	A2
De Selby Lawns	122	A2
De Selby Ri **1**	122	A2
De Selby Rd	122	A2
Desmond Av	119	C3
Desmond Cotts **4**	134	B3
Desmond St	89	D3
Devenish Rd	100	B2
Deverell Pl	145	E1
Deverys La	77	D2
De Vesci Ter	119	C3
Devitt Vil **11**	134	A1
Devon Cl **6**	132	B1
Devoy Rd	88	A3
Dewberry Pk	27	C1
Digges La *off Stephen St*	144	C4
Digges St	90	A3
Digges St Lwr *off Cuffe La*	90	A3
Dillon's Row	65	C1
Dingle, The	73	C3
Dingle Rd	76	B2
Dispensary La *Dublin 14*	113	C3

Name	Page	Grid
Dispensary La **1** *Lucan*	70	A3
Distillery La	68	B1
Distillery Rd	78	B2
Distributor Rd	36	B3
Diswellstown Rd	46	A3
Dixon Vil **12**	134	A1
Docklands Innovation Pk	79	D3
Dock Pl S *off Dock St S*	91	D2
Dock St S	91	C2
Doctor's La	65	C2
Dodder Av	124	B2
Dodderbank	102	B3
Dodder Ct	124	B2
Dodder Cres	124	B2
Dodder Dale	113	C2
Dodder Grn	124	B2
Dodder Lawn	124	B2
Dodder Pk Dr	113	D1
Dodder Pk Gro	113	D1
Dodder Pk Rd	113	C1
Dodder Ter	91	D2
Dodder Vw Rd	113	C2
D'Olier St	145	D2
Dollymount Av	81	D2
Dollymount Gro	81	C2
Dollymount Pk	81	D2
Dollymount Ri	81	D2
Dolmen Ct	37	D3
Dolphin Av	89	C3
Dolphin Mkt *off Dolphin's Barn St*	89	C3
Dolphin Rd	88	B3
Dolphin's Barn	89	C3
Dolphin's Barn St	89	C3
Dominican Conv	76	A1
Dominick La	144	C1
Dominick Pl	144	C1
Dominick St	119	C3
Dominick St Lwr	144	C1
Dominick St Upr	77	D3
Domville Dr	112	A2
Domville Gro **2**	139	C3
Domville Rd	112	A2
Donabate Sta	13	C2
Donaghmede Av	56	B1
Donaghmede Dr	56	B1
Donaghmede Pk	56	B1
Donaghmede Rd	56	A1
Donaghmede Shop Cen	56	A1
Donard Rd	99	D1
Donelan Av	88	B2
Donnybrook Castle Ct	103	D3
Donnybrook Cl	103	D3
Donnybrook Grn	103	D3
Donnybrook Manor	103	C2
Donnybrook Rd	103	C2
Donnycarney Rd	53	D3
Donnycastle	103	D2
Donomore Av	122	B2
Donomore Cres	123	C2
Donomore Grn	122	B2
Donomore Pk	123	C2
Donore Av	89	C3
Donore Rd	89	C3
Donore Ter *off Brown St S*	89	C3
Donovan La *off Clanbrassil St Lwr*	89	D3
Doonamana Rd	138	A1
Doonanore Pk	138	A1
Doon Av	77	C3
Doon Ct	37	D3
Doonsalla Dr	138	A1
Doonsalla Pk	138	A1
Doris St	91	C2
Dornden Rd	104	B3
Dorney Ct	141	C2
Dorset La	78	A3
Dorset Pl *off Dorset St Lwr*	78	A3
Dorset St Lwr	78	A3
Dorset St Upr	78	A3
Double La	65	C1
Dowkers La	89	C3
Dowland Rd	99	D2
Dowling's Ct *off Lombard St E*	145	F2
Dowling's Ct S *off Lombard St E*	145	F2
Downpatrick Rd	100	B1

Name	Page	Grid
Downs, The *Celbr.*	66	B3
Downs, The *Dunb.*	28	A3
Dowth Av	77	C2
Doyle's La	81	D2
Drapier Grn	51	D2
Drapier Rd	51	D2
Drayton Cl	118	B3
Drimnagh Castle	99	C1
Drimnagh Rd	99	D1
Drimnagh Sta	87	D3
Drinagh Av	136	A2
Drinagh More Av	136	A2
Drinagh More Cl **2**	136	A2
Drinagh More Ct **3**	136	A2
Drive, The (Ballinteer) *Dublin 16*	128	B2
Drive, The (Ballyboden) *Dublin 16*	126	B1
Drive, The *Dublin 24*	124	A1
Drive, The (Castletown) *Celbr.*	66	B2
Drive, The (Oldtown Mill) *Celbr.*	66	A2
Drive, The (Lutterell Hall) *Dunb.*	28	B1
Drive, The (Sadlier Hall) *Dunb.*	28	A1
Drive, The *Gra M.*	82	B2
Drive, The *Kins.*	18	A2
Drive, The *Manor.*	31	C3
Drive, The *Mulh.*	32	A2
Drive, The *Swords*	15	D3
Droim Na Coille Ct **4**	83	D1
Dromard Rd	99	D1
Dromawling Rd	53	D2
Dromcarra Av	122	B1
Dromcarra Dr	122	B1
Dromcarra Grn	122	B1
Dromcarra Gro	122	B2
Dromdawn Av	53	C2
Dromeen Av	53	D2
Dromheath Av	32	B2
Dromheath Dr	32	B2
Dromheath Gdns	32	B2
Dromheath Gro	32	B2
Dromheath Pk	32	B2
Dromlee Cres	53	D2
Dromnanane Pk	53	D2
Dromnanane Rd	53	D2
Dromore Rd	100	A1
Druid Ct	37	D3
Druid Valley	138	A3
Drumahill	129	D1
Drumalee Av	77	C3
Drumalee Ct off Drumalee Rd	77	C3
Drumalee Dr off Drumalee Rd	77	C3
Drumalee Gro off Drumalee Rd	77	C3
Drumalee Pk	77	C3
Drumalee Rd	77	C3
Drumcairn Av	108	B3
Drumcairn Dr	108	B3
Drumcairn Gdns	108	B3
Drumcairn Pk	108	B3
Drumcliffe Dr	76	B2
Drumcliffe Rd	76	B2
Drumcondra Pk	78	B2
Drumcondra Rd Lwr	78	A2
Drumcondra Rd Upr	78	B1
Drumcondra Sta	78	B2
Drumfinn Av	85	D1
Drumfinn Pk	86	B1
Drumfinn Rd (Bothar Drom Finn)	86	A2
Drumkeen Manor	133	C3
Drummartin Cl	115	D3
Drummartin Cres **1**	115	D3
Drummartin Link Rd, The *Dublin 14*	129	D1
Drummartin Link Rd, The *Dublin 16*	129	D1
Drummartin Pk	129	D1
Drummartin Rd	115	D3
Drummartin Ter	115	D3
Drummond Pl off Mount Drummond Av	101	D1
Drumnigh Rd	42	B1
Drumnigh Wd	42	B1
Druncondra Br	78	B1
Drury St	144	C4
Drynam Cl **1**	18	A3
Drynam Ct	17	D2
Drynam Cres	18	A3
Drynam Dr	18	A3
Drynam Glen **3**	18	B3
Drynam Grn **4**	18	B3
Drynam Gro	18	A3
Drynam Pl	18	A3
Drynam Ri	18	A3
Drynam Rd	17	D1
Drynam Sq	18	A3
Drynam Vw **2**	18	B3
Drynam Wk **2**	18	A3
Drynam Way **3**	18	A3
Drysdale Cl	124	A2
Dubber Cross	36	B2
Dublin City Uni	52	A2
Dublin Corporation Food Mkt off St. Michan's St	144	B2
Dublin Ind Est	51	C3
Dublin Port Tunnel	79	D3
Dublin Rd *Dublin 13*	57	C2
Dublin Rd *Ashb.*	11	C3
Dublin Rd *Celbr.*	66	B3
Dublin Rd *Dunb.*	29	C3
Dublin Rd *Mala.*	19	C3
Dublin Rd *Mayn.*	65	D2
Dublin Rd *Shank.*	140	B1
Dublin St *Dublin 13*	43	D3
Dublin St *Swords*	17	C1
Dublin Zoo	76	A3
Dufferin Av	89	D3
Duggan Pl off Rathmines Rd Upr	102	A2
Duke La	145	D4
Duke La Lwr off Duke St	145	D3
Duke Row off Summerhill	78	B3
Duke St	145	D4
Dun Aengusa	123	C3
Dunamase	117	C1
Dún An Óir	123	D1
Dunard Av	76	B3
Dunard Ct	76	B2
Dunard Dr	76	B2
Dunard Pk	76	B3
Dunard Rd	76	B3
Dunard Wk	76	B3
Dunawley Av	96	A1
Dunawley Dr	96	A1
Dunawley Gro	96	A1
Dunawley Way	96	A1
Dunbo Ter off Church St	60	B2
Dunboy	136	B2
Dunboyne Business Pk	28	B1
Dunboyne Castle	28	B3
Dunbur Ter **8**	142	A1
Duncairn Av	142	A1
Duncairn Ter	142	A1
Duncarrig	59	C2
Dundaniel Rd	53	D1
Dundela Av	134	A1
Dundela Cres	134	A1
Dundela Haven	134	A1
Dundela Pk	134	A1
Dundrum Business Pk	115	C1
Dundrum Bypass	129	C1
Dundrum Castle	128	B1
Dundrum Gate Apts **4**	128	B1
Dundrum Rd	114	B1
Dundrum Shop Cen	114	B3
Dundrum Sta	115	C3
Dundrum Town Cen	129	C1
Dundrum Wd	128	B1
Dunedin Ct **7**	132	B1
Dunedin Dr **8**	132	B1
Dunedin Pk	132	B1
Dunedin Ter	132	B1
Dun Emer Dr	129	C1
Dun Emer Pk	129	C1
Dun Emer Rd	129	C1
Dunes, The	27	C3
Dungar Ter off Northumberland Av	119	D3
Dungriffan Rd	61	C3
Dun Laoghaire Ind Est	132	B2
Dun Laoghaire Sta	119	D2
Dunleary Hill	119	C3
Dunleary Rd	119	C2
Dunluce Rd	80	B1
Dunmanus Rd	76	B2
Dunmore Gro	109	D1
Dunmore Lawn	109	D1
Dunmore Pk	109	D1
Dunne St	78	B3
Dunree Pk	55	C1
Dunsandle Ct	74	A1
Dunsandle Gro	74	A1
Dunseverick Rd	80	B1
Dunsink Av	50	A2
Dunsink Dr	50	A2
Dunsink Gdns	50	B2
Dunsink Grn	50	A2
Dunsink La	49	C2
Dunsink Observatory	49	C2
Dunsink Pk	50	A2
Dunsink Rd	50	B2
Dunsoghly Av	49	D1
Dunsoghly Cl	49	D1
Dunsoghly Ct	49	D1
Dunsoghly Dr	49	D1
Dunsoghly Grn	49	D1
Dunsoghly Gro	49	D1
Dunsoghly Pk	49	D1
Dunstaffnage Hall Apts **2**	131	C1
Dunville Av	102	A2
Dunville Ter off Mountpleasant Av Upr	102	A1
Durham Pl **8**	133	D1
Durham Rd	104	A1
Durrow Rd	100	B2
Dursey Row	47	D1
Dwyer Pk	142	A1

E

Name	Page	Grid
Eagle Hill	117	D2
Eagle Hill Av	101	C3
Eagle Pk	54	A1
Eagle Ter **2**	115	C3
Eaglewood **1**	133	C3
Earl Pl	145	D1
Earls Ct	76	B2
Earlscourt Ind Est	114	A3
Earlsfort Av	83	D2
Earlsfort Cl	83	D2
Earlsfort Ct	83	D1
Earlsfort Dr	83	D2
Earlsfort Gdns	83	D1
Earlsfort Gro	83	D2
Earlsfort La	83	D2
Earlsfort Lawn	83	D1
Earlsfort Mans off Adelaide Rd	90	A3
Earlsfort Meadows	83	D1
Earlsfort Pk	83	D1
Earlsfort Ri	83	D2
Earlsfort Rd	83	D2
Earlsfort Ter	90	A3
Earlsfort Vale	83	D2
Earlsfort Vw	83	D2
Earlsfort Way	83	D2
Earl St N	145	D1
Earl St S	144	A4
Eastern Breakwater	92	B2
East Link	91	D2
Eastmoreland La	91	C3
Eastmoreland Pl	91	C3
East Oil Jetty	92	B2
East Pt Business Pk	79	D3
East Rd	91	D1
East Rd Ind Est	91	D1
East Wall Rd	79	C2
Eastwood Cl	49	D2
Eastwood Cres	49	D2
Eastwood Pk	49	D2
Eaton Brae *Dublin 14*	114	A1
Eaton Brae *Shank.*	141	C2
Eaton Ct	142	B3
Eaton Pl	118	A2
Eaton Rd	101	C3
Eaton Sq *Dublin 6W*	101	C3
Eaton Sq *Black.*	118	A2
Eaton Wd Av	141	C2
Eaton Wd Ct	141	C2
Eaton Wd Grn	141	C2
Eaton Wd Gro	141	C2
Ebenezer Ter	89	C3
Eblana Av	119	D3
Eblana Vil off Grand Canal St Lwr	91	C2
Eccles Ct off Eccles Pl	78	A3
Eccles Pl	78	A3
Eccles St	78	A3
Echlin St	89	C2
Eden Av	127	D1
Edenbrook Ct **1**	113	C3
Edenbrook Dr	112	B3
Edenbrook Pk	112	B3
Eden Ct	127	D1
Eden Cres	127	D1
Eden Gro *Dublin 16*	127	D1
Eden Gro *D'bate*	13	C1
Edenmore Av	55	C2
Edenmore Cres	55	D2
Edenmore Dr	55	D2
Edenmore Gdns	55	D2
Edenmore Grn	55	D2
Edenmore Gro	55	D2
Edenmore Pk	55	C2
Eden Pk	133	C1
Eden Pk Av	129	D1
Eden Pk Dr	115	D3
Eden Pk Rd	115	D3
Eden Quay	145	D2
Eden Rd	143	D1
Eden Rd Lwr	133	D1
Eden Rd Upr	133	D1
Eden Shop Cen	127	D1
Eden Ter	133	D1
Edenvale Rd	102	B2
Eden Vil **3**	133	D1
Edgewood Lawns	33	C3
Edmondstown Ct **1**	71	C3
Edmondstown Grn	126	B2
Edmondstown Pk	126	B2
Edmondstown Rd	126	B3
Edward Rd	142	B2
Edwards Ct	126	B2
Edwin Ct **5**	134	A2
Effra Rd	101	D2
Eglantine Rd	142	A1
Eglinton Ct	103	C2
Eglinton Pk *Dublin 4*	103	C2
Eglinton Pk *D.L.*	133	C1
Eglinton Rd	103	C2
Eglinton Sq	103	C2
Eglinton Ter *Dublin 4*	103	C2
Eglinton Ter *Dublin 14*	115	C3
Eglinton Wd	103	C2
Elderberry	82	A2
Elderwood Rd	73	C3
Eldon Ter off South Circular Rd	89	C3
Elgin Rd	103	C1
Elizabeth St	78	B2
Elkwood	112	A3
Ellenfield Rd	53	C2
Ellensborough	123	D3
Ellensborough Av	123	D3
Ellensborough Cl	123	D3
Ellensborough Copse	123	D3
Ellensborough Ct	123	D3
Ellensborough Cres	123	D3
Ellensborough Dale	123	D3
Ellensborough Downs	123	D3
Ellensborough Gra	123	D3
Ellensborough Grn	123	D3
Ellensborough Gro	123	D3
Ellensborough La	123	D3
Ellensborough Lo	123	D3
Ellensborough Meadows	123	D3
Ellensborough Pk	123	D3
Ellensborough Ri	123	D3
Ellensborough Vw	123	D3
Ellensborough Wk	123	D3
Ellesmere **1**	130	B2
Ellesmere Av	77	C3
Ellis Quay	89	C1
Ellis St off Benburb St	89	C1
Elmbrook	83	C1

Elmbrook Cres	83	C1
Elmbrook Lawn	83	C1
Elmbrook Wk	83	C1
Elmcastle Cl	110	A2
Elmcastle Ct	110	A2
Elmcastle Dr	110	A2
Elmcastle Grn	110	A2
Elmcastle Pk	110	A2
Elmcastle Wk	110	A2
Elm Cl	83	C2
Elm Ct *Jobs.*	122	A2
Elm Ct *Lucan*	83	C2
Elmdale Cl	85	D2
Elmdale Cres	85	D2
Elmdale Dr	85	D2
Elmdale Pk	85	C2
Elm Dene	83	C2
Elm Dr *Jobs.*	122	A2
Elm Dr *Lucan*	83	C2
Elmfield Av	42	A3
Elmfield Cl **5**	42	A3
Elmfield Ct **4**	42	A3
Elmfield Cres **1**	42	A3
Elmfield Dr **2**	42	A3
Elmfield Grn	42	A3
Elmfield Ind Est	96	B1
Elmfield Lawn	42	A3
Elmfield Pk		
off *Elmfield Av*	42	A3
Elmfield Ri	42	A3
Elmfield Vale **3**	42	A3
Elmfield Wk	42	A3
Elmfield Way	42	A3
Elm Grn	82	B2
Elmgrove *B'brack*	138	B2
Elm Gro *Black.*	117	D3
Elm Gro *Jobs.*	122	A2
Elm Gro *Lucan*	83	C2
Elm Gro Cotts		
off *Blackhorse Av*	76	A2
Elmgrove Ter **9**	142	A1
Elm Mt Av	53	D3
Elm Mt Cl	53	D3
Elm Mt Ct	54	A3
Elm Mt Cres	53	D2
Elm Mt Dr	53	D3
Elm Mt Gro	53	D2
Elm Mt Hts	53	D2
Elm Mt Lawn	53	D2
Elm Mt Pk	53	D2
Elm Mt Ri	53	D2
Elm Mt Rd	53	D3
Elm Mt Vw	53	D2
Elm Pk *Dublin 4*	104	A2
Elm Pk *Celbr.*	66	B2
Elmpark Av	102	B1
Elmpark Ter	101	C3
Elm Rd *Dublin 9*	53	D3
Elm Rd *Dublin 12*	98	A2
Elms, The *Dublin 4*	104	A3
Elms, The **14** *Abb.*	139	C3
Elms, The *Black.*	117	C2
Elms, The *Celbr.*	66	B1
Elms, The *Dunb.*	29	C2
Elms, The *Shank.*	141	C3
Elm Vale	83	C2
Elm Way *Dublin 16*	128	A2
Elm Way *Lucan*	83	C2
Elm Wd	83	C2
Elmwood Av Lwr		
off *Elmwood Av Upr*	102	B1
Elmwood Av Upr	102	B2
Elmwood Cl	45	C1
Elmwood Ct	14	B3
Elmwood Dr	14	B3
Elmwood Pk	14	B3
Elmwood Rd	14	B3
Elner Ct	27	C1
Elton Ct *Dublin 13*		
off *Clonrosse Dr*	55	D1
Elton Ct *Dunb.*	29	C2
Elton Ct *D.L.*	134	B1
Elton Ct *Leix.*	68	A2
Elton Dr *Dublin 13*	55	D1
Elton Dr *Dunb.*	29	C2
Elton Gro	29	C2
Elton Pk *Dublin 13*	55	D1
Elton Pk *D.L.*	134	A1
Elton Wk		
off *Clonrosse Dr*	55	D1
Ely Cres	124	B3
Ely Dr	124	B3
Ely Grn **1**	124	B3
Ely Gro	124	B3
Ely Manor	124	B3
Ely Pl	90	B3
Ely Pl Upr *off Ely Pl*	90	B3
Ely Vw	124	B3
Embassy Lawn	115	C1
Emerald Cotts	91	C3
Emerald Pl		
off *Sheriff St Lwr*	91	C1
Emerald Sq	89	C3
Emerald St	91	C1
Emily Pl		
off *Sheriff St Lwr*	145	F1
Emmet Ct	87	D3
Emmet Rd	87	D2
Emmet Sq	117	C1
Emmet St *Dublin 1*	78	B3
Emmet St (Haroldscross)		
Dublin 6	101	D1
Emmet St **1** *Sally.*	133	D2
Emor St	89	D3
Emorville Av	89	D3
Emorville Sq		
off *South Circular Rd*	89	C3
Empress Pl	78	B3
Enaville Rd	79	C2
Engine All	144	A4
English Row	66	B3
Ennafort Av		
(Ascal Dun Eanna)	55	C3
Ennafort Ct	55	C3
Ennafort Dr		
(Ceide Dun Eanna)	55	C3
Ennafort Gro	55	C3
Ennafort Pk	55	C3
Ennafort Rd	55	C3
Ennel Av	55	C2
Ennel Ct **3**	139	C3
Ennel Dr	55	C2
Ennel Pk	55	C2
Ennis Gro	91	D3
Enniskerry Rd	77	D2
Erne Pl	91	C2
Erne Pl Little	145	F3
Erne St Lwr	91	C2
Erne St Upr	91	C2
Erne Ter Front		
off *Erne St Upr*	91	C2
Erne Ter Rere		
off *Erne St Upr*	91	C2
Errigal Gdns	99	D1
Errigal Rd	99	D1
Erris Rd	77	C2
Erskine Av	143	D2
Esker Dr	82	A1
Esker La (north) *Lucan*	71	C3
Esker La (south) *Lucan*	83	C1
Esker Lawns	70	B3
Esker Lo	83	C1
Esker Lo Av	83	C1
Esker Lo Cl	83	C1
Esker Lo Vw	83	C1
Esker Manor	82	B1
Esker Meadow	83	C1
Esker Meadow Cl	83	C1
Esker Meadow Ct	83	C1
Esker Meadow Grn	83	C1
Esker Meadow Gro	83	C1
Esker Meadow Lawn	83	C1
Esker Meadow Ri	83	C1
Esker Meadow Vw	83	C1
Esker Pk	83	C1
Esker Pines	71	C3
Esker Rd	82	B1
Esker S	82	B2
Esker Wds Ct	83	C1
Esker Wds Dr	83	C1
Esker Wds Gro	83	C1
Esker Wds Ri	83	C1
Esker Wds Vw	83	C1
Esker Wds Wk	83	C1
Esmond Av	79	C2
Esplanade Ter **14**	142	B2
Esposito Rd	99	D2
Essex Quay	144	B3
Essex St E	144	C3
Essex St W	144	B3
Estate Av	104	B3
Estate Cotts	91	C3
Estuary Business Pk	15	D2
Estuary Ct	15	D3
Estuary Rd	19	C2
Estuary Rbt	15	D3
Estuary Row	20	A1
Estuary Wk	19	C2
Eugene St	89	C3
Eustace St	144	C3
Everton Av	77	C3
Evora Cres	60	B2
Evora Pk	60	B2
Evora Ter		
off *St. Lawrence Rd*	60	B2
Ewington La	89	C2
Excalibur Dr	143	D1
Exchange Ct		
off *Dame St*	144	C3
Exchange St Lwr	144	B3
Exchange St Upr		
off *Lord Edward St*	144	C3
Exchequer St	144	C3

F

Faber Gro **3**	132	B1
Fade St	144	C4
Fagan's La **1**	65	C2
Fairbrook Lawn	113	C3
Fairfield Av	79	C3
Fairfield Pk	101	D3
Fairfield Rd (Glasnevin)	78	A1
Fairgreen	120	B2
Fairgreen Ct **10**	142	A1
Fairgreen Ter **11**	142	A1
Fair Haven **1**	20	A2
Fairlawn Pk		
off *Fairlawn Rd*	50	B2
Fairlawn Rd	50	B2
Fairlawns	134	A2
Fairview	79	C2
Fairview Av (Irishtown)	91	D2
Fairview Av Lwr	79	C2
Fairview Av Upr	79	C2
Fairview Grn	79	C2
Fairview Lawn	138	A3
Fairview Pas		
off *Fairview Strand*	79	C2
Fairview Strand	79	C2
Fairview Ter	79	C2
Fairways *Dublin 14*	112	B2
Fairways *D'bate*	13	C2
Fairways, The *Port.*	26	A3
Fairways Av	51	C2
Fairways Grn	51	C2
Fairways Gro	51	C2
Fairways Pk	51	C2
Fairy Hill	131	D1
Faith Av	79	C3
Falcarragh Rd	52	B2
Falls Rd	140	B1
Farmhill Dr	115	C2
Farmhill Pk	115	D3
Farmhill Rd	115	C2
Farmleigh Av *Dublin 15*	74	A1
Farmleigh Av *Black.*	131	C1
Farmleigh Cl *Dublin 15*	74	A1
Farmleigh Cl *Black.*	131	C1
Farmleigh Ct	74	A1
Farmleigh Pk *Dublin 15*	74	A1
Farmleigh Pk *Black.*	131	C1
Farmleigh Vw	74	A1
Farmleigh Wds	74	A1
Farney Pk	92	A3
Farnham Cres	50	B2
Farnham Dr	50	B2
Farrenboley Cotts	114	B1
Farrenboley Pk	114	B1
Father Colohan Ter **4**	142	A2
Father Kitt Ct	100	A2
Father Matthew Br	144	A3
Fatima Mans	88	B3
Fatima Sta	89	C3
Fatima Ter	142	A1
Faughart Rd	100	B2
Faussagh Av	76	B1
Faussagh Rd	77	C2
Feltrim Ind Pk	18	A2
Feltrim Rd	18	B3
Fenian St	145	F4
Ferguson Rd	78	A1
Fergus Rd	113	C1
Ferncourt Av	124	B3
Ferncourt Cl	124	B3
Ferncourt Cres **2**	124	B3
Ferncourt Dr **3**	124	B3
Ferncourt Grn	124	B3
Ferncourt Pk	124	B3
Ferncourt Vw	124	B3
Ferndale *Dublin 24*	123	C1
Ferndale *Manor.*	31	D3
Ferndale Av	51	C2
Ferndale Glen	140	B3
Ferndale Hill	140	B3
Ferndale Rd *Dublin 11*	51	C2
Ferndale Rd *Shank.*	140	B3
Fernhill Av	111	D1
Fernhill Pk	111	D1
Fernhill Rd	111	D1
Fernleigh	72	A1
Fernleigh Cl	46	A3
Fernleigh Ct	72	A1
Fernleigh Dale	72	A1
Fernleigh Dr	46	A3
Fernleigh Grn	72	A1
Fernleigh Gro	72	A1
Fernleigh Pk	72	A1
Fernleigh Pl **3**	72	A1
Fernleigh Vw	72	A1
Ferns Rd	100	B2
Fernvale Dr	99	D1
Fernwood Av	109	C3
Fernwood Cl	123	C1
Fernwood Ct	109	C3
Fernwood Lawn	109	C3
Fernwood Pk	109	C3
Fernwood Way	123	C1
Ferrard Rd	101	D3
Ferrycarrig Av	40	B3
Ferrycarrig Dr	40	B3
Ferrycarrig Grn **2**	40	B3
Ferrycarrig Pk	40	B3
Ferrycarrig Rd	40	B3
Ferrymans Crossing	91	C1
Fertullagh Rd	77	C2
Fettercairn Rd	108	B3
Fey Yerra **1**	131	C2
Fforester	83	C1
Fforester Cl	83	C1
Fforester Ct	83	C1
Fforester Lawn	83	C1
Fforester Pk	83	C1
Fforester Wk	83	C1
Fforester Way	83	C1
Field Av	99	D2
Fields Ter		
off *Ranelagh Rd*	102	B1
Finches Ind Pk	99	C1
Findlater Pl		
off *Marlborough St*	145	D1
Findlaters St	88	B1
Findlater St **14**	134	A1
Fingal Pl	77	C3
Fingal St	89	C3
Finglas Business Cen	36	B3
Finglas Business Pk	51	C1
Finglas Pk	51	C1
Finglas Pl	50	B2
Finglas Rd	51	C3
Finglas Rd Old	51	D3
Finglas Shop Cen	50	B1
Finglaswood Rd	50	A1
Finlay Sq	116	A2
Finneber Fort	50	B2
Finneber Fort Sq **1**	50	B2
Finnscourt	82	A3
Finnsgreen	82	A2
Finnsgrove	82	A2
Finnslawn	82	A3
Finnspark	82	A3
Finnstown Fairways	82	A2
Finn St	77	C3
Finnsvale	82	A2
Finnsview	82	A2
Finnswood	82	A3
Finsbury Grn	114	B3
Finsbury Pk	114	B3
Firgrove **1**	140	B3
Firhouse Rd *Dublin 16*	111	D3
Firhouse Rd *Dublin 24*	111	D3
Firhouse Rd W	123	D1

Name	Page	Grid
First Av *Dublin 1*	91	C1
First Av (Inchicore) *Dublin 10*	87	C2
First Av *Dublin 24*	109	C2
Fishamble St	144	B3
Fitzgerald Pk **2**	133	C1
Fitzgibbon St	101	D1
Fitzgibbon La	78	B3
Fitzgibbon St	78	B3
Fitzmaurice Rd *Dublin 11*	51	D2
Fitzmaurice Rd *R'coole*	120	A1
Fitzroy Av	78	A2
Fitzwilliam Ct *off Pembroke St Upr*	90	B3
Fitzwilliam La	90	B3
Fitzwilliam Pl	90	B3
Fitzwilliam Quay	91	D2
Fitzwilliam Sq E	90	B3
Fitzwilliam Sq N	90	B3
Fitzwilliam Sq S	90	B3
Fitzwilliam Sq W	90	B3
Fitzwilliam St (Ringsend)	91	D2
Fitzwilliam St Lwr	90	B3
Fitzwilliam St Upr	90	B3
Fleet St	145	D3
Fleming Pl	90	B3
Fleming Rd	78	A1
Flemings La *off Haddington Rd*	91	C3
Flemingstown Pk	114	B2
Fleurville	117	D3
Floraville Av	96	B2
Floraville Dr	97	C3
Floraville Est	96	B2
Floraville Lawn	97	C2
Florence Rd	142	A1
Florence St *off Lennox St*	102	A1
Florence Ter **2**	142	B1
Florence Vil **12**	142	A1
Flower Gro	133	D3
Foley St	145	E1
Fontenoy St	77	D3
Fontenoy Ter	142	B2
Fonthill Abbey **2**	113	C3
Fonthill Ct **3**	113	C3
Fonthill Pk	113	C3
Fonthill Retail Pk	84	A1
Fonthill Rd *Dublin 14*	113	C3
Fonthill Rd *Clond.*	84	A1
Fonthill Rd S	96	B3
Forbes La	89	C2
Forbes St	91	C2
Forest Av *Dublin 24*	110	A1
Forest Av *Swords*	16	B2
Forest Boul	16	A2
Forest Cl	110	A1
Forest Ct	16	A2
Forest Cres	16	B2
Forest Dale	16	B2
Forest Dr *Dublin 24*	110	A1
Forest Dr *Swords*	16	B2
Forest Flds Rd	16	B2
Forest Grn *Dublin 24*	110	A1
Forest Grn *Swords*	16	B2
Forest Gro	16	A2
Forest Lawn	110	A1
Forest Pk *Leix.*	68	A2
Forest Pk *Dublin 24*	110	A1
Forest Pk *Swords*	16	B2
Forest Rd	16	A3
Forest Vw **1**	16	B2
Forest Wk	16	B2
Forest Way **2**	16	B2
Forestwood Av	38	A3
Forestwood Cl	38	B3
Fortfield Av	112	B1
Fortfield Ct	112	B1
Fortfield Dr	112	B2
Fortfield Gdns	102	A3
Fortfield Gro	112	B1
Fortfield Pk	112	B2
Fortfield Rd	112	B1
Fortfield Sq	112	B1
Fortfield Ter	102	A3
Forth Rd	79	D3
Fortlawn	46	A1
Fortlawn Av	46	A1
Fortlawn Dr	46	A1
Fortlawn Pk	46	A1
Fortlawns	134	A3
Fortrose Pk	112	A2
Fortunestown Cl	121	D1
Fortunestown Cres	121	D1
Fortunestown Lawns	121	C1
Fortunestown Rd	122	A2
Fortunestown Wk	121	C1
Fortview Av	81	C3
Fosterbrook	116	B1
Foster Cotts *off Phibsborough Rd*	77	D3
Foster Pl S	145	D3
Fosters, The	116	A2
Fosters Av	116	A2
Foster Ter	78	B3
Fountain Pl	89	C1
Fountain Rd	88	B1
Four Cts (Courts of Justice)	144	B2
Four Cts Sta	144	B2
Fourth Av *Dublin 1*	91	C1
Fourth Av *Dublin 24*	109	C3
Fownes St	145	D3
Foxborough Av	83	C2
Foxborough Cl	83	D2
Foxborough Ct	83	C3
Foxborough Cres **1**	83	C2
Foxborough Downes	83	C2
Foxborough Dr	83	C2
Foxborough Gdns	83	D2
Foxborough Glen	83	D2
Foxborough Grn	83	D2
Foxborough Gro	83	D2
Foxborough Hts	83	D2
Foxborough Hill	83	C2
Foxborough La	83	C2
Foxborough Lawn	83	D3
Foxborough Meadows	83	C2
Foxborough Pk	83	C2
Foxborough Pl	83	C2
Foxborough Ri	83	C2
Foxborough Rd	83	C3
Foxborough Row	83	D2
Foxborough Wk	83	D2
Foxborough Way	83	C3
Foxdene Av	83	D3
Foxdene Dr	84	A3
Foxdene Gdns	84	A3
Foxdene Grn	83	D2
Foxdene Gro	84	A3
Foxdene Pk	84	A3
Foxes Gro	141	C2
Foxfield	82	A2
Foxfield Av	56	A2
Foxfield Cres	56	B2
Foxfield Dr	56	B2
Foxfield Grn	56	B2
Foxfield Gro	56	B2
Foxfield Hts	56	A2
Foxfield Lawn	56	B2
Foxfield Pk	56	B2
Foxfield Rd	56	B2
Foxfield St. John	56	B2
Foxford	83	D1
Foxhill Av	55	D1
Foxhill Cl	55	D1
Foxhill Ct	55	D1
Foxhill Cres	55	D1
Foxhill Dr	55	D1
Foxhill Grn	41	D3
Foxhill Gro	41	D3
Foxhill Lawn	55	D1
Foxhill Pk	55	D1
Foxhill Way	55	D1
Foxpark	82	A2
Foxrock Av	131	D2
Foxrock Cl	132	A2
Foxrock Ct	131	D2
Foxrock Cres	132	A2
Foxrock Grn	132	A2
Foxrock Gro	132	A2
Foxrock Manor	131	C2
Foxrock Mt **1**	131	D2
Foxrock Pk	131	D2
Foxrock Wd	132	A2
Foxs La	56	B3
Foxwood *Lucan*	82	A2
Foxwood *Swords*	17	D1
Foyle Rd	79	C2
Francis St	144	A3
Frankfort	114	B2
Frankfort Av	101	D2
Frankfort Ct	101	D3
Frankfort Pk	114	B2
Frascati Pk	117	D2
Frascati Rd	117	D2
Frascati Shop Cen	117	D2
Frederick Ct *off Hardwicke St*	78	A3
Frederick La	145	E4
Frederick La N	78	A3
Frederick St	10	B2
Frederick St N	78	A3
Frederick St S	145	E4
Frenchmans La *off Gardiner St Lwr*	145	E1
Friarsland Av	115	C2
Friarsland Rd	115	C2
Friar's Wk **8**	96	B2
Friary Av	144	A2
Friel Av	86	A3
Fumbally La	89	D3
Furry Pk Ct	80	B1
Furry Pk Ind Est	38	B2
Furry Pk Rd	80	B1
Furze Rd *Dublin 8*	74	B2
Furze Rd *Sandy.*	130	A3

G

Name	Page	Grid
Gables, The *Clond.*	95	C2
Gables, The **4** *Fox.*	131	D3
Gaelic St	79	C3
Gailtrim Gra	26	A1
Gainsborough	18	B2
Gainsborough Av	19	C2
Gainsborough Cl **3**	19	C2
Gainsborough Ct	18	B2
Gainsborough Cres	18	B2
Gainsborough Downs	18	B2
Gainsborough Grn	18	B2
Gainsborough Lawn	19	C2
Gainsborough Pk	19	C2
Gairdini Sheinleasa	52	A1
Gallaun Rd	37	D3
Gallery, The	13	C2
Galloping Grn **3**	131	C2
Galmoy Rd	77	C2
Galtrim Pk	142	A1
Galtrim Rd	142	A1
Galtymore Cl	87	D3
Galtymore Dr	88	A3
Galtymore Pk	99	D1
Galtymore Rd	88	A3
Gandon Cl	101	D1
Gandon Ms	70	B3
Garden Croath	117	D3
Garden La	144	A4
Gardens, The	136	B3
Gardiner La	78	B3
Gardiner Row	78	A3
Gardiner's Pl	78	A3
Gardiner St Lwr	78	B3
Gardiner St Mid	78	A3
Gardiner St Upr	78	A3
Gardini Lein (Lein Gdns)	55	D3
Gardini Phairc An Bhailtini (Villa Park Gdns)	76	A2
Garnett Hall	28	A2
Garnish Sq	47	D1
Garrynisk Cl	109	D2
Garrynisk Est	109	D2
Garrynure	102	B3
Garryowen Rd	86	A3
Gartan Av	78	A2
Garter La	120	B1
Garth, The *Dublin 24*	109	D1
Garth, The (Cookstown) *Dublin 24*	109	C2
Garville Av	101	D3
Garville Av Upr	101	D3
Garville Rd	101	D3
Gas Yd La	20	A1
Gateway Ct **4**	52	A1
Gateway Cres	52	A1
Gateway Gdns **3**	52	A1
Gateway Ms **2**	52	A1
Gateway Pl **1**	52	A1
Gateway Vw **5**	52	A1
Gaybrook Lawns	19	C2
Gaywood Ind Est	32	B1
Geoffrey Keating Rd *off O'Curry Rd*	89	D3
George's Av	117	D2
George's Hill	144	B2
George's La	144	A1
George's Pl *Dublin 1*	78	A3
George's Pl *Black.*	117	D2
George's Pl *D.L.*	119	C3
George's Quay	145	E2
Georges Rd	50	B1
George's St Lwr	119	C3
George's St Upr	119	C3
Georgian Hamlet	43	D3
Georgian Village	74	A1
Geraldine Ct **4**	65	C2
Geraldine St	77	D3
Geraldine Ter	102	B3
Geraldstown Wds	38	A3
Geraldstown Wds Apts **1**	38	A3
Gerald St	91	C2
Gilbert Rd	89	D3
Gilford Av	104	A1
Gilford Ct	104	A1
Gilford Dr	104	A1
Gilford Pk	104	A1
Gilford Rd	104	A1
Giltspur Brook	142	A3
Glade, The *Dublin 16*	128	B2
Glade, The (Cookstown) *Dublin 24*	109	C2
Glade, The (Oldtown Mill) *Celbr.*	66	A1
Glade, The (St. Wolstan's Abbey) *Celbr.*	66	B3
Glade, The *Palm.*	73	C3
Glandore Pk	133	C1
Glandore Rd	53	C3
Glasanaon Ct *off Glasanaon Pk*	51	C2
Glasanaon Pk	51	C2
Glasanaon Rd	51	C1
Glasaree Rd	51	C1
Glasilawn Av	51	D2
Glasilawn Rd	51	C3
Glasmeen Rd	51	C3
Glasmore Pk	14	B3
Glasnamana Pl	51	C2
Glasnamana Rd	51	C3
Glasnevin Av	51	C1
Glasnevin Br	77	D1
Glasnevin Business Pk	50	A3
Glasnevin Ct	51	C3
Glasnevin Downs	51	C3
Glasnevin Dr	51	D2
Glasnevin Hill	52	A3
Glasnevin Pk	51	D1
Glasnevin Wds	51	C3
Glasson Ct	114	B1
Glasthule Bldgs **15**	134	A1
Glasthule Rd	134	A1
Glaunsharoon	103	C2
Gleann Na Ri	138	A3
Gleann Na Smol *Dublin 24*	123	D1
Gleann Na Smol *D.L.*	118	A3
Glebe, The	82	B1
Glebe Vw	50	B1
Gledswood Av	115	C1
Gledswood Cl	115	C1
Gledswood Dr	115	C1
Gledswood Pk	115	C1
Glen, The (Ballinteer) *Dublin 16*	128	B3
Glen, The (Ballyboden) *Dublin 16*	126	B1
Glen, The **14** *D.L.*	133	D1
Glen, The *Lou.V.*	68	A1
Glenaan Rd	52	B2
Glen Abbey Complex	109	D2
Glenabbey Rd	116	A3
Glenageary Av	133	D2
Glenageary Ct	133	D2
Glenageary Hall	134	A2
Glenageary Lo	133	D2
Glenageary Office Pk	133	C2
Glenageary Pk	133	D2
Glenageary Rd Lwr	133	D1

180

Glenageary Rd Upr	133	C1
Glenageary Sta	133	D1
Glenageary Wds	133	C1
Glenalbyn Rd	131	C1
Glenalua Hts	139	C1
Glenalua Rd	139	C1
Glenalua Ter	139	C1
Glenamuck Rd	137	C2
Glenanne	100	B3
Glenard Av *Dublin 7*	77	C3
Glenard Av *Bray*	142	B2
Glenarm Av	78	B2
Glenarm Sq	78	A2
Glenarriff Rd	75	D1
Glenart Av	117	C3
Glenaulin	74	A3
Glenaulin Dr		
(Ceide Glennaluinn)	86	A1
Glenaulin Grn	85	D1
Glenaulin Pk		
(Pairc Gleannaluinn)	74	A3
Glenaulin Rd	85	D1
Glen Av	137	C1
Glenavon Pk	138	B3
Glenavy Pk	100	B3
Glenayle Rd	55	D1
Glenayr Rd	113	D1
Glenbeigh Pk	76	B3
Glenbeigh Rd	76	B3
Glenbourne Gro	136	A1
Glenbower Pk	114	B3
Glenbrook Pk	113	C3
Glenbrook Rd	49	D3
Glencairn	130	B3
Glencarr Ct **4**	139	C3
Glencarrig	59	C1
Glencarrig Ct	124	B2
Glencarrig Dr	124	B2
Glencarrig Grn	124	A2
Glencarr Lawn	139	C3
Glencar Rd	76	B3
Glen Cl	137	D1
Glenclog Rd	52	B2
Glencorp Rd	53	C2
Glen Dale *Cabin.*	137	C1
Glendale *Leix.*	68	B1
Glendale Dr	142	A3
Glendale Meadows	69	C1
Glendale Pk	112	A1
Glendalough Rd	78	A1
Glendhu Pk	49	D3
Glendhu Rd	49	D3
Glendoher Av	127	C1
Glendoher Cl	126	B1
Glendoher Dr	127	C1
Glendoher Pk	127	C1
Glendoher Rd	126	B1
Glendoo Cl		
off Lugaquilla Av	110	B1
Glendown Av	111	D1
Glendown Cl		
off Glendown Gro	111	D1
Glendown Ct	111	D1
Glendown Cres	111	D1
Glendown Grn		
off Glendown Gro	112	A1
Glendown Gro	111	D1
Glendown Lawn	112	A1
Glendown Pk	111	D1
Glendown Rd	111	D2
Glen Dr	137	D1
Glen Druid	141	C1
Glendun Rd	52	B2
Glenealy Downs	31	D3
Glenealy Rd	101	C1
Glen Easton	67	D1
Gleneaston Av	67	D2
Gleneaston Gdns	67	D1
Gleneaston Gro	67	D2
Gleneaston Pk	67	D2
Gleneaston Ri	67	D2
Gleneaston Wds	67	D1
Glen Ellan Av	15	C2
Glen Ellan Cl	15	C3
Glen Ellan Ct	15	C3
Glen Ellan Cres	15	C3
Glen Ellan Dr	15	C2
Glen Ellan Gdns	14	B2
Glen Ellan Grn	15	C2
Glen Ellan Gro	14	B2
Glen Ellan Pk	15	C2
Glen Ellan Pines	15	C2
Glen Ellan Wk	14	B2
Glenfarne Rd	55	C1
Glenfield Av	84	A1
Glenfield Cl	84	A1
Glenfield Dr	84	A1
Glenfield Gro	84	A1
Glenfield Pk	84	A1
Glengara Cl **4**	133	D1
Glengara Pk	133	D1
Glengariff Par	78	A2
Glen Garth	137	C1
Glen Gro	137	D1
Glenhill Av	51	C2
Glenhill Ct	51	C2
Glenhill Dr	50	B2
Glenhill Gro	51	C2
Glenhill Rd	50	B2
Glenhill Vil		
off Glenhill Rd	50	B2
Glen Lawn Dr	137	C1
Glenlyon Cres	125	C2
Glenlyon Gro	125	C2
Glenlyon Pk	125	C2
Glenmalure Pk	88	B3
Glenmalure Sq	102	B3
Glenmaroon Pk	85	D1
Glenmaroon Rd	85	D1
Glenmore Ct	127	C2
Glenmore Pk	127	C2
Glenmore Rd	76	B3
Glen Na Smol	142	A3
Glenomena Gro	116	A1
Glenomena Pk	104	A3
Glenpark Cl	73	C3
Glenpark Dr	73	C3
Glenpark Rd	73	C3
Glens, The	136	B3
Glenshane Cl	122	A1
Glenshane Cres	122	A1
Glenshane Gdns	122	A1
Glenshane Grn	122	A1
Glenshane Gro	122	B1
Glenshane Lawns	122	A1
Glenshane Pk	122	A1
Glensheshek Rd	53	C2
Glenside Vil **2**	73	D3
Glen Ter **16**	134	A1
Glenties Dr	50	A2
Glenties Pk	50	A3
Glentow Rd	52	B2
Glentworth Pk	41	D3
Glenvale	83	C2
Glenvara Pk	125	C2
Glenvar Pk	117	C2
Glenview	133	D3
Glenview Dr **4**	124	B1
Glenview Ind Est	88	B3
Glenview Lawn	111	C3
Glenview Pk	110	B3
Glenville Av	47	C2
Glenville Ct	46	B3
Glenville Dr	46	B3
Glenville Garth	46	B3
Glenville Grn	47	C2
Glenville Gro	47	C2
Glenville Ind Est	116	A2
Glenville Lawn	46	B2
Glenville Rd	46	B3
Glenville Way	47	C2
Glen Wk	137	C1
Glenwood Rd	55	C1
Glin Av	40	B3
Glin Cres	40	B3
Glin Dr	40	B3
Glin Glen	40	B3
Glin Gro	40	B3
Glin Pk	40	B3
Glin Rd	40	B3
Gloucester La *off Sean*		
McDermott St Lwr		
Gloucester Pl	78	B3
Gloucester Pl Lwr	78	B3
Gloucester Pl N	78	B3
Gloucester Pl Upr		
off Gloucester Pl	78	B3
Gloucester St S	145	E2
Glovers All	144	C4
Goatstown Av	115	C2
Goatstown Rd	115	D2
Gofton Hall	50	B1
Golden Br	87	D2
Goldenbridge Av	88	A3
Goldenbridge Gdns	88	A3
Goldenbridge Sta	88	A3
Goldenbridge Ter		
off Connolly Av	88	A3
Golden La	144	B4
Goldsmith St	77	D3
Goldsmith Ter **13**	142	A1
Golf La	131	D3
Golf Links Rd	27	C3
Gordon Av	132	A3
Gordon Pl		
off Richmond St S	90	A3
Gordon St	91	C2
Gorsefield Ct	55	C2
Gortbeg Av	50	B3
Gortbeg Dr	50	B3
Gortbeg Pk	50	B3
Gortbeg Rd	50	B3
Gortmore Av	50	B3
Gortmore Dr	50	B3
Gortmore Pk		
off Gortmore Rd	50	B3
Gortmore Rd	50	B3
Gort Na Mona Dr	132	A3
Gosworth Pk	134	A2
Government Bldgs	90	B3
Gowrie Pk	133	C1
Gracefield Av	55	C3
Gracefield Ct	54	B3
Gracefield Rd	54	B2
Grace O'Malley Dr	60	B2
Grace O'Malley Rd	60	B2
Grace Pk Av	78	B1
Grace Pk Ct	53	C2
Grace Pk Gdns	78	B1
Grace Pk Hts	53	C3
Grace Pk Meadows	53	D3
Grace Pk Rd	78	B1
Grace Pk Ter	79	C1
Grafton St	145	D4
Graham Ct	78	A3
Graigue Ct	37	D2
Granard Br	47	D2
Granby La	78	A3
Granby Pl	144	C1
Granby Row	78	A3
Grand Canal Bk		
Dublin 8	89	C2
Grand Canal Bk (Ranelagh)		
Dublin 8	102	A1
Grand Canal		
Business Cen	87	C3
Grand Canal Dock Sta	91	C2
Grand Canal Harbour		
off James's St	88	B2
Grand Canal Pl N	89	C2
Grand Canal Quay	91	C2
Grand Canal St Lwr	91	C2
Grand Canal St Upr	91	C3
Grand Canal Vw	88	A3
Grand Par	102	B1
Grange, The *Deans Gra*	132	B2
Grange, The *Still.*	131	C1
Grange Abbey Cres	42	B3
Grange Abbey Dr	42	B3
Grange Abbey Gro	42	B3
Grange Abbey Rd	42	B3
Grange Av	43	C3
Grange Brook	127	C2
Grangebrook Av	127	C2
Grangebrook Cl	127	C2
Grangebrook Pk	127	C2
Grangebrook Vale	127	C2
Grange Castle		
Int Business Park	94	B1
Grange Cl *Dublin 13*	57	C1
Grange Cl *Sally.*	133	C3
Grange Cotts **1**	132	A1
Grange Ct	127	D2
Grange Cres	132	B2
Grange Downs	113	C3
Grange Dr	57	C1
Grangefield	128	B3
Grangegorman Lwr	144	A1
Grangegorman Upr	77	C3
Grange Gro **2**	132	A1
Grange Hall	128	B3
Grange Lo Av	42	B3
Grange Manor	82	B2
Grange Manor Av	127	D1
Grange Manor Cl	127	D1
Grange Manor Dr	127	D1
Grange Manor Gro	127	D1
Grange Manor Rd	127	D1
Grangemore	42	A3
Grangemore Av	42	A3
Grangemore Ct	42	A3
Grangemore Cres	42	A3
Grangemore Dr	42	A3
Grangemore Gro	42	A3
Grangemore Lawn	42	A3
Grangemore Pk	42	A3
Grangemore Ri	42	A3
Grangemore Rd	42	A3
Grange Par	57	C1
Grange Pk *Dublin 13*	43	C3
Grange Pk *Dublin 14*	113	C3
Grange Pk *Corn.*	132	A2
Grange Pk Av	56	A2
Grange Pk Cl	56	A2
Grange Pk Cres	56	A2
Grange Pk Grn	56	A2
Grange Pk Gro	56	A2
Grange Pk Par	56	A2
Grange Pk Ri	56	A2
Grange Pk Rd	56	A2
Grange Pk Wk	56	A2
Grange Ri	43	C3
Grange Rd *Dublin 13*	56	A1
Grange Rd (Baldoyle)		
Dublin 13	42	B3
Grange Rd *Dublin 14*	113	C2
Grange Rd *Dublin 16*	113	C3
Grange Vw Cl	95	C1
Grange Vw Ct	95	C1
Grange Vw Grn	95	C1
Grange Vw Gro	95	C1
Grange Vw Lawn	95	C2
Grange Vw Pk	95	C2
Grange Vw Rd	95	C2
Grange Vw Wk	95	C1
Grange Vw Way	95	C1
Grange Vw Wd	95	C1
Grange Way	57	C1
Grange Wd *Dublin 16*	128	A2
Grangewood *D.L.*	132	B2
Granitefield	133	C3
Granite Hall **5**	133	D1
Granite Pl	103	D1
Granite Ter		
off Inchicore Ter S	87	D2
Grantham Pl	90	A3
Grantham St	90	A3
Grants Row	91	C2
Granville Cl	138	A1
Granville Cres	138	A1
Granville Pk	131	D1
Granville Rd *Cabin.*	138	A1
Granville Rd *Deans Gra*	131	D2
Grattan Br	144	C2
Grattan Ct E		
off Grattan St	91	C2
Grattan Cres	87	D2
Grattan Hall	42	A3
Grattan Lo	42	A3
Grattan Par	78	A2
Grattan Pl	143	C2
Grattan Pl		
off Grattan St	91	C2
Grattan St	91	C2
Gray La *off Gray St*	144	A4
Gray St	144	A4
Great Clarence Pl	91	C2
Great Western Av		
off North Circular Rd	77	D3
Great Western Sq	77	D3
Great Western Vil	77	D3
Greek St	144	B2
Green, The *Dublin 9*	53	D1
Green, The (Ballinteer)		
Dublin 16	128	B2
Green, The (Ballyboden)		
Dublin 16	126	A1
Green, The *Dublin 17*	39	D3
Green, The *Dublin 24*	109	D1
Green, The *Ashb.*	11	C3
Green, The *Carrick.*	136	B3

Green, The *Celbr.*	66	A2
Green, The (Dunboyne Castle) *Dunb.*	28	B3
Green, The (Lutterell Hall) *Dunb.*	28	B1
Green, The *Kins.*	18	A3
Green, The *Mala.*	20	A2
Green, The (Robswall) **2** *Mala.*	21	C3
Green, The *Manor.*	31	C3
Green, The *Mayn.*	64	A1
Green, The *Mulh.*	32	A2
Green, The *Swords*	15	D3
Greenacre Ct	111	D3
Greencastle Av	54	B1
Greencastle Cres	40	B3
Greencastle Dr	40	B3
Greencastle Par	55	C1
Greencastle Pk	40	B3
Greencastle Rd	40	B3
Greendale Av	56	B2
Greendale Rd	56	B2
Greendale Shop Cen	56	B2
Greenfield Cl	64	B3
Greenfield Cres	103	D3
Greenfield Dr	65	C3
Greenfield Gro	11	C3
Greenfield Manor	103	D3
Greenfield Pk *Dublin 4*	103	D3
Greenfield Pk *Dublin 24*	125	C2
Greenfield Rd *Dublin 13*	58	B1
Greenfield Rd *Still.*	116	B2
Greenfort Av	84	A1
Greenfort Cl	84	B1
Greenfort Cres	84	B1
Greenfort Dr	84	B1
Greenfort Gdns	84	B1
Greenfort Lawns	84	B1
Greenfort Pk	84	A1
Greenhills Business Cen	110	B2
Greenhills Business Pk	110	B3
Greenhills Ind Est	99	C3
Greenhills Rd *Dublin 12*	98	B3
Greenhills Rd *Dublin 24*	110	B2
Green Isle Business Pk	108	A1
Green Isle Ct **1**	108	A1
Greenlands *Dublin 16*	129	D2
Greenlands, The *Dublin 14*	113	D2
Green La	68	A2
Greenlawns **1**	40	B3
Greenlea Av	112	B1
Greenlea Dr	112	B1
Greenlea Gro	112	B1
Greenlea Rd	112	B1
Greenmount Av	101	D1
Greenmount Ct *off Greenmount Av*	101	D1
Greenmount La	101	D1
Greenmount Lawns	113	C1
Greenmount Rd	101	D3
Greenmount Sq *off Greenmount La*	101	D1
Greenore Ter *off Hogan Av*	91	C2
Green Pk	114	A1
Greenridge Ct	47	C1
Green Rd *Black.*	117	C2
Green Rd, The *Dalkey*	135	C2
Green St	144	B1
Green St E	91	D2
Green St Little	144	B2
Greentrees Dr	111	D1
Greentrees Pk	99	D3
Greentrees Rd	99	D3
Greenview	26	A3
Greenville Av	89	C3
Greenville Rd	118	A3
Greenville Ter	89	D3
Greenwich Ct	102	A2
Greenwood Av	41	D3
Greenwood Cl	41	D3
Greenwood Ct	41	D3
Greenwood Dr	41	D3
Greenwood Lawn *off Greenwood Dr*	41	D3
Greenwood Pk **2**	41	D3
Greenwood Wk	41	D3
Greenwood Way	41	D3
Grenville La	78	A3
Grenville St	78	A3
Greygates	116	B2
Greyhound Racing Stadium	101	D1
Greys La	61	C3
Greystones Sta	143	D2
Greythorn Pk	133	D1
Griffeen	83	C2
Griffeen Av	82	B2
Griffeen Glen Av	82	B2
Griffeen Glen Boul	83	C2
Griffeen Glen Chase	82	B2
Griffeen Glen Ct	83	C2
Griffeen Glen Ct Yd	83	C2
Griffeen Glen Cres	82	B2
Griffeen Glen Dale	82	B2
Griffeen Glen Dene	82	B2
Griffeen Glen Dr	83	C2
Griffeen Glen Grn	82	B2
Griffeen Glen Gro	83	C2
Griffeen Glen Lawn	83	C2
Griffeen Glen Pk	82	B2
Griffeen Glen Rd (east) *Lucan*	83	C2
Griffeen Glen Rd (west) *Lucan*	82	B2
Griffeen Glen Vale	83	C2
Griffeen Glen Vw	82	B2
Griffeen Glen Way	83	C2
Griffeen Rd	83	C2
Griffeen Way	83	C1
Griffin Rath Hall	65	C3
Griffin Rath Manor	65	C3
Griffith Av *Dublin 9*	52	B3
Griffith Av *Dublin 11*	51	D3
Griffith Br	88	A3
Griffith Cl	51	C3
Griffith Ct	79	C1
Griffith Downs	52	B3
Griffith Dr	51	C2
Griffith Hts	51	C3
Griffith Lawns	52	A3
Griffith Par	51	C2
Griffith Rd	51	C2
Griffith Sq *off Wesley Pl*	89	D3
Griffith Sq S *off South Circular Rd*	89	C3
Griffith Wk	79	C1
Grosvenor Av	142	B2
Grosvenor Ct *Dublin 3*	80	B1
Grosvenor Ct *Dublin 6W*	112	A1
Grosvenor Lo	101	D2
Grosvenor Pk	101	D2
Grosvenor Pl	101	D2
Grosvenor Rd	101	D2
Grosvenor Sq	101	D1
Grosvenor Ter **5** *Dalkey*	135	C2
Grosvenor Ter *D.L.*	119	C3
Grosvenor Vil	101	D2
Grotto Av	117	C1
Grotto Pl	116	B1
Grove, The *Dublin 5*	56	A3
Grove, The *Dublin 9*	53	C3
Grove, The (Ballinteer) *Dublin 16*	128	B2
Grove, The (Meadow Mt) *Dublin 16*	128	A1
Grove, The *Dublin 24*	124	A1
Grove, The (Cookstown) *Dublin 24*	109	C2
Grove, The (Kilnamanagh) *Dublin 24*	109	C1
Grove, The *Celbr.*	66	B3
Grove, The (Abbeyfarm) *Celbr.*	66	A3
Grove, The (Dunboyne Castle) *Dunb.*	28	B3
Grove, The (Lutterell Hall) *Dunb.*	28	B1
Grove, The (Plunkett Hall) *Dunb.*	28	A1
Grove, The (Sadleir Hall) *Dunb.*	28	A2
Grove, The *Gra M.*	82	B2
Grove, The *Kins.*	18	A3
Grove, The *Lou.V.*	68	A1
Grove Av *Dublin 6* *off Grove Rd*	101	D1
Grove Av (Finglas) *Dublin 11*	51	C1
Grove Av *Black.*	117	C2
Grove Av *Mala.*	20	B2
Grove Ct **1**	16	A1
Grove Ho	136	B1
Grove Ho Gdns	117	C3
Grove Ind Est	36	B1
Grove La	41	D3
Grove Lawn *Black.*	117	C3
Grove Lawn *Mala.*	20	B2
Grove Pk *Dublin 6*	101	D1
Grove Pk *Dublin 13*	41	D3
Grove Pk Av	51	C1
Grove Pk Cres	51	D1
Grove Pk Dr	51	C1
Grove Pk Rd	51	C1
Grove Rd (Rathmines) *Dublin 6*	101	D1
Grove Rd (Finglas) *Dublin 11*	51	C1
Grove Rd (Blanchardstown) *Dublin 15*	46	B3
Grove Rd *Mala.*	20	A2
Grove Wd	51	C1
Guild St	91	C1
Guilford Ter	141	C2
Guinness Brewery	89	C2
Guinness Enterprise Cen	89	C2
Gulistan Cotts	102	A1
Gulistan Pl	102	A1
Gulistan Ter	102	A1
Gullivers Retail Pk	38	A2
Gurteen Av	86	A2
Gurteen Pk	86	A2
Gurteen Rd	86	A1

H

Hacketsland	141	C1
Haddington Lawns	134	A2
Haddington Pk **6**	134	A2
Haddington Pl	91	C3
Haddington Rd	91	C3
Haddinton Ter	119	D3
Haddon Pk *off Seaview Av N*	80	A2
Haddon Rd	80	A2
Hadleigh Ct	48	A3
Hadleigh Grn	48	A3
Hadleigh Pk	48	A3
Hagans Ct	90	B3
Haigh Ter	119	D3
Hainault Dr	137	C1
Hainault Gro	137	C1
Hainault Lawn	137	C1
Hainault Pk	136	B1
Hainault Rd	131	D3
Halliday Rd	89	C1
Halliday Sq	89	C1
Halston St	144	B1
Hamilton Ct **1**	29	C2
Hamilton Hall	29	C3
Hamilton St	89	C3
Hammond La	144	A2
Hammond St	89	D3
Hampstead Av	52	A2
Hampstead Ct	52	A2
Hampstead Pk	52	A3
Hampton Ct	81	C1
Hampton Cres	116	B1
Hampton Grn	76	B2
Hampton Hermitage & Theresian Trust	79	C1
Hampton Pk	116	B2
Hampton Wd Av	37	C2
Hampton Wd Ct	37	C2
Hampton Wd Cres	37	C2
Hampton Wd Dr	37	C2
Hampton Wd Grn	37	C2
Hampton Wd Lawn	37	C2
Hampton Wd Pk	37	C2
Hampton Wd Rd	37	C2
Hampton Wd Sq	37	C2
Hampton Wd Way	37	C2
Hanbury La *Dublin 8*	144	A3
Hanbury La **2** *Lucan*	70	A3
Hannaville Pk	101	C3
Hanover La	144	B4
Hanover Quay	91	C2
Hanover Sq W *off Hanover La*	144	B4
Hanover St E	145	F3
Hanover St W *off Carmans Hall*	144	A4
Hansfield	31	C3
Hansfield Rd	30	B3
Hansted Cl **1**	82	A3
Hansted Cres	82	A3
Hansted Dale	82	A3
Hansted Pk	82	A3
Hansted Pl **2**	82	A3
Hansted Rd	82	A3
Hansted Way	82	A3
Ha'penny Br	145	D2
Harbour Ct *off Marlborough St*	145	D2
Harbour Cres	134	B2
Harbourmaster Pl	145	F1
Harbour Rd *Dublin 13*	60	B1
Harbour Rd *Dalkey*	134	B1
Harbour Rd *D.L.*	119	C2
Harbour Ter	119	C2
Harbour Vw *off St. Lawrence Rd*	61	C2
Harcourt Grn	90	A3
Harcourt La *off Adelaide Rd*	90	A3
Harcourt Rd	90	A3
Harcourt Sta	90	A3
Harcourt St	90	A3
Harcourt Ter	90	A3
Harcourt Ter La	90	B3
Hardbeck Av	99	C2
Hardiman Rd	78	A1
Hardwicke Pl	78	A3
Hardwicke St	78	A3
Harelawn Av	84	B2
Harelawn Cres	84	B2
Harelawn Dr	84	B1
Harelawn Grn	84	B2
Harelawn Gro	84	B1
Harelawn Pk	84	B2
Harlech Cres	115	D2
Harlech Downs	115	D2
Harlech Gro	115	D2
Harlech Vil	115	D2
Harman St	89	C3
Harmonstown Rd	55	C3
Harmonstown Sta	55	C3
Harmony Av	103	C2
Harmony Row	91	C2
Harold Rd	89	C1
Harolds Cross Rd	101	D1
Harold's Gra Rd	128	A3
Haroldville Av	89	C3
Harrington St	90	A3
Harrison Row	101	D3
Harry St	145	D4
Hartstown Rd	45	D1
Harty Av	99	D2
Harty Ct	99	D2
Harty Pl	89	D3
Harvard	115	D2
Hastings St	91	D2
Hastings Ter **17**	134	A1
Hatch La	90	A3
Hatch Pl *off Hatch La*	90	B3
Hatch St Lwr	90	A3
Hatch St Upr	90	A3
Havelock Pl *off Bath Av*	91	D3
Havelock Sq E	91	D3
Havelock Sq N	91	D3
Havelock Sq S	91	D3
Havelock Sq W	91	D3
Havelock Ter *off Bath Av*	91	D3
Haven, The *Dublin 9*	52	A3
Haven, The *Mala.*	19	D1
Haven Vw **2**	19	D1
Haverty Rd	79	D2
Hawkins La	143	D2
Hawkins St	145	E2
Hawthorn Av	79	C3
Hawthorn Dr	128	B1
Hawthorn Lawn	48	A3
Hawthorn Lo	48	A3
Hawthorn Manor **1**	117	D3
Hawthorn Pk	17	C2
Hawthorn Rd	97	D2
Hawthorns, The **15** *Abb.*	139	C3

Name	Page	Grid
Hawthorns, The *Ashb.*	11	C2
Hawthorns Rd	129	D2
Hawthorn Ter	79	C3
Hawthorn Vw	66	A1
Hayden's La	82	A2
Haydens Pk	82	B3
Haydens Pk Av	82	B3
Haydens Pk Cl	82	B2
Haydens Pk Dale	82	B3
Haydens Pk Dr	82	B3
Haydens Pk Glade	82	B3
Haydens Pk Grn	82	B2
Haydens Pk Lawn	82	B3
Haydens Pk Vw	82	B3
Haydens Pk Wk	82	B2
Haydens Pk Way	82	B3
Hayden Sq	116	A2
Haymarket	144	A2
Hayworth Dr	44	B1
Hayworth Ms	44	B1
Hayworth Ter	44	B1
Hazel Av	130	A1
Hazelbrook Ct	101	C3
Hazelbrook Dr	100	B3
Hazelbrook Pk	110	B2
Hazelbrook Rd	100	B3
Hazelbury Grn	31	C2
Hazelbury Pk	31	C3
Hazel Ct **6**	26	B3
Hazelcroft Gdns	50	B2
Hazelcroft Pk	50	B3
Hazelcroft Rd	50	B2
Hazeldene	103	D2
Hazelgrove *Jobs.*	122	B2
Hazel Gro *Port.*	26	B3
Hazelgrove Ct	122	B2
Hazel Lawn (Blanchardstown)		
Dublin 15	47	C2
Hazel Lawn **5** *D.L.*	133	C2
Hazel Pk	100	B3
Hazel Rd	53	D3
Hazel Vil	130	A1
Hazelwood *D'bate*	13	C1
Hazelwood *Shank.*	141	C2
Hazelwood Av	45	D1
Hazelwood Cl	96	A3
Hazelwood Ct *Dublin 5*	54	A1
Hazelwood Ct *Clons.*	45	D1
Hazelwood Cres *Clond.*	96	A3
Hazelwood Cres *Clons.*	45	D1
Hazelwood Dr	54	A2
Hazelwood Grn	45	D1
Hazelwood Gro	54	A2
Hazelwood La	96	A3
Hazelwood Pk	54	A2
Hazelwood Vw	96	A3
Headford Gro	114	A3
Healthfield Rd	101	D3
Healy St		
off Rutland Pl N	78	B3
Heaney Av	85	D3
Heany Av	135	C2
Heath, The *Dublin 6W*	112	A2
Heath, The *Dublin 24*	109	C2
Heath Cres	75	D1
Heather Cl	128	A2
Heather Dr	128	A2
Heather Gdns	27	D1
Heather Gro *Dublin 16*	128	A2
Heather Gro *Palm.*	85	C1
Heather Lawn	128	A2
Heather Pk	128	A2
Heather Rd *Dublin 16*	128	A2
Heather Rd *Sandy.*	130	A3
Heather Vw Av	123	D2
Heather Vw Cl	123	D2
Heather Vw Dr	123	D2
Heather Vw Lawn	123	D2
Heather Vw Pk	123	D2
Heather Vw Rd	123	D2
Heathervue	143	C2
Heather Wk	27	D1
Heathfield	118	B3
Heath Gro	76	A3
Hedgerows, The	131	D3
Heidelberg	115	D2
Heights, The *Dublin 16*	128	B3
Heights, The *Dunb.*	28	B3
Heights, The *Kins.*	18	A3
Heights, The *Mala.*	20	B3
Hellers Copse	117	C3
Hendrick La		
off Benburb St	89	C1
Hendrick Pl	89	C1
Hendrick St	89	C1
Henley Ct	114	B2
Henley Pk	114	B2
Henley Vil	114	B2
Henrietta La	77	D3
Henrietta Pl	144	B1
Henrietta St	144	B1
Henry Pl	145	D1
Henry Rd	86	A3
Henry St	144	C1
Herbert Av	104	B3
Herbert Cotts	103	D1
Herbert Hill	129	C1
Herbert La	91	C3
Herberton Dr	88	B3
Herberton Pk	88	B3
Herberton Rd *Dublin 8*	88	B3
Herberton Rd *Dublin 12*	88	B3
Herbert Pk	103	C1
Herbert Pl	91	C3
Herbert Rd *Dublin 4*	91	D3
Herbert Rd (Blanchardstown)		
Dublin 15	47	D2
Herbert St	90	B3
Hermitage Av	127	D1
Hermitage Cl	127	D1
Hermitage Ct	127	D1
Hermitage Cres	71	D3
Hermitage Downs	127	D1
Hermitage Dr	127	D1
Hermitage Gdn	71	D3
Hermitage Grn	127	D1
Hermitage Gro	127	D1
Hermitage Lawn	127	D1
Hermitage Manor	71	D3
Hermitage Pk		
Dublin 16	127	D1
Hermitage Pk *Lucan*	71	D3
Hermitage Pl	71	D3
Hermitage Rd	71	D3
Hermitage Valley	71	D3
Hermitage Vw	127	D1
Hermitage Way	71	D3
Heuston Luas Sta	89	C1
Heuston Sta	88	B1
Hewardine Ter		
off Killarney St	78	B3
Heytesbury La	103	C1
Heytesbury Pl		
off Long La	89	D3
Heytesbury St	90	A3
Hibernian Av	79	C3
Hibernian Ind Est	110	A3
Highfield Av	127	D2
Highfield Cl	17	C1
Highfield Ct	101	D3
Highfield Cres	17	C1
Highfield Downs	17	C1
Highfield Dr	127	D2
Highfield Grn	17	C1
Highfield Gro	102	A3
Highfield Lawn	17	C1
Highfield Pk *Dublin 14*	114	B2
Highfield Pk *Leix.*	68	A2
Highfield Rd	101	D3
Highland Av	137	C1
Highland Gro	137	C1
Highland Lawn	137	C1
Highland Vw	137	C1
High Pk	53	C3
Highridge Grn	130	A1
High St *Dublin 8*	144	B3
High St *Dublin 24*	109	D3
Highthorn Pk	133	C1
Highthorn Wds **3**	133	C1
Hill, The *Dublin 16*	128	B3
Hill, The *Black.*	119	C3
Hill, The *Mala.*	20	A3
Hill, The **6** *Mulh.*	32	A3
Hill, The *Still.*	117	C3
Hillbrook Wds	46	A1
Hill Cotts **1**	139	D1
Hill Ct	27	C1
Hillcourt Pk	133	D2
Hillcourt Rd	133	D2
Hillcrest *Dublin 6W*	112	A3
Hillcrest *Lucan*	82	A1
Hillcrest (Mooretown) **1**		
Swords	19	C1
Hillcrest Av	82	A1
Hillcrest Ct	82	A1
Hillcrest Dr	82	A1
Hillcrest Grn	82	A1
Hillcrest Hts	82	A1
Hillcrest Lawns	82	A1
Hillcrest Pk *Dublin 11*	51	D1
Hillcrest Pk *Lucan*	82	A1
Hillcrest Rd	82	A1
Hillcrest Vw	82	A1
Hillcrest Wk	82	A1
Hillcrest Way	82	A1
Hill Dr	20	A3
Hillsbrook Av	99	D3
Hillsbrook Cres	99	D3
Hillsbrook Dr	100	A3
Hillsbrook Gro	99	D3
Hillside *Dalkey*	134	B2
Hillside *Grey.*	143	C1
Hillside Dr	113	D2
Hillside Pk	126	B1
Hillside Rd	143	D2
Hillside Vw	57	C2
Hills Ind Est	70	B2
Hill St	78	A3
Hilltop Lawn	140	B3
Hilltop Shop Cen	55	D2
Hilltown Cl	16	B1
Hilltown Ct **4**	16	B1
Hilltown Grn **5**	16	B1
Hilltown Gro	16	B1
Hilltown Lawn	16	B1
Hilltown Pk	16	B1
Hilltown Rd	16	B1
Hilltown Way	16	B1
Hill Vw	128	A1
Hillview Cotts **3**	132	B3
Hillview Dr	132	B3
Hillview Glade **2**	128	A1
Hillview Gro	128	A1
Hillview Lawn	132	B3
Hilton Gdns	128	B2
Hoeys Ct		
off Castle St	144	B3
Hogan Av	91	C2
Hogan Pl	91	C2
Hole In The Wall Rd,		
The	42	A2
Holles Row	145	F4
Holles St	145	F4
Hollows, The **7**	70	A3
Holly Av	130	A2
Holly Pk	141	C2
Holly Pk Av	131	D1
Holly Rd *Dublin 9*	79	D1
Holly Rd *Dublin 12*	97	D2
Hollyville Lawn	73	C3
Hollywell	37	C3
Hollywood Dr	115	D2
Hollywood Pk	115	D3
Holmston Av	133	D1
Holmwood	137	D2
Holycross Av	78	B2
Holy Cross Coll	78	B2
Holyrood Pk		
off Sandymount Av	104	A1
Holywell *Dublin 14*	129	D1
Holywell *Swords*	17	D3
Holywell Av *Dublin 13*	56	A1
Holywell Av *Swords*	17	D2
Holywell Cl	18	A3
Holywell Ct **1**	17	D3
Holywell Cres *Dublin 13*	56	A1
Holywell Cres *Swords*	17	D3
Holywell Dr	17	D2
Holywell Gdns	17	D2
Holywell Glen	18	A3
Holywell Gro	18	A3
Holywell Heath	17	D3
Holywell Pk	17	D3
Holywell Pl **2**	17	D3
Holywell Ri	17	D3
Holywell Rd *Dublin 13*	56	A1
Holywell Rd *Swords*	17	D3
Holywell Row	17	D3
Holywell Sq	18	A2
Holywell Vw	18	A3
Holywell Wk	17	D3
Holywell Way	18	A3
Holywell Wd	17	D3
Home Fm Pk	78	B1
Home Fm Rd	52	A3
Homelawn Av	124	B1
Homelawn Dr	124	B1
Homelawn Gdns	124	B1
Homelawn Rd	124	B1
Homelawn Vil	124	A1
Homeleigh	72	B1
Home Vil	103	C1
Homeville *Dublin 6*	102	A2
Homeville, The **1**		
Dublin 24	125	C1
Homeville Ct **4**	125	C1
Honey Pk **8**	133	C2
Hope Av	79	C3
Hope St	91	C2
Hopkins Sq	116	A2
Horseman's Row		
off Parnell St	78	A3
Horton Ct	113	C1
Hospital Sta	109	C3
Hotel Yd	144	C2
House of Retreat	87	D3
House of St. John		
of God	131	C1
Howard St	91	C2
Howth Castle	59	D2
Howth Golf Course	59	D3
Howth Junct	56	B1
Howth Rd *Dublin 3*	79	D2
Howth Rd *Dublin 5*	55	C3
Howth Rd (Howth)		
Dublin 13	59	D1
Howth Sta	60	B1
Howth Vw Pk	56	A1
H.S. Reilly Br	50	A3
Huband Br	91	C3
Huband Rd	99	C1
Hudson Rd	134	A1
Hughes Rd E	99	D2
Hughes Rd N	99	D2
Hughes Rd S	99	D2
Hume Av	97	D1
Hume Cen	86	A3
Hume St	90	B3
Hunters Av	125	C3
Hunters Ct	125	C3
Hunters Cres	125	C3
Hunters Grn	125	C3
Hunters Gro	125	C3
Hunters Hill	125	C3
Hunters La *Dublin 24*	125	C3
Hunters La *Ashb.*	11	C2
Hunters Meadow	125	C3
Hunters Par	125	C3
Hunters Pl	125	C3
Hunters Rd	125	C3
Hunter's Run	31	D2
Hunter's Run The Cl	31	D2
Hunter's Run The Dr	31	D2
Hunter's Run The Glade	31	D2
Hunter's Run The Gro	31	C2
Hunter's Run The Pk	31	D2
Hunter's Run The Ri	31	D3
Hunter's Run The Vw	31	D3
Hunter's Run The Way	31	D3
Hunters Wk	125	C3
Hunters Way	125	C3
Huntsgrove	11	C2
Huntstown Av	31	D3
Huntstown Cl	32	A3
Huntstown Ct	31	D3
Huntstown Dr	31	D3
Huntstown Glen	31	D3
Huntstown Grn	32	A3
Huntstown Gro	32	A3
Huntstown Lawn	32	A3
Huntstown Pk	32	A3

Name	Page	Grid
Huntstown Ri	32	A3
Huntstown Rd	32	A3
Huntstown Way	32	A3
Huntstown Wd	31	D3
Huxley Cres	89	C3
Hyacinth St	79	C3
Hyde Pk *Dublin 6W*	112	B2
Hyde Pk *D.L.*	134	B1
Hyde Pk Av	117	C2
Hyde Pk Gdns	117	C2
Hyde Rd	134	B1
Hyde Sq	116	A2

I

Name	Page	Grid
I.D.A. Ind Cen	77	C3
I.D.A. Small Ind Cen	39	D3
Idrone Av	125	D1
Idrone Cl	126	A1
Idrone Dr	125	D1
Idrone Pk	125	D1
Idrone Ter	117	D2
ILAC Cen	144	C1
Imaal Rd	77	C2
Inagh Ct	139	C3
Inagh Rd	86	A2
Inbhir Ide	19	D2
Inbhir Ide Cl	19	D1
Inbhir Ide Dr	19	D1
Inchicore Par	87	D2
Inchicore Rd	88	A2
Inchicore Sq	87	D2
Inchicore Ter N	87	D2
Inchicore Ter S	87	D2
Infirmary Rd	88	B1
Inglewood	45	D1
Inglewood Cl	45	D1
Inglewood Cres	45	D1
Inglewood Dr	46	A1
Inglewood Rd	46	A1
Ingram Rd	89	D3
Inis Fail	123	D2
Innisfallen Par	78	A2
Innishmaan Rd	52	B2
Innismore	99	D2
Inns Quay	144	B2
Invermore Gro *off Carraroe Av*	56	A1
Inverness Rd	79	C2
Inver Rd	76	B2
Iona Cres	78	A1
Iona Dr	78	A1
Iona Pk	78	A2
Iona Rd	77	D2
Iona Vil	78	A1
Iris Gro	116	A2
Irishtown Rd	91	D2
Irvine Cres *off Church Rd*	91	C1
Irvine Ter	91	C1
Irwin Ct	88	B2
Irwin St	88	B2
Island St	89	C1
Island Vw *Dublin 5*	57	C2
Island Vw *Mala.*	20	B2
Island Vil *off Hogan Av*	91	C1
Isolda Rd	92	A2
Iuar St	89	C1
Iveagh Bldgs *off Kevin St Upr*	89	D3
Iveagh Gdns	100	A1
Iveleary Rd	52	B2
Iveragh Ct	91	D3
Iveragh Rd	52	B2

J

Name	Page	Grid
James Connolly Pk	96	B1
James Connolly Sq	142	A1
James Joyce Ct	57	C2
James Larkin Rd *Dublin 3*	105	C1
James Larkin Rd *Dublin 5*	56	A3
James McCormack Gdns	58	A1
James Pl E	90	B3
James's Gate *off James's St*	88	B2
James's Sta	88	B2
James's St	88	B2
James's St E	90	B3
James's Ter 6	20	A2
James St N	79	C3
Jamestown Av	87	C3
Jamestown Business Pk	50	B1
Jamestown Ind Est	87	C3
Jamestown Rd (Inchicore) *Dublin 8*	87	C3
Jamestown Rd (Finglas) *Dublin 11*	50	B1
Jamestown Sq	87	C3
Janelle Shop Cen	50	B2
Jane Ville *off Tivoli Rd*	119	C3
Jerome Connor Pl *off Sullivan St*	88	B1
Jervis La Lwr	144	C2
Jervis La Upr	144	C1
Jervis Sta	144	C2
Jervis St	144	C1
Jetty Rd	92	B1
Jobstown Rd	122	A2
John Dillon St	144	B4
John F. Kennedy Av	98	A1
John F. Kennedy Dr	98	B1
John F. Kennedy Ind Est	98	A1
John F. Kennedy Pk	98	A1
John F. Kennedy Rd	98	A1
John McCormack Av	99	D2
Johnsbridge	82	B2
Johnsbridge Av	82	B2
Johnsbridge Cl	82	B2
Johnsbridge Grn	82	B2
Johnsbridge Gro	82	B2
Johnsbridge Meadows	82	B2
Johnsbridge Pk	82	B2
Johnsbridge Wk	82	B2
Johns La W	144	A3
Johnsons Ct *off Grafton St*	145	D4
Johnsons Pl *off William St S*	145	D4
Johnstown Av	133	C3
Johnstown Ct	133	C3
Johnstown Gro	133	C3
Johnstown La	133	C3
Johnstown Pk *Dublin 11*	51	D2
Johnstown Pk *Corn.*	133	C3
Johnstown Rd	138	A1
John St S	89	C2
John St W	144	A3
Jones's Rd	78	B2
Jones Ter 15	142	B2
Josephine Av *off Leo St*	78	A3
Joshua La *off Dawson St*	145	D4
Joyce Av	136	B1
Joyce Rd	78	A1
Joyce Way	97	D1
Joy St *off Barrow St*	91	C2
Jugback Cl	15	C2
Jugback Cres	15	C3
Jugback Grn	15	C2
Jugback La	15	C2

K

Name	Page	Grid
KCR Ind Est	100	B3
Keadeen Av	110	B1
Kearns Pl	88	B2
Keeper Rd	88	B3
Kells Rd	100	B2
Kelly's Av	119	C3
Kelly's La	64	B2
Kellys Row	78	A3
Kellystown Rd	128	A3
Kelston Av	131	D2
Kelston Dr	131	D2
Kelston Hall 9	131	D2
Kelston Pk	131	C2
Kelston Vw 10	131	D2
Kelvin Cl	27	C1
Kempton Av	75	D1
Kempton Ct	75	D1
Kempton Grn	75	C1
Kempton Gro	75	D1
Kempton Heath	75	D1
Kempton Lawn	75	D1
Kempton Pk	75	D1
Kempton Ri	75	D1
Kempton Vw	75	D1
Kempton Way	75	D1
Kenah Hill	139	C1
Kenilworth La	101	D2
Kenilworth Pk	101	C2
Kenilworth Rd	101	D2
Kenilworth Sq E	101	D2
Kenilworth Sq N	101	D2
Kenilworth Sq S	101	D2
Kenilworth Sq W	101	D2
Kenmare Par *off Killarney Par*	78	A2
Kennedy Pk 2	142	A3
Kennelsfort Grn	85	C1
Kennelsfort Rd	85	C1
Kennelsfort Rd Lwr	73	D3
Kennelsfort Rd Upr	85	C1
Kennington Cl	111	C2
Kennington Cres	111	C2
Kennington Lawn	111	D2
Kennington Rd	111	C2
Kentfield	140	B1
Keogh Sq	87	D2
Kerlogue Rd	92	A2
Kerrymount Av	136	B1
Kerrymount Cl 1	137	C1
Kerrymount Grn	137	C1
Kerrymount Mall	137	C1
Kerrymount Ri	137	C1
Kettles La	17	D3
Kevanagh Av	86	A3
Kevin St Lwr	90	A3
Kevin St Upr	144	B4
Kew Pk	69	D3
Kew Pk Av	69	D3
Kew Pk Cres	69	D3
Kickam Rd	88	A2
Kilakea Cl *off Tibradden Dr*	110	B1
Kilakea Dr *off Tibradden Dr*	110	B1
Kilbarrack Av	56	B2
Kilbarrack Gdns	57	C2
Kilbarrack Gro	56	B2
Kilbarrack Ind Est	56	B1
Kilbarrack Par	56	B1
Kilbarrack Rd	56	A1
Kilbarrack Shop Cen	56	A1
Kilbarrack Sta	56	A2
Kilbarrack Way	56	B1
Kilbarron Av	53	D1
Kilbarron Dr	53	D1
Kilbarron Pk	53	D1
Kilbarron Rd	53	D1
Kilbegnet Cl	134	B2
Kilbogget Gro	138	A2
Kilbogget Vil 1	138	A1
Kilbride Rd	80	B1
Kilbrina	28	B2
Kilcarberry Av	95	D2
Kilcarberry Cl	95	D2
Kilcarberry Ct	95	D2
Kilcarberry Ind Est	94	B2
Kilcarberry Ind Pk	95	C2
Kilcarberry Lawn	95	D2
Kilcarrig Av	108	B3
Kilcarrig Cl	108	B3
Kilcarrig Cres	108	B3
Kilcarrig Grn	108	B3
Kilclare Av	122	B1
Kilclare Cres	122	B1
Kilclare Dr	122	B1
Kilclare Gdns	122	B1
Kilcock Maynooth Leixlip Bypass	68	A3
Kilcock Rd	64	A2
Kilcolman Ct 7	134	A2
Kilcronan Av	95	C1
Kilcronan Cl	95	C1
Kilcronan Ct	95	C1
Kilcronan Cres	95	C1
Kilcronan Gro	95	C1
Kilcronan Lawns 1	95	C1
Kilcronan Vw	95	C1
Kilcross Av	129	D3
Kilcross Cl 2	129	D3
Kilcross Ct	129	C3
Kilcross Cres	129	D3
Kilcross Dr	129	D3
Kilcross Gro	129	C3
Kilcross Lawn	129	D3
Kilcross Pk	129	C3
Kilcross Rd	129	D3
Kilcross Sq	129	D3
Kilcross Way 1	129	D3
Kildare Br	65	D1
Kildare Pk	100	A1
Kildare Rd	100	B1
Kildare St	145	E4
Kilderry Hall	10	B2
Kildonan Av	50	A1
Kildonan Dr	50	A1
Kildonan Rd	50	A1
Kilfenora Dr	42	A3
Kilfenora Rd	100	B2
Kilgobbin Rd	130	A3
Kilkieran Ct	76	B1
Kilkieran Rd	76	B1
Kill Abbey	132	A1
Killakee Av	124	B2
Killakee Ct	124	B2
Killakee Gdns	124	B2
Killakee Grn	124	B2
Killakee Gro	124	B2
Killakee Lawns	124	B2
Killakee Pk	124	B2
Killakee Ri	124	B2
Killakee Vw	124	B2
Killakee Wk	124	B2
Killakee Way	124	B2
Killala Rd	76	B2
Killan Rd	91	C1
Killarney Av	78	B3
Killarney Par	78	A2
Killarney St	78	B3
Killarney Vil 5	142	A2
Killary Gro *off Ardara Av*	56	A1
Kill Av	132	B1
Killeen	19	C2
Killeen Av	19	C2
Killeen Ct 2	19	C2
Killeen Cres	19	C2
Killeen Ms	20	A2
Killeen Pk	19	C2
Killeen Rd *Dublin 6*	102	C2
Killeen Rd *Dublin 10*	98	A1
Killeen Rd *Dublin 12*	98	A1
Killeen Ter	20	A2
Killegland Ct	10	B2
Killegland Pk	10	B2
Killegland Ri	11	C3
Killegland Rd	11	C3
Killester Av	80	B1
Killester Ct	54	B3
Killester Pk	54	B3
Killester Sta	80	B1
Killinarden Est	122	B2
Killinarden Hts	123	C2
Killinarden Rd	122	B3
Killinarden Enterprise Pk	123	C2
Killincarrick Rd	143	C2
Killincarrig Manor	143	C2
Killiney Av	139	C2
Killiney Cen	133	D3
Killiney Ct 5	139	C3
Killiney Gate	139	C2
Killiney Gro	134	A3
Killiney Heath	139	C2
Killiney Hill Pk	134	B3
Killiney Hill Pk	139	C1
Killiney Oaks 6	139	C3
Killiney Rd	134	A2
Killiney Sta	139	D2
Killiney Ter 2	134	B1
Killiney Twrs 8	134	A2
Killiney Vw	134	A1
Killininny Cotts	124	B2
Killininny Ct Apts 1	124	B2
Killininny Rd	124	B2
Kill La	132	A2
Kilmacud Av	130	A1
Kilmacud Pk	116	A3
Kilmacud Rd Upr *Dublin 14*	115	D3
Kilmacud Rd Upr *Still.*	130	A1
Kilmacud Sta	129	D1
Kilmahuddrick Av	95	C1
Kilmahuddrick Cl	95	C1
Kilmahuddrick Ct	95	C1
Kilmahuddrick Cres	95	C1
Kilmahuddrick Dr	95	C1

Kilmahuddrick Grn	95	C1
Kilmahuddrick Gro	95	C1
Kilmahuddrick Lawn	95	C1
Kilmahuddrick Pl	95	C1
Kilmahuddrick Rd	95	C1
Kilmahuddrick Wk	95	C1
Kilmahuddrick Way	95	C1
Kilmainham Br	88	A2
Kilmainham La	88	A2
Kilmantain Pl **6**	142	A2
Kilmartin Av	108	A3
Kilmartin Cres	108	B3
Kilmartin Dr	108	A3
Kilmartin Gdns	108	A3
Kilmartin Pk	108	A3
Kilmashogue Br	127	D3
Kilmashogue Cl		
off Kilmashogue Dr	110	B1
Kilmashogue Dr	110	B1
Kilmashogue Gro	110	B1
Kilmore Av *Dublin 5*	54	A1
Kilmore Av *Kill.*	139	C2
Kilmore Cl	54	A1
Kilmore Cres	54	A1
Kilmore Dr	54	A1
Kilmore Rd	54	A2
Kilmorony Cl	56	A1
Kilnamanagh Rd	99	C2
Kilnamarragh		
Shop Cen	110	A2
Kilohan Gro	111	C1
Kilrock Rd	61	C2
Kilshane Rd *Dublin 11*	49	D2
Kilshane Rd *Kilsh.*	34	B1
Kiltalown Av	122	A2
Kiltalown Cl	122	A2
Kiltalown Ct	122	A2
Kiltalown Cres	122	A2
Kiltalown Dr	122	A2
Kiltalown Grn	122	A2
Kiltalown Gro	122	A2
Kiltalown Hts	122	A2
Kiltalown Pk	122	A2
Kiltalown Rd	122	A2
Kiltalown Vw	122	A2
Kiltalown Wk	122	A2
Kiltalown Way	122	A2
Kilteragh Dr	136	B1
Kilteragh Pines **3**	131	D3
Kilteragh Rd	137	C1
Kiltipper Av	124	A2
Kiltipper Cl	124	A2
Kiltipper Dr	124	A2
Kiltipper Gate **3**	123	D3
Kiltipper Ri **1**	123	D3
Kiltipper Rd	123	D3
Kiltipper Vw **2**	123	D3
Kiltipper Way	123	D2
Kiltuck Pk **2**	141	C3
Kilvere	112	B2
Kilworth Rd	87	D3
Kimberley Rd	143	D1
Kimmage Ct	100	B3
Kimmage Gro	101	C3
Kimmage Manor Way	112	A1
Kimmage Rd Lwr	101	C2
Kimmage Rd W	100	A3
Kinahan St	88	B1
Kincora Av	80	A2
Kincora Ct	81	C2
Kincora Dr	80	B2
Kincora Gro	80	B2
Kincora Pk	80	B2
Kincora Rd	80	B2
Kindlestown Lwr	143	C1
Kindlestown Pk	143	C1
King Edward Ct **7**	142	A2
Kingram La	90	B3
Kings Av	79	C3
Kingsbury	64	B3
Kings Hall *Dublin 20*	86	B1
Kings Hall **2** *Swords*	18	A2
Kings Inns St	144	C1
Kingsland Par	102	A1
Kingsland Pk Av	90	A3
Kingsmill Rd	142	B1

Kingston	128	B3
Kingston Av	128	B3
Kingston Cl	128	B3
Kingston Ct	127	C1
Kingston Cres	128	B3
Kingston Dr	128	B3
Kingston Grn	128	B3
Kingston Gro	128	B3
Kingston Hall	128	B3
Kingston Hts	128	B3
Kingston Lawn	128	B3
Kingston Pk	128	B3
Kingston Ri	128	B3
Kingston Vw	128	B3
Kingston Wk	128	B3
King St N	144	B1
King St S	145	D4
Kingswood Av		
Dublin 24	109	D1
Kingswood Av *City W*	107	C3
Kingswood Castle	97	D3
Kingswood Dr		
Dublin 24	109	D1
Kingswood Dr *Kings.*	107	D3
Kingswood Rd	107	D3
Kingswood Sta	110	A1
Kingswood Vw	109	C1
Kinlen Rd	143	D2
Kinsaley Br	25	D2
Kinsaley Business Pk	25	D2
Kinsaley La	25	D2
Kinsaley Research Cen	25	C3
Kinsealy Ct	18	B2
Kinsealy Downs	18	A3
Kinvara Av	75	D1
Kinvara Dr	75	D1
Kinvara Gro	75	D1
Kinvara Pk	75	D1
Kinvara Rd	75	D1
Kippure Av	110	B1
Kippure Pk	50	A3
Kirkfield **1**	46	A2
Kirkpatrick Av	46	B3
Kirkpatrick Dr	46	B3
Kirkwood	104	A1
Kirwan St	89	C1
Kirwan St Cotts		
off Kirwan St	77	C3
Kitestown Rd	61	C3
Knapton Ct		
off Vesey Pl	119	C3
Knapton Lawn	119	C3
Knapton Rd	119	C3
Knights Br	80	B2
Knights Wd	39	C3
Knockaire	126	A1
Knockaulin	68	A2
Knockcullen	112	A3
Knockcullen Dr	112	A3
Knockcullen Lawn	112	A3
Knockcullen Pk	112	A3
Knockcullen Ri	126	A1
Knockdara	20	B3
Knockfield Grn	125	D1
Knockfield Manor	125	D1
Knocklyon Av	111	D3
Knocklyon Cl	125	D1
Knocklyon Ct	125	D1
Knocklyon Cres	125	C2
Knocklyon Dr	112	A3
Knocklyon Gate Apts **1**	125	C2
Knocklyon Grn	125	D1
Knocklyon Gro	125	D1
Knocklyon Hts	125	D1
Knocklyon Hill	125	C2
Knocklyon Ms	111	D3
Knocklyon Pk	125	D1
Knocklyon Rd	126	A1
Knockmaroon Hill	74	A3
Knockmaroon Rd	74	A3
Knockmeenagh La	97	C3
Knockmeenagh Rd	96	B3
Knockmitten Cl	97	D1
Knockmitten La	97	D1
Knockmitten La N	97	D1
Knockmore Av	122	B2
Knockmore Cres	122	B2
Knockmore Dr	122	B2
Knockmore Gdns	122	B2
Knockmore Grn	122	B2
Knockmore Gro	122	B2
Knockmore Pk	122	B2

Knock-na-Cree Gro	135	C3
Knock-na-Cree Pk	134	B2
Knock-na-Cree Rd	134	B3
Knocknarea Av	100	A1
Knocknarea Rd	99	D1
Knocknashee	115	D3
Knock Riada	86	B1
Knocksinna	131	D1
Knocksinna Ct **8**	131	D2
Knocksinna Cres	131	D2
Knocksinna Gro **4**	131	D2
Knocksinna Pk	131	D2
Knowth Ct	37	D3
Kor Dev Pk	98	B1
Kyber Rd	75	D3
Kyle-Clare Rd	92	A2
Kylemore Av	86	A3
Kylemore Dr	86	B3
Kylemore Pk Ind Est	86	B3
Kylemore Pk N	86	A3
Kylemore Pk S	86	B3
Kylemore Pk W	86	B3
Kylemore Rd *Dublin 10*	86	B2
Kylemore Rd *Dublin 12*	86	B2
Kylemore Rd *Dublin 20*	86	A1
Kylemore Sta	98	B1

L

Labre Pk	86	B3
Laburnum Rd	103	C3
Laburnum Wk	73	C3
Lad La	90	B3
Lady's Well Rd	32	B2
Lagan Rd	50	B3
Lake Dr	107	D3
Lakelands, The	113	C2
Lakelands Av	130	A1
Lakelands Cl	130	A1
Lakelands Cres	130	A1
Lakelands Dr	130	A1
Lakelands Gro	130	A1
Lakelands Lawn	130	A1
Lakelands Pk	113	C1
Lakelands Rd	130	A1
Lakeshore Dr	17	D2
Lakeview Dr	17	D2
Lally Rd	87	C2
Lambay Cl	139	C3
Lambay Ct	21	C2
Lambay Dr	139	C3
Lambay Rd	52	A3
Lambourne Av	45	D2
Lambourne Ct	45	D2
Lambourne Dr	45	D2
Lambourne Pk *Clons.*	45	D2
Lambourne Pk *D'bate*	13	D1
Lambourne Rd	45	D2
Lambourne Village	80	B2
Lambourne Wd	137	D2
Lambs Ct		
off James's St	88	B2
Landen Rd	86	B3
Landscape Av	114	A2
Landscape Cres	114	A2
Landscape Gdns	114	A2
Landscape Pk	114	A2
Landscape Rd	114	A2
Landys Ind Est	112	A3
Lanesborough Av	36	B2
Lanesborough Dr	37	C2
Lanesborough Gdns	36	B2
Lanesborough Gro	37	C2
Lanesborough Pk	36	B3
Lanesborough Rd	36	B2
Lanesborough Ter	36	B2
Lanesborough Vw	36	B3
Lanesville	132	B1
Langrishe Pl		
off Summerhill	78	B3
Lanndale Lawns	109	C3
Lansdowne Gdns		
off Shelbourne Rd	91	D3
Lansdowne Hall		
off Tritonville Rd	91	D3
Lansdowne La	91	D3
Lansdowne Pk		
Dublin 4	91	C3
Lansdowne Pk		
Dublin 16	112	A3
Lansdowne Rd	91	C3
Lansdowne Rd Stadium	91	D3
Lansdowne Rd Sta	91	D3

Lansdowne Ter		
off Shelbourne Rd	91	D3
Lansdowne Valley Apts	99	C1
Lansdowne Valley Cres		
off Kilworth Rd	99	D1
Lansdowne Village	91	D3
Lansdown Valley Pk	87	D3
Laracor Gdns	56	A1
Laragh	139	C2
Laragh Cl	56	A1
Laraghcon	70	A2
Laragh Gro		
off Laragh Cl	56	A1
Larch Dr **4**	126	B2
Larchfield *Dublin 14*	114	B2
Larchfield *Dunb.*	29	C3
Larchfield Pk	115	C2
Larchfield Rd	115	C2
Larch Gro	102	B2
Larkfield	71	D3
Larkfield Av *Dublin 6W*	101	C2
Larkfield Av *Lucan*	83	D1
Larkfield Cl	71	D3
Larkfield Ct	83	D1
Larkfield Gdns	101	C2
Larkfield Grn	71	D3
Larkfield Gro		
Dublin 6W	101	C3
Larkfield Gro (Ballyowen)		
Lucan	71	D3
Larkfield Ms	66	B2
Larkfield Pk	101	C2
Larkfield Ri	83	D1
Larkfield Vw	83	D1
Larkfield Way	71	D3
Larkhill Rd	52	A2
Latchford Cl	30	B3
Latchford Grn	31	C3
Latchford Pk	31	C3
Latchford Sq	31	C3
Latchford Ter	31	C3
La Touche Ct	143	D2
La Touche Ct	128	A2
La Touche Dr	87	C3
La Touche Pk	143	C1
La Touche Pl	143	D1
La Touche Rd *Dublin 12*	99	C1
La Touche Rd *Grey.*	143	D1
Lauderdale Est	142	A3
Lauderdale Ter **3**	142	A3
Lauders La	58	B1
Laundry La	101	C2
Laurel Av *Dublin 14*	114	B3
Laurel Av *Lough.*	138	B3
Laurel Ct	47	C3
Laurel Dr	114	B3
Laurel Hill	133	D1
Laurel Lo Rd	47	D3
Laurel Pk	96	B2
Laurel Rd	114	B3
Laurels, The *Dublin 6W*	101	C3
Laurels, The *Dublin 14*	114	B3
Laurelton *Dublin 6*	113	C1
Laurelton *Swords*	14	B2
Laurence Brook	86	B1
Laurleen	131	C2
Lavarna Gro	112	B1
Lavarna Rd	100	B3
Laverna Av	47	C3
Laverna Dale	47	C3
Laverna Gro	47	C3
Laverna Way	73	C3
Lavery Av	85	D3
Lavista Av (Killester)		
Dublin 5	80	B1
La Vista Av *Dublin 13*	59	C3
Lawn, The *Dublin 11*	50	B3
Lawn, The (Ballinteer)		
Dublin 16	128	B2
Lawn, The (Ballyboden)		
Dublin 16	126	A1
Lawn, The (Cookstown)		
Dublin 24	109	C2
Lawn, The *Celbr.*	66	A2
Lawn, The *Dunb.*	28	A1
Lawn, The *Kins.*	18	A2
Lawn, The *Mayn.*	64	A1
Lawns, The		
(Abbeyfarm)	66	A3
Lawnswood Pk	131	C1
Lawrence's Av	65	C3

Lawson Spinney	19	C2
Lawson Ter **18**	134	A1
Lea Cres	104	A1
Leahys Ter	92	A3
Lealand Av	95	D2
Lealand Cl	95	D2
Lealand Cres	95	D2
Lealand Dr	95	D2
Lealand Gdns	95	D2
Lealand Gro	95	D2
Lealand Rd	95	D1
Lealand Wk	95	D2
Lea Rd	104	A1
Le Bas Ter		
off Leinster Rd W	101	D2
Le Broquay Av	86	A3
Lee Rd	77	C1
Leeson Cl	90	B3
Leeson La	90	B3
Leeson Pk	102	B1
Leeson Pk Av	102	B1
Leeson Pl	90	B3
Leeson St Br	90	B3
Leeson St Lwr	90	B3
Leeson St Upr	90	B3
Leeson Village	102	B1
Le Fanu Dr	86	A3
Le Fanu Rd	86	A2
Lehaunstown Rd	137	D3
Leicester Av	101	D2
Leighlin Rd	100	B2
Lein Gdns		
(Gairdini Lein)	55	D3
Lein Pk	55	C2
Lein Rd	55	C2
Leinster Av	79	C3
Leinster Ct	65	C1
Leinster La		
off Leinster St S	145	E4
Leinster Lawn	115	C1
Leinster Mkt		
off D'Olier St	145	D2
Leinster Pk	65	C2
Leinster Pl	101	D2
Leinster Rd	101	D2
Leinster Rd W	101	D2
Leinster Sq	102	A2
Leinster St	64	B2
Leinster St E	79	C3
Leinster St N	77	D2
Leinster St S	145	E4
Leinster Ter **2**	96	B2
Leitrim Pl off Grand		
Canal St Upr	91	C3
Leixlip Br	68	B2
Leixlip Pk	68	A2
Leixlip Rd	69	D3
Leix Rd	77	C2
Leland Pl	91	C1
Lemon St	145	D4
Lennox Pl	102	A1
Lennox St	102	A1
Lentisk Lawn	56	A1
Leo Av off Leo St	78	A3
Leopardstown Av	131	C2
Leopardstown		
Business Cen	136	A1
Leopardstown Ct **2**	130	B2
Leopardstown Dr	131	C2
Leopardstown Gdns	131	C2
Leopardstown Gro	131	C2
Leopardstown Lawns	130	A3
Leopardstown Lawn **3**	131	C2
Leopardstown Oaks	131	C2
Leopardstown		
Office Pk	130	B2
Leopardstown Pk	131	C2
Leopardstown		
Retail Pk	130	B3
Leopardstown Ri	130	A3
Leopardstown Rd	130	B3
Leopardstown Valley	136	A1
Leo St	78	A3
Leslie Av	135	C2
Leslies Bldgs	77	D3
Leukos Rd	92	A2
Le Vere Ter	101	D1
Liberty La	90	A3
Library Rd D.L.	119	C3
Library Rd Shank.	140	B2
Liffey Cl	83	D1
Liffey Ct	83	D1
Liffey Cres	83	D1
Liffey Dale	83	D1
Liffey Dockyard	91	D1
Liffey Downs **1**	71	D3
Liffey Dr	83	D1
Liffey Gdns	83	D1
Liffey Glen **2**	83	D1
Liffey Grn	83	D1
Liffey Hall	83	D1
Liffey Lawn	84	A1
Liffey Pk	83	D1
Liffey Pl **3**	83	D1
Liffey Ri	83	D1
Liffey Rd	83	D1
Liffey Row	71	D3
Liffey St	87	C2
Liffey St Lwr	144	C2
Liffey St Upr	144	C2
Liffey St W		
off Benburb St	89	C1
Liffey Vale	83	D1
Liffey Valley Av	83	D1
Liffey Valley Pk	83	D1
Liffey Vw	83	D1
Liffey Vw Apts **2**	68	B2
Liffey Wk	84	A1
Liffey Way	83	D1
Liffey Wd	83	D1
Lilys Rd	30	B3
Limekiln Av	111	C1
Limekiln Cl	111	D1
Limekiln Dr	111	D1
Limekiln Gro	99	D3
Limekiln La	111	D1
Limekiln Pk	111	D1
Limekiln Rd	111	C1
Limelawn Pk	46	A2
Limelawn Pk Ct	46	A2
Limelawn Pk Glade	46	A2
Limelawn Pk Grn	46	A2
Limelawn Pk Hill	46	A2
Limelawn Pk Ri	46	A2
Limelawn Pk Wd	46	A2
Limes Rd	129	D2
Lime St	91	C2
Limetree Av	27	C1
Limewood Av	55	D1
Limewood Pk	55	D1
Limewood Rd	55	C1
Lincoln Hall	15	C1
Lincoln La	144	A2
Lincoln Pl	145	E4
Linden	117	C3
Linden Gro	117	C3
Linden Lea Pk	130	B1
Linden Vale	117	D3
Lindisfarne Av	95	D1
Lindisfarne Dr	95	D1
Lindisfarne Grn	95	D1
Lindisfarne Gro	95	D1
Lindisfarne Lawns	95	D1
Lindisfarne Pk	95	D1
Lindisfarne Vale	95	D1
Lindisfarne Wk	95	D1
Lindsay Ms	11	C3
Lindsay Rd	77	D2
Linenhall Par	144	B1
Linenhall Ter	144	B1
Link Rd	134	A1
Links, The D'bate	13	D1
Links, The Port.	26	B3
Linnetfields	30	B3
Linnetfields Av	30	B3
Linnetfields Cl	31	C3
Linnetfields Ct	30	B3
Linnetfields Dr	30	B3
Linnetfields Pk	30	B3
Linnetfields Ri	30	B3
Linnetfields Sq	30	B3
Linnetfields Vw	30	B3
Linnetfields Wk	30	B3
Lios Cian	14	B3
Lios Na Sidhe	123	D2
Lisburn St	144	B1
Liscannor Rd	76	A3
Liscanor **1**	135	C1
Liscarne Ct	84	B2
Liscarne Gdns	84	B2
Lisle Rd	99	D2
Lismore Rd	100	B2
Lissadel Av	88	A3
Lissadel Ct	100	A1
Lissadel Cres	18	B1
Lissadel Dr	100	A1
Lissadel Gro	18	B2
Lissadel Pk	18	B2
Lissadel Rd	100	A1
Lissadel Wd	18	B2
Lissenfield	102	A1
Lissen Hall Av	15	D3
Lissenhall Br Swords	15	D2
Lissen Hall Br (bridge)		
Swords	15	D2
Lissen Hall Ct	15	D3
Litten La	145	D2
Little Britain St	144	B1
Little Gro, The	66	B3
Little Meadow **5**	132	B3
Littlepace	31	C2
Littlepace Cl	31	C2
Littlepace Ct	31	C2
Littlepace Cres	31	C2
Littlepace Dr	31	C2
Littlepace Gallops	31	C2
Littlepace Meadow	31	C2
Littlepace Pk	31	C2
Littlepace Rd	31	C2
Littlepace Vw	31	C2
Littlepace Wk	31	C2
Littlepace Way	31	C2
Littlepace Wds	31	C2
Little Strand St	144	B2
Llewellyn Cl	128	A1
Llewellyn Ct	128	A1
Llewellyn Gro	128	A1
Llewellyn Lawn	128	A1
Llewellyn Pk	128	A1
Llewellyn Way	128	A1
Lockkeepers Wk	50	A3
Lock Rd	82	A2
Lodge, The	133	D1
Loftus La	144	C1
Lohunda Cres	46	A2
Lohunda Dale	46	A2
Lohunda Downs	46	A2
Lohunda Dr	46	A2
Lohunda Gro	46	A2
Lohunda Pk	45	D1
Lohunda Rd	46	A2
Lombard Ct	145	F2
Lombard St E	145	F3
Lombard St W	89	D3
Lomond Av	79	C2
London Br	91	D3
Londonbridge Dr		
off Londonbridge Rd	91	D3
Londonbridge Rd	91	D3
Longdale Ter	52	A1
Longfield Rd	43	C3
Longford La		
off Longford St Gt	144	C4
Longford Pl	119	C3
Longford St Gt	144	C4
Longford St Little	144	C4
Longford Ter	118	B3
Longlands	17	D1
Long La Dublin 7	78	A3
Long La Gro	89	D3
Longmeadow	137	D1
Longmeadow Gro	133	C3
Long Mile Rd	98	B2
Longs Pl	89	C2
Longwood Av	89	D3
Longwood Pk	113	D3
Lorcan Av	53	C1
Lorcan Cres	53	C1
Lorcan Dr	53	C1
Lorcan Grn	53	D1
Lorcan Gro	53	C1
Lorcan O'Toole Pk	100	A3
Lorcan Pk	53	C1
Lorcan Rd	53	C1
Lorcan Vil	53	D1
Lord Edward St	144	B3
Lordello Rd	140	B3
Lord's Wk	76	A3
Loreto Av Dublin 14	113	D3
Loreto Av Dalkey	135	C2
Loreto Ct	113	D3
Loreto Cres	113	D3
Loreto Gra	142	A3
Loreto Pk	113	D3
Loreto Rd	89	C3
Loreto Row	113	D3
Loreto Ter	113	D3
Loretto Av **2**	142	B2
Loretto Ter **3**	142	B2
Loretto Vil **4**	142	B2
Lorne Ter		
off Brookfield Rd	88	B2
Lotts	145	D2
Lough Conn Av	86	A1
Lough Conn Dr	86	A1
Lough Conn Rd		
(Bothar Loch Con)	86	A1
Lough Conn Ter	86	A1
Lough Derg Rd	55	D2
Loughlinstown Dr	138	B3
Loughlinstown Ind Est	138	B3
Loughlinstown Pk	138	B3
Loughlinstown Wd	138	B3
Loughsallagh Br	30	A1
Lourdes Rd	89	C3
Louvain	115	D2
Louvain Glade	115	D2
Love La E	91	C3
Lower Dodder Rd	113	D1
Lower Glen Rd	74	A3
Lower Kilmacud Rd		
Dublin 14	115	D3
Lower Kilmacud Rd		
Still.	116	A3
Lower Lucan Rd	71	D1
Lower Rd Dublin 20	73	D2
Lower Rd Shank.	141	C3
Luby Rd	88	A2
Lucan	70	B3
Lucan Br	70	B3
Lucan Bypass	82	B1
Lucan Hts	70	B3
Lucan Rd Dublin 20	74	A3
Lucan Rd Lucan	71	D3
Lucan Rd Palm.	73	C3
Lucan Shop Cen	82	A1
Ludford Dr	128	B1
Ludford Pk	128	B2
Ludford Rd	128	B1
Lugaquilla Av	110	B1
Lugmore La	121	D3
Luke St	145	E2
Lullymore Ter	89	C3
Lurgan St	144	B1
Lutterell Hall	28	B1
Luttrell Pk	46	B3
Luttrell Pk Cl	46	B3
Luttrell Pk Ct	46	B3
Luttrell Pk Cres	72	B1
Luttrell Pk Dr	46	B3
Luttrell Pk Grn	46	B3
Luttrell Pk Gro	46	B3
Luttrell Pk La	46	B3
Luttrell Pk Vw	46	B3
Luttrellstown Av	72	B1
Luttrellstown Beeches	72	A1
Luttrellstown Chase	72	A1
Luttrellstown Cl	72	B1
Luttrellstown Ct	72	A1
Luttrellstown Dale	72	A1
Luttrellstown Dr	72	B1
Luttrellstown Glade	72	B1
Luttrellstown Grn	72	B1
Luttrellstown Gro	72	B1
Luttrellstown Heath	72	B1
Luttrellstown Hts	72	B1
Luttrellstown Lawn	72	B1
Luttrellstown Oaks	72	B1
Luttrellstown Pk	72	B1
Luttrellstown Pl	72	B1
Luttrellstown Ri	72	B1
Luttrellstown Thicket	72	B1
Luttrellstown Vw	72	B1
Luttrellstown Wk	72	B1
Luttrellstown Way	72	B1
Luttrellstown Wd	72	B1
Lymewood Ms	38	A2
Lynchs La	86	B2
Lynchs Pl	77	D3

Lyndon Gate 76 A2
Lynwood 129 C1
Lyreen Ct **5** 65 C2
Lyreen Pk 65 C1

M

M50 Business Pk 110 A1
Mabbot La 145 E1
Mabel St 78 B2
Macartney Br 90 B3
McAuley Av 55 C2
McAuley Dr 55 C2
McAuley Pk 55 C2
McAuley Rd 55 C2
McCabe Vil 116 B1
McCarthy's Bldgs
  off Cabra Rd 77 D2
McCreadie's La 19 D2
McDowell Av 88 B2
McGrane Ct **3** 129 C1
McKee Av 36 B3
McKee Barracks 76 B3
McKee Dr 76 B3
McKee Pk 76 B3
McKee Rd 50 B1
McKelvey Av 36 A3
McKelvey Rd 36 B3
Macken St 91 C2
Macken Vil 91 C2
Mackies Pl 90 B3
Mackintosh Pk 132 B3
McMahon St 89 D3
McMorrough Rd 101 C3
Macroom Av 40 B3
Macroom Rd 40 B3
Mac Uilliam Av 121 D1
Mac Uilliam Cl **11** 121 D1
Mac Uilliam Ct **1** 121 D1
Mac Uilliam Cres 121 D1
Mac Uilliam Dale **3** 121 D1
Mac Uilliam Dr **10** 121 D1
Mac Uilliam Grn **8** 121 D1
Mac Uilliam Gro **7** 121 D1
Mac Uilliam Lawns **4** 121 D1
Mac Uilliam Ms **2** 121 D1
Mac Uilliam Par **5** 121 D1
Mac Uilliam Rd 121 D1
Mac Uilliam Wk **6** 121 D1
Mac Uilliam Way **9** 121 D1
Madden's La 138 B2
Madeleine Ter 87 D2
Madison Rd 88 B3
Magennis Pl 145 F3
Magennis Sq
  off Magennis Pl 145 F3
Magenta Cres 39 C3
Magenta Hall 53 C1
Magenta Pl 133 D1
Mageough Home 102 A3
Magna Business Pk 121 D1
Magna Dr 121 D2
Mahers Pl
  off Macken St 91 C2
Maiden Row 86 B1
Main Rd 110 A3
Main Rd Tallaght 110 B3
Main St (Raheny)
  Dublin 5 55 D3
Main St (Ballymun)
  Dublin 9 38 A3
Main St (Finglas)
  Dublin 11 50 B1
Main St (Baldoyle)
  Dublin 13 43 D3
Main St (Clongriffin)
  Dublin 13 42 B2
Main St (Howth)
  Dublin 13 61 C2
Main St (Dundrum)
  Dublin 14 114 B3
Main St (Rathfarnham)
  Dublin 14 113 C2
Main St Dublin 20 86 B1
Main St Dublin 24 110 A3
Main St Black. 117 D2
Main St Bray 142 A2

Main St Celbr. 66 B3
Main St Clond. 96 B2
Main St D'bate 13 D2
Main St Dunb. 28 B2
Main St Leix. 68 B2
Main St Lucan 70 A3
Main St Mala. 20 A1
Main St Mayn. 64 B2
Main St Swords 17 C1
Malachi Rd 89 C1
Malahide Rd Dublin 3 79 D2
Malahide Rd Dublin 5 54 A3
Malahide Rd Dublin 17 55 C1
Malahide Rd Balg. 41 D1
Malahide Rd Swords 17 D1
Malahide Rbt 17 D1
Malahide Sta 20 A2
Malborough Ct **9** 134 A2
Mall, The Dublin 15 46 B2
Mall, The Leix. 68 B2
Mall, The Lucan 70 A3
Mall, The Mala. 20 A2
Mallin Av 89 C3
Malone Gdns 91 D2
Malpas Pl
  off Malpas St 89 D3
Malpas St 89 D3
Malpas Ter
  off Malpas St 89 D3
Maltings, The 142 A1
Mander's Ter
  off Ranelagh Rd 102 B1
Mangerton Rd 99 C1
Mannix Rd 78 A1
Manor Av Dublin 6W 112 B1
Manor Av Grey. 143 D2
Manor Cl 128 A2
Manor Ct 65 C2
Manor Cres 31 C3
Manor Dr 42 A3
Manorfields 31 C3
Manorfields Pk 31 C3
Manorfields Ter 31 C3
Manor Grn 127 D2
Manor Heath 128 A1
Manor Grn (Ballinteer)
  Dublin 16 127 D2
Manor Pk Dublin 20 85 D1
Manor Pl Dublin 7 89 C1
Manor Pl Clons. 30 B3
Manor Ri 128 A2
Manor Rd 85 D1
Manor Sq 30 B3
Manor St 77 D2
Mansion Ho 145 D4
Mantua Pk 15 D3
Maolbuille Rd 52 A2
Mapas Av 134 A2
Mapas Rd 134 B2
Maple Av Castle. 47 C3
Maple Av Still. 130 A3
Maple Cl 47 C3
Maple Dr Dublin 6W 101 C3
Maple Dr Castle. 47 C3
Maple Dr Dunb. 29 C3
Maple Glen 47 C3
Maple Grn 47 C3
Maple Gro Ashb. 11 C2
Maple Gro Castle. 47 C3
Maple Lawn 47 C3
Maple Manor 138 A1
Maple Rd 103 C3
Maples, The Dublin 14 115 C1
Maples, The D.L. 118 A3
Maples Rd 129 D2
Maplewood Av 123 C1
Maplewood Cl 123 C1
Maplewood Ct 123 C1
Maplewood Dr 123 C1
Maplewood Grn 123 C1
Maplewood Lawn 123 C1
Maplewood Pk 123 C1
Maplewood Rd 122 B1
Maplewood Way 123 C1
Maquay Br 91 C3
Maretimo Gdns E 118 A2
Maretimo Gdns W
  off Newtown Av 118 A2
Maretimo Pl
  off Newtown Av 118 A2
Maretimo Rd
  off Newtown Av 118 A2

Maretimo Vil
  off Newtown Av 117 D2
Marewood Cres 37 D3
Marewood Dr
  off Belclare Cres 37 D3
Marfield Cl **5** 123 D3
Marfield Ct **6** 123 D3
Marfield Cres **8** 123 D3
Marfield Grn 123 D3
Marfield Gro **7** 123 D3
Marfield Lawn **4** 123 D3
Marfield Pl 123 D3
Margaret Pl 91 D2
Marguerite Rd 78 A1
Marian Cres 112 B3
Marian Dr 112 B3
Marian Gro 112 B3
Marian Pk Dublin 13 57 C1
Marian Pk (Rathfarnham)
  Dublin 14 112 B3
Marian Pk Black. 131 D1
Marian Rd 112 B3
Marie Vil **5** 142 B2
Marigold Av 41 C3
Marigold Ct **4** 41 C3
Marigold Cres **5** 41 C3
Marigold Gro **6** 41 C3
Marigold Pk **7** 41 C3
Marina Village 20 A1
Marine Av 134 A1
Marine Ct 134 A1
Marine Dr 92 A3
Marine Par 134 A1
Marine Rd 119 D3
Mariners Cove 61 C3
Mariner's Port 91 C1
Marine Ter **9** Bray 142 B1
Marine Ter D.L. 119 D3
Marine Ter Grey. 143 D1
Marino Av 79 D1
Marino Av E 139 D2
Marino Av W 139 C2
Marino Grn 79 D1
Marino Inst of Ed 79 C1
Marino Mart 79 D2
Marino Pk 79 C2
Marino Pk Av 79 C2
Marion Vil 89 C2
Market Sq **8** 142 A2
Market St S 89 C2
Marks All W 144 B4
Marks La 145 F3
Mark St 145 F3
Marlay Vw 128 A3
Marlborough Ms 76 B3
Marlborough Pk **2** 133 D2
Marlborough Pl 145 D1
Marlborough Rd (Donnybrook)
  Dublin 4 102 B2
Marlborough Rd
  Dublin 7 76 B3
Marlborough Rd
  G'geary 134 A2
Marlborough St 145 D1
Marlborough Ter **10** 142 B1
Marley Av 127 D1
Marley Cl 128 A1
Marley Ct N 128 A1
Marley Ct S 128 A1
Marley Dr 127 D1
Marley Gro 127 D1
Marley Lawn 127 D1
Marley Ri 127 D1
Marley Vil **1** 127 D1
Marley Wk 127 D1
Marlfield 137 D1
Marne Vil 77 D3
Marrowbone La 89 C3
Marrowbone La Cl 89 C2
Marshal La 89 C2
Marsham Ct 130 A1
Martello Av 119 D3
Martello Ct 27 C1
Martello Ms 104 B2
Martello Ter Boot. 117 C1
Martello Ter **1** Bray 142 B1
Martello Vw 104 A1
Martello Wd 104 B1
Martin Savage Pk 49 C3
Martin Savage Rd 75 D2
Martins Row 86 B1
Martin St 102 A1

Mart La 132 A3
Maryfield Av 54 A2
Maryfield Coll 53 C3
Maryfield Cres 54 A2
Maryfield Dr 54 A2
Maryland **3** 141 C2
Mary's Abbey 144 B2
Mary's La 144 B2
Mary St 144 C2
Mary St Little 144 B2
Maryville Rd 55 C3
Mask Av (Ascal Measc) 54 B2
Mask Cres 54 B2
Mask Dr 54 B2
Mask Grn 54 B2
Mask Rd 54 B2
Mastersons La
  off Charlemont St 90 A3
Mather Rd N 116 A2
Mather Rd S 116 A2
Maunsell Pl
  off Mountjoy St 78 A2
Maxwell Rd 102 A2
Maxwell St 89 C3
Mayberry Pk 109 D2
Mayberry Rd 109 D2
Mayeston Boul 37 C2
Mayeston Cl 37 C2
Mayeston Ct 37 C2
Mayeston Cres 37 C2
Mayeston Downs 37 C2
Mayeston Dr 37 C2
Mayeston Lawn 37 C2
Mayeston Ri 37 C2
Mayeston Sq 37 C2
Mayeston Wk 37 C2
Mayfair 20 B2
Mayfield 113 D1
Mayfield Rd (Terenure)
  Dublin 6W 101 C3
Mayfield Rd (Kilmainham)
  Dublin 8 88 B3
Mayfield Ter Dublin 16 128 B2
Mayfield Ter **4** Bray 142 A3
May La 144 A2
Mayne Br 43 D2
Mayne River Av 41 D2
Mayne Rd 42 B1
Maynooth Pk 65 C3
Maynooth Rd 28 A3
Maynooth Sta 65 C2
Mayola Ct 114 B2
Mayor St Lwr 91 C1
Mayor St Upr 91 C1
May St 78 B2
Mayville Ter **1** 135 C2
Maywood Av 56 A3
Maywood Cl 56 A3
Maywood Cres 56 A3
Maywood Dr 56 A3
Maywood Gro 56 A3
Maywood La 56 A3
Maywood Pk 56 A3
Maywood Rd 56 A3
Meades Ter 91 C2
Meadow, The
  Dublin 16 128 B2
Meadow, The Mala. 21 C3
Meadow Av **2** 128 B1
Meadowbank 113 D1
Meadowbrook 64 B3
Meadowbrook Av
  Dublin 13 57 D1
Meadowbrook Av
  Mayn. 64 B3
Meadow Brook Cl 64 B3
Meadow Brook Ct Ashb. 11 C3
Meadowbrook Ct Mayn. 64 B3
Meadowbrook Cres 64 B3
Meadowbrook Dr 64 B3
Meadowbrook Lawn 57 D1
Meadowbrook Lawns 64 B3
Meadowbrook Pk 57 D1
Meadowbrook Rd 64 B3
Meadow Cl Dublin 16 128 A1
Meadow Cl Black. 131 D1
Meadow Copse 31 D3
Meadow Ct **1** 138 B3
Meadow Dale **1** 31 D3
Meadow Downs 45 D3
Meadow Dr 31 D3
Meadow Grn 45 D3

Name	Page	Grid
Meadow Gro	128	A1
Meadow Mt	128	A1
Meadow Pk	128	A1
Meadow Pk Av	128	A1
Meadows, The *Dublin 5*	55	C3
Meadows, The *Celbr.*	66	A1
Meadows, The *Dunb.*	28	B2
Meadows E, The	109	C2
Meadows W, The	109	C2
Meadow Vale	132	B3
Meadow Vw *Dublin 14*	128	A1
Meadow Vw *Dunb.*	28	B2
Meadow Vil **1**	128	A1
Meadow Way	31	D3
Meakstown Cotts	36	B2
Meath Pl *Dublin 8*	144	A4
Meath Pl *Bray*	142	B2
Meath Rd	142	B2
Meath Sq *off Gray St*	144	A4
Meath St	144	A3
Meehan Sq	116	A1
Meetinghouse La		
off Mary's Abbey	144	C2
Méile An Rí Cres	83	D2
Méile An Rí Dr	83	D2
Méile An Rí Grn	83	D2
Méile An Rí Pk	83	D2
Méile An Rí Rd	83	D3
Mellifont Av	119	D3
Mellowes Av	50	A1
Mellowes Ct	50	B1
Mellowes Cres	50	B1
Mellowes Pk	50	A1
Mellowes Rd	50	A1
Mellows Br	89	C1
Melrose Av *Dublin 3*	79	C2
Melrose Av *Clond.*	95	D1
Melrose Cres	95	D1
Melrose Grn	95	D1
Melrose Gro	95	D1
Melrose Lawn	95	D1
Melrose Pk *Clond.*	95	D1
Melrose Pk *Swords*	18	A3
Melrose Rd	95	D1
Melville Cl	37	C3
Melville Ct	36	B3
Melville Cres	36	B3
Melville Dr	36	B3
Melville Grn	36	B3
Melville Gro	37	C3
Melville Pk	36	B3
Melville Ter	36	B3
Melville Vw	36	B3
Melville Way	36	B3
Melvin Rd	101	C3
Memorial Rd	145	E2
Mercer St Lwr	144	C4
Mercer St Upr	90	A3
Merchamp	81	C2
Merchants Quay	144	A3
Merchants Rd	91	D1
Meretimo Vil **26**	142	B2
Meridianpoint	143	D2
Merlyn Dr	104	A2
Merlyn Pk	104	A2
Merlyn Rd	104	A2
Merrion Cres	104	B3
Merrion Gro	116	B1
Merrion Pk	116	B2
Merrion Pl	145	E4
Merrion Rd	103	D1
Merrion Row	90	B3
Merrion Shop Cen	104	A2
Merrion Sq E	90	B3
Merrion Sq N	145	F4
Merrion Sq S	145	F4
Merrion Sq W	145	E4
Merrion Strand	104	B2
Merrion St Lwr		
off Lincoln Pl	145	F4
Merrion St Upr	90	B3
Merrion Vw Av	104	A2
Merrion Village	104	A2
Merrywell Business Pk	98	A3
Merrywell Ind Est	98	A3
Merton Av	89	C3
Merton Cres	102	B3
Merton Dr	102	B2
Merton Rd	102	B3
Merton Wk	102	B3
Merville Av *Dublin 3*	79	C2
Merville Av *Still.*	130	B1
Merville Rd	130	B1
Mespil Rd	90	B3
Mews, The *Dublin 3*	80	B2
Mews, The (Dollymount)		
Dublin 3	81	D2
Mews, The **6** *Mala.*	21	C3
Mews, The *Sally.*	133	C3
Michael Collins Pk	96	A1
Middle Ill	80	B2
Milesian Av	18	A2
Milesian Ct	18	A2
Milesian Gro	18	A2
Milesian Lawn	18	A2
Milford	19	C1
Military Cem	76	A2
Military Rd (Rathmines)		
Dublin 6	102	A1
Military Rd (Kilmainham)		
Dublin 8	88	B2
Military Rd (Phoenix Pk) *Dublin 8*		
87		C1
Military Rd *Kill.*	139	C2
Millbank	26	B3
Millbourne Av	78	A1
Millbrook Av	55	D1
Millbrook Ct	88	B2
Millbrook Dr	56	A1
Millbrook Gro	55	D1
Millbrook Lawns	124	A1
Millbrook Rd	55	D1
Millbrook Village		
off Prospect La	103	C3
Mill Cen	96	B1
Mill Ct Av	95	D2
Mill Ct Dr	95	D2
Mill Ct Way	95	D2
Millennium Br	144	A2
Millennium Business Pk	34	B2
Millfarm	29	C2
Millfield	26	B3
Millgate Dr	111	D1
Mill Gro	143	C3
Mill La *Dublin 8*	89	D3
Mill La *Dublin 15*	49	C3
Mill La *Dublin 20*	73	D3
Mill La *Leix.*	68	B2
Mill La *Lough.*	141	C1
Mill La Business Pk	69	C2
Millmount Av	78	A1
Millmount Gro	114	B1
Millmount Pl	78	B1
Millmount Ter (Drumcondra)		
Dublin 9		
off Millmount Av	78	B1
Millmount Ter (Dundrum)		
Dublin 14		
off Millmount Gro	114	B1
Millmount Vil	78	A1
Mill Pk	96	A1
Mill Pond Apts, The **4**	96	B2
Mill Race Av	120	A2
Millrace Cl	75	C1
Mill Race Ct	120	A2
Mill Race Cres	120	A2
Mill Race Dr	120	A2
Mill Race Gdn	120	A2
Mill Race Grn	120	A2
Mill Race Pk	120	A2
Millrace Rd	75	C1
Mill Race Vw	120	A2
Mill Race Wk	120	A2
Mill Rd *Dublin 15*	47	D2
Mill Rd *Grey.*	143	C3
Mill Rd *Sagg.*	120	A2
Millstead	47	D2
Millstream	26	B3
Millstream Rd	69	D3
Mill St	89	D3
Milltown Av	102	B3
Milltown Br	11	D3
Milltown Br Rd	102	B3
Milltown Dr	114	A2
Milltown Est	11	C3
Milltown Gro	114	A2
Milltown Hill		
off Milltown Rd	102	B3
Milltown Path	102	B3
Milltown Rd *Dublin 6*	102	B3
Milltown Rd *Ashb.*	11	D3
Milltown Sta	102	B3
Millview Cl **1**	19	C2
Millview Ct	19	C2
Millview Lawns	19	C2
Millview Rd	19	C2
Millwood Pk	55	D1
Millwood Vil	55	D1
Milners Sq	52	B1
Milton Ter **14**	142	A1
Milward Ter **16**	142	B2
Misery Hill	91	C2
Moatfield Av	55	C1
Moatfield Pk	55	C1
Moatfield Rd	55	C1
Moatview Av	40	B3
Moatview Ct	40	B2
Moatview Dr	40	B2
Moatview Gdns	40	B3
Moeran Rd	99	D2
Moira Rd	89	C1
Moland Pl		
off Talbot St	145	E1
Molesworth Pl		
off Schoolhouse La	145	E4
Molesworth St	145	D4
Molyneux Yd	144	A3
Monalea Dr	125	C1
Monalea Gro	125	C1
Monalea Pk	125	C1
Monalea Wd	125	C1
Monaloe Av	137	D1
Monaloe Ct **1**	137	D1
Monaloe Cres **2**	132	B3
Monaloe Dr	132	B3
Monaloe Pk	132	B3
Monaloe Pk Rd	132	B3
Monaloe Way	132	B3
Monarch Ind Est	109	D3
Monasterboice Rd	100	A1
Monastery Cres	97	C2
Monastery Dr	97	C2
Monastery Gate	97	D2
Monastery Gate Av	97	C2
Monastery Gate Cl	97	D2
Monastery Gate Copse	97	C2
Monastery Gate Grn	97	C2
Monastery Gate Lawns	97	D2
Monastery Gate Vil	97	C2
Monastery Heath	97	C2
Monastery Heath Av	97	C2
Monastery Heath Ct	97	C2
Monastery Heath Grn	97	C2
Monastery Heath Sq	97	C2
Monastery Hts **1**	97	C2
Monastery Pk	96	B2
Monastery Ri	96	B2
Monastery Rd	96	B2
Monastery Shop Cen	96	B2
Monastery Wk	97	C2
Monck Pl	77	D3
Monksfield	97	C2
Monksfield Ct	97	C2
Monksfield Downs	97	C1
Monksfield Gro	97	C1
Monksfield Hts	97	C2
Monksfield Lawn	97	C1
Monksfield Meadows	97	C2
Monksfield Wk	97	C2
Monks Meadow	21	D3
Monkstown Av	132	B3
Monkstown Cres	118	B3
Monkstown Fm	132	B1
Monkstown Gate	119	C3
Monkstown Gro	132	B1
Monkstown Rd	118	A2
Monkstown Sq **4**	132	B1
Monkstown Valley	118	B3
Montague Ct		
off Protestant Row	90	A3
Montague La	90	A3
Montague Pl		
off Montague La	90	A3
Montague St	90	A3
Montebello Ter **17**	142	B2
Monte Vella **4**	134	B2
Montgomery Vw	18	A1
Montone Business Pk	97	D1
Montpelier Dr	88	B1
Montpelier Gdns	88	B1
Montpelier Hill	88	B1
Montpelier Par	118	A3
Montpelier Pk	89	C1
Montpelier Pl	118	A3
Montpelier Vw	122	A2
Montrose Av	53	D2
Montrose Cl	53	D2
Montrose Ct	53	D2
Montrose Cres	54	A1
Montrose Dr	53	D1
Montrose Gro	53	D2
Montrose Pk	53	D2
Moorefield	138	B2
Moore La	145	D1
Moore's Cotts **4**	131	D1
Moore St	145	D1
Mooretown Av	15	C3
Mooretown Gro	15	C3
Mooretown Pk	14	B3
Mooretown Rd	15	C3
Moorfield	84	A3
Moorfield Av	84	B3
Moorfield Cl **2**	84	B3
Moorfield Dr	84	B3
Moorfield Grn	84	B3
Moorfield Gro	84	A3
Moorfield Lawns	84	B3
Moorfield Par	84	B3
Moorfield Wk	84	A3
Moorings, The	20	B2
Moreen Av	129	D2
Moreen Cl	129	D3
Moreen Lawn **3**	129	D3
Moreen Pk	129	D3
Moreen Rd	129	D3
Moreen Wk	129	D3
Morehampton La	103	C1
Morehampton Rd	103	C1
Morehampton Sq	102	B1
Morehampton Ter	103	C1
Morgan Pl		
off Inns Quay	144	B2
Morgan's Pl	48	B3
Morning Star Av	144	A1
Morning Star Rd	89	C3
Mornington Av	134	B1
Mornington Gro	54	B2
Mornington Rd	102	B2
Morrogh Ter	79	C1
Moss St	145	E2
Mountain Pk	124	A1
Mountain Vw	140	B3
Mountain Vw Apts **5**	142	A3
Mountain Vw Av		
off Shamrock Vil	101	D2
Mountain Vw Cotts		
Dublin 6	102	B2
Mountain Vw Cotts		
Castle.	72	B1
Mountain Vw Dr	114	A3
Mountain Vw Pk		
Dublin 14	114	A3
Mountainview Pk *Grey.*	143	C1
Mountain Vw Rd		
Dublin 6	102	B2
Mountain Vw Rd **1** *Kill.*	139	C2
Mountain Vil **2**	139	C2
Mount Albany	131	D1
Mount Albion Rd	114	A3
Mount Albion Ter **1**	114	A3
Mount Alton	125	D1
Mount Alton Ct	125	D1
Mount Andrew	71	D3
Mount Andrew Av	72	A3
Mount Andrew Cl	72	A3
Mount Andrew Ct	71	D3
Mount Andrew Dale	72	A3
Mount Andrew Gro	72	A3
Mount Andrew Ri	72	A3
Mount Annville	116	A3
Mount Annville Conv	115	D3
Mount Annville Lawn	115	D3
Mount Annville Pk	116	A3
Mount Annville Rd	115	D3
Mount Annville Wd	116	A3
Mount Argus Cl	101	C2
Mount Argus Ct	101	C2
Mount Argus Cres	101	C2
Mount Argus Grn	101	C2
Mount Argus Gro	101	C2
Mount Argus Pk	101	C2
Mount Argus Rd	101	C2

Mount Argus Ter	101	C2
Mount Argus Vw	101	C2
Mount Argus Way	101	C2
Mount Auburn **1**	134	A3
Mount Bellew Cres **1**	83	D1
Mount Bellew Grn **2**	83	C1
Mount Bellew Ri **1**	83	C1
Mount Bellew Way	83	C1
Mount Brown	88	B2
Mount Carmel Av	115	C2
Mount Carmel Pk	125	C1
Mount Carmel Rd	115	C2
Mount Dillon Ct	54	B2
Mountdown Dr	111	D1
Mountdown Pk	111	D1
Mountdown Rd	111	D1
Mount Drinan Av	18	A3
Mount Drinan Cres	18	A3
Mount Drinan Gro **5**	18	A3
Mount Drinan Lawn **1**	18	B3
Mount Drinan Pk	18	A3
Mount Drinan Wk	18	A3
Mount Drummond Av	101	D1
Mount Drummond Sq	101	D1
Mount Eagle Dr	130	A3
Mount Eagle Grn	130	A3
Mount Eagle Gro	130	A3
Mount Eagle Lawn	130	A3
Mount Eagle Ri	130	A3
Mount Eagle Vw	130	A3
Mount Eden Rd	103	C2
Mountfield	20	A3
Mount Gandon	70	A3
Mount Harold Ter	101	D2
Mount Jerome Cem	101	C1
Mountjoy Cotts	78	A2
Mountjoy Par		
off North Circular Rd	78	B2
Mountjoy Pl	78	B3
Mountjoy Prison	78	A2
Mountjoy Prison Cotts		
off Cowley Rd	78	A2
Mountjoy Sq E	78	B3
Mountjoy Sq N	78	A3
Mountjoy Sq S	78	A3
Mountjoy Sq W	78	A3
Mountjoy St	77	D3
Mountjoy St Mid	77	D3
Mount Merrion Av	116	B2
Mount Norris Vil **18**	142	B2
Mount Olive Gro	56	A1
Mount Olive Pk	56	A1
Mount Olive Rd	56	A1
Mountpleasant Av Lwr	102	A1
Mountpleasant Av Upr	102	A1
Mountpleasant Par		
off Prices La	102	A1
Mountpleasant Pl	102	A1
Mountpleasant Sq	102	A1
Mount Prospect Av	81	C2
Mount Prospect Dr	81	C1
Mount Prospect Gro	81	D1
Mount Prospect Lawns	81	C2
Mount Prospect Pk	81	C2
Mount Sackville Conv	74	A2
Mount Salus Rd	135	C3
Mountsandel	137	C2
Mount Sandford	103	C2
Mount Shannon Rd	88	B3
Mount St Cres	91	C3
Mount St Lwr	91	C2
Mount St Upr	90	B3
Mount Symon Av	45	C1
Mount Symon Cl	45	D2
Mount Symon Cres	45	C1
Mount Symon Dale	45	C1
Mount Symon Dr	45	C2
Mount Symon Grn	45	C2
Mount Symon Lawn	45	D2
Mount Symon Pk	45	C1
Mount Symon Ri	45	D1
Mount Tallant Av	101	C3
Mount Tallant Ter		
off Harolds Cross Rd	101	D1
Mount Temple Rd	89	C1

Mount Town Lwr	133	C1
Mounttown Pk **4**	133	C1
Mount Town Rd Upr	118	B3
Mount Vw Rd	46	A1
Mount Wd	133	C1
Mourne Rd	88	B3
Moyclare Av	57	D1
Moyclare Cl	57	D1
Moyclare Dr	57	D1
Moyclare Gdns	58	A1
Moyclare Pk	57	D1
Moyclare Rd	57	D1
Moycullen Rd	85	D2
Moy Elta Rd	79	C3
Moyglare Abbey	64	A1
Moyglare Meadows	64	B1
Moyglare Rd	64	B1
Moyglare Village	64	B1
Moy Glas Av	83	C2
Moy Glas Chase	83	C2
Moy Glas Cl	83	C2
Moy Glas Ct	83	C2
Moy Glas Dale	83	C2
Moy Glas Dene	83	C2
Moy Glas Dr	83	C2
Moy Glas Glen	83	C2
Moy Glas Grn	83	C2
Moy Glas Gro	83	C2
Moy Glas Lawn	83	C2
Moy Glas Pk	83	C2
Moy Glas Rd	83	C2
Moy Glas Vale	83	C2
Moy Glas Vw	83	C2
Moy Glas Way	83	C2
Moy Glas Wd	83	C2
Moyle Cres	96	B2
Moyle Rd	76	B1
Moyne Pk	43	C2
Moyne Rd	102	B2
Moynihan Ct	110	B3
Moyville	126	B2
Moyville Lawns	126	B1
Muckross Av	99	D3
Muckross Cres	99	D3
Muckross Dr	100	A3
Muckross Grn	100	A3
Muckross Gro	99	D3
Muckross Par		
off Killarney Par	78	A2
Muckross Pk	99	D3
Muirfield Dr	99	C1
Mulberry Cres	73	C1
Mulberry Dr	73	C1
Mulberry Pk	73	C1
Mulcahy Keane Est	99	C3
Muldowney Ct	20	B2
Mulgrave St	119	D3
Mulgrave Ter	133	D1
Mulhuddart Wd	32	A2
Mullinastill Rd	140	A1
Mulroy Rd	77	C1
Mulvey Rd	115	C2
Munster St	77	D2
Munster Ter **3**	134	B1
Murphystown Rd	130	A3
Murray's Cotts		
off Sarsfield Rd	87	D2
Murtagh Rd	89	C1
Museum of Modern Art		
(Royal Hospital)	88	A2
Museum Sta	89	C1
Muskerry Rd	86	B2
Mygan Business Pk	36	B3
Mygan Pk Ind Est	36	B3
Myra Cotts	88	A2
Myra Manor	25	C3
Myrtle Av Dublin 13	43	C3
Myrtle Av **16** D.L.	133	D1
Myrtle Ct	43	C3
Myrtle Dr	43	C3
Myrtle Gro	130	B1
Myrtle Pk	133	D1
Myrtle Sq	43	C3
Myrtle St	77	D3

N

Naas Rd Dublin 12	98	A2
Naas Rd Dublin 22	97	D2
Naas Rd Sagg.	106	B3
Naas Rd Business Pk	99	C1
Naas Rd Ind Pk	99	C1
Nangor Cres **1**	96	A2

Nangor Pl **2**	95	D2
Nangor Rd Dublin 12	97	C1
Nangor Rd Clond.	96	A2
Nangor Rd		
Business Cen	97	D1
Nanikin Av	55	D3
Nash St	87	C3
Nashville Pk	61	C2
Nashville Rd	61	C2
Nassau Pl	145	E4
Nassau St	145	D3
National Mus Dublin 2	145	E4
National Mus		
(Collins Barracks)		
Dublin 7	89	C1
National Transport Mus	59	D2
National Uni Ireland		
Maynooth	64	A1
Naul Rd	22	B1
Navan Rd Dublin 7	75	D1
Navan Rd Dublin 15	48	A3
Navan Rd (Blanchardstown)		
Dublin 15	32	B3
Navan Rd Clonee	31	C2
Navan Rd Dunb.	28	B2
Navan Rd Mulh.	31	D2
Neagh Rd	101	C3
Neillstown Av	84	B3
Neillstown Cres	84	B3
Neillstown Dr	84	B2
Neillstown Gdns	84	B2
Neillstown Pk	84	B3
Neilstown Cotts **2**	96	B1
Neilstown Rd	84	B2
Neilstown Shop Cen	84	A3
Neilstown Village Ct **1**	84	A3
Nelson St	78	A3
Nephin Rd	76	A2
Neptune Ter **4**	134	B1
Nerano Rd	135	C3
Nerneys Ct	78	A3
Neville Rd	102	A3
Nevinstown La	17	C3
New Bawn Dr	124	A1
New Bawn Pk	124	A1
New Bride St	90	A3
Newbridge Av Dublin 4	91	D3
Newbridge Av D'bate	13	C2
Newbridge Rd	91	D3
New Brighton Ter **9**	142	A2
Newbrook Av	56	B1
Newbrook Rd	56	B1
Newbury Av	40	A3
Newbury Dr	40	A3
Newbury Gro	40	A3
Newbury Lawns	40	A3
Newbury Pk	40	A3
Newbury Ter **1**	40	A3
Newcastle Rd	82	A1
New Ch St	144	A2
Newcomen Av	79	C3
Newcomen Br	79	C3
Newcomen Ct		
off Newcomen Av	79	C3
Newcourt	15	D3
Newcourt Av	142	B3
Newcourt Business Pk	36	A1
Newcourt Ms	15	D3
Newcourt Rd	142	B3
Newcourt Vil **6**	142	A3
New Gra Rd Dublin 7	77	C2
New Gra Rd Black.	131	D1
Newgrove Av	92	A3
New Gro Est	42	B3
Newhall Ct	122	A2
New Ireland Rd	88	B3
Newlands Av	97	C3
Newlands		
Business Cen	96	B3
Newlands Dr	96	B3
Newlands Manor	108	A1
Newlands Manor Ct	108	A1
Newlands Manor Dr	108	A1
Newlands Manor		
Fairway	108	A1
Newlands Manor Grn	108	A1
Newlands Manor Pk	108	A1
Newlands Pk	96	B3
Newlands Retail Cen	96	B3
Newlands Rd Clond.	96	B3
Newlands Rd Lucan	70	B3
Newlands Rd Ronan.	83	D2

New Lisburn St		
off Coleraine St	144	B1
New Lucan Rd	72	B3
Newman Pl	65	C2
Newmarket	89	D3
Newmarket St	89	D3
New Nangor Rd	96	A1
New Pk Lo **7**	131	D2
New Pk Rd	131	D1
Newport St	89	C2
New Rd (Inchicore)		
Dublin 8	87	C3
New Rd Dublin 13	61	C3
New Rd Clond.	96	B2
New Rd (Killincarrig)		
Grey.	143	C3
New Rd **1** Swords	17	D1
New Rd, The Dublin 11	34	B3
New Row S	89	D3
New Row Sq	144	B4
New St	20	A2
New St Gdns	89	D3
New St S	89	D3
Newtown	28	A2
Newtown Av Dublin 17	41	C3
Newtown Av Black.	118	A2
Newtown Br	15	D2
Newtown Cotts		
Dublin 17	55	C1
Newtown Cotts Swords	15	C1
Newtown Ct	64	B1
Newtown Dr	55	C1
Newtown Glendale	68	B1
Newtown Gro	64	B2
Newtown Ind Est	41	C3
Newtown Pk Dublin 17	41	C3
Newtown Pk Dublin 24	110	B3
Newtown Pk Black.	131	D1
Newtown Pk Leix.	68	B1
Newtownpark Av	117	C3
Newtown Pk Ct **5**	131	D1
Newtown Rd Dublin 17	41	C3
Newtown Rd Celbr.	66	B2
Newtown Rd Mayn.	64	A3
Newtown Vil	118	A2
New Vale	140	B2
New Vale Cotts	140	B3
New Vale Cres	140	B2
New Wapping St	91	C1
Niall St	77	C3
Nicholas Av		
off Church St	144	B1
Nicholas Pl		
off Patrick St	144	B4
Nicholas St	144	B4
Ninth Lock Rd	96	B2
Nore Rd	76	B1
Norfolk Mkt		
off Parnell St	78	A3
Norfolk Rd	77	D2
Norseman Pl	89	C1
North Av	116	A2
Northbrook Av	102	B3
Northbrook Av Lwr		
off North Strand Rd	79	C3
Northbrook Av Upr	79	C3
Northbrook La	102	B3
Northbrook Rd	102	A1
Northbrook Ter	79	C3
Northbrook Vil		
off Northbrook Rd	102	A1
Northbrook Wk	102	B3
North Circular Rd		
Dublin 1	78	A3
North Circular Rd		
Dublin 7	78	A2
Northcote Av	119	C3
Northcote Pl	119	C3
North Dublin		
Docklands	92	A1
Northern Cl	40	B2
Northern Cross		
Business Pk	36	A3
North Gt Clarence St	78	B3
North Gt Georges St	78	A3
Northland Dr	51	C3
Northland Gro	51	C3
North Pk Business &		
Office Pk	36	A3
North Quay Ext	91	D1
North Rd Dublin 8	75	C1
North Rd Dublin 11	36	A3

Name	Page	Grid
Northside Shop Cen	40	A3
North Strand Rd *Dublin 1*	78	B3
North Strand Rd *Dublin 3*	78	B3
North St	15	D3
North St Business Pk	15	D3
Northumberland	119	D3
Northumberland Pk	119	D3
Northumberland Pl off *Northumberland*	119	D3
Northumberland Rd	91	C3
North Wall Quay	91	C1
Northway Est	36	A3
North W Business Pk	34	A1
Nortons Av	77	D3
Norwood	139	C3
Norwood Pk	102	B2
Nottingham St	79	C3
Novara Av	142	A1
Novara Ms **15**	142	A1
Novara Pk **10**	142	A2
Novara Ter **11**	142	A2
Nugent Rd	114	A3
Nurney Lawn	42	A3
Nurseries, The **4** *B'brack*	139	C2
Nurseries, The *Mulh.*	32	B2
Nurseries, The *Swords*	16	B2
Nutgrove Av (Ascal An Charrain Chno)	113	D3
Nutgrove Cres	114	A3
Nutgrove Enterprise Pk	114	A3
Nutgrove Office Pk	114	A3
Nutgrove Pk	115	C1
Nutgrove Shop Cen	114	A3
Nutgrove Way	114	A3
Nutley Av	103	D2
Nutley La	104	A3
Nutley Pk	104	A3
Nutley Rd	103	D2
Nutley Sq	103	D3

O

Name	Page	Grid
Oak Apple Grn	101	D3
Oak Av	39	C3
Oak Cl	97	D1
Oak Ct	39	C3
Oakcourt Av	85	D1
Oakcourt Cl	85	D1
Oakcourt Dr	85	D1
Oakcourt Gro	85	D1
Oakcourt Lawn	85	D1
Oakcourt Lawns	85	D1
Oakcourt Pk	85	D1
Oak Cres	39	C2
Oakdale Cl	125	C3
Oakdale Cres	124	B3
Oakdale Dr *Dublin 24*	125	C3
Oakdale Dr *Corn.*	133	C3
Oakdale Gro	125	C3
Oakdale Pk	124	B3
Oakdale Rd	124	B3
Oak Dene	134	A3
Oakdown Rd	114	A3
Oak Downs	96	A3
Oak Dr *Dublin 9*	39	C3
Oak Dr *Dublin 12*	97	D2
Oakfield	96	B1
Oakfield Ind Est	96	B1
Oakfield Pl	89	D3
Oak Grn	39	C3
Oak Gro	39	C3
Oaklands	143	C1
Oaklands Av	17	D1
Oaklands Cres	102	A3
Oaklands Dr *Dublin 4*	103	D1
Oaklands Dr *Dublin 6*	102	A3
Oaklands Pk *Dublin 4*	103	D1
Oaklands Pk *Swords*	17	D1
Oaklands Ter *Dublin 4* off *Serpentine Av*		
Oaklands Ter *Dublin 6*	101	D3
Oak Lawn *Dublin 9*	39	C3
Oak Lawn *Dublin 15*	47	D3
Oak Lawn *Castle.*	48	A3
Oaklawn *Leix.*	68	A2
Oaklawn Cl	68	A2
Oaklawn W	68	A2
Oakleigh	66	A3
Oakley Gro	117	D3
Oakley Pk *Dublin 3*	81	C2
Oakley Pk *Black.*	117	D3
Oakley Rd	102	B1
Oak Lo	74	A1
Oak Pk Av	53	C1
Oak Pk Cl	53	C1
Oak Pk Dr	39	C3
Oak Pk Gro	39	C3
Oak Ri *Dublin 9*	39	C3
Oak Ri *Clond.*	96	A3
Oak Rd *Dublin 9*	79	D1
Oak Rd *Dublin 12*	97	D2
Oak Rd Business Pk	97	D1
Oaks, The *Dublin 3*	81	D2
Oaks, The *Dublin 14*	114	B3
Oaks, The *Dublin 16*	128	B2
Oaks, The (Cookstown) *Dublin 24*	109	C2
Oaks, The **16** *Abb.*	139	C3
Oaks, The *Celbr.*	66	B2
Oaks, The **5** *Lough.*	138	B3
Oaks, The (Hilltown) *Swords*	16	B2
Oakton Ct	138	B2
Oakton Dr	138	B2
Oakton Grn **2**	138	B2
Oakton Pk	138	B2
Oaktree Av	47	C3
Oaktree Dr	47	C3
Oaktree Grn	47	C3
Oaktree Gro	47	C3
Oaktree Lawn	47	C3
Oaktree Rd	130	B2
Oak Vw	39	C3
Oakview Av	45	D1
Oakview Cl	45	D1
Oakview Ct	45	D1
Oakview Dr	45	D1
Oakview Gro **1**	45	D1
Oakview Lawn	45	D1
Oakview Pk	45	D1
Oakview Ri	45	D1
Oakview Wk	45	D1
Oakview Way	45	D1
Oak Way	46	A3
Oakwood Av *Dublin 11*	51	C1
Oakwood Av *Swords*	17	C1
Oakwood Cl	37	C3
Oakwood Gro Est	96	A1
Oakwood Pk	37	C3
Oakwood Rd	37	C3
Oatfield Av	84	B2
Oatfield Cl	84	B2
Oatfield Cres	84	B2
Oatfield Dr	84	B2
Oatfield Gro	84	B2
Oatfield Lawn	84	B2
Oatfield Pk	84	B2
Obelisk Ct **6**	131	D1
Obelisk Gro	117	D3
Obelisk Ri	131	D1
Obelisk Vw	131	C1
Obelisk Wk	117	D3
O'Brien Rd	99	D2
O'Brien's Inst	79	D1
O'Brien's Pl N	78	A1
O'Brien's Ter off *Prospect Rd*	77	D2
Observatory La	102	A1
O'Byrne Rd	142	A3
O'Byrne Vil **7**	142	A3
O'Carolan Rd	89	D3
Ocean Pier	92	A1
O'Connell Av	77	D3
O'Connell Br	145	D2
O'Connell Gdns	91	D3
O'Connell Gdns **9**	133	D1
O'Connell St Lwr	145	D1
O'Connell St Upr	145	D1
O'Curry Av	89	D3
O'Curry Rd	89	D3
O'Daly Rd	52	A3
Odd Lamp Rd	75	D2
O'Devaney Gdns	88	B1
O'Donnell Gdns **9**	133	D1
O'Donoghue St	87	C3
O'Donovan Rd	89	D3
O'Donovan Rossa Br	144	B3
O'Dwyer Rd	99	D2
Offaly Rd	77	C2
Offington Av	59	C1
Offington Ct	59	C1
Offington Dr	59	C2
Offington Lawn	59	C2
Offington Pk	59	C1
O'Hanlon's La	20	A2
O'Hogan Rd	87	C2
Olaf Rd	89	C1
Olcovar	140	B3
Old Ballycullen Rd	125	C1
Old Bawn Av	123	D1
Old Bawn Cl	124	A2
Old Bawn Ct	124	A1
Old Bawn Dr	124	A2
Old Bawn Pk	123	D2
Old Bawn Rd	124	A1
Old Bawn Ter **1**	124	A2
Old Bawn Way	123	D1
Old Belgard Rd	109	C2
Old Belgard Rd Business Pk	109	C2
Oldbridge	83	C3
Oldbridge Cl	83	C2
Oldbridge Ct	82	B3
Oldbridge Glen	83	C3
Oldbridge Grn	83	C3
Oldbridge Gro	83	C3
Oldbridge Pk	82	B3
Old Br Rd	112	A2
Oldbridge Vw	83	C3
Oldbridge Wk	83	C3
Oldbridge Way	82	B3
Old Brighton Ter **12**	142	A2
Old Cabra Rd	76	B2
Old Camden St off *Harcourt Rd*	90	A3
Old Castle Av	59	C3
Oldcastle Dr	95	C2
Oldcastlepark	95	C2
Oldcastlepark Cl	95	C2
Oldcastlepark Grn	95	C2
Oldcastlepark Gro	95	C2
Oldcastlepark Lawn	95	C2
Oldcastlepark Vw	95	C2
Oldchurch Av	95	D2
Oldchurch Cl	95	D2
Oldchurch Ct	95	D2
Oldchurch Cres	95	D2
Oldchurch Dr	95	D2
Oldchurch Gro	95	D2
Oldchurch Lawn	95	D2
Oldchurch Pk	95	D2
Oldchurch Way	95	D2
Old Corduff Rd	47	C1
Old Cornmill Rd	69	D3
Old Co Glen	100	B1
Old Co Rd	100	A1
Oldcourt Av	124	B3
Oldcourt Cl	124	B2
Oldcourt Cotts	124	B3
Oldcourt Fm	124	B2
Oldcourt Lawn	124	A2
Oldcourt Lo	124	B2
Oldcourt Manor	124	B3
Oldcourt Rd	125	C3
Oldcourt Ter **8**	142	A3
Oldcourt Vw	124	B2
Old Dublin Rd	116	B3
Old Dunleary	119	C3
Old Fairgreen	28	B2
Old Fm, The	115	D3
Old Forge, The	82	B3
Old Golf Links, The	20	A2
Old Greenfield	64	B2
Old Hill *Leix.*	68	A2
Old Hill, The *Lucan*	70	B3
Old Kilmainham	88	B2
Old Kilmainham Village	88	B2
Old Malahide Rd	54	B1
Old Mill Ct	89	D3
Old Mountpleasant off *Ranelagh Rd*	102	B1
Old Naas Rd *Dublin 12*	98	B1
Old Naas Rd *Kings.*	107	D2
Old Orchard	112	A3
Old Quarry	134	B2
Old Rathmichael	140	A3
Old Rectory	70	B3
Old Rectory Pk	115	C3
Old Rd	26	A3
Old Sawmills Ind Est	99	C3
Old St	20	A2
Oldtower Cres	84	A1
Oldtown Av	52	A1
Oldtown Cotts	66	A2
Oldtown Mill	66	A2
Oldtown Mill Rd	66	A2
Oldtown Pk	52	A1
Oldtown Rd	52	A1
Old Yellow Walls Rd	19	C1
O'Leary Rd	88	A3
Olivemount Gro	115	C1
Olivemount Rd	115	C1
Oliver Bond St	144	A3
Oliver Plunkett Av (Irishtown) *Dublin 4*	91	D2
Oliver Plunkett Av *D.L.*	132	B3
Oliver Plunkett Rd	132	B3
Oliver Plunkett Sq **9**	132	B3
Oliver Plunkett Ter **10**	132	B3
Oliver Plunkett Vil **5**	132	B1
Olney Cres	113	C3
Omac Business Cen	96	B2
Omni Pk	52	B1
Omni Pk Shop Cen	52	B1
O'Moore Rd	87	C2
O'Neachtain Rd	78	A1
O'Neill Pk	65	C1
O'Neill's Bldgs	90	A3
Ongar Chase	30	A3
Ongar Grn	44	B1
Ongar Pk	45	C1
Ongar Village	44	B1
Ontario Ter	102	A1
Onward Cl	27	C1
Onward Wk	27	C1
Ophaly Ct	115	C2
O'Quinn Av	88	B2
O'Rahilly Par off *Moore St*	145	D1
Oranmore Rd	85	D2
Orchard, The *Dublin 3*	79	C2
Orchard, The *Dublin 5*	54	B3
Orchard, The *Dublin 6W*	100	B3
Orchard, The **3** *Dublin 13*	41	D3
Orchard, The *Black.*	131	D1
Orchard, The **3** *Cool.*	46	B3
Orchard, The *Palm.*	73	C2
Orchard Av *City W*	107	C3
Orchard Av *Clons.*	46	A2
Orchard Cl (Blanchardstown) *Dublin 15*	46	B2
Orchard Cl *D'bate*	13	D1
Orchard Cotts **2**	117	D3
Orchard Ct	46	B2
Orchard Grn	46	B2
Orchard Gro (Blanchardstown)	46	B2
Orchard La *Dublin 6*	102	A1
Orchard La *Black.*	131	D1
Orchard Lawns	85	D2
Orchard Pk	37	D3
Orchard Rd *Dublin 3*	79	C2
Orchard Rd *Dublin 5*	56	B3
Orchard Rd *Dublin 5*	102	A3
Orchard Rd *Clond.*	96	B2
Orchardston	112	B3
Orchardstown Av	112	B3
Orchardstown Dr	112	A3
Orchardstown Pk	112	B3
Orchardstown Vil	112	B3
Orchard Ter **9**	142	A3
Orchardton **1**	126	B1
Ordnance Survey Office	74	B2
Ordnance Survey Rd	74	B2
O'Reilly's Av	88	B2
Oriel Pl	79	C3
Oriel St Lwr	91	C1
Oriel St Upr	91	C1
Orlagh Av	125	D2
Orlagh Cl	126	A2
Orlagh Ct	125	D2
Orlagh Cres	125	D2
Orlagh Downs	126	A2
Orlagh Gra	126	A2
Orlagh Grn	125	D2
Orlagh Gro	125	D2
Orlagh Lawn	125	D2
Orlagh Lo	126	A2
Orlagh Meadows	126	A2
Orlagh Pk	125	D2

Orlagh Pines	125	D2
Orlagh Ri	125	D2
Orlagh Vw	126	A2
Orlagh Way	125	D2
Orlagh Wd	126	A2
Ormeau Dr	134	B2
Ormeau St		
off Gordon St	91	C2
Ormond Av	14	A3
Ormond Cl	14	A3
Ormond Cres	14	A3
Ormond Dr	14	A3
Ormond Gro	14	A3
Ormond Lawn	14	A3
Ormond Mkt Sq *off*		
Ormond Quay Upr	144	B2
Ormond Quay Lwr	144	C2
Ormond Quay Upr	144	B3
Ormond Rd N	78	B1
Ormond Rd S		
(Rathmines)	102	A2
Ormond Sq	144	B2
Ormond St	89	C3
Ormond Vw	14	A3
Ormond Way	14	A3
O'Rourke Pk	133	C2
Orpen Cl	117	C3
Orpen Dale	117	C3
Orpen Grn	131	C1
Orpen Hill	131	C1
Orpen Ri	131	C1
Orwell Gdns	114	A1
Orwell Pk	114	A1
Orwell Pk Av	111	D2
Orwell Pk Cl	111	D2
Orwell Pk Cres	111	D2
Orwell Pk Dale	111	D2
Orwell Pk Dr	111	D2
Orwell Pk Glade	111	D2
Orwell Pk Glen	111	D2
Orwell Pk Grn	111	D2
Orwell Pk Gro	111	D2
Orwell Pk Hts	111	D2
Orwell Pk Lawns	111	D2
Orwell Pk Ri	111	D2
Orwell Pk Vw	111	D2
Orwell Pk Way	111	D2
Orwell Rd *Dublin 6*	101	D3
Orwell Rd *Dublin 6W*	111	D2
Orwell Rd *Dublin 14*	114	A1
Orwell Shop Cen	111	D2
Orwell Wk	114	A1
Orwell Wds	114	A1
Oscar Sq	89	D3
Oscar Traynor Rd	40	A3
O'Shea's Cotts **3**	137	D1
Osprey Av	111	C1
Osprey Dr	111	D2
Osprey Lawn	111	D1
Osprey Pk	111	C1
Osprey Rd	111	D2
Ossory Rd	79	C3
Ossory Sq	89	D3
Ostman Pl	77	C3
O'Sullivan Av	78	B2
Oswald Rd	92	A3
Otranto Pl	134	A1
Otterbrook	113	C3
Oulart	17	C2
Oulton Rd	80	B2
Our Ladys Cl	89	C2
Our Lady's Hospice	101	C1
Our Lady's Rd	89	C3
Oval, The	73	D3
Ovoca Rd	89	D3
Owendoher Haven	126	B1
Owendoher Lo	126	B1
Owendore Av	113	C2
Owendore Cres	113	C2
Owens Av	88	B2
Owenstown Pk	116	A2
Oxford Rd	102	A1
Oxford Ter *Dublin 3*		
off Church Rd	91	C1
Oxford Ter *Dublin 6*		
off Oxford Rd	102	A1

Oxmantown La		
off Blackhall Pl	89	C1
Oxmantown Rd	77	C3
Oxmantown Rd Lwr		
off Arbour Hill	89	C1

P

Pace Av	31	C2
Pace Cres	31	C2
Pacelli Av	57	C2
Pace Rd	31	C2
Pace Vw	31	C2
Packenham	119	C3
Paddock, The *Dublin 7*	75	C1
Paddock, The *Celbr.*	66	A1
Paddocks, The **4** *Clons.*	30	B3
Paddocks, The *Dalkey*	134	B1
Paddocks, The *Dunb.*	28	B2
Pairc Baile Munna	51	D1
Pairc Clearmont		
(Claremont Pk)	92	A3
Pairc Gleannaluinn		
(Glenaulin Pk)	74	A3
Pairc Gleann Trasna	123	D2
Pairc Mhuire	120	B2
Pairc Na Cuilenn	51	D1
Pakenham Br	44	B2
Pakenham Rd	118	B3
Palace St		
off Dame St	144	C3
Palmer Pk	127	C1
Palmers Av	85	C1
Palmers Cl	85	C1
Palmers Copse	85	C1
Palmers Ct	85	C1
Palmers Cres	85	C1
Palmers Dr	85	C1
Palmers Glade	85	C1
Palmers Gro	85	C1
Palmers Lawn	85	C1
Palmers Pk	85	C1
Palmers Rd	85	C1
Palmerston Av	85	D1
Palmerston Gdns	102	A3
Palmerston Gro	103	C3
Palmerston La	102	A3
Palmerston Pk		
Dublin 6	102	A3
Palmerston Pk *Palm.*	85	C1
Palmerston Pl	77	D3
Palmerston Rd	102	A2
Palmerston Vil	102	A3
Palmerstown Av	85	C1
Palmerstown Cl	85	C1
Palmerstown Ct	85	C1
Palmerstown Dr	73	D3
Palmerstown Grn	85	C1
Palmerstown Hts	85	C1
Palmerstown Lawn	85	C1
Palmerstown Manor	85	C1
Palmers Wk	85	C1
Palms, The	115	D2
Paradise Pl	78	A3
Parc Na Silla Av	140	B1
Parc Na Silla Cl	140	B1
Parc Na Silla La	140	B1
Parc Na Silla Ri	140	B1
Park, The *Dublin 9*	53	D2
Park, The *Dublin 17*	39	D3
Park, The *Dublin 24*	124	B1
Park, The (Greenhills)		
Dublin 24	109	D1
Park, The (Oldtown Mill Rd)		
Celbr.	66	A2
Park, The (Wolstan Haven Av)		
Celbr.	66	A2
Park, The (Dunboyne Castle)		
Dunb.	28	B3
Park, The (Lutterell Hall)		
Dunb.	28	B1
Park, The (Plunkett Hall)		
Dunb.	28	A1
Park, The *Gra M.*	82	B2
Park, The *Kins.*	18	A3
Park, The *Lou.V.*	68	A1
Park, The *Mala.*	21	C3
Park Av *Dublin 4*	104	A1
Park Av (Willbrook)		
Dublin 14	127	C1
Park Av *Dublin 15*	73	D1
Park Av *Deans Gra*	132	A2

Park Av (Hilltown)		
Swords	16	B1
Park Cl	133	D2
Park Ct	133	D2
Park Cres *Dublin 8*	76	A2
Park Cres *Dublin 12*	100	A3
Park Dr *Dublin 6*	102	B2
Park Dr *Cabin.*	137	C1
Park Dr Av	47	D3
Park Dr Cl	47	D3
Park Dr Ct	47	D3
Park Dr Cres	47	D3
Park Dr Grn	73	D1
Park Dr Gro	47	D3
Park Dr Lawn	47	D3
Parker Hill	102	A1
Parkgate Pl		
Business Cen	88	B1
Parkgate St	88	B1
Parkhill Av	109	D2
Parkhill Cl		
off Parkhill Ri	109	D2
Parkhill Ct	109	D2
Parkhill Dr	109	D2
Parkhill Grn	109	D2
Parkhill Lawn	109	D2
Parkhill Ri	109	D2
Parkhill Rd	109	D2
Parkhill Way	109	D2
Parklands *Castle.*	47	D3
Parklands *Mayn.*	65	D2
Parklands, The		
Dublin 14	113	C2
Parklands Av	124	B2
Parklands Cl	65	C2
Parklands Ct		
Dublin 24	124	B2
Parklands Ct *Mayn.*	65	C2
Parklands Cres	65	C2
Parklands Dr	124	B3
Parklands Gro	65	D2
Parklands Lawns	65	C2
Parklands Ri	65	C2
Parklands Rd	125	C2
Parklands Sq	65	C2
Parklands Vw	124	B2
Parklands Way	65	C2
Park La *Dublin 4*	104	A1
Park La *Dublin 20*	86	B1
Park La E	145	E3
Park Lawn	81	D1
Park Lo	47	D3
Park Manor	73	C1
Parkmore	48	A3
Parkmore Dr	112	B1
Parkmore Ind Est	98	C2
Park Pl		
off South Circular Rd	88	A1
Park Rd *Dublin 7*	75	D1
Park Rd *D.L.*	119	D3
Park Rd *Sally.*	133	D3
Park Shop Cen	77	C3
Park St	87	C2
Park Ter	144	A4
Parkvale *Dublin 13*	57	C2
Parkvale *Dublin 16*	129	C2
Parkview *Dublin 7*	76	B3
Park Vw *Dublin 15*	74	B1
Park Vw *Clons.*	46	A2
Park Vw *Mala.*	21	C3
Parkview *Port.*	27	C1
Parkview *Swords*	16	A1
Parkview (Harold'scross)		
Dublin 6	101	D2
Park Vw Av (Rathmines)		
Dublin 6	102	A2
Park Vw Lawns	96	A3
Park Vil *Dublin 15*	48	A3
Park Vil *Black.*	117	C3
Parkway Business Cen	98	A3
Park W Av *Dublin 10*	97	D2
Park W Av *Dublin 22*	97	D1
Park W Business Pk	85	D3
Park W Ind Pk	86	A3
Park W Rd	85	D3
Parkwood Av	124	A2
Parkwood Gro	124	A2
Parkwood Lawn	124	A2
Parkwood Rd **2**	124	A2
Parliament Row		
off Fleet St	145	D2
Parliament St	144	C3

Parnell Av		
off Parnell Rd	101	D1
Parnell Cotts	20	A3
Parnell Ct	101	D1
Parnell Pl	78	A3
Parnell Rd *Dublin 12*	89	C3
Parnell Rd *Bray*	142	A1
Parnell Sq E	78	A3
Parnell Sq N	78	A3
Parnell Sq W	78	A3
Parnell St *Dublin 1*	144	C1
Parnell St *Sally.*	133	D2
Parochial Av **2**	43	D3
Parslickstown Av	32	B2
Parslickstown Cl	32	B2
Parslickstown Ct	32	B2
Parslickstown Dr	32	B2
Parslickstown Gdns	32	A2
Parslickstown Grn	32	B2
Parson Ct	64	B2
Parson Lo	64	B2
Parsons Hall	64	A2
Parson St	64	B2
Partridge Ter	87	C3
Patrician Pk **5**	133	C1
Patrician Vil	117	C3
Patrick Doyle Rd	114	B1
Patrick's Row		
off Carysfort Av	117	D2
Patrick St *Dublin 8*	144	B4
Patrick St *D.L.*	119	D3
Patrickswell Pl	50	B2
Patriotic Ter		
off Brookfield Rd	88	B2
Paul St	144	A2
Pavilion Rd	143	D2
Pavilions Shop Cen, The	17	C1
Pavillion Gate **1**	137	C2
Pea Fld	117	C2
Pearse Av	133	C3
Pearse Brothers Pk	127	C1
Pearse Cl **9**	133	C2
Pearse Dr	133	C3
Pearse Gdns	133	C2
Pearse Grn **10**	133	C2
Pearse Gro		
off Great Clarence Pl	91	C1
Pearse Ho	145	F3
Pearse Pk	133	C2
Pearse Rd	133	C2
Pearse Sq	91	C2
Pearse Sta	145	F3
Pearse St *Dublin 2*	145	E3
Pearse St *Sally.*	133	C3
Pearse Vil	133	C3
Pear Tree Fld **3**	131	C1
Pebble Hill	65	C1
Pecks La	48	A3
Pelletstown Av	49	D3
Pembroke Cotts (Donnybrook)		
Dublin 4	103	C2
Pembroke Cotts (Ringsend)		
Dublin 4	91	D2
Pembroke Cotts (Dundrum)		
Dublin 14	115	C3
Pembroke Cotts *Boot.*	116	B1
Pembroke Gdns	91	C3
Pembroke La *Dublin 2*	90	B3
Pembroke La *Dublin 4*	91	C3
Pembroke Pk	103	C1
Pembroke Pl		
off Pembroke St Upr	90	B3
Pembroke Rd	91	C3
Pembroke Row	90	B3
Pembroke St	91	D2
Pembroke St Lwr	90	B3
Pembroke St Upr	90	B3
Penrose St	91	C2
Percy French Rd	99	D2
Percy La	91	C3
Percy Pl	91	C3
Peter Row	144	C4
Petersons Ct	145	F2
Peters Pl	90	A3
Peter St	144	C4
Petrie Rd	89	D3
Pheasant Run	31	D2
Pheasant Run The Dr	31	D2
Pheasant Run The Grn	31	D2
Pheasant Run The Gro	31	D2
Pheasant Run The Pk	31	D2
Phelan Av	50	A3

Name	Page	Grid
Phibsborough	77	D2
Phibsborough Av	77	D3
Phibsborough Pl	77	D3
Phibsborough Rd	77	D3
Philipsburgh Av	79	C2
Philipsburgh Ter	79	C1
Philomena Ter	91	D2
Phoenix Av	48	A3
Phoenix Ct *Dublin 7*		
off Slade Row	89	C1
Phoenix Ct *Dublin 15*	48	A3
Phoenix Dr	48	A3
Phoenix Gdns	48	A3
Phoenix Manor	76	B3
Phoenix Pk Av	75	C1
Phoenix Pk Way	75	C1
Phoenix Pl	48	A3
Phoenix St *Dublin 7*	144	A2
Phoenix St *Dublin 10*	87	C2
Phoenix Ter	117	C1
Pigeon Ho Rd	91	D2
Pig La	78	B3
Piles Bldgs		
off Golden La	144	B4
Piles Ter		
off Sandwith St Upr	145	F3
Pilot Vw	134	B1
Pimlico	144	A4
Pimlico Sq		
off The Coombe	144	A4
Pim St	89	C2
Pine Av	131	D3
Pinebrook	31	D3
Pinebrook Av	54	A3
Pinebrook Cl	31	D3
Pinebrook Cres		
off Pinebrook Av	54	A2
Pinebrook Downs	31	D3
Pinebrook Glen	31	D3
Pinebrook Gro		
off Pinebrook Rd	54	A3
Pinebrook Hts	31	D3
Pinebrook Lawn	32	A3
Pinebrook Ri	54	A3
Pinebrook Rd	54	A3
Pinebrook Vale	31	D3
Pinebrook Vw	31	D3
Pinebrook Way	32	A3
Pine Copse Rd	128	B1
Pine Ct *Black.*	131	D1
Pine Ct *Port.*	27	C2
Pine Gro	112	A3
Pine Gro Pk	14	B3
Pine Gro Rd	14	B3
Pine Haven	117	C1
Pine Hurst	76	B2
Pine Lawn *Dublin 24*	124	A1
Pine Lawn *Black.*	131	D1
Pine Rd	92	A2
Pines, The *Dublin 5*	54	B3
Pines, The **2** *Dublin 14*	129	D1
Pines, The *Dublin 15*	48	A3
Pines, The *Dublin 16*	128	A3
Pinetree Cres	109	D2
Pinetree Gro	109	D2
Pine Valley Av	128	A3
Pine Valley Dr	128	A3
Pine Valley Gro	128	A3
Pine Valley Pk	128	A3
Pine Valley Way	128	A3
Pineview Av	123	D2
Pineview Dr	123	D2
Pineview Gro	123	D2
Pineview Lawn	123	D2
Pineview Pk	124	A2
Pineview Ri	124	A2
Pineview Rd	123	D2
Pinewood	138	B2
Pinewood Av	51	D1
Pinewood Cl	142	A3
Pinewood Ct *Ashb.*	11	C3
Pinewood Ct *Mulh.*	32	A3
Pinewood Cres	51	D1
Pinewood Dr	51	D1
Pinewood Grn	51	D1
Pinewood Gro	51	D1
Pinewood Pk	112	B3
Pinewoods	96	A3
Pinewood Vil	51	D1
Pinnockhill Rbt	17	C2
Place, The *Carrick.*	136	B3
Place, The *Dunb.*	28	B3
Plato Business Pk	32	A1
Plaza Shop Cen, The	17	D1
Pleasants La	90	A3
Pleasants Pl	90	A3
Pleasants St	90	A3
Plums Rd	129	D2
Plunkett Av *Dublin 11*	36	A3
Plunkett Av *Fox.*	131	D3
Plunkett Cres	36	A3
Plunkett Dr	36	A3
Plunkett Grn	36	A3
Plunkett Gro	36	A3
Plunkett Hall	28	A1
Plunkett Rd	50	A1
Poddle Pk	100	B3
Polo Rd	76	A3
Poolbeg St	145	E2
Poole St	89	C2
Poplar Row	79	C2
Poplars, The	118	A3
Poppintree Ind Est	37	C3
Poppintree Pk La W	37	C3
Porters Av	46	B2
Portersfield	46	B2
Porters Gate	45	C2
Porters Gate Av	45	D2
Porters Gate Cl	45	C2
Porters Gate Ct	45	C2
Porters Gate Cres	45	C2
Porters Gate Dr	45	C2
Porters Gate Grn	45	C2
Porters Gate Gro	45	D2
Porters Gate Hts	45	D2
Porters Gate Ri	45	D2
Porters Gate Vw	45	C2
Porters Gate Way	45	D2
Porters Rd	46	A2
Porterstown Rd	46	A2
Portland Cl	78	B3
Portland Pl	78	A2
Portland Rd	143	D2
Portland Rd N	143	D2
Portland Row	78	B3
Portland St N	78	B3
Portmahon Dr	88	B3
Portmarnock Av **2**	27	C1
Portmarnock Br	26	B3
Portmarnock Cres	27	C1
Portmarnock Dr	27	C1
Portmarnock Gro	27	C1
Portmarnock Pk	27	C2
Portmarnock Ri	27	C2
Portmarnock Sta	26	A3
Portmarnock Wk	27	C1
Portobello Harbour	102	A1
Portobello Pl	102	A1
Portobello Rd	101	D1
Portobello Sq		
off Clanbrassil St Upr	101	D1
Portraine Rd	13	C1
Portside Business Cen	79	D3
Port Side Ct	79	C3
Potato Mkt		
off Green St Little	144	B2
Pottery Rd	132	B3
Pound La	64	B2
Pound Pk	64	B1
Pound St	68	B2
Powers Ct		
off Warrington Pl	91	C3
Powers Sq		
off John Dillon St	144	B4
Prebend St	144	B1
Preston St	78	B3
Price's La *Dublin 2*	145	D2
Prices La *Dublin 6*	102	A1
Priestfield Cotts	89	C3
Priestfield Dr		
off Dolphin Av	89	C3
Priestfield Ter		
off South Circular Rd	89	C3
Primrose Av	77	D3
Primrose Gro	41	D3
Primrose Hill *Celbr.*	66	B3
Primrose Hill *D.L.*	119	C3
Primrose La	70	A3
Primrose St	77	D3
Prince Arthur Ter	102	A2
Prince of Wales Ter		
Dublin 4	103	D1
Prince Of Wales Ter **16**		
Bray	142	A1
Princes St N	145	D2
Princes St S	145	F2
Princeton	115	D2
Priorswood Rd	40	B3
Priory, The *Dublin 7*	76	A1
Priory, The *Dublin 16*	127	D1
Priory, The **4** *Mala.*	20	A2
Priory Av	117	C2
Priory Chase	66	A3
Priory Cl	66	A3
Priory Ct **1** *Dublin 16*	127	D2
Priory Ct *Celbr.*	66	A3
Priory Cres	66	A3
Priory Dr *Black.*	116	B3
Priory Dr *Celbr.*	66	A3
Priory E	76	A1
Priory Grn	66	A3
Priory Gro *Black.*	116	B3
Priory Gro *Celbr.*	66	A3
Priory Hall *Dublin 12*	112	A1
Priory Hall *Black.*	116	B3
Priory Lo	66	A3
Priory N	76	A1
Priory Rd	101	C2
Priory Vw	66	A3
Priory Wk *Dublin 12*	100	A3
Priory Wk *Celbr.*	66	A3
Priory Way *Dublin 12*	112	A1
Priory Way *Celbr.*	66	A2
Priory W	76	A1
Proby Pk	134	A2
Probys La	144	C2
Proby Sq	117	D3
Promenade Rd	80	A3
Prospect Av *Dublin 9*	77	D1
Prospect Av *Dublin 16*	126	B2
Prospect Cem	77	D1
Prospect Ct	126	B3
Prospect Dr	126	B2
Prospect Glen	126	B3
Prospect Gro	126	B2
Prospect Heath	126	B3
Prospect Hts	126	B3
Prospect Hill	13	C2
Prospect La	103	C3
Prospect Lawn	137	D1
Prospect Meadows	126	B2
Prospect Rd	77	D1
Prospect Sq	77	D1
Prospect Ter (Sandymount)		
off Beach Rd	92	A3
Prospect Vw	126	B2
Prospect Way	77	D1
Protestant Row	90	A3
Prouds La	145	D4
Prussia St	77	C3
Purley Pk	27	C1
Purser Gdns	102	A2
Putland Rd	142	A3
Putland Vil **10**	142	A3
Q		
Quarry Dr	99	D3
Quarryfield Ct	97	C3
Quarry Rd (Cabra)		
Dublin 7	77	C2
Quarry Rd *Grey.*	143	D2
Queens Pk	118	A3
Queens Rd	119	D3
Queen St	144	A2
Quinns La	90	B3
Quinn's Rd	141	C3
Quinsborough Rd	142	A1
R		
Racecourse Shop Cen	43	C3
Race Hill Cl	10	B1
Race Hill Cres	11	C2
Race Hill La	10	B1
Race Hill Lo	10	B1
Race Hill Manor	11	C1
Race Hill Pk	10	B1
Race Hill Rd	10	B2
Race Hill Vw	10	B2
Radlett Gro	27	C1
Rafters Av	100	A1
Rafters La	100	A1
Rafters Rd	100	A1
Raglan La	103	C1
Raglan Rd	103	C1
Raheen Av	122	B1
Raheen Cl	122	B1
Raheen Ct	122	B1
Raheen Cres	122	B1
Raheen Dr *Dublin 10*	86	A3
Raheen Dr *Dublin 24*	122	B1
Raheen Lawn	142	B3
Raheen Pk *Dublin 10*	86	A3
Raheen Pk *Dublin 24*	122	B1
Raheen Pk *Bray*	142	B3
Raheen Rd	122	B1
Raheny Pk	56	A3
Raheny Rd	55	D2
Raheny Sta	55	D3
Rail Pk	65	C3
Railway Av *Dublin 8*		
off Tyrconnell Rd	87	D3
Railway Av (Inchicore)		
Dublin 8	87	C3
Railway Av *Dublin 13*	58	A1
Railway Av **3** *Mala.*	20	A2
Railway Cotts		
off Serpentine Av	103	D1
Railway Ct **2**	20	A2
Railway Ms	42	B3
Railway Rd *Dublin 13*	43	C3
Railway Rd **5** *Dalkey*	134	B2
Railway St	145	E1
Railway Ter		
off Grattan St	91	C2
Rainsford Av	89	C2
Rainsford La **3**	139	C2
Rainsford St	89	C2
Ralahine	138	B2
Raleigh Sq	100	A1
Ralph Sq **1**	68	B2
Ramillies Rd	86	B2
Ramleh Cl	103	C3
Ramleh Pk	103	C3
Ramleh Vil	102	B3
Ramor Pk	47	C2
Ranelagh Av	102	B1
Ranelagh Rd	102	A1
Ranelagh Sta	102	B1
Raphoe Rd	100	A1
Rathbeale Ct	15	C3
Rathbeale Cres	15	C3
Rathbeale Ri	17	C1
Rathbeale Rd	14	B2
Rathbone Av	49	D3
Rathbone Cl	49	D3
Rathbone Dr	49	D3
Rathbone Pl	49	D3
Rathbone Way	49	D3
Rath Cross Rds	10	B1
Rathdown Av	113	C1
Rathdown Cl	143	C1
Rathdown Ct		
Dublin 6W	101	C3
Rathdown Ct *Grey.*	143	C1
Rathdown Cres	113	C1
Rathdown Dr	113	C1
Rathdown Gro **6**	129	D2
Rathdown Pk		
Dublin 6W	113	C1
Rathdown Rd *Grey.*	143	C1
Rathdown Rd *Dublin 7*	77	D3
Rathdown Rd *Grey.*	143	C1
Rathdown Sq	77	C3
Rathdown Ter **7**	129	D2
Rathdown Vil	113	C1
Rathdrum Rd	101	C1
Rathfarnham Gate	113	C2
Rathfarnham Castle	113	C2
Rathfarnham Mill	113	C2
Rathfarnham Pk	113	C1
Rathfarnham Rd		
Dublin 6W	113	C1
Rathfarnham Rd		
Dublin 14	113	C1
Rathfarnham		
Shop Cen	112	B2
Rathfarnham Wd	113	D2
Rathgar Av	101	D2
Rathgar Pk	101	D3
Rathgar Rd	101	D3
Rathgar Vil	101	D3
Rathingle Rd	16	B2

Rathland Rd		
(Bothar Raitleann)	100	B3
Rathlin Rd	52	A3
Rath Lo	10	B1
Rathlyon	125	C2
Rathlyon Pk	125	C2
Rathmichael Dales	140	A2
Rathmichael Haven	140	A2
Rathmichael Hill	140	A2
Rathmichael La	140	A2
Rathmichael Manor	140	B1
Rathmichael Pk	141	C2
Rathmichael Wds	141	C2
Rathmines Av	102	A2
Rathmines Cl	102	A3
Rathmines Pk	102	A2
Rathmines Rd Lwr	102	A1
Rathmines Rd Upr	102	A2
Rathmintan Cl **3**	122	A2
Rathmintan Ct	122	A2
Rathmintan Cres	122	A2
Rathmintan Dr	122	A2
Rathmore	26	B3
Rathmore Av	130	A1
Rathmore Pk	56	A3
Rathmore Vil	101	C3
Rath Row	145	E2
Rathsallagh Av	141	C1
Rathsallagh Br	141	C1
Rathsallagh Dr	141	C2
Rathsallagh Gro	141	C1
Rathsallagh Pk	141	C1
Rathvale Av	55	C1
Rathvale Dr	55	C1
Rathvale Gro		
off Rathvale Av	55	C1
Rathvale Pk	55	C1
Rathvilly Dr	50	A2
Rathvilly Pk	50	A2
Rathvilly Rd	50	A2
Ratoath Av		
(Ascal Ratabhachta)	49	D2
Ratoath Dr	49	D1
Ratoath Est	76	A1
Ratoath Rd Dublin 7	76	B2
Ratoath Rd Dublin 11	49	D2
Ratra Rd	75	D1
Ravens Ct	50	A1
Ravensdale Cl	100	B3
Ravensdale Pk	100	B3
Ravensdale Rd	79	D3
Ravens Rock Rd	130	A2
Ravenswell Rd	142	A1
Ravenswood	31	C3
Ravenswood Av	45	C1
Ravenswood Cres	45	C1
Ravenswood Dr	45	C1
Ravenswood Grn	45	C1
Ravenswood Lawn	45	C1
Ravenswood Ri	31	C3
Ravenswood Rd	45	C1
Ravenswood Vw	45	C1
Raymond St	89	D3
Red Arches Av	43	C3
Red Arches Dr	43	C3
Redberry	82	A2
Red Brick Ter **3**	117	D3
Redcourt Oaks	81	D2
Red Cow Business Pk	98	A2
Red Cow La	144	A1
Red Cow Sta	97	D3
Redesdale Cres	116	A3
Redesdale Rd	116	A3
Redfern Av	27	C1
Redmonds Hill	90	A3
Redwood Av	110	A2
Redwood Cl		
off Redwood Av	110	A2
Redwood Ct Dublin 14	114	A2
Redwood Ct Dublin 24		
off Parkhill Rd	109	D2
Redwood Dr	109	D2
Redwood Gro	117	C2
Redwood Hts		
off Redwood Pk	110	A2
Redwood Lawn	109	D2
Redwood Pk	110	A2
Redwood Ri		
off Redwood Pk	110	A2
Redwood Vw		
off Redwood Av	110	A2
Redwood Wk	109	D2
Reginald Sq		
off Gray St	144	A4
Reginald St	144	A4
Rehoboth Av	89	C3
Rehoboth Pl	89	C3
Reillys Av		
off Dolphin's Barn St	89	C3
Reuben Av	88	B3
Reuben St	89	C3
Rialto Br	88	B3
Rialto Bldgs		
off Rialto Cotts	88	B3
Rialto Cotts	88	B3
Rialto Dr	88	B3
Rialto Sta	88	B3
Rialto St	88	B3
Ribh Av	55	C3
Ribh Rd	55	C3
Richelieu Pk	104	A2
Richmond	131	D1
Richmond Av	118	B3
Richmond Av N	79	C2
Richmond Av S	102	B3
Richmond Cotts		
Dublin 1	78	B3
Richmond Cotts (Inchicore)		
Dublin 8	88	A2
Richmond Cotts N		
off Richmond Cotts	78	B3
Richmond Ct	114	B1
Richmond Cres	78	B3
Richmond Est	79	C2
Richmond Grn	118	B3
Richmond Gro	118	B3
Richmond Hill Dublin 6	102	A1
Richmond Hill Black.	118	B3
Richmond La		
off Russell St	78	B3
Richmond Ms	102	A1
Richmond Par	78	B3
Richmond Pk	118	B3
Richmond Pl	102	A1
Richmond Pl S		
off Richmond St S	102	A1
Richmond Rd	78	B1
Richmond Row	102	A1
Richmond Row S		
off Richmond St S	90	A3
Richmond St N	78	B3
Richmond St S	90	A3
Richmond Ter **19**	142	B3
Richview Office Pk	103	C3
Richview Pk	102	B3
Ridge Hill	139	C3
Ridgewood Av	16	A2
Ridgewood Cl	16	A2
Ridgewood Ct	16	A2
Ridgewood Grn	16	A3
Ridgewood Gro	16	B3
Ridgewood Pk	16	A2
Ridgewood Pl	16	A2
Ridgewood Sq	16	A2
Rinawade Lawns	67	D2
Ringsend Br	91	D2
Ringsend Pk	91	D2
Ringsend Rd	91	C2
Ring St	87	C3
Ring Ter	87	D3
Rise, The (Drumcondra)		
Dublin 9	52	A3
Rise, The (Ballinteer)		
Dublin 16	128	B3
Rise, The (Ballyboden)		
Dublin 16	126	B2
Rise, The (Cookstown)		
Dublin 24	109	C2
Rise, The (Kilnamanagh)		
Dublin 24	109	D1
Rise, The Carrick.	136	B3
Rise, The Dalkey	134	B3
Rise, The Kins.	18	A2
Rise, The Leix.	68	A1
Rise, The Mala.	20	A2
Rise, The (Robswall) **3**		
Mala.	21	C3
Rise, The Manor.	31	D3
Rise, The Still.	116	B2
Riverbank Hall	51	D3
River Cl **2**	141	C1
River Ct **1**	29	C3
Riverdale	68	B2
River Forest	68	B1
River Gdns	52	A3
River La	141	C1
River Rd Dublin 11	49	D3
River Rd Dublin 15	48	A2
Riversdale	73	C3
Riversdale Av Dublin 6	113	D1
Riversdale Av Clond.	96	B1
Riversdale Av Palm.	73	C3
Riversdale Ct	73	C3
Riversdale Cres	96	B1
Riversdale Dr	96	B1
Riversdale Grn	96	B1
Riversdale Gro		
Dublin 6W	100	B3
Riversdale Gro Palm.	73	C3
Riversdale Ind Est	98	B1
Riversdale Pk Clond.	96	B1
Riversdale Pk Palm.	73	C3
Riversdale Rd	96	B1
Riverside **3**	96	B1
Riverside Av	40	A3
Riverside Cotts	112	B2
Riverside Cres	40	A3
Riverside Dr Dublin 14	113	D2
Riverside Dr Dublin 17	40	A3
Riverside Dr Palm.	73	C3
Riverside Gro	40	A3
Riverside Pk	40	A3
Riverside Rd	40	A3
Riverside Wk	103	C3
Riverston Abbey	76	A1
River Valley Av	17	C1
River Valley Cl	16	B1
River Valley Ct	16	B1
River Valley Dr	16	B1
River Valley Gro	16	B2
River Valley Hts	16	B1
River Valley Lawn	17	C2
River Valley Pk	16	B1
River Valley Ri	16	B2
River Valley Rd	16	B1
River Valley Vw	16	B1
River Valley Way	16	B1
Riverview Dublin 24	124	A3
Riverview Palm.	73	D3
Riverview Business Cen	97	D1
Riverview Ct	86	B1
Riverwood Chase	46	A3
Riverwood Cl	46	A3
Riverwood Copse	46	A3
Riverwood Ct	46	A3
Riverwood Cres	72	B1
Riverwood Dale	46	B3
Riverwood Dene	46	A3
Riverwood Dr	46	B3
Riverwood Gdns	72	B1
Riverwood Glebe	72	A1
Riverwood Glen	46	B3
Riverwood Grn	46	B3
Riverwood Gro	46	B3
Riverwood Heath	46	A3
Riverwood Lawn	46	B3
Riverwood Pk	46	B3
Riverwood Pl	72	A1
Riverwood Rd	46	B3
Riverwood Ter	46	A3
Riverwood Vale	46	B3
Riverwood Vw	46	B3
Riverwood Way	46	B3
Road, The	31	C3
Robert Emmet Br	101	D1
Robert Pl		
off Clonliffe Rd	78	B2
Robert St Dublin 3		
off Clonliffe Rd	78	B2
Robert St Dublin 8	89	C2
Robinhood Business Pk	98	A2
Robinhood Ind Est	98	A2
Robinhood Rd	98	B2
Robinsons Ct	144	A4
Robin Vil	73	D3
Robswall	21	C3
Rochestown Av	133	C3
Rochestown Pk	133	C3
Rochfort Av	83	D1
Rochfort Cl	83	D1
Rochfort Cres	83	D2
Rochfort Downs	83	D1
Rochfort Grn	83	D1
Rochfort Pk	83	D1
Rochfort Way	83	D2
Rock Br	66	A3
Rock Enterprise Cen	106	B2
Rockfield Dublin 14	129	C1
Rockfield Lucan	82	A2
Rockfield Mayn.	65	C3
Rockfield Av Dublin 12	111	D1
Rockfield Av Mayn.	65	C3
Rockfield Cl	46	B3
Rockfield Ct Dublin 12	100	A3
Rock Fld Dr Clond.	96	B3
Rockfield Dr Cool.	46	B3
Rockfield Gdns	65	C2
Rockfield Grn	65	C2
Rockfield Lo	65	C3
Rockfield Manor	65	C3
Rockfield Pk Clons.	46	B3
Rockfield Pk Mayn.	65	C3
Rockfield Ri	65	C2
Rockfield Sq	65	C2
Rockfield Wk	65	C2
Rockford Pk	118	A3
Rockfort Av	135	C2
Rock Hill	117	D2
Rockingham Av	68	A1
Rockingham Grn	68	A1
Rockingham Gro	68	A1
Rockingham Pk	68	A1
Rocklands **2**	135	C1
Rock Lo	134	A3
Rock Rd	104	A3
Rockview	129	C3
Rockville Cres	118	A3
Rockville Dr	118	A3
Rockville Pk	118	A3
Rockville Rd	118	A3
Rockwood	82	A2
Rocwood	131	C2
Roebuck Av	116	B2
Roebuck Castle	115	C2
Roebuck Downs	115	C2
Roebuck Dr	99	D3
Roebuck Hall	115	D2
Roebuck Rd	115	C1
Roe La	89	C2
Roger's La	90	B3
Rollins Ct **7**	133	C2
Rollins Vil	133	C2
Roncalli Rd	57	C2
Rookery, The	126	A1
Roosevelt Cotts	76	B3
Rooske Ct	28	B3
Rooske Rd	28	B3
Rope Wk Pl	91	D2
Rory O'Connor Pk	132	B1
Rory O'More Br	89	C1
Rosapenna Dr	42	A3
Rosary Gdns E	119	C3
Rosary Gdns W	119	C3
Rosary Rd	89	C3
Rosary Ter	91	D2
Rosbeg Ct	57	C2
Rosberry	82	B3
Rosberry Av	82	B3
Rosberry Ct	82	B3
Rosberry La	82	B3
Rosberry Pk	82	B3
Rosberry Pl	82	B3
Rosebank	123	D1
Rosedale (Hartstown)		
Clons.	30	B3
Rosedale Dunb.	28	B2
Rosedale Dr	30	B3
Rose Glen Av	56	B2
Rose Glen Rd	56	A2
Rosehaven	46	B3
Rosehill **7**	131	D1
Roselawn	71	C3
Roselawn Av	47	C2
Roselawn Cl	47	D2
Roselawn Ct	47	D2
Roselawn Cres	47	C2
Roselawn Dr Bray	142	A3
Roselawn Dr Castle.	47	C2
Roselawn Glade	47	C2
Roselawn Gro	47	C2
Roselawn Pk	142	A3

Name	Page	Grid
Roselawn Rd	47	D2
Roselawn Shop Cen	47	C2
Roselawn Vw	47	C2
Roselawn Wk	47	C2
Roselawn Way	47	D2
Rosemount	114	B2
Rosemount Av	54	B3
Rosemount Business Pk	34	B3
Rosemount Ct *Dublin 14*	115	C3
Rosemount Ct *Boot.*	116	B1
Rosemount Cres	115	C1
Rosemount Pk	115	C2
Rosemount Pk Rd	34	A3
Rosemount Rd	77	D3
Rosemount Ter	116	B1
Rose Pk	132	B1
Rosevale Ct *off Brookwood Glen*	55	C3
Rosevale Mans	55	C3
Rosewood Gro	83	D2
Rosmeen Gdns	119	D3
Rosmeen Pk	133	D1
Rossecourt Av **2**	83	D2
Rossecourt Grn **6**	83	D2
Rossecourt Gro **1**	83	D2
Rossecourt La **5**	83	D2
Rossecourt Ri **8**	83	D2
Rossecourt Sq **4**	83	D2
Rossecourt Ter **7**	83	D2
Rossecourt Way **3**	83	D2
Rossfield Av	108	A3
Rossfield Cres	122	A1
Rossfield Dr	108	A3
Rossfield Gdns	122	A1
Rossfield Grn	122	A1
Rossfield Gro	122	A1
Rossfield Pk	108	A3
Rossfield Way	122	A1
Rosslyn **13**	142	A2
Rosslyn Ct	142	A2
Rosslyn Gro **14**	142	A2
Rossmore Av *Dublin 6W*	111	D2
Rossmore Av *Dublin 10*	86	A2
Rossmore Cl	111	D3
Rossmore Cres	111	D2
Rossmore Dr *Dublin 6W*	111	D2
Rossmore Dr *Dublin 10*	86	A1
Rossmore Gro	111	D3
Rossmore Lawns	111	D2
Rossmore Pk	111	D3
Rossmore Rd *Dublin 6W*	111	D2
Rossmore Rd *Dublin 10*	86	A1
Ross Rd	144	B4
Ross St	76	B3
Ross Vw	73	C3
Rostrevor Rd	113	D1
Rostrevor Ter	113	D1
Rothe Abbey	88	A3
Rowan Av	130	A2
Rowanbyrn	118	A3
Rowan Cl	66	B2
Rowan Hall *off Prospect La*	103	C3
Rowan Pk Av	118	A3
Rowans, The **17**	139	C3
Rowans Rd	129	D2
Rowlagh Av	84	A2
Rowlagh Cres	84	A2
Rowlagh Gdns	84	A2
Rowlagh Grn	84	A2
Rowlagh Pk	84	A2
Roxboro Cl	134	A3
Royal Canal Av	49	D3
Royal Canal Bk	77	D3
Royal Canal Ter	77	D3
Royal Liver Retail Pk	98	B1
Royal Marine Ter **3**	142	B1
Royal Oak	39	C3
Royal Ter *off Inverness Rd*	79	C2
Royal Ter E	133	D1
Royal Ter La **9**	133	C1
Royal Ter N **10**	133	D1
Royal Ter W	133	D1
Royse Rd	77	D2
Royston	100	A3
Ruby Hall	132	B2
Rugby Rd	102	A1
Rugby Vil *off Rugby Rd*	102	A1
Rugged La	72	A1
Rushbrook	47	C2
Rushbrook Av	111	C2
Rushbrook Ct	111	D2
Rushbrook Dr	111	D2
Rushbrooke Cres	111	C2
Rushbrooke Rd	111	C2
Rushbrook Gro	111	D2
Rushbrook Pk	111	D2
Rushbrook Vw	111	C2
Rushbrook Way	111	D2
Rusheeney	31	C3
Rusheeney Av	31	D3
Rusheeney Cl	31	D3
Rusheeney Ct	31	D3
Rusheeney Cres	31	C3
Rusheeney Grn	31	D3
Rusheeney Gro	31	D3
Rusheeney Manor	31	C3
Rusheeney Pk	31	C3
Rusheeney Vw	31	D3
Rusheeney Way	31	D3
Rus-in-Urbe Ter **11**	133	D1
Russell Av *Dublin 3*	78	A2
Russell Av *Jobs.*	122	A1
Russell Av E	79	C3
Russell Cl	122	A1
Russell Ct	122	A1
Russell Cres	122	A1
Russell Downs	122	A1
Russell Dr	122	A1
Russell Gro	122	A1
Russell Grn	122	A1
Russell La	122	A1
Russell Lawns	122	A1
Russell Meadows	122	A1
Russell Pl	78	B3
Russell Ri	122	A1
Russell St	78	B3
Russell Vw	122	A1
Russell Wk	122	A1
Rutland Av	101	C1
Rutland Gro	101	C1
Rutland Pl *off Clontarf Rd*	80	B3
Rutland Pl N	78	B3
Rutland Pl W	78	A3
Rutland St Lwr	78	B3
Rutledges Ter	89	C3
Ryders Row *off Parnell St*	144	C1
Rye Br	68	B2
Ryecroft	142	A2
Ryemont Abbey	68	A1
Rye River	68	B1
Rye River Av	68	B2
Rye River Cl	68	B2
Rye River Ct	68	B2
Rye River Cres	68	B2
Rye River Gdns	68	B2
Rye River Gro	68	B2
Rye River Mall	68	B2
Rye River Pk	68	B2
Ryevale Lawns	68	B1

S

Name	Page	Grid
Sackville Av	78	B3
Sackville Gdns	78	B3
Sackville La *off O'Connell St Lwr*	145	D1
Sackville Pl	145	D2
Saddlers Av	32	B3
Saddlers Cl	32	B3
Saddlers Cres	32	B3
Saddlers Dr **1**	32	B3
Saddlers Glade	32	B3
Saddlers Gro	32	B3
Saddlers Lawn	32	B3
Sadleir Hall	28	A3
Saggart Abbey	121	C2
St. Agnes Pk	100	A2
St. Agnes Rd	100	A2
St. Aidan's Dr	115	D2
St. Aidan's Pk	79	D1
St. Aidan's Pk Av	79	D2
St. Aidan's Pk Rd	79	D2
St. Aidan's Ter **20**	142	A1
St. Alban's Pk	104	B2
St. Alban's Rd	89	D3
St. Alphonsus Av	78	B2
St. Alphonsus Rd	78	A2
St. Andoens Ter *off Cook St*	144	A3
St. Andrews	71	C3
St. Andrews Dr	71	D3
St. Andrews Fairway	83	D1
St. Andrews Grn	71	D3
St. Andrew's Gro	20	A2
St. Andrew's La *off Trinity St*	145	D3
St. Andrews Pk	14	B3
St. Andrew's St	145	D3
St. Andrews Wd	71	D3
St. Annes	100	A3
St. Anne's Av	55	D3
St. Anne's Dr	55	D3
St. Annes Pk	141	C3
St. Annes Rd	89	C3
St. Clement's Rd	117	D2
St. Anne's Sq	78	A2
St. Anne's Ter	55	D3
St. Ann's Sq N	26	B3
St. Ann's Sq Lwr **4**	26	B3
St. Anthony's Av	96	B3
St. Anthony's Business Pk	97	D2
St. Anthony's Cres	99	C3
St. Anthony's Pl *off Temple St N*	78	A3
St. Anthony's Rd	88	B3
St. Aongus Av	110	B2
St. Aongus Grn	110	B2
St. Aongus Gro	110	B2
St. Aongus Lawn	110	B2
St. Aongus Rd	110	B2
St. Assam's Av	56	A3
St. Assam's Dr	56	A3
St. Assam's Pk	56	A2
St. Assam's Rd E	56	A3
St. Assam's Rd W	56	A3
St. Attracta Rd	77	C2
St. Aubyn's Ct **9**	139	C3
St. Audoens Ter *off School Ho La W*	144	B3
St. Augustine's Pk	131	D1
St. Augustine St	144	A3
St. Barnabas Gdns	79	C3
St. Begnet's Vil	134	B2
St. Brendan's Av	54	B2
St. Brendan's Cotts	91	D2
St. Brendan's Cres	111	C1
St. Brendan's Dr	54	B2
St. Brendan's Pk	55	C2
St. Brendan's Ter *Dublin 5*	54	B1
St. Brendan's Ter *D.L.* *off St. Mary's St*	119	C3
St. Bricin's Pk	89	C1
St. Bridget's Av	79	C3
St. Bridget's Dr	99	C3
St. Bridget's Pk	143	C1
St. Brigid's Av **3**	26	B3
St. Brigid's Ch Rd	131	C1
St. Brigid's Cotts *off St. Brigid's Dr*	54	B3
St. Brigid's Cotts Clond.	97	C3
St. Brigid's Cres	54	B3
St. Brigid's Dr *Dublin 5*	54	B3
St. Brigid's Dr *Clond.*	96	B3
St. Brigids Flats	103	C3
St. Brigids Gdns	91	C1
St. Brigids Grn	54	B3
St. Brigids Gro	54	B3
St. Brigids Lawn	54	B3
St. Brigid's Pk (Blanchardstown) *Dublin 15*	47	D2
St. Brigid's Pk **1** *Clond.*	96	B3
St. Brigid's Pk *Corn.*	132	A3
St. Brigid's Rd *Dublin 9*	54	B2
St. Brigid's Rd *Clond.*	96	B3
St. Brigid's Rd Lwr	78	A2
St. Brigid's Rd Upr	78	A2
St. Brigids Shop Mall	54	B2
St. Brigid's Ter **21**	142	A1
St. Broc's Cotts	103	C2
Saintbury Av	139	C2
St. Canice's Pk	51	D2
St. Canice's Rd	51	D2
St. Catherine's Av	89	C3
St. Catherines Gro **3**	95	D2
St. Catherine's La W	144	A3
St. Catherine's Pk *Dalkey*	134	A2
St. Catherine's Pk *D.L.*	134	A1
St. Catherine's Rd	134	A2
St. Catherine's Vw	69	C1
St. Clare's Av *off Harolds Cross Rd*	101	D1
St. Clare's Home	51	D2
St. Clare's Ter *off Mount Drummond Av*	101	D1
St. Clement's Rd	78	A2
St. Colmcilles Ct **1**	17	C1
St. Colmcille's Way	125	C2
St. Columbanus Av	114	B1
St. Columbanus Pl	114	B1
St. Columbanus Rd	114	B1
St. Columbas Hts	17	C1
St. Columbas Ri	17	C1
St. Columba's Rd	99	C3
St. Columba's Rd Lwr	78	A2
St. Columba's Rd Upr	78	A2
St. Columcille's Cres **2**	17	D1
St. Columcille's Dr	17	D1
St. Columcille's Ter **22**	142	A1
St. Columcills Pk	17	D1
St. Conleth's Rd	99	C3
St. Cronan's Av	14	B3
St. Cronan's Cl **1**	16	B1
St. Cronan's Ct	14	B3
St. Cronan's Gro	14	B3
St. Cronan's Lawn	14	B3
St. Cronan's Rd **23**	142	A1
St. Cronan's Vw **2**	16	B1
St. Cronan's Way **3**	16	B1
St. Davids	54	A3
St. Davids Pk	54	A3
St. David's Ter *Dublin 7* *off Blackhorse Av*	76	B3
St. David's Ter (Glasnevin) *Dublin 9*	52	A3
St. Davids Wd	52	A3
St. Declan Rd	79	C1
St. Declan Ter	79	D1
St. Dominic's Av	124	A1
St. Dominic's Cen	124	A1
St. Dominic's Ct **3**	124	A1
St. Dominic's Rd	124	A1
St. Dominic's Ter	124	A1
St. Donagh's Cres	56	A1
St. Donagh's Pk	56	B1
St. Donagh's Rd	56	A1
St. Edmunds	72	A3
St. Eithne Rd	77	C2
St. Elizabeth's Ct *off North Circular Rd*	77	C3
St. Enda's Dr	113	C3
St. Enda's Pk	113	C3
St. Enda's Rd	101	C3
St. Finbar's Cl	111	C1
St. Finbar's Rd	76	B1
St. Finian's	82	B1
St. Finian's Av	82	B1
St. Finian's Cl	82	B1
St. Finian's Cres	82	B1
St. Finian's Gro	82	B1
St. Fintan Rd	77	C2
St. Fintan's Cres	59	C3
St. Fintan's Gro	59	C3
St. Fintan's Pk *Dublin 13*	59	C3
St. Fintan's Pk *Black.*	132	A1
St. Fintan's Rd	59	C3
St. Fintan's Ter **4**	73	D3
St. Fintan's Vil	132	A1
St. Fintan Ter	77	C1
St. Gabriel's	137	D1
St. Gabriels Ct	81	D2
St. Gabriel's Rd	81	D2
St. Gall Gdns N	114	B1

St. Gall Gdns S 114 B1
St. Gatien Ct 127 C1
St. Gatien Rd **2** 127 C1
St. George's Av
Dublin 3 78 B2
St. George's Av *Kill.* 139 C1
St. Gerard's Rd 99 C3
St. Helena's Av 50 B2
St. Helena's Rd 50 B2
St. Helen's 134 A1
St. Helen's Rd 116 B1
St. Helens Wd 116 B2
St. Ignatius Av 78 A2
St. Ignatius Rd 78 A2
St. Ita's Rd 78 A1
St. Ive's 20 A2
St. James Pl 87 D2
St. James's Av *Dublin 3* 78 B2
St. James's Av *Dublin 8* 89 C2
St. James's Pl
off Tyrconnell Rd 87 D3
St. James's Rd 99 C3
St. James's Ter 89 C3
St. James's Wk 88 B3
St. Jarlath Rd 77 C2
St. Johns 104 A2
St. John's Av *Dublin 8*
off John St S 144 A4
St. John's Av *Clond.* 96 A3
St. John's Cl 96 A3
St. John's Ct *Dublin 3* 80 A1
St. Johns Ct *Dublin 5* 54 A1
St. John's Ct *Clond.* 96 A3
St. John's Cres 96 A3
St. John's Dr 96 A3
St. John's Grn 96 A3
St. John's Lawn 96 A3
St. John's Pk *Clond.* 96 A3
St. John's Pk *D.L.* 119 C3
St. John's Pk W 96 A3
St. John's Rd *Dublin 4* 104 A1
St. John's Rd *Clond.* 96 A3
St. John's Rd W 88 A2
St. John St
off Blackpitts 89 D3
St. Johns Wd *Dublin 3* 80 B2
St. John's Wd *Clond.* 96 A2
St. Johns Wd Ct 10 B2
St. Johns Wd Dr 10 B2
St. Johns Wd Pk 10 B2
St. John's Wd W 96 A2
St. Joseph's 49 D2
St. Joseph's Av
Dublin 3 78 B2
St. Joseph's Av
Dublin 9 78 A2
St. Joseph's Conv 101 C3
St. Josephs Ct 77 C3
St. Josephs Gro 115 C3
St. Joseph's Par 78 A3
St. Joseph's Pl
off St. Joseph's Par 78 A3
St. Joseph's Rd
Dublin 7 77 C3
St. Joseph's Rd
Dublin 12 99 C3
St. Joseph's Sq
off Vernon Av 81 C2
St. Joseph's St
off Synnott Pl 78 A3
St. Joseph's Ter *Dublin 1*
off North Circular Rd 78 B3
St. Joseph's Ter
Dublin 3 79 C2
St. Kevins Ct 102 A3
St. Kevins Gdns 102 A3
St. Kevins Par 89 D3
St. Kevins Pk (Rathgar)
Dublin 6 102 A3
St. Kevin's Pk *Still.* 130 A1
St. Kevin's Rd 101 D1
St. Kevin's Sq 142 A1
St. Kevin's Ter **15** 142 A2
St. Kevin's Vil 133 C1
St. Killian's Av 98 B3
St. Killian's Pk **1** 96 B2

St. Laurence Gro 86 B1
St. Laurence Rd 86 B1
St. Laurence's Mans 91 C1
St. Laurences Pk 116 B3
St. Laurence's Ter **24** 142 A1
St. Laurence St N
off Sheriff St Lwr 145 F1
St. Laurence Gro 80 A2
St. Laurence
O'toole Av **1** 26 B3
St. Laurence Pl
off Sheriff St Lwr 145 F1
St. Laurence Rd (Clontarf)
Dublin 3 80 A2
St. Laurence Rd (Howth)
Dublin 13 60 B2
St. Lawrences Ct 80 A2
St. Lawrences St
off Sheriff St Lwr 145 F1
St. Lawrence Ter 61 C2
St. Lomans Rd 71 D3
St. Luke's Av 144 A4
St. Luke's Cres 114 B1
St. Maelruans Pk 124 A1
St. Magdalene Ter 91 D2
St. Malachy's Dr 99 C3
St. Malachy's Rd 78 A1
St. Margaret's Av
Dublin 5 56 B2
St. Margaret's Av *Mala.* 20 A2
St. Margaret's Av N
off North Circular Rd 78 B3
St. Margaret's
Business Pk 36 A3
St. Margaret's Cl **5** 134 B1
St. Margaret's Cl **1** 36 B3
St. Margaret's
Halting Site 37 D2
St. Margaret's Pk 20 A2
St. Margaret's Rd
Dublin 11 36 B3
St. Margaret's Rd *Mala.* 20 A2
St. Margaret's Ter 89 C3
St. Mark's Av 84 A1
St. Mark's Cres 84 A2
St. Mark's Dr 84 B2
St. Mark's Gdns 84 A2
St. Mark's Grn 84 A2
St. Mark's Gro 84 A2
St. Marnock's Av 26 B3
St. Martin's Dr 100 B3
St. Martin's Pk 100 B2
St. Mary's Av
(Rathfarnham) 113 C2
St. Mary's Av N 78 A3
St. Mary's Av W 87 D2
St. Mary's Coll 102 A1
St. Mary's Cres 99 D1
St. Mary's Dr 99 D1
St. Mary's La 91 C3
St. Mary's Pk *Dublin 12* 99 D2
St. Mary's Pk *Dublin 15* 49 D2
St. Mary's Pk *Leix.* 68 B1
St. Mary's Pl
off Main St 61 C2
St. Mary's Pl N 78 A3
St. Mary's Rd *Dublin 3* 79 C3
St. Mary's Rd *Dublin 12* 99 D2
St. Mary's Rd *Dublin 13*
off Main St 61 C2
St. Mary's Rd N 79 C3
St. Mary's Rd S 91 C3
St. Mary's St 79 C3
St. Mary's Ter *Dublin 7* 78 A3
St. Marys Ter **22** *Bray* 142 B2
St. Mary's Ter **1** *Dunb.* 28 B2
St. Mel's Av 111 C1
St. Michael's Est 88 A3
St. Michael's Hill 144 B3
St. Michael's La
off High St 144 B3
St. Michael's Rd 78 A1
St. Michael's Ter 89 D3
St. Michan's St 144 B2
St. Mobhi Boithirin 52 A3
St. Mobhi Ct 52 A3
St. Mobhi Dr 78 A1
St. Mobhi Gro 78 A1
St. Mobhi Rd 78 A1
St. Mobhis Br 78 A1
St. Mochtas 46 B3
St. Mochtas Av 46 B2

St. Mochtas Chase 46 B2
St. Mochtas Dr 46 A3
St. Mochtas Grn 46 B3
St. Mochtas Gro 46 B3
St. Mochtas Lawn 46 A2
St. Mochtas Rd 46 A3
St. Mochtas Vale 46 B2
St. Nessan's Ter
off Tuckett's La 60 B2
St. Nicholas Pl 144 B4
St. Oliver's Pk 85 C3
St. Pappin Grn 51 D2
St. Pappin Rd 51 D2
St. Patrick Av
off Annesley Av 79 C3
St. Patrick's Av **1**
Clond. 96 A1
St. Patrick's Av **6**
Dalkey 134 B2
St. Patrick's Av *Port.* 26 B3
St. Patrick's Cath 144 B4
St. Patrick's Cl *Dublin 8* 144 B4
St. Patrick's Cl **11** *D.L.* 132 B1
St. Patrick's Coll
Maynooth 64 B2
St. Patrick's Cotts 113 C3
St. Patrick's Cres 132 B1
St. Patrick's Nat Sch 78 B1
St. Patrick's Par 78 A2
St. Patrick's Pk
(Blanchardstown)
Dublin 15 47 C2
St. Patrick's Pk *Celbr.* 66 B2
St. Patrick's Pk *Clond.* 96 A1
St. Patricks Pk *D'bate* 13 D2
St. Patrick's Pk *Dunb.* 28 B2
St. Patrick's Rd
Dublin 9 78 A2
St. Patrick's Rd
Dublin 12 99 C3
St. Patrick's Rd *Clond.* 96 A1
St. Patrick's Rd *Dalkey* 134 B2
St. Patrick's Sq **1** *Bray* 142 A1
St. Patrick's Sq **7**
Dalkey 134 B2
St. Patrick's Ter *Dublin 1*
off Russell St 78 B3
St. Patrick's Ter *Dublin 3*
off North Strand Rd 79 C3
St. Patrick's Ter
Dublin 8 87 D2
St. Patricks Ter *D'bate* 13 D2
St. Patrick's Ter **6** *D.L.* 133 C1
St. Patrick's Vil 91 D2
St. Paul's Dr 99 D3
St. Paul's Ter **21** 134 A1
St. Peters Av 77 D2
St. Peters Cl 77 D3
St. Peter's Cres 99 D3
St. Peter's Dr 99 D3
St. Peter's Pk 28 B2
St. Peter's Rd *Dublin 7* 77 D2
St. Peter's Rd *Dublin 12* 99 C3
St. Peter's Ter *Dublin 13* 60 B2
St. Peter's Ter **6** *D.L.* 134 A1
St. Philomena's Rd 77 D2
St. Raphaels Av 66 A3
St. Ronan's Av 84 A3
St. Ronan's Cl 84 A2
St. Ronan's Cres 84 A2
St. Ronan's Dr 84 A2
St. Ronan's Gdns 84 A2
St. Ronan's Grn 84 A2
St. Ronan's Gro 84 A2
St. Ronan's Pk 84 A2
St. Ronan's Way 84 A3
St. Samson Ct 41 D2
St. Samson Sq 41 D2
St. Stephen's Grn 90 B3
St. Stephen's Grn N 145 D4
St. Stephen's Grn Pk 90 A3
St. Stephen's Grn
Shop Cen 145 D4
St. Stephen's Grn Sta 90 A3
St. Stephen's Grn Sta 145 D4
St. Stephen's Grn W 90 A3
St. Stephen's Pl 90 B3
St. Sylvester Vil 20 A3
St. Teresa's La 100 A3
St. Teresa's Pl
off Prospect Av 77 D1
St. Teresa's Rd *Dublin 9* 77 D1

St. Teresa's Rd (Crumlin)
Dublin 12 100 A3
St. Theresa Gdns 89 C3
St. Thomas's Mead 116 B2
St. Thomas' Rd (Tenter Flds)
Dublin 8 89 D3
St. Thomas' Rd *Still.* 116 A2
St. Thomas's Av
off Constitution Hill 144 B1
St. Vincent's Home 75 D1
St. Vincent's Pk 118 A2
St. Vincents Rd 143 D2
St. Vincent St N 77 D3
St. Vincent St S
(Tenter Flds) 89 D3
St. Vincent St W 87 D2
St. Werburghs 18 A1
St. Wolstan's Abbey 66 B3
Salamanca 115 D2
Sallowood Vw 38 B3
Sallyglen Rd 133 D2
Sallymount Av 102 A3
Sallymount Gdns 102 B1
Sallynoggin Pk 133 C2
Sallynoggin Rd 133 C2
Sally Pk 125 C1
Sally Pk Cl 125 C1
Sally's Br 101 C1
Salthill &
Monkstown Sta 118 B2
Salzburg 115 D2
Sampsons La 144 C1
Sandford Av (Donnybrook)
Dublin 4 103 C2
Sandford Av *Dublin 8* 89 C3
Sandford Cl 102 B2
Sandford Gdns *Dublin 4* 103 C2
Sandford Gdns *Dublin 8*
off Donore Av 89 C3
Sandford Rd 102 B2
Sandford Ter 102 B2
Sandford Wd 14 B2
Sand Holes, The 73 D1
Sandon Cove 80 B2
Sandwith Pl 145 F3
Sandwith St Lwr 145 F3
Sandwith St Upr 145 F3
Sandycove Av E 134 B2
Sandycove Av W 134 A1
Sandycove Av E La 134 A1
Sandycove Glastule Sta 133 D1
Sandycove Rd 134 A1
Sandyford
Business Cen 130 A2
Sandyford Downs 129 D3
Sandyford Ind Est 130 A2
Sandyford Office Pk 130 B2
Sandyford Pk
Dublin 16 129 D3
Sandyford Pk *Leo.* 130 B2
Sandyford Rd 129 C1
Sandyford Sta 130 B2
Sandyford Vw 129 C3
Sandyford Village 129 D3
Sandyhill Ct 37 D3
Sandyhill Gdns 37 D3
Sandymount Av 103 D1
Sandymount Castle Dr 104 A1
Sandymount Castle Rd 104 A1
Sandymount Grn 92 A3
Sandymount Rd 92 A3
Sandymount Sta 104 A1
Sans Souci Pk 116 B1
Sans Souci Wd 142 A2
Santa Sabina Manor 59 C2
Santry Av 38 A3
Santry Av Ind Est 38 B3
Santry Business Pk 39 C3
Santry Cl 39 C3
Santry Ct 39 C3
Santry Hall Ind Est 52 B1
Santry Vil 39 C3
Santry Way 38 B3
Sarah Curran Av 127 C1
Sarah Curran Rd **1** 127 C1
Sarah Pl 88 A1
Sarsfield Ct 70 A3
Sarsfield Pk 70 B3
Sarsfield Quay 89 C1
Sarsfield Rd *Dublin 8* 87 D2
Sarsfield Rd *Dublin 10* 87 C2
Sarsfield St *Dublin 7* 77 D3

Sarsfield St *Sally.*	133	C2	Seamus Ennis Rd	50	B1	Shankill Shop Cen	141	C2
Sarsfield Ter **4**	70	A3	Sean Heuston Br	88	B1	Shankill Sta	141	C2
Sarto Lawn	57	C1	Sean McDermott St Lwr	78	B3	Shankill Vw **19**	142	A1
Sarto Pk	57	C1	Sean McDermott St Upr	145	D1	Shanliss Av	52	B1
Sarto Ri	57	C2	Sean More Rd	92	A3	Shanliss Dr	52	B1
Sarto Rd	57	C2	Sean O'Casey La	78	B3	Shanliss Gro	52	B1
Saul Rd	100	B1	Seapark *Dublin 3*	81	C2	Shanliss Pk	52	B1
Saval Pk Cres	134	A3	Seapark *Mala.*	20	B2	Shanliss Rd	52	A1
Saval Pk Dr	134	A3	Seapark Dr	81	C2	Shanliss Wk	52	B1
Saval Pk Gdns	134	A2	Seapark Hill	20	B3	Shanliss Way	52	B1
Saval Pk Rd	134	A2	Seapark Rd	81	C2	Shannon Ter	88	B2
Scholarstown Pk	126	A2	Seapoint Av **1**			Shanowen Av	52	A2
Scholarstown Rd	126	A2	*Dublin 13*	43	D3	Shanowen Cres	52	B1
School La	54	B3	Seapoint Av *Black.*	118	A2	Shanowen Dr	52	B1
Schoolhouse La	145	D4	Seapoint Ct **5**			Shanowen Gro	52	A1
Sch Ho La W	144	B3	*Dublin 13*	43	D3	Shanowen Pk	52	A1
School St	89	C2	Seapoint Ct *Bray*	142	A1	Shanowen Rd	52	B1
Scotchstone Br	15	D3	Seapoint Rd	142	A1	Shanowen Rd Ind Est	52	B2
Scott Pk	142	B3	Seapoint Sta	118	A2	Shanrath Rd	53	C1
Scriblestown	49	D3	Seapoint Ter **17**	142	A1	Shantalla Av	53	C2
Scriblestown Rd	49	C3	Seapoint Vil **18**	142	A1	Shantalla Dr	53	C2
Seabank Ct	134	A1	Sea Rd	19	D1	Shantalla Pk	53	C2
Seabrook Manor	26	A3	Seatown Pk	15	D3	Shantalla Rd	53	C2
Seabury	104	B2	Seatown Rd	15	D3	Shanvarna Rd	53	C1
Seabury Av	19	C1	Seatown Rbt	15	D3	Sharavogue	134	A2
Seabury Cl	19	C1	Seatown Ter	17	D1	Shaws La	91	D3
Seabury Ct **5**	19	C1	Seatown Vil	15	D3	Shaw St	145	E3
Seabury Cres	19	C2	Seatown Wk	17	D1	Sheelin Av	139	C3
Seabury Dale **3**	19	C1	Seatown W	15	D3	Sheelin Dr	139	C3
Seabury Downs	19	C2	Seaview Av	79	C3	Sheelin Gro	139	C3
Seabury Dr	19	C1	Seaview Av N	80	A2	Sheelin Hill **8**	139	C3
Seabury Gdns	18	B1	Seaview Lawn	140	B1	Sheelin Wk	139	C3
Seabury Glen	19	C1	Seaview Pk	140	B1	Sheephill Av	33	D3
Seabury Grn	19	C1	Sea Vw Ter *Dublin 4*	103	D2	Sheephill Grn	33	D3
Seabury Gro **4**	19	C2	Seaview Ter *Dublin 13*	61	C2	Sheephill Pk	33	D3
Seabury Hts	18	B1	Seaview Wd	140	B1	Sheepmoor Av	46	A1
Seabury La	19	C2	Second Av *Dublin 1*	91	C1	Sheepmoor Cl	46	A1
Seabury Lawns **1**	18	B1	Second Av (Cookstown)			Sheepmoor Cres	46	A1
Seabury Meadows	18	B1	*Dublin 24*	109	C2	Sheepmoor Gdns	46	A1
Seabury Orchard	19	C1	Sefton Grn	132	B2	Sheepmoor Grn	46	A1
Seabury Par	19	C1	Selskar Ter	102	A1	Sheepmoor Gro	46	A1
Seabury Pk	18	B1	Serpentine Av	103	D1	Sheepmoor Lawn	46	A1
Seabury Pl	19	C2	Serpentine Pk	91	D3	Sheepmoor Way	46	A1
Seabury Rd	19	C1	Serpentine Rd	91	D3	Shelbourne Av	91	D3
Seabury Vale	19	C1	Serpentine Ter	103	D1	Shelbourne La	91	C3
Seabury Vw	18	B1	Seskin Vw Av	124	A1	Shelbourne Pk		
Seabury Wk	19	C1	Seskin Vw Dr	124	A1	Greyhound Stadium	91	D2
Seabury Wd	18	B1	Seskin Vw Pk	124	A2	Shelbourne Rd	91	D3
Seacliff Av	57	D1	Seskin Vw Rd	124	A1	Shelerin Rd	46	A2
Seacliff Dr	57	C1	Seven Hos **12**	133	D1	Shellysbanks Rd	92	B3
Seacliff Rd	57	C1	Seven Oaks	52	B3	Shelmalier Rd	79	C3
Seacourt	81	C2	Seville Pl	79	C3	Shelmartin Av	79	C2
Seacrest	142	B2	Seville Ter	78	B3	Shelmartin Ter	79	C1
Seafield	141	C1	Seymour Rd	142	A1	Shelton Dr	100	A3
Seafield Av *Dublin 3*	81	C2	Shamrock Cotts			Shelton Gdns	100	A3
Seafield Av *Black.*	118	B3	off *Shamrock Pl*	79	C3	Shelton Gro	100	A3
Seafield Cl	116	A1	Shamrock Pl	79	C3	Shelton Pk	100	A3
Seafield Ct *Dublin 13*	58	A1	Shamrock St			Sheriff St Lwr	145	F1
Seafield Ct *Kill.*	139	C3	off *Primrose St*	77	D1	Sheriff St Upr	91	C1
Seafield Ct *Mala.*	20	A2	Shamrock Ter	79	C3	Sherkin Gdns	52	B3
Seafield Cres	116	B1	Shamrock Vil	101	D2	Sherrard Av	78	A2
Seafield Down	81	D2	Shanard Av	52	A1	Sherrard St Lwr	78	A3
Seafield Dr	116	A1	Shanard Rd	52	A1	Sherrard St Upr	78	A3
Seafield Gro	81	D2	Shanboley Rd	53	C1	Shielmartin Dr	59	C3
Seafield Pk	116	B1	Shancastle Av	84	A1	Shielmartin Pk	62	A2
Seafield Rd *Boot.*	116	A1	Shancastle Cl	84	A1	Shielmartin Rd	62	A2
Seafield Rd *Kill.*	139	C3	Shancastle Cres	84	A1	Ship St Gt	144	C3
Seafield Rd E	81	C2	Shancastle Dr	84	A1	Ship St Little	144	B3
Seafield Rd W	80	B2	Shancastle Lawns	84	A1	Shrewsbury	104	A1
Seafield Ter **6**	135	C2	Shancastle Pk	84	A1	Shrewsbury Hall	141	C3
Seafort Av	92	A3	Shandon Cres	77	D2	Shrewsbury Lawn	138	A1
Seafort Cotts			Shandon Dr	77	D2	Shrewsbury Pk	104	A1
off *Seafort Av*	92	A3	Shandon Gdns	77	C1	Shrewsbury Rd		
Seafort Gdns	92	A3	Shandon Pk *Dublin 7*	77	C2	*Dublin 4*	103	D2
Seafort Vil			Shandon Pk *Black.*	118	A2	Shrewsbury Rd *Shank.*	141	C3
off *Seafort Av*	92	A3	Shandon Rd	77	D2	Shrewsbury Wd	138	A1
Seagrange Av	43	C3	Shanganagh Cliffs	141	C1	Sibthorpe La	102	B1
Seagrange Dr	57	D1	Shanganagh Gro	141	C1	Sidbury Ct **20**	142	B2
Seagrange Rd	57	C2	Shanganagh Rd	139	C3	Sidmonton Av	142	B2
Seagrave	26	B3	Shanganagh Ter	139	C2	Sidmonton Ct	142	B2
Seagrave Cl	37	C2	Shanganagh Vale	138	A2	Sidmonton Gdns	142	A2
Seagrave Ct	36	B2	Shanganagh Wd	141	C2	Sidmonton Pk	142	B2
Seagrave Dr	36	B2	Shangan Av	52	B1	Sidmonton Pl **6**	142	B2
Seagrave Ri	37	C2	Shangan Cres	38	B3	Sidmonton Rd *Bray*	142	B2
Seagrave Ter	37	C2	Shangan Gdns	52	B1	Sidmonton Rd *Grey.*	143	D1
Seagrave Way	36	B2	Shangangh Rd	78	A2	Sidmonton Sq **7**	142	B2
Seamount Dr	20	B3	Shangan Grn	52	B1	Sigurd Rd	77	C3
Seamount Gro	20	B3	Shangan Pk	52	B1	Silchester Ct	133	D1
Seamount Hts	20	B3	Shangan Rd	52	A1	Silchester Cres	133	D1
Seamount Pk	20	B3	Shanglas Rd	53	C1	Silchester Pk	133	D1
Seamount Rd	20	B3	Shanid Rd	101	C3	Silchester Rd	133	D1
Seamount Vw	18	A1	Shankill Business Cen	141	C2	Silchester Wd **3**	133	D2

Silken Vale	64	B2
Silleachain La	69	C1
Silloge Av	51	D1
Silloge Gdns	52	A1
Silloge Rd	37	D3
Silverberry	82	B2
Silver Birches *Dublin 14*	115	C3
Silver Birches *Dunb.*	29	C2
Silver Birches Cl	29	C2
Silver Birches Cres	29	C2
Silverdale	82	A2
Silver Pines **3**	130	B2
Silverwood	82	B2
Silverwood Dr *Dublin 6W*		
off *Templeville Dr*	112	A2
Silverwood Dr *Dublin 14*	112	B3
Silverwood Rd	112	B3
Simmon's Ct off		
Simmonscourt Castle	103	D2
Simmonscourt Av	103	D2
Simmonscourt Castle	103	D1
Simmonscourt Rd	103	D1
Simmonscourt Ter	103	D2
Simmonstown Manor	66	B3
Simmonstown Pk	66	B3
Simonscourt Sq	103	D1
Simonscourt Vw	103	D1
Simons Ridge	129	C3
Sion Hill	117	C1
Sion Hill Av	101	C2
Sion Hill Ct	53	C3
Sion Hill Rd	53	C3
Sion Rd	133	D3
Sir Ivor Mall **1**	131	C3
Sir John Rogersons		
Quay	91	C1
Sitric Rd	89	C1
Skelligs Ct	33	D3
Skellys La	53	D2
Skippers All	144	B3
Skreen Rd	76	A2
Slade Av	120	B2
Slade Castle	120	B2
Slade Cl	120	B2
Slade Hts	120	B2
Slademore Av	41	C3
Slademore Cl	55	D1
Slademore Ct	41	C3
Slademore Dr	55	D1
Slade Row	89	C1
Slane Rd	100	B1
Slaney Cl	77	C1
Slaney Rd	77	C1
Slemish Rd	76	A2
Slieve Bloom Pk	99	D1
Slieve Bloom Rd	99	D1
Slievemore Rd	100	A1
Slievenamon Rd	88	A3
Slieve Rua Dr	116	A3
Sloan Ter **21**	142	B2
Sloperton	119	C3
Slopes, The	119	C3
Smithfield	144	A2
Smithfield Sta	144	A2
Smiths Vil	119	C3
Snowdrop Wk	41	C3
Snugborough Rd	33	D3
Snugborough Rd		
(extension)	46	B2
Somerby Rd	143	D2
Somerset St		
off *Doris St*	91	D2
Somerton *D'bate*	13	D1
Somerton *Sally.*	133	C2
Somerville Av	99	D2
Somerville Grn	99	D2
Somerville Pk	99	D2
Summerton La	72	B2
Sommerville	114	B2
Sonesta	19	C1
Sorbonne	115	D2
Sorrel Dale	46	A2
Sorrel Dr	46	A2
Sorrel Heath	46	A2
Sorrento Cl **7**	135	C2
Sorrento Ct **8**	135	C2

Name	Ref
Sorrento Dr	134 B2
Sorrento Hts 1	135 C3
Sorrento Lawn 9	135 C2
Sorrento Ms 2	135 C3
Sorrento Rd	134 B2
South Av	116 A3
South Bk Rd	92 A2
South Circular Rd	88 A1
South Co Business Pk	130 B3
Southdene	118 B3
South Docks Rd	91 D2
Southern Cross Av	88 A2
Southern Cross Route	128 A3
South Esplanade	142 B2
South Gt Georges St	144 C4
South Hill *Dublin 6*	102 A3
South Hill *Dublin 13*	59 C3
South Hill Av	116 B2
South Hill Pk	116 B2
South Lotts Rd	91 D3
South Pk *Corn.*	132 A3
South Pk *Swords*	15 C2
South Pk Dr	132 A3
South Winds 11	134 B1
Southwood Pk	117 C2
Spade Enterprise Cen	89 C1
Spafield Ter	103 D1
Spa Rd (Kilmainham) *Dublin 8*	87 D2
Spa Rd (Phoenix Pk) *Dublin 8*	76 A3
Spawell Br	112 A3
Spencer Dock	91 C1
Spencer St *off South Circular Rd*	89 C3
Spencer St N	79 C3
Spencer Vil	134 A1
Sperrin Rd	87 D3
Spiddal Pk	85 D2
Spiddal Rd	85 D2
Spires, The	13 C3
Spire Vw Ct	101 D2
Spire Vw La	101 D2
Spitalfields	144 A4
Spring Bk Cotts	120 A1
Springdale Rd	55 C1
Springfield *Dublin 7*	76 A2
Springfield *Dublin 24*	109 C3
Springfield Av	112 B2
Springfield Cl	66 A3
Springfield Cres	112 B2
Springfield La	136 B3
Springfield Pk *Dublin 6W*	112 B2
Springfield Pk *Deans Gra*	131 D3
Springfield Rd	112 B2
Spring Gdn La	145 E3
Spring Gdn St	79 C3
Springhill Av	132 A1
Springhill Cotts 3	132 A1
Springhill Pk *Dalkey*	134 A3
Springhill Pk *Deans Gra*	132 A1
Springlawn	47 C1
Springlawn Cl	47 C1
Springlawn Ct	47 C2
Springlawn Dr	47 C2
Springlawn Hts	47 C1
Springlawn Rd	47 C1
Springvale	126 B2
Spruce Av	130 A2
Square, The *Dublin 4*	91 D2
Square, The *Dublin 6W*	101 C2
Square, The *Dublin 17*	39 D3
Square, The *Dublin 24*	123 D1
Square, The 3 *Lucan*	70 A3
Square Ind Complex, The	109 D3
Stable La *Dublin 2*	90 A3
Stable La *Dublin 4 off Londonbridge Rd*	91 D3
Stables, The	116 B1
Stadium Business Pk	35 C3
Stamer St	90 A3
Stanford Grn	99 D2
Stanhope Cen	77 D3
Stanhope Grn	89 C1
Stannaway Av	100 A2
Stannaway Dr	100 B2
Stannaway Rd	100 A2
Stapolin Av	43 C3
Stapolin Lawns	43 C3
Station Cl	96 B1
Stationcourt *Cool.*	46 B3
Station Ct *D'bate*	13 C2
Stationcourt Pk	46 B3
Stationcourt Vw	46 B3
Stationcourt Way	46 B3
Station Rd *Dublin 5*	55 D2
Station Rd *Dublin 13*	58 A1
Station Rd *Clond.*	96 B1
Station Rd *Dunb.*	29 C2
Station Rd *D.L.*	134 A1
Station Rd *Kill.*	139 D2
Station Rd *Lou.V.*	68 A1
Station Rd *Port.*	26 A3
Station Rd 4 *Shank.*	141 C2
Station Rd Business Pk	84 B3
Station Vw 2	46 B3
Station Way	42 B3
Steeple, The	64 A1
Steeples, The	87 C2
Steevens La	89 C2
Stella Av	52 A3
Stephens La	91 C3
Stephens Pl *off Merrion Sq E*	145 F4
Stephens Rd	88 A3
Stephen St	144 C4
Stephen St Upr	144 C4
Stiles Ct, The *off The Stiles Rd*	80 A2
Stiles Rd, The	80 A2
Stillorgan Ct 2	130 B1
Stillorgan Gro	131 C1
Stillorgan Heath	130 B1
Stillorgan Ind Est	129 D2
Stillorgan Pk	117 C3
Stillorgan Pk Av	117 C3
Stillorgan Rd *Dublin 4*	103 D2
Stillorgan Rd *Still.*	116 B2
Stillorgan Shop Cen	116 B3
Stillorgan Sta	130 A2
Stillorgan Wd	130 A1
Stirling Pk	114 A1
Stirrup La *off Beresford St*	144 B1
Stockhole La	23 C1
Stocking Av	126 A3
Stocking La	126 A3
Stocking Wd	125 D3
Stockton Ct	48 A3
Stockton Dr	74 A1
Stockton Grn	74 A1
Stockton Gro	74 A1
Stockton Lawn	48 A3
Stockton Pk	74 A1
Stonebridge	45 C1
Stonebridge Av	45 D1
Stonebridge Cl 1	141 C3
Stonebridge Dr	45 C1
Stonebridge La 1	140 B2
Stonebridge Rd *Clons.*	45 C1
Stonebridge Rd *Shank.*	140 B2
Stonemasons Grn 2	128 A2
Stonemasons Way	128 A2
Stonepark Abbey	113 D3
Stonepark Ct	113 D3
Stonepark Dr	113 D3
Stonepark Grn	113 D3
Stonepark Orchard	113 D3
Stoneview Pl	119 D3
Stoneybatter	89 C1
Stoneylea Ter 11	142 A3
Stoney Rd *Dublin 3 off Northbrook Av Upr*	79 C3
Stoney Rd (Dundrum) *Dublin 14*	115 C3
Store St	145 E1
Stormanstown Rd	51 D2
Stradbrook Cl	132 A1
Stradbrook Gdns	118 A3
Stradbrook Hill 4	132 A1
Stradbrook Lawn	118 A3
Stradbrook Pk	118 A3
Stradbrook Rd	118 A3
Straffan Av	64 B3
Straffan Cl	64 B3
Straffan Ct	64 B3
Straffan Cres	64 B3
Straffan Dr	64 B3
Straffan Grn	64 B3
Straffan Gro	64 B3
Straffan Lawn	64 B3
Straffan Way	65 C3
Stralem Ct	45 C1
Stralem Gro	45 C1
Stralem Ms	45 C1
Stralem Ter	45 C1
Strand, The	13 D2
Strandmill Av	27 C3
Strandmill Rd 1	27 C3
Strandmill Rd	27 C3
Strand Rd (Sandymount) *Dublin 4*	92 A3
Strand Rd *Dublin 13*	59 C2
Strand Rd *Bray*	142 B1
Strand Rd *Kill.*	139 D2
Strand Rd *Mala.*	19 D1
Strand Rd *Port.*	26 B3
Strand St *Dublin 4*	91 D2
Strand St *Mala.*	20 A2
Strand St Gt	144 C2
Strandville Av E	80 A2
Strandville Av N	79 C3
Strandville Ho	80 A2
Strangford Gdns	79 C3
Strangford Rd E	79 C3
Strathmore Rd	139 C1
Streamstown La	19 C3
Streamville Ct 10	139 C3
Streamville Rd	56 A1
Suffolk St	145 D3
Sugarloaf Cres	142 A3
Sugarloaf Ter 12	142 A3
Suir Rd	88 A2
Suir Rd Sta	88 A3
Sullivan St	88 B1
Summerfield (Blanchardstown) *Dublin 15*	47 C2
Summerfield 2 *Dublin 24*	124 A1
Summerfield Av	47 C2
Summerfield Cl (Blanchardstown) *Dublin 15*	47 C2
Summerfield Cl 8 *Dalkey*	134 B2
Summerfield Grn	47 C2
Summerfield Lawns	47 C2
Summerfield Meadows	47 C2
Summerfield Pk	47 C2
Summerfield Ri	47 C1
Summerhill	78 B3
Summerhill Par *Dublin 1*	78 B3
Summerhill Par *D.L.*	119 D3
Summerhill Pl	78 B3
Summerhill Rd *Dunb.*	28 A1
Summerhill Rd *D.L.*	119 D3
Summer Pl	78 B3
Summerseat Ct	30 B2
Summer St N	78 B3
Summer St S	89 C2
Summerville	80 B2
Summerville Pk	102 A2
Sunbury Gdns	102 A3
Suncroft Av 2	27 C3
Suncroft Dr	122 A1
Suncroft Pk	122 A1
Sundale Av	122 A2
Sundale Cl	122 A2
Sundale Cres	122 A1
Sundale Grn	122 A1
Sundale Gro	122 A1
Sundale Hts	122 A1
Sundale Lawn	121 D1
Sundale Meadows 12	121 D1
Sundale Par	121 D1
Sundale Pk	122 A1
Sundale Rd	122 A2
Sundale Vil	122 A1
Sundale Wk	122 A1
Sunday Well Br	15 D1
Sundrive Pk	101 C2
Sundrive Rd	100 B1
Sundrive Shop Cen	101 C2
Sunnybank Ter	114 B3
Sunshine Ind Est	100 A1
Superquinn Shop Cen *Dublin 12*	99 C2
Superquinn Shop Cen *Dublin 16*	126 A1
Susan Ter	89 C3
Susanville Rd	78 B2
Sussex Rd	102 B1
Sussex St	119 D3
Sussex Ter Lwr *off Mespil Rd*	90 B3
Sussex Ter Upr *off Sussex Rd*	90 B3
Sutton Ct	57 D1
Sutton Cross Shop Cen	58 B1
Sutton Downs	57 D1
Sutton Gro	57 D1
Sutton Lawns	57 D1
Sutton Pk	57 D1
Sutton Sta	58 A1
Swallowbrook	31 D2
Swallowbrook Cres	31 D2
Swallowbrook Pk	31 D2
Swallowbrook Vw	31 D2
Swan Pl *off Morehampton Rd*	103 C1
Swan Shop Cen	102 A2
Swans Nest Av	56 B1
Swans Nest Ct	56 B1
Swans Nest Rd	56 A1
Swanville Pl	102 A2
Swanward Business Cen	98 A3
Swanward Ct	101 C1
Swan Yd *off Harry St*	145 D4
Sweeneys Ter *off Mill St*	89 D3
Sweetbriar La	130 A1
Sweetmans Av	117 D2
Sweetmount Av	114 B3
Sweetmount Dr	114 B3
Sweetmount Pk	114 B3
Swiftbrook	122 A1
Swiftbrook Av	122 A1
Swiftbrook Cl	122 A1
Swiftbrook Dr	122 A1
Swiftbrook Pk	122 A1
Swifts All	144 A4
Swift's Gro	40 A2
Swifts Row *off Ormond Quay Upr*	144 B1
Swiftwood	120 B1
Swilly Rd	76 B2
Swords Business Campus	15 D2
Swords Business Pk	15 D3
Swords Manor Av	14 B3
Swords Manor Ct	14 B3
Swords Manor Cres	14 B3
Swords Manor Dr	14 B3
Swords Manor Gro	14 B3
Swords Manor Vw	14 B3
Swords Manor Way	14 B3
Swords Rd *Dublin 9*	52 B3
Swords Rd *Collins.*	22 B3
Swords Rd *Mala.*	19 C2
Swords St	77 C3
Sybil Hill Av	55 C3
Sybil Hill Rd	55 C3
Sycamore Av *Dublin 24*	109 D1
Sycamore Av *Cabin.*	137 C1
Sycamore Av *Castle.*	47 C3
Sycamore Cl *Dublin 24*	109 D1
Sycamore Cl *Cabin.*	137 C1
Sycamore Cl 6	133 C2
Sycamore Cres *Cabin.*	137 C1
Sycamore Cres *Still.*	116 B2
Sycamore Dr 1 *Dublin 16*	128 B1
Sycamore Dr *Dublin 24*	110 A1
Sycamore Dr *Cabin.*	137 C1
Sycamore Dr *Castle.*	47 C3
Sycamore Grn	137 C1
Sycamore Gro *Cabin.*	137 C1
Sycamore Gro 3 *Fox.*	131 D2
Sycamore Lawn *Cabin.*	137 C1
Sycamore Lawn *Castle.*	47 C3
Sycamore Pk *Dublin 11*	37 C3
Sycamore Pk *Dublin 24*	110 A1

Sycamore Pk Castle. 47 C3
Sycamore Rd (Finglas)
  Dublin 11 37 C3
Sycamore Rd Dublin 12 98 A2
Sycamore Rd Dublin 16 128 B1
Sycamore Rd Still. 116 B2
Sycamores, The 18 Abb. 139 C3
Sycamores, The Mala. 20 B2
Sycamore St 144 C3
Sycamore Vw 47 C3
Sycamore Wk 137 C1
Sydenham Ms Bray 142 B2
Sydenham Ms D.L. 119 D3
Sydenham Rd (Sandymount)
  Dublin 4 103 D1
Sydenham Rd (Dundrum)
  Dublin 14 115 C3
Sydenham Vil
  Dublin 14 115 C3
Sydenham Vil 27 Bray 142 B2
Sydney Av 117 D2
Sydney Par Av 104 A2
Sydney Par Sta 104 A2
Sydney Ter 117 D2
Sykes La 101 D3
Sylvan Av 109 D1
Sylvan Cl 109 D1
Sylvan Dr 109 D1
Synge La 90 A3
Synge Pl 90 A3
Synge St 90 A3
Synge Way 97 C1
Synnott Pl 78 A3
Synnott Row 78 A2

T

Tailor's Mkt 144 B3
Talbot Av 19 C2
Talbot Ct Dublin 15 47 D2
Talbot Ct 6 Mala. 19 C2
Talbot Downs 47 D2
Talbot Hall 14 B1
Talbot La Dublin 1
  off Talbot St 145 D1
Talbot La Kill. 134 A3
Talbot Lo 117 C3
Talbot Mem Br 145 E2
Talbot Pk 19 C2
Talbot Pl 145 E1
Talbot Rd 2 Kill. 139 C1
Talbot Rd Mala. 19 C2
Talbot St 145 D1
Tallaght Business Pk 123 C1
Tallaght Bypass 124 A1
Tallaght Enterprise Cen 110 A3
Tallaght Retail Cen 109 D3
Tallaght Rd 111 C3
Tallaght Sta 109 C3
Tallagt Rd 111 D3
Tamarisk Av 110 A1
Tamarisk Cl
  off Tamarisk Way 110 A1
Tamarisk Ct 110 A2
Tamarisk Dale
  off Tamarisk Dr 110 A1
Tamarisk Dr 110 A1
Tamarisk Gro
  off Tamarisk Pk 110 A2
Tamarisk Hts 110 A2
Tamarisk Lawn 110 A2
Tamarisk Pk 110 A2
Tamarisk Vw
  off Tamarisk Pk 110 A2
Tamarisk Wk
  off Tamarisk Dr 110 A1
Tamarisk Way 110 A1
Tandys La 82 A2
Taney Av 115 C3
Taney Ct 115 C3
Taney Cres 115 C3
Taney Dr 115 C3
Taney Gro 115 D3
Taney Lawn 115 C3
Taney Manor 115 C3
Taney Pk 115 C3
Taney Ri 115 C3
Taney Rd 115 C3
Tara Hill Cres 113 C3
Tara Hill Gro 113 C3
Tara Hill Rd 113 C3
Tara Lawn 56 A1
Tara St 145 E2

Tara St Sta 145 E2
Tassagard Grns 120 B2
Tassagart Dr 120 B2
Taylor's Hill 128 A3
Taylors La Dublin 8 89 C2
Taylor's La Dublin 16 126 B1
Temple Bar 144 C3
Temple Cotts 77 D3
Temple Ct Dublin 7 89 C1
Temple Ct Dublin 9 38 B2
Temple Cres 118 A2
Temple Gdns Dublin 6 102 A3
Temple Gdns Dublin 9 38 B2
Temple Hill 118 A2
Temple La N 78 A3
Temple La S 144 C3
Temple Lawns Dublin 9 38 B2
Temple Lawns Celbr. 66 B3
Temple Manor 29 C1
Temple Manor Av 111 C1
Temple Manor Cl 111 C1
Temple Manor Ct 111 C1
Temple Manor Dr 111 C1
Temple Manor Gro 111 C1
Temple Manor Way 111 C1
Templemore Av 101 D3
Templeogue Lo 111 D2
Templeogue Rd 112 B2
Templeogue Wd 112 A2
Temple Pk 102 B3
Temple Pk Av 118 A2
Temple Pl 102 B1
Temple Rd Dublin 6 102 A3
Temple Rd Black. 117 D2
Templeroan 126 A1
Templeroan Av 126 A1
Templeroan Cl 126 A1
Templeroan Ct 126 A1
Templeroan Cres 126 A1
Templeroan Downs 126 B1
Templeroan Dr 126 A1
Templeroan Grn 126 A1
Templeroan Gro 126 A1
Templeroan Lo
  off Ballyboden Way 126 A2
Templeroan Meadows 126 B1
Templeroan Ms 126 A1
Templeroan Pk 126 A1
Templeroan Vw 126 A1
Templeroan Way 126 A1
Temple Sq 102 A3
Temple St N 78 A3
Temple St W 89 C1
Temple Ter 10 135 C2
Templeview Av 41 D3
Templeview Cl 41 D3
Templeview Copse 41 D3
Templeview Ct 41 D3
Templeview Cres 41 D3
Templeview Downs 41 D3
Templeview Dr 42 A3
Templeview Grn 41 D3
Templeview Gro 41 D3
Templeview Lawn 41 D3
Templeview Pk 41 D3
Templeview Pl 41 D3
Templeview Ri 41 D3
Templeview Row 41 D3
Templeview Sq 41 D3
Templeview Vale 1 41 D3
Templeview Wk 42 A3
Templeview Way 42 A3
Temple Vil
  off Palmerston Rd 102 A2
Templeville Av 112 A2
Templeville Dr 112 A2
Templeville Pk 112 B1
Templeville Rd 111 D1
Terenure Coll 112 B1
Terenure Pk 101 C3
Terenure Pl 113 C1
Terenure Rd E 101 C3
Terenure Rd N 101 C3
Terenure Rd W 100 B3
Terminal Rd N 93 C1
Terminal Rd S 93 C1
Termon Ct 1 37 D3
Terrace, The 136 B3
Tetrarch Gro 29 C1
Texas La 19 D2
Thatch Rd, The 53 C2
Thicket, The 136 B1

Third Av Dublin 1 91 C1
Third Av Dublin 8
  off Dolphin's Barn 89 C3
Third Av (Cookstown)
  Dublin 24 109 C3
Thomas St 89 C2
Thomas Davis St S 144 B4
Thomas Davis St W 87 D3
Thomas La
  off Cathedral St 145 D1
Thomas Moore Rd 99 C3
Thomas St E 91 D2
Thomas St W 89 C2
Thomastown Cres 11 133 C2
Thomastown Rd 133 D3
Thomond 5 141 C2
Thomond Rd 86 B2
Thormanby Lawns 61 C3
Thormanby Lo 61 D3
Thormanby Rd 61 C2
Thormanby Wds 61 C3
Thornbury Apts 32 A2
Thorncastle St 91 D2
Thorncliffe 114 B1
Thorncliffe Pk 114 A1
Thorndale Av
  off Elm Mt Rd 54 A3
Thorndale Ct 53 C2
Thorndale Cres
  off Elm Mt Rd 54 A3
Thorndale Dr 52 A3
Thorndale Gro 52 A3
Thorndale Lawns
  off Elm Mt Rd 54 A3
Thorndale Pk
  off Elm Mt Rd 54 A3
Thornhill Gdns 66 A1
Thornhill Hts 66 A1
Thornhill Meadows 66 A1
Thornhill Rd 116 A3
Thornleigh 15 C2
Thornleigh Av 15 C2
Thornleigh Grn 14 B2
Thornleigh La 15 C2
Thornleigh Pl 15 C2
Thornleigh Rd 15 C2
Thornleigh Row 15 C2
Thornleigh Sq 14 B2
Thornville Av 56 B2
Thornville Dr 56 B2
Thornville Pk 56 B2
Thornville Rd 56 B2
Thor Pl 89 C1
Three Rock Cl 110 B1
Three Rock Rd 130 A2
Thundercut All
  off Smithfield 144 A1
Tibradden Cl
  off Tibradden Dr 110 B1
Tibradden Dr 110 B1
Tibradden Gro
  off Tibradden Dr 110 B1
Ticknock Av 129 C3
Ticknock Dale 129 C3
Ticknock Gro 128 B3
Ticknock Hill 128 B3
Ticknock Way 129 C3
Timber Quay 92 A1
Tinkler's Path 74 B2
Tionscail Ind Est 17 D1
Tivoli Av 101 D2
Tivoli Cl 133 C1
Tivoli Rd 119 C3
Tivoli Ter E 119 C3
Tivoli Ter N 119 C3
Tivoli Ter S 119 C3
Tolka Cotts 51 C3
Tolka Est Rd 51 C3
Tolka Quay Rd 91 D1
Tolka Rd 78 B2
Tolka Vale 51 C3
Tolka Valley
  Business Pk 50 B3
Tolka Valley Grn 50 B3
Tolka Valley Ind Est 50 B3
Tolka Valley Rd 50 A3
Tom Clarke Ho 79 C2
Tom Kelly Rd 102 A1
Tonduff Cl
  off Lugaquilla Av 110 B1
Tonguefield Rd 100 B2
Tonlegee Av 55 D1

Tonlegee Dr 55 C1
Tonlegee Rd 55 C1
Torca Rd 135 C3
Torlogh Gdns 79 C2
Torlogh Par 79 C1
Torquay Rd 131 C2
Torquay Wd 131 C2
Tory Sq 47 C1
Tourmakeady Rd 52 B2
Tower Av 101 D3
Tower Rd Dublin 15 74 A2
Tower Rd Clond. 96 B2
Tower Shop Cen 96 B2
Tower Vw Cotts 77 D1
Townsend St 145 E2
Townyard La 20 A2
Trafalgar La 118 A2
Trafalgar Rd 143 D1
Trafalgar Ter Black. 118 A2
Trafalgar Ter 4 Bray 142 B1
Tram Ter 81 C3
Tramway Cotts 77 D2
Tramway Ct
  off Station Rd 58 A1
Tramway Ter 104 A1
Tranquility Gro 54 A1
Treepark Av 110 A2
Treepark Cl 110 A2
Treepark Dr 110 A2
Treepark Rd 110 A2
Trees Av 116 B3
Trees Rd Lwr 116 B3
Trees Rd Upr 116 A3
Tresilian 136 B1
Trevor Ter
  off Grattan St 91 C2
Trimbleston 115 D2
Trimleston Av 104 B3
Trimleston Dr 104 B3
Trimleston Gdns 104 B3
Trimleston Pk 104 B3
Trimleston Rd 116 B1
Trim Rd 53 D1
Trinity Coll 145 D3
Trinity Coll
  Enterprise Cen 91 C2
Trinity St 145 D3
Trinity Ter 79 C2
Tritonville Av 92 A3
Tritonville Ct 91 D3
Tritonville Cres 92 A3
Tritonville Rd 91 D3
Trosyrafon Ter 23 142 B2
Tryconnell Pk 87 D2
Tubbermore Av 11 135 C2
Tubbermore Rd 134 B2
Tuckett's La 60 B2
Tudor Ct 2 19 C1
Tudor Cres 10 B2
Tudor Gro 10 B2
Tudor Hts 10 B2
Tudor Lawns 131 C3
Tudor Rd 102 B3
Tulip Ct 41 C3
Tullyhall 82 B3
Tullyhall Av 82 B3
Tullyhall Cl 82 B3
Tullyhall Ct 82 B3
Tullyhall Cres 82 B3
Tullyhall Dr 82 B3
Tullyhall Grn 82 B3
Tullyhall Pk 82 B3
Tullyhall Ri 82 B3
Tullyhall Way 82 B3
Tullyvale 138 A3
Turnapin Cotts 39 D2
Turnapin Grn 39 D2
Turnapin Gro 39 D2
Turnapin La 39 C2
Turnberry 57 D1
Turnpike Rd 97 C2
Turret Rd 85 D1
Turrets, The 91 D3
Turrets Flats
  off Rathmines Rd Upr 102 A2
Turvey Av 12 A1

Turvey Cl 13 C1
Turvey Cres 13 C2
Turvey Dr 13 C2
Turvey Gdn 13 C2
Turvey Gro 13 C2
Turvey Pk 13 C2
Turvey Wds 13 C1
Tuscany Downs 55 D2
Tuscany Pk 57 D1
Tymon Cl 123 D2
Tymon Cres 123 D1
Tymon Gro 123 D1
Tymon Hts 124 B2
Tymon La 111 C2
Tymon Lawn 123 D2
Tymon N Av 110 B2
Tymon N Gdns 110 B3
Tymon N Grn 110 B2
Tymon N Gro 110 B2
Tymon N Lawn 110 B2
Tymon N Pk 110 B3
Tymon N Rd 110 B2
Tymonville Av 110 B2
Tymonville Ct 110 A2
Tymonville Cres 110 A2
Tymonville Dr 110 B2
Tymonville Gro 110 B2
Tymonville Pk 110 B2
Tymonville Rd 110 B2
Tynan Hall 109 D1
Tynan Hall Av 109 D1
Tynan Hall Gro 109 C1
Tynan Hall Pk 109 C1
Tyrconnell Rd 87 D3
Tyrconnell St 87 D3
Tyrconnell Vil
  off Grattan Cres 87 D2
Tyrone Pl 87 D3

U
Ullardmor 9 134 B2
Ulster St 77 D2
Ulster Ter 1 117 C3
Ulverton Cl 134 B1
Ulverton Ct 12 134 B1
Ulverton Rd 134 B1
University Coll Dublin 2 90 A3
University Coll Dublin 4 115 D1
University Coll
  (Sch of Nursing &
  Midwifery) Dublin 4 91 D3
Upper Cliff Rd 61 C2
Uppercross 71 D3
Uppercross Rd 88 B3
Upper Glen Rd 74 B3
Upper Portraine Rd 13 D1
Urney Gro 134 A3
U.S.A. Embassy
  (Residence) 75 C3
Ushers Island 89 C1
Ushers Quay 144 A2
Usher St 144 A3

V
Vale, The Celbr. 66 A2
Vale, The Palm. 73 C3
Valentia Par 78 A2
Valentia Rd 52 A3
Vale Vw Av 137 C1
Vale Vw Cl 137 C1
Valeview Cres 50 A2
Valeview Dr 50 A2
Valeview Gdns 50 A2
Vale Vw Gro 137 C1
Vale Vw Lawn 137 C1
Valley Av 138 A3
Valley Cl 138 A3
Valley Dr 138 A3
Valley Pk Av 49 D2
Valley Pk Dr 49 D3
Valley Pk Rd 49 D3
Valley Vw Lough. 138 A3
Valley Vw Swords 14 B3
Valley Wk 138 A3
Vanessa Cl 66 A2
Vanessa Lawns 66 A2

Vauxhall Av 89 C3
Vavasour Sq 91 D3
Venetian Hall 54 B3
Ventry Dr 76 B1
Ventry Pk 76 B1
Ventry Rd 76 B1
Verbena Av Dublin 13 57 C2
Verbena Av Fox. 131 D3
Verbena Gro 57 C1
Verbena Lawns 57 C1
Verbena Pk 57 C1
Verdemont 46 B2
Vergemount
  off Clonskeagh Rd 103 C3
Vergemount Hall 103 C3
Vergemount Pk 103 C2
Vernon Av (Clontarf)
  Dublin 3 81 C2
Vernon Av Dublin 6
  off Frankfort Av 101 D2
Vernon Ct 81 C3
Vernon Dr 81 C1
Vernon Gdn 81 C2
Vernon Gro Dublin 3 81 C2
Vernon Gro (Rathgar)
  Dublin 6 102 A3
Vernon Heath 81 C1
Vernon Par
  off Clontarf Rd 80 A2
Vernon Pk 81 C2
Vernon Ri 81 C1
Vernon St 89 D3
Vernon Ter
  off Frankfort Av 102 A3
Veronica Ter 91 D2
Verschoyle Av 121 C2
Verschoyle Cl 121 D2
Verschoyle Ct
  off Verschoyle Pl 91 C3
Verschoyle Cres 121 D2
Verschoyle Glen 121 D2
Verschoyle Grn 121 C2
Verschoyle Hts 121 C2
Verschoyle Pk 121 D2
Verschoyle Pl 91 C3
Verschoyle Ri 121 C2
Verschoyle Vale 121 C2
Vesey Ms 119 C3
Vesey Pk 82 A1
Vesey Pl 119 C3
Vevay Cres 16 142 A2
Vevay Rd 142 A3
Vevay Vil 13 142 A3
Vicar St 144 A3
Vico Rd 139 D1
Victoria Av Dublin 4 103 C2
Victoria Av Bray 142 B2
Victoria Br 91 C2
Victoria Quay 89 C1
Victoria Rd (Clontarf)
  Dublin 3 80 A2
Victoria Rd (Terenure)
  Dublin 6 113 D1
Victoria Rd Dalkey 135 C2
Victoria Rd Grey. 143 C1
Victoria Rd Kill. 139 D1
Victoria St 89 D3
Victoria Ter Dublin 3
  off Clontarf Rd 81 C3
Victoria Ter Dublin 14 114 B3
Victoria Ter 1 Dalkey 134 B2
Victoria Vil Dublin 3 79 D2
Victoria Vil (Rathgar)
  Dublin 6 101 D3
View, The Dublin 16 128 B3
View, The Dublin 17 39 D3
View, The Dublin 24 124 B1
View, The (Cookstown)
  Dublin 24 109 C2
View, The (Oldtown Mill)
  Celbr. 66 A2
View, The
  (St. Wolstan's Abbey)
  Celbr. 66 B3
View, The Dunb. 28 A3
View, The Mala. 21 C3
View, The Manor. 31 C3
Viking Pl off Viking Rd 89 C1
Viking Rd 89 C1
Villa, The 18 A2
Villa Blanchard 47 D2
Village, The Dublin 5 56 A3

Village, The Dublin 9 52 B3
Village, The Clons. 45 D2
Village Cen Clond. 96 B2
Village Cen, The 5
  Lucan 70 A3
Village Ct Dublin 14 113 C2
Village Ct, The 6 Lucan 70 A3
Village Gate, The 134 B2
Village Grn 110 A3
Village Hts 32 B3
Village Sq 124 A1
Villa Pk Av (Ascal Pairc
  An Bhailtini) 76 A2
Villa Pk Dr (Ceide Pairc
  An Bhailtini) 76 A2
Villa Pk Gdns (Gardini Pairc
  An Bhailtini) 76 A2
Villa Pk Rd (Bothar Pairc
  An Bhailtini) 76 A2
Villarea Pk 134 A1
Villiers Rd 102 A3
Vincent Ter 78 A1
Violet Hill Dr 51 C3
Violet Hill Pk 51 C3
Violet Hill Rd 51 C3
Virginia Dr
  off Virginia Pk 50 A2
Virginia Hts 109 C3
Virginia Pk 50 A2
Viscount Av 39 C2

W
Wad Br 52 A2
Wadelai Grn 52 A2
Wadelai Rd 51 D2
Wade's Av 55 D3
Wainsfort Av 112 A1
Wainsfort Cres 112 A1
Wainsfort Dr 100 A3
Wainsfort Gdns
  off Wainsfort Cres 112 A1
Wainsfort Gro 112 B1
Wainsfort Manor Cres 112 A1
Wainsfort Manor Dr 112 A1
Wainsfort Manor Grn 112 A1
Wainsfort Manor Gro 112 A1
Wainsfort Pk 112 A1
Wainsfort Rd 112 A1
Waldemar Ter 114 B3
Waldrons Br 114 A1
Walk, The Dublin 6W 112 A2
Walk, The Dublin 16 128 B3
Walk, The Dublin 24 124 A1
Walk, The Carrick. 136 B3
Walk, The Celbr. 66 A2
Walk, The Dunb. 28 B3
Walk, The Kins. 18 A3
Walk, The Lou.V. 68 A1
Walk, The Mala. 21 C3
Walk, The Manor. 31 C3
Walkinstown Av 99 C2
Walkinstown Cl 99 C2
Walkinstown Cres 99 C2
Walkinstown Cross 99 C2
Walkinstown Dr 99 C2
Walkinstown Grn 99 C2
Walkinstown Mall 99 C2
Walkinstown Par 99 C2
Walkinstown Pk 99 C2
Walkinstown Rd (Bothar
  Chille Na Manac) 99 C2
Wallace Rd 99 D2
Walled Gdns, The 66 B1
Walnut Av Dublin 9 52 B3
Walnut Av 1 Dublin 24 109 D1
Walnut Cl 109 D1
Walnut Ct 52 B3
Walnut Dr 2 109 D1
Walnut Lawn 52 B3
Walnut Pk 52 B3
Walnut Ri 52 B3
Walnut Vw 5 126 B2
Walsh Rd 52 A3
Waltersland Rd 130 B1
Waltham Ter 117 C2
Walton Hall 15 C1
Walworth Rd
  off Victoria St 101 D1
Warburton Ter 24 142 B2
Wards Hill 89 D3
Warners La 90 B3
Warren, The 19 C2

Warren Av 72 B1
Warren Cl 72 B1
Warren Cres 72 B1
Warren Grn Dublin 13 58 A1
Warren Grn Carp. 72 B1
Warrenmount 89 D3
Warrenmount Pl 89 D3
Warren Pk 72 B1
Warrenpoint 80 A2
Warrenstown 33 C3
Warrenstown Cl 33 C3
Warrenstown Ct 33 C3
Warrenstown Downs 33 C3
Warrenstown Dr 33 C2
Warrenstown Garth 32 B3
Warrenstown Grn 33 C3
Warrenstown Gro 33 C3
Warrenstown Lawn 33 C3
Warrenstown Pk 33 C3
Warrenstown Pl 32 B3
Warrenstown Ri 33 C3
Warrenstown Row 33 C3
Warrenstown Vale 33 C3
Warrenstown Vw 32 B3
Warrenstown Wk 33 C3
Warrenstown Way 33 C3
Warren St 102 A1
Warrington La
  off Warrington Pl 91 C3
Warrington Pl 91 C3
Warwick Ter
  off Sallymount Av 102 B1
Wasdale Gro 113 D1
Wasdale Pk 113 C1
Washington La 112 B3
Washington Pk 112 B2
Washington St 89 D3
Watercourse 111 D2
Waterfall Av 78 B2
Waterfall Rd 55 D3
Watergate Est 123 D1
Waterloo Av 79 C3
Waterloo La 102 B1
Waterloo Rd 103 C1
Watermeadow Dr 123 D1
Watermeadow Pk 123 D1
Watermill Av 55 D3
Watermill Cl 124 A2
Watermill Dr 55 D3
Watermill Gro 124 A2
Watermill Lawn
  Dublin 5 56 A3
Watermill Lawn
  Dublin 24 124 A2
Watermill Pk 55 D3
Watermill Rd
  (Bothar An Easa) 55 D3
Waterside Av 18 A2
Waterside Cl 18 A2
Waterside Ct 18 A2
Waterside Cres Port. 27 C1
Waterside Cres Swords 18 B2
Waterside Dr 18 A2
Waterside Grn 18 A2
Waterside Lawn 18 A2
Waterside Pk 18 A2
Waterside Ri 4 18 A2
Waterside Rd 1 18 A2
Waterside Wk 18 A2
Waterside Way 3 18 A2
Waterstown Av 73 D3
Waterville Rd 33 D3
Waterville Row 47 C1
Waterville Ter 47 D1
Watery La Clond. 96 B1
Watery La Swords 15 C3
Watling St 89 C2
Watson Av 138 B3
Watson Dr 138 B3
Watson Pk 138 B3
Watson Rd 138 B3
Watson's Est 138 B3
Waverley Av 79 C2
Waverley Business Pk 98 B1
Waverley Ter Dublin 6
  off Kenilworth Rd 101 D2
Waverley Ter 5 Bray 142 B1
Way, The 28 B3
Weatherwell Ind Est 84 B3
Weaver La
  off Phibsborough Rd 77 D3
Weaver's Row 45 D2

Name	Page	Grid
Weavers Sq	89	C3
Weaver's St	144	A4
Wedgewood Est	129	D2
Weirview	70	A2
Weirview Dr	130	B1
Weldon's La **8**	43	D3
Wellesley Pl		
off Russell St	78	B3
Wellfield Br	42	A2
Wellington Ct **17**	142	A2
Wellington La Dublin 4	103	C1
Wellington La		
Dublin 6W	111	D2
Wellington Monument	88	B1
Wellington Pl	111	D1
Wellington Pl		
(Donnybrook)	103	C1
Wellington Pl N	77	D3
Wellington Quay	144	C3
Wellington Rd		
Dublin 4	103	C1
Wellington Rd		
Dublin 6W	111	D2
Wellington Rd		
Dublin 8	88	A1
Wellington St	119	C3
Wellington St Lwr	78	A3
Wellington St Upr	77	D3
Wellmount Av	50	A2
Wellmount Ct	50	A2
Wellmount Cres	50	A2
Wellmount Dr	50	A2
Wellmount Grn	50	A2
Wellmount Par	50	A2
Wellmount Pk	50	A2
Wellmount Rd	50	A2
Wellpark Av	52	B3
Well Rd **2**	17	C1
Wellview Av	32	B2
Wellview Cres	32	B2
Wellview Grn	32	B1
Wellview Gro	32	B1
Wellview Pk	32	B2
Wendell Av	27	C1
Wentworth Ter		
off Hogan Pl		
Werburgh St	144	B3
Wesbury	130	B1
Wesley Hts	129	C2
Wesley Lawns	129	C2
Wesley Pl	89	D3
Wesley Rd	101	D3
Westbourne	95	D2
Westbourne Av	95	D2
Westbourne Cl	95	D2
Westbourne Dr	95	D2
Westbourne Gro	95	D2
Westbourne Lo	125	D1
Westbourne Ri	95	D2
Westbourne Rd	113	C1
Westbourne Ter **25**	142	A1
Westbourne Vw	95	D2
Westbrook	100	A3
Westbrook Lawns	121	D2
Westbrook Rd	114	B2
Westbury	82	A1
Westbury Av	82	A1
Westbury Cl	82	A2
Westbury Dr	82	A1
Westbury Pk	82	A2
Westcourt		
off Basin St Upr	89	C2
Westcourt La	89	C2
Westend Village	46	B1
Western Ind Est	98	A2
Western Parkway		
Dublin 15	73	C1
Western Parkway		
Dublin 20	85	C1
Western Parkway		
Dublin 22	97	D3
Western Parkway		
Dublin 24	97	D3
Western Parkway		
Business Cen	98	B3
Western Parkway		
Business Pk	98	B3
Western Rd	89	C3
Western Way	77	D3
Westerton Ri **5**	128	B1
Westfield Av	69	C3
Westfield Grn	10	B2
Westfield Pk	142	B2
Westfield Rd	101	C2
Westfield Vw	10	B2
Westgate Business Pk	98	A3
Westhampton Pl	101	C3
Westhaven	31	D3
Westland Ct		
off Cumberland St S	145	F4
Westland Row	145	F3
Westlink Ind Est	86	B3
Westminster Ct **4**	136	B1
Westminster Lawns	131	C2
Westminster Pk	131	D2
Westminster Rd	131	D3
Westmoreland Pk	102	B1
Westmoreland St	145	D3
West Oil Jetty	92	B2
Weston Av	114	B3
Weston Cl Dublin 14	114	B3
Weston Cl Lucan	69	D3
Weston Ct	69	C3
Weston Cres	69	C3
Weston Dr	69	C3
Weston Grn	69	C3
Weston Gro	114	B3
Weston Hts	69	C3
Weston La	69	C3
Weston Lawn	69	C3
Weston Meadow	69	C3
Weston Pk Dublin 14	114	B3
Weston Pk Lucan	69	D3
Weston Rd	114	B3
Weston Ter	114	B3
Weston Way	69	C3
West Pk Dublin 5	55	C2
Westpark Dublin 24	124	A1
West Pk Dr	51	D3
Westpoint Business Pk	31	D2
Westpoint Ct		
Business Pk	98	B1
West Rd	79	C3
West Row	144	C1
West Ter	87	D2
Westview	10	B3
Westview Ter **6**	142	B1
Westway	33	D3
Westway Cl	33	D3
Westway Gro	33	D3
Westway Lawns		
off Westway Gro	33	D3
Westway Pk	33	D3
Westway Ri	33	D3
Westway Vw	33	D3
Westwood Av	49	D2
Westwood Rd	49	D2
Wexford St	90	A3
Wharton Ter		
off Harolds Cross Rd	101	D1
Whately Pl	130	A1
Wheatfield Gro	27	C1
Wheatfield Rd		
Dublin 20	85	D1
Wheatfield Rd Port.	27	C1
Wheatfields Av	84	B2
Wheatfields Cl	84	B2
Wheatfields Ct	84	B2
Wheatfields Cres	84	B2
Wheatfields Dr	84	B2
Wheatfields Gro	84	B2
Wheatfields Pk	84	B2
Whiteacre Ct	52	B1
Whiteacre Cres	52	B1
Whitebank Rd	92	B2
Whitebarn Rd	114	A2
Whitebeam Av	103	C3
Whitebeam Rd	103	C3
Whitebeams Rd	129	D2
Whitebrook Pk	122	B1
Whitechapel Av	46	A1
Whitechapel Ct	46	A1
Whitechapel Cres	46	A1
Whitechapel Grn	46	A1
Whitechapel Gro	46	A1
Whitechapel Lawn	46	A1
Whitechapel Pk	46	A1
Whitechapel Rd	46	A1
Whitechurch	127	C2
Whitechurch Abbey **7**	113	C3
Whitechurch Av	127	C2
Whitechurch Cl	127	C2
Whitechurch Ct	127	C2
Whitechurch Cres	127	C2
Whitechurch Dr	127	C2
Whitechurch Grn	127	C2
Whitechurch Gro	127	C2
Whitechurch Hill	127	C3
Whitechurch Lawn	127	C2
Whitechurch Pk	127	C2
Whitechurch Pines	113	C3
Whitechurch Pl	127	C2
Whitechurch Rd		
Dublin 14	113	C3
Whitechurch Rd		
Dublin 16	113	C3
Whitechurch Stream **5**	113	C3
Whitechurch Vw	127	C2
Whitechurch Wk	127	C2
Whitechurch Way	127	C2
Whitecliff	127	C1
Whitefriar Pl		
off Peter Row	144	C4
Whitefriar St	144	C4
White Hall	109	C1
Whitehall Cl	111	D1
Whitehall Gdns	100	A3
Whitehall Ms	131	D3
Whitehall Pk	111	D1
Whitehall Rd		
(Rathfarnham)	114	A3
Whitehall Rd E	111	D1
Whitehall Rd W	111	D1
White Oak	115	C1
Whites La N	77	D3
Whites Rd	74	A2
Whitestown		
Business Pk	123	C2
Whitestown Cres	32	B3
Whitestown Dr		
Dublin 24	123	C1
Whitestown Dr Mulh.	32	A3
Whitestown Gdns	46	B1
Whitestown Grn	32	B3
Whitestown Gro	32	B3
Whitestown Pk	32	B3
Whitestown Rd	123	C1
Whitestown Wk	46	B1
Whitestown Way	123	D1
White's Vil	134	B2
Whitethorn	85	C1
Whitethorn Av	54	A2
Whitethorn Cl	53	D2
Whitethorn Cres		
Dublin 5	54	A2
Whitethorn Cres		
Dublin 10	85	C2
Whitethorn Dr	85	C2
Whitethorn Gdns	85	C2
Whitethorn Gro	54	A2
Whitethorn La		
off Thorncastle St	91	D2
Whitethorn Pk		
Dublin 5	54	A2
Whitethorn Pk		
Dublin 10	85	C2
Whitethorn Ri	54	A2
Whitethorn Rd		
Dublin 5	53	D2
Whitethorn Rd		
Dublin 14	103	C3
Whitethorn Wk **1** D.L.	132	B2
Whitethorn Wk **2** Fox.	131	D3
Whitethorn Way	85	C2
Whitshed Rd	143	C2
Whitton Rd	101	C3
Whitworth Av		
off Whitworth Pl	78	A2
Whitworth Pl	78	A2
Whitworth Rd Dublin 1		
off Seville Pl	79	C3
Whitworth Rd Dublin 9	77	D2
Whyteleaf Gro	42	A3
Wicklow La		
off Wicklow St	145	D3
Wicklow St	145	D3
Wigan Rd	78	A2
Wikeford Hall	15	C1
Wilderwood Gro	111	D2
Wilfield	104	A1
Wilfield Rd	104	A1
Wilfrid Rd	101	C2
Willans Av	44	B1
Willans Dr	44	B1
Willans Grn	44	B1
Willans Ri	44	B1
Willans Row	44	B1
Willans Way	44	B1
Willbrook	127	C1
Willbrook Downs	127	C1
Willbrook Gro	113	C3
Willbrook Lawn	113	C3
Willbrook Pk	113	C3
Willbrook Rd	113	C3
Willbrook St	113	C3
Willfield Pk	104	A1
William's La		
off Princes St N	145	D2
William's Pk	102	A1
William's Pl S	89	D3
William's Pl Upr	78	A2
William's Row		
off Abbey St Mid	145	D2
William St N	78	B3
William St S	145	D4
Willie Nolan Rd	43	D1
Willington Av	111	D2
Willington Ct	111	D1
Willington Cres	111	D2
Willington Dr	111	D2
Willington Grn	111	D1
Willington Gro	111	D2
Willington Pk		
off Willington Gro	111	D2
Willmont Av	134	A1
Willow Av Clond.	96	A3
Willow Av Lough.	138	A3
Willowbank Dublin 16	129	C1
Willow Bk D.L.	119	C3
Willowbank Dr	127	C1
Willowbank Pk	112	B3
Willowbrook	13	D1
Willowbrook Gro	66	A2
Willowbrook Lawns	66	A2
Willowbrook Lo	66	A1
Willowbrook Pk	66	A1
Willow Business Pk	98	A1
Willow Ct Clond.	96	A3
Willow Ct Lough.	138	A3
Willow Cres	138	A3
Willow Dr	96	A3
Willowfield	104	A1
Willowfield Av	115	D2
Willowfield Pk	115	D2
Willow Gate	128	B1
Willow Gro Clond.	96	A3
Willow Gro Corn.	132	A3
Willow Gro **4** D.L.	133	C2
Willow Ms	104	B2
Willow Pk Dunb.	29	C2
Willow Pk **5** Fox.	131	D2
Willow Pk Lough.	138	A3
Willow Pk Av	51	D1
Willow Pk Cl	51	D1
Willow Pk Cres	51	C1
Willow Pk Dr	51	D1
Willow Pk Gro	51	D1
Willow Pk Lawn	51	D1
Willow Pk Rd	51	D1
Willow Pl Boot.	117	C1
Willow Pl Lough.	138	A3
Willow Rd Dublin 12	97	D1
Willow Rd Dublin 16	128	B1
Willows, The Dublin 11	77	C1
Willows, The **19** Abb.	139	C3
Willows, The Celbr.	66	B2
Willows, The D.L.	118	A3
Willows Ct	45	D1
Willows Dr	45	D1
Willows Grn	45	D1
Willows Rd	45	D1
Willow Ter		
off Rock Rd	117	C1
Willow Vale	138	B2
Willow Wd Cl	45	D1
Willow Wd Downs	45	D1
Willow Wd Grn	45	D1
Willow Wd Gro	45	D1
Willow Wd Lawn	45	D1
Willow Wd Pk	45	D1

Willow Wd Ri	45	D1	
Willow Wd Vw	45	D1	
Willow Wd Wk	45	D1	
Willsborough Ind Est	39	D2	
Willsbrook Av	71	C3	
Willsbrook Cres	71	D3	
Willsbrook Dr	71	C3	
Willsbrook Gdns	71	C3	
Willsbrook Grn	71	C3	
Willsbrook Gro	71	C3	
Willsbrook Pk	71	C3	
Willsbrook Pl	71	C3	
Willsbrook Rd	83	C1	
Willsbrook Vw	71	C3	
Willsbrook Way	71	C3	
Wilson Cres	116	A2	
Wilson Rd	116	A2	
Wilsons Pl			
off Grants Row	91	C2	
Wilton Pl	90	B3	
Wilton Ter	90	B3	
Windele Rd	78	A1	
Windermere	45	C1	
Windgate Ri	63	D2	
Windgate Rd	61	C3	
Windmill Av Dublin 12	100	A2	
Windmill Av Swords	17	C1	
Windmill Cres	100	A1	
Windmill La	145	F2	
Windmill Pk	100	A2	
Windmill Ri	17	C1	
Windmill Rd	100	A2	
Windrush	141	C2	
Windsor Av	79	C2	
Windsor Ct 12	132	B1	
Windsor Dr	132	B1	
Windsor Ms 5	20	A2	
Windsor Pk	132	B1	
Windsor Pl	90	B3	
Windsor Rd	102	A2	
Windsor Ter Dublin 8	101	D1	
Windsor Ter D.L.	119	D3	
Windsor Ter Mala.	20	A2	
Windsor Vil	79	C2	
Windy Arbour Sta	114	B2	
Winetavern St	144	B3	
Winton Av	101	D3	
Winton Rd	102	B1	
Wogans Fld	68	A2	
Wolfe Tone Av	119	C3	
Wolfe Tone Quay	89	C1	
Wolfe Tone Sq E	142	A3	
Wolfe Tone Sq Mid	142	A3	
Wolfe Tone Sq N	142	A3	
Wolfe Tone Sq S	142	A3	
Wolfe Tone Sq W	142	A3	
Wolfe Tone St	144	C2	
Wolseley St	89	D3	
Wolstan Haven Av	66	A2	
Wolstan Haven Rd	66	A2	
Wolverton Glen	134	A2	
Wood, The Dublin 24	124	A1	
Wood, The Carrick.	136	B3	
Wood, The Shank.	140	B3	
Wood Avens	84	A3	
Woodbank Av	49	D2	
Woodbank Dr	49	D2	

Woodberry Castle.	73	C1	
Woodberry Lucan	82	A2	
Woodbine Av	104	A3	
Woodbine Cl	55	D1	
Woodbine Dr	55	D2	
Woodbine Pk Dublin 5	55	D2	
Woodbine Pk Boot.	104	B3	
Woodbine Rd Dublin 5	56	A1	
Woodbine Rd Boot.	104	A3	
Woodbrook Ct	46	A3	
Woodbrook Cres	46	A3	
Woodbrook Hall	46	A3	
Woodbrook Lawn	142	A3	
Woodbrook Pk			
Dublin 16	112	A3	
Woodbrook Pk Carp.	46	A3	
Woodbrook Sq	46	A3	
Woodcliff Hts	61	C3	
Wood Dale Cl	125	C2	
Wood Dale Cres	125	C2	
Wood Dale Dr	125	C2	
Wood Dale Grn	125	C2	
Wood Dale Gro	125	C2	
Wood Dale Oak 2	125	C2	
Wood Dale Vw	125	C2	
Woodfarm Av	85	D1	
Woodfarm Dr	85	D1	
Woodfield	126	A2	
Woodfield Av	87	D2	
Woodfield Pl			
off Woodfield Av	87	D2	
Woodford	130	B2	
Woodford Av	97	C2	
Woodford Business Pk	39	C2	
Woodford Cl	97	C2	
Woodford Ct	97	C2	
Woodford Cres	97	C1	
Woodford Downs	97	C2	
Woodford Dr	97	C2	
Woodford Garth	97	C2	
Woodford Grn	97	C2	
Woodford Gro	97	C2	
Woodford Hts	97	C2	
Woodford Hill	97	C2	
Woodford Lawn	97	C2	
Woodford Meadows	97	C1	
Woodford Par	97	C1	
Woodford Pk	97	C1	
Woodford Pk Rd	97	C2	
Woodford Ri	97	C2	
Woodford Rd	97	C2	
Woodford Ter	97	C2	
Woodford Vw	97	C2	
Woodford Vil	97	C2	
Woodford Wk	97	C2	
Woodford Way	97	C1	
Woodhaven	102	B3	
Woodhazel Cl	38	A3	
Woodhazel Ter	38	A3	
Woodhazel Way	38	A3	
Woodlands Dublin 6	113	D1	
Woodlands Grey.	143	D3	
Woodlands Mayn.	64	A2	
Woodlands 5 Mulh.	32	A3	
Woodlands Port.	27	C2	
Woodlands, The			
Dublin 14	113	D2	
Woodlands, The Celbr.	66	B2	
Woodlands Av Corn.	138	A1	
Woodlands Av Still.	116	B3	
Woodlands Ct	27	C2	
Woodlands Dr Corn.	138	A1	
Woodlands Dr Still.	116	B3	

Woodlands Pk Black.	116	B2	
Woodlands Pk Corn.	138	A1	
Woodlands Rd	138	A1	
Woodland Vil	102	B1	
Woodlawn	39	C3	
Woodlawn Av	39	D3	
Woodlawn Cl	39	D3	
Woodlawn Ct	39	D3	
Woodlawn Cres			
Dublin 14	114	B2	
Woodlawn Cres			
Dublin 17	39	D3	
Woodlawn Dr	39	D3	
Woodlawn Grn	39	D3	
Woodlawn Gro			
Dublin 14	114	B2	
Woodlawn Gro			
Dublin 17	39	D3	
Woodlawn Ind Est	39	C1	
Woodlawn Pk			
Dublin 14	114	B2	
Woodlawn Pk			
Dublin 17	39	D3	
Woodlawn Pk			
Dublin 24	125	C2	
Woodlawn Pk 7 D.L.	133	C1	
Woodlawn Pk Av	124	B1	
Woodlawn Pk Dr	125	C1	
Woodlawn Pk Gro	125	C1	
Woodlawn Ri	39	D3	
Woodlawn Ter	114	B3	
Woodlawn Vw	39	D3	
Woodlawn Wk	39	D3	
Woodlawn Way	39	D3	
Woodley Dr	129	D1	
Woodley Rd	138	A1	
Woodpark Dublin 15	47	D2	
Woodpark Dublin 16	128	B2	
Wood Quay	144	B3	
Woodscape	82	A2	
Woodside Dublin 3	81	C1	
Woodside Dublin 14	113	D2	
Woodside Leix.	68	A1	
Woodside Dr	113	D2	
Woodside Gro	113	D2	
Woodstock Gdns	102	B2	
Woodstock Pk	126	A1	
Woodstown	125	C2	
Woodstown Abbey	125	C2	
Woodstown Av	125	C2	
Woodstown Cl	125	D2	
Woodstown Ct 3	125	C2	
Woodstown Dale	125	C2	
Woodstown Dr	125	D2	
Woodstown Gdns	125	D2	
Woodstown Grn	125	D2	
Woodstown Heath	125	C2	
Woodstown Height	125	D3	
Woodstown La	125	D3	
Woodstown Lawn	125	C2	
Woodstown Meadow	125	D2	
Woodstown Par	125	D2	
Woodstown Pk	125	C2	
Woodstown Pl	125	D3	
Woodstown Ri	125	D2	
Woodstown Rd 2	125	D2	
Woodstown Vale	125	D3	
Woodstown Village Cen	125	C2	
Woodstown Wk 1	125	D2	
Woodstown Way	125	D3	
Wood St	144	C4	
Woodthorpe 4	130	B1	
Woodtown Pk	126	A3	

Woodvale Av	46	A1	
Woodvale Cres	46	A1	
Woodvale Dr	46	A1	
Woodvale Garth	46	A1	
Woodvale Grn	32	A3	
Woodvale Gro	46	A1	
Woodvale Pk	32	A3	
Woodvale Way	32	A3	
Woodview Black.	117	C2	
Woodview Celbr.	66	B1	
Woodview Lucan	69	D3	
Woodview Cl	56	A1	
Woodview Cotts	113	C2	
Woodview Ct 4	131	C1	
Woodview Dr 14	142	A3	
Woodview Gro	47	C2	
Woodview Hts	28	B3	
Woodview Pk Dublin 13	56	A1	
Woodview Pk Dublin 15	48	A3	
Woodville Av	71	C3	
Woodville Cl	71	C3	
Woodville Ct	54	A1	
Woodville Grn	71	C3	
Woodville Gro	71	C3	
Woodville Lawn	71	C3	
Woodville Rd			
off Botanic Av	78	A1	
Woodville Wk	71	C3	
Wyattville Cl	138	B3	
Wyattville Hill	138	B3	
Wyattville Pk	138	B3	
Wyattville Rd	138	B3	
Wyckham Pk Rd	128	B1	
Wyckham Pl	129	C1	
Wyckham Pt	129	C1	
Wyckham Way	129	C2	
Wynberg Pk	118	A3	
Wyndham Pk	142	A1	
Wynnefield Rd	102	A2	
Wynnsward Dr	115	C1	
Wynnsward Pk	115	C1	
Wyvern Est	134	A3	

X

Xavier Av	79	C3	

Y

Yale	115	D2	
Yankee Ter	117	D3	
Yeates Way	85	D3	
Yellow Meadows Av	97	C1	
Yellow Meadows Dr	97	C1	
Yellow Meadows Est	97	C1	
Yellow Meadows Gro	97	C1	
Yellow Meadows Lawn	97	C1	
Yellow Meadows Pk	97	C1	
Yellow Meadows Vale	97	C1	
Yellow Rd	53	C2	
Yellow Walls Rd	19	D1	
Yewland Ter	101	C3	
York Av	102	A2	
York Rd Dublin 4	91	D2	
York Rd Dublin 6	102	A2	
York Rd D.L.	119	C3	
York St	144	C4	
York Ter	119	C3	

Z

Zion Rd	113	D1	
Zoo Rd	88	B1	